Taking Ethno-Cultural Diversity Seriously in Constitutional Design

Studies in International Minority and Group Rights

Series Editors

Gudmundur Alfredsson
Kristin Henrard

VOLUME 4

The titles published in this series are listed at brill.nl/imgr

Taking Ethno-Cultural Diversity Seriously in Constitutional Design

A Theory of Minority Rights for Addressing Africa's Multiethnic Challenge

By

Solomon A. Dersso

MARTINUS
NIJHOFF
PUBLISHERS

LEIDEN • BOSTON
2012

Library of Congress Cataloging-in-Publication Data

Dersso, Solomon A.
Taking ethno-cultural diversity seriously in constitutional design : a theory of minority rights for addressing Africa's multiethnic challenge / by Solomon A. Dersso.
p. cm. — (Studies in international minority and group rights ; 4)
Includes bibliographical references and index.
ISBN 978-90-04-20535-2 (hardback : alk. paper) — ISBN 978-90-04-23553-3 (e-book)
1. Minorities—Legal status, laws, etc.—Africa. 2. Minorities—Civil rights—Africa. 3. Africa—Ethnic relations. I. Title.
KQC575.D47 2012
342.608'73—dc23

2012041543

ISSN 2210-2132
ISBN 978-90-04-20535-2
e-ISBN 978-90-04-23553-3

Koninklijke Brill NV incorporates the imprints Brill, Global Oriental, Hotei Publishing, IDC Publishers and Martinus Nijhoff Publishers.

This book is printed on acid-free paper.

PRINTED IN THE NETHERLANDS

To my wife Emezat Hailu Mengesha
and my daughter Bethel Solomon Ayele

ACKNOWLEDGEMENT

This work would not have been possible without the support I received from various institutions and individuals.

I owe special gratitude to my doctoral supervisors Prof. Catherine Albertyn and Prof. Theunis Roux. They have provided me with their unfailing support throughout the course of writing this book. Had it not been for their detailed, constructive criticisms and comments on the various chapters and various drafts, it would not have been possible to have this book in its current and highly improved form.

My greatest debt is to my wife, Emezat Hailu Mengesha and my daughter Bethel Solomon for bearing with me through the difficult times of writing this book. Many aspects of this work have been improved in the discussions I had with my wife and her observations were very valuable.

I would like to acknowledge the South African Institute for Advanced Constitutional, Public, Human Rights and International Law (SAIFAC) for giving me the special privilege of working on my PhD project at one of South Africa's most special historical sites, the Constitution Hill. I would like to thank the Institute for providing me with what has been one of the most exceptional academic atmosphere and institutional facilities including my own fully furnished office and generous funding that supported not only mine but also in many ways the PhD project of my wife. I extend my special thanks to the Director of the Institute, Prof. Theunis Roux, for having been there whenever I called upon him both for academic and non-academic matters.

Last but not least, I would like also to thank my friends from home particularly Wondwosen Michago and my family for their constant support and all my colleagues at SAIFAC for their academic and other contributions and the other doctoral fellows for all the times, the good and the bad, we shared together.

CONTENTS

CHAPTER I

INTRODUCTION

1.1. Background and Objectives of the Study

Since the end of direct European colonial rule, the post-colonial state has been beset by various crises, including civil wars, authoritarianism, brutal human rights violations and pervasive socio-economic malaise.[1] At no other time, however, have these crises reached more devastating proportions than during the post-Cold War period. As Makau Wa Mutua succinctly states: '[i]t is as though the African state has gone from the frying pan and into the fire.'[2] Africa has been engulfed from north to south and from west to east by violent upheavals of severe intensity, with consequences that include genocide and the disintegration of states. As inequalities more often than not followed ethno-cultural or regional lines, most of these strifes involve ethnic-based claims for political inclusion, socio-economic justice and autonomy.[3] Even a cursory look at many of these conflicts would attest to this fact.

In Algeria, while political violence erupted following the cancellation of the 1992 elections, the Berbers continued their agitation and protest against the non-recognition of their distinct identity and the policy of assimilation into the dominant Arab culture that was aggressively pursued by successive post-colonial governments.[4] In Mauritania, the largely black communities were brutally massacred and forcibly removed from their land, dispossessed of their property and expelled from their country while being stripped of their citizenship.[5] While fighting involving ethnic-based rebel groups led to the implosion of Liberia[6] and Sierra Leone, Senegal continues to contend with an intermittent violence

---

[1] See Basil Davidson *The Black Man's Burden: Africa and the Curse of the Nation-State* (1992) 8.

[2] MW Mutua 'Putting Humpty Dumpty Back Together: The Dilemmas of the Post-colonial African State' (1995) 21 *Brooklyn J of Int L* 505, 506.

[3] For an analysis of the relationship between ethnic based exclusion or inequality in access to state power and resources and conflicts see Andreas Wimmer, Lars-Erik Cederman, and Brian Min 'Ethnic Diversity, Political Exclusion and Armed Conflict: A Quantitative Analysis of a Global Dataset' in Marc Weller and Katherine Nobbs (eds.) *Political Participation of Minorities: A Commentary on International Standards and Practice* (2010) 3.

[4] See M Meredith *The State of Africa: A History of Fifty Years of Independence* (2005, 2006) 447–461; J McDougal *History and the culture of nationalism in Algeria* (2006) 184–216.

[5] See Human Rights Watch/Africa *Mauritania's Campaign of Terror: State-Sponsored Repression of Black Africans* (1994).

[6] See M Soolisa 'Standing on Sinking Sand: ECOMOGC and the Liberian Internal Conflict' in PA Nyong'o (ed.) *Arms and Daggers in the Heart of Africa: Studies on Internal Conflicts* (1993) 285; B Berkeley *Liberia: A Promise Betrayed* (1986).

by groups agitating for the independence of Casamance.[7] In Nigeria, despite the apparent return to democratic governance, agitation by and the intermittently violent protests of national minority groups such as the Ogoni, the Atyab, and the Bajju have been on the rise.[8]

While the struggle of South Sudan against religious bigotry and ethno-cultural discrimination as well as political and socio-economic marginalisation went on intermittently since 1956 until the signing of the 2005 Comprehensive Peace Agreement, another violent civil war erupted in the Darfur region following a rebellion against political and socio-economic marginalisation by Khartoum.[9] Its neighbour Chad endured civil strife that pitted ethno-regional groups of the south against those of the north,[10] and the country continues to experience ethno-regional and political insurgencies. Hostilities between armed clan militias rendered Somalia a state without government, the prototype of a failed state in the world.[11]

After years of authoritarian rule under Mobutu, the Democratic Republic of Congo (DRC), formerly Zaire, descended into one of Africa's brutal civil wars.[12] The historical rivalry between Hutus and Tutsis for domination and control of the state degenerated into a genocidal civil war in Rwanda[13] and has until recently left Burundi in a vicious circle of genocidal strife.[14] Despite the conclusion of the long civil war in Angola between the government and UNITA

[7] See JB Forrest *Subnationalism in Africa: Ethnicity, Alliance, and Politics* (2004) 88–97; B Sonko 'The Casamance Conflict: A Forgotten Civil War? 3 & 4 *CODESERA Bulletin* (2004) 30.

[8] See OC Okwa-Okafor 'Self-determination and the struggle for ethno-cultural autonomy in Nigeria: The Zangon-Kafaf and Ogoni problems' (1994) 6 *ASIL Proceedings* 52; A Raufu Mustapha 'Ethnicity and the Politics of Democratization in Nigeria' in Bruce Berman et al. (eds.) *Ethnicity and Democracy in Africa* (2004) 257.

[9] See FM Deng 'Sudan's Turbulent Road to Nationhood' in RR Larémont (ed.) *Borders, Nationalism and the African State* (2005) 33–86; Jack Kalpakian 'War over Identity: The Case of Sudan' in Christopher Clapham et al. (eds.) *Big African States* (2001) 39; Report of the AU High Level Panel on Darfur, *Darfur: The Quest for Peace, Justice and Reconciliation*, AU Doc. PSC/AHG/2(CCVII), 29 October 2009.

[10] See S Decalo 'Chad: The roots of centre periphery strife' (1980) 79 *African Affairs* 317.

[11] D Compagnon 'Somali Armed Movements: The Interplay of Political Entrepreneurship and Clan-Based Factions' in C Clapham (ed.) *African Guerrillas* (1998) 73–90. According to Ali A. Mazrui in Somalia, the conflict is often subethnic. Ali A Mazrui 'Black Berlin and the Curse of Fragmentation: From Bismark to Barack', Preface to Adekeye Adebajo's *The Curse of Berlin: Africa after the Cold War* (2010) xiv.

[12] See HF Weiss & T Carayannis 'The Enduring Idea of the Congo' in Larémont (ed.) (note 9 above) 135–178.

[13] See The International Panel of Eminent Personalities to Investigate the 1994 Genocide in Rwanda and the Surrounding Events *Rwanda: The Preventable Genocide* (1994) <http://www.africa-union.org/Official_documents/Reports/OUA-Rapport%20sur%20le%20genocide%20au%20Rwanda.pdf> ; G Prunier *The Rwanda Crisis: History of a Genocide* (1995); Meredith (note 4 above) Chapter 27.

[14] See M Dravis 'Burundi in the 1990s – from democratization to communal war' in TR Gurr *Peoples versus states: Minorities at risk in the new century* (2000) 188–194; R Lemarchand *Burundi: Ethnic conflict and Genocide* (1996).

following the death of Sabimbi, secessionist violence in the resource rich enclave of Cabinda remains unresolved. Others, including Cameroon, Djibouti, South Africa, Uganda, Congo, Ethiopia and Kenya have to contend with low-level ethnic and political conflict. The recent spat of election-related instability and violence in several African countries, most notably Kenya, Guinea and Côte d'Ivoire, often take ethnic or regional cues as various ethnic or regional blocks wrestle against perceived marginalisation and historical injustice and the threat of loss of power and potential exclusion.

The crises that have engulfed the post-colonial African state are not simply products of Africa's authoritarian, ethnically biased and highly corrupt regimes. Rather, both the crises and these regimes are the result and manifestation of the profound crisis of the failure of the post-colonial African state to achieve legitimate statehood.[15] At the heart of this problem, in turn, is the issue of minorities. In Africa, this structurally manifests itself through the disconnection between the post-colonial African state and its ethno-culturally diverse population, and the unsuitability of the basic structures of governance to accommodate the identity and interests of its diverse population in the political, socio-economic and cultural processes of the state.[16] In other words, the issue of minorities is about the demands for political inclusion, socio-economic justice, recognition and autonomy defined by the processes of the making of the African state as a colonially contrived, ethnically diverse and divided entity and of its illegitimate structures of governance and post-colonial misguided and undemocratic approach to nation-building. As such, the issue of minorities in Africa is more about the organisation and distribution of state power in relation to ethnic diversity than about diversity and recognition of difference alone.

Although it is a problem that is defined by Africa's historical, political, economic and socio-cultural conditions, the issue of minorities is not a problem that is unique to Africa. Despite the conventional view that ethnic or national movements emerge in only developing countries, even established Western democracies did not escape the rise of ethnic-based claims. In Canada, separatist claims in Quebec subsided only following various constitutional reforms and a referendum by a small majority of Quebecois to remain part of Canada. While the conflict in Northern Ireland challenged the territorial integrity of the UK, Scottish and Welsh nationalist claims led to the introduction of autonomous

---

[15] As Davidson aptly puts it, while human blunders and corruption involving post-colonial leadership supply some easy explanation, the more fundamental source of the problem arises 'from the social and political institutions within which decolonised Africans have lived and tried to survive. Primarily, this is a crisis of institutions'. Davidson (note 1 above) 10. See Mutua (note 2 above); MW Mutua 'Why Redraw the Map of Africa: A Moral and Legal Inquiry' (1995)16 *Michigan J Int L* 1113,1122–1141; AM Abdulahi 'The Refugee Crisis in Africa as a Crisis of the Institution of the State'(1994) 6 (4) *Int J Refugee L* 562.

[16] Davidson refers to this phenomenon as alienation. Davidson (note 1 above), 10.

self-government structures. The institutionalised rivalry between the two major communities, Flemish and French, continues to threaten the survival of Belgium to this date. In Spain, the Basques have been fighting for independence for a number of decades. In other countries such as the US, Germany, Mexico and Australia, the question of whether and how to accommodate ethno-cultural diversity was seriously debated.

With this worldwide resurgence of ethnic-based claims, the issue of minority rights and the accommodation of group interests and identity in multi-ethnic societies has come to attract enormous attention in a number of fields, particularly political philosophy and legal theory. At a theoretical level, the interest in the subject focuses on the question of whether liberalism, with its focus on individual rights and majoritarian democracy, provides an adequate framework for dealing with identity-based claims for equality and justice. For proponents of minority rights and multicultural liberalism, individual rights and majoritarian democracy are inadequate for ensuring real equality between dominant groups and members of minorities, and much less for resolving ethno-cultural conflicts in multi-ethnic societies. At a practical level, the interest in the subject focuses on the basic structure that a multi-ethnic state ought to take in order to achieve social justice and inclusive democracy. Although the works of multicultural liberal theorists such as Charles Taylor, Will Kymilcka, Iris Marion Young, Bhikhu Parekh, and many others focus on the context of established Western democracies, the insights from their works has important theoretical resonance and potential application to other parts of the world as well.

Notwithstanding the fact that the post-colonial African state is by far the most seriously affected, in the discourse on human rights and democratisation, as well as in the political framework of African states, very little attention is paid to the question of accommodation of the interests and identity of the communities constituting it. As Bertram G Ramcharan observed, '[t]he protection of minorities in Africa is a subject practically untouched in the literature or in African policy documents even though it involves one of the core causes of conflicts and of gross violations of human rights throughout the continent.'[17] Violent conflicts and the overall problem of the sustainability and legitimacy of the African state for social justice and democracy are not only not analysed and problematised as minority issues; more importantly, the relevance and potential role of the framework of minority rights that is being articulated in normative political theory and international law is not sufficiently examined.

[17] BG Ramcharan 'The Protection of Minorities in Africa' in G Alfredsson & M Stavropoulous (eds.) *Justice Pending: Indigenous Peoples and Other Good Causes: Essays in Honour of Erica-Irene A Daes* (2002) 99, 100.

As the civil wars and incidents of state collapse referred to above, and the continuing socio-economic and political ills of the post-colonial African state show, the issue of minorities is an essential part and a core manifestation of the crisis of legitimacy of the African state. As Obiora Chinedu Okafor maintains, the issue of minorities 'has been, and will for the foreseeable future remain, the central problem of post-colonial African state craft'.[18] But as political developments during the post-colonial period, particularly since the end of the Cold War, such as the tragic post-electoral violence of 2007 in Kenya, have made clear, the issue of minorities is not something that the African state can continue to ignore without incurring serious cost, including its own demise. Without properly addressing this issue at the constitutional and political level, the state cannot guarantee social justice, substantive equality and inclusion for all members of its diverse population in the processes of the state. As Alemante G Selassie puts it, 'no issue is more perplexing or more critical than how African societies should treat ethnic identity'. He goes on to warn that, '[n]othing less than the future hope of Africa for stability, democracy, and development is at stake'.[19]

It is evident from the foregoing that it is well worth interrogating the need for and potential of minority rights as a framework for addressing the claims of ethno-cultural groups for social justice and inclusive democracy, and generally for reconfiguring the structure of the post-colonial African state. At one level, this aims at avoiding evil. Accordingly, it advances the framework of minority rights as articulated in this book as the normative basis for preventing conflicts. At another level, the purpose of this investigation is to promote the good. It therefore looks at the possibilities of identifying constitutional design that enhances social justice, equality and cooperation among various sections of society.

In engaging with this task from a legal perspective, this book seeks to address the following questions: What are the factual bases and the normative frameworks for articulating and responding to the claims of minorities (or ethno-cultural groups in general) in Africa? How might minority rights be best conceptualised and translated in multi-ethnic African states into a democratic constitutional design for recognising and accommodating such claims? What insights can be drawn from the individual and group-based models of constitutional accommodation of diversity represented by South Africa and Ethiopia respectively?

The main objective of this study is, accordingly, to articulate and defend a robust constitutional democratic framework for the accommodation of ethno-cultural diversity in Africa using a reconceptualised minority rights framework.

---

[18] OC Okafor '"Righting", Restructuring, and Rejuvenating the Post-colonial African State: The Case for the Establishment of an AU Special Commission on National Minorities' (2007) 13 *African Yearbook of International Law* 2005 43, 46.

[19] AG Selassie 'Ethnic Identity and Constitutional Design for Africa' (Fall 1992–1993) 29 (1) *Stanford J of Int L.* 1, 5.

To this end, this study seeks: (a) to identify the nature of ethno-cultural diversity in the post-colonial African state and the demands arising from it; (b) to establish the historical, social and political conditions and the normative bases for the recognition and accommodation of ethno-cultural diversity in Africa; and (c) to define the form that such recognition should take as well as its institutional implications (i.e. the principles and structures of a democratic constitution committed to the accommodation of ethno-cultural diversity).

1.2. The Concept of Minorities

Although the term minorities has a long pedigree in international law and many efforts have been made to define it, so far, there is not universal agreement about its definition. As Francesco Capotorti puts it, '[t]he preparation of a definition capable of being universally accepted has always proved a task of such difficulty and complexity that neither the experts in this field nor the organs of the international agencies have been able to accomplish it today'.[20] This does not, however, dispense with the need for a definition altogether. Thornberry, while admitting the importance of a definition for reasons of clarity, reiterated the view that 'the lack of a universal definition does not, however, prevent a description of what is and has been understood by the terms'.[21] Similarly, Hannum expressed the view that the absence of a widely accepted definition of the term 'minority' does not bar scholars, judicial bodies and international organisations from using a common-sense conception of the term.[22] There is therefore the implicit recognition that some understanding of what constitutes a minority is a prerequisite for determining the application and subject of minority rights as set out in international law.[23] For the purposes of this study as well, an elaboration of the concept of a minority, particularly as it applies to Africa, is necessary to elaborate the form that a constitutional recognition and accommodation of ethno-cultural diversity should take.

In international legal discourse and official documents, the most widely acknowledged definition is the one formulated by Special Rapporteur Capotorti.[24] This definition is also used in this study to develop a working definition of the

[20] F Capotorti *Study on the Rights of Persons Belonging To Ethnic, Religious, and Linguistic Minorities* (1979) UN Docs. E/CN.4/Sub.2/384/Rev.1, Sales No E78XIV1 p. 5.

[21] P Thornberry *International Law and the Rights of Minorities* (1991) 164.

[22] H Hannum 'Contemporary Developments in the International Protection of the Rights of Minorities' (1991) 66 *Notre Dame LR* 1431.

[23] See M Nowak *UN Covenant on Civil and Political Rights: CCPR Commentary* (1993) 487; MN Shaw 'The Definition of Minorities in International Law' in Y Dinstien (ed.) *The Protection of Minorities and Human Rights* (1992) 1, 1–2.

[24] See Nowak (ibid) 487; J Pejic 'Minority Rights In International Law' (1997) 19 *Human Rights Quarterly* 666, 670.

term and for elaborating the nature and type of groups that this term covers, as used in this book. In his highly regarded study for the UN on the rights of persons belonging to minorities based on Article 27 of the International Covenant on Civil and Political Rights (ICCPR), Capotorti defined a minority for purposes of Article 27 of the ICCPR as

> A group numerically inferior to the rest of the population of a state, in a non-dominant position, whose members – being nationals of the state – possess ethnic, religious or linguistic characteristics differing from those of the rest of the population and show, if only implicitly, a sense of solidarity, directed towards preserving their culture, traditions, religion or language.[25]

For the purposes of this study, the most important elements of this definition are: the numerical inferiority of the group; the non-dominant position that it has in the society; the ethnic, religious and linguistic characteristics distinguishing the group from those of the rest of the population of the state; and the collective will to preserve its culture, traditions, religion or language.

In the context of this study, the numerical factor raises some important issues. The first relates to its importance in determining a group's minority status in a country. The idea that a group constitutes a minority if it is less than 50 percent of the total population of the state is very difficult to sustain, particularly in the African context, for various reasons.[26] Firstly, it is not always the case that the relative size of the group necessarily impinges on its dominant or subordinated position in a society. Even in those African states having numerically majority groups (50 plus), a group that is numerically a minority can actually be politically and economically dominant. This was the case in South Africa during the apartheid era. Today, it is also the case in Rwanda and Burundi. In these countries as well as in Niger and Zimbabwe, numerical strength is not generally accompanied by political and socio-economic strength. The numerical majority can be and in most of these states is, in a politically vulnerable position. In Africa, it is only in very few countries such as Botswana, Egypt, Algeria and possibly Djibouti, that the minority-majority dichotomy in terms of population size may have clear application. Secondly, in countries composed only of numerical minorities, as is the case in the majority of African countries, the relative population size of groups says little, if anything, about the issue of minorities. Some suggest that in such cases each group in a state is a minority vis-à-vis the aggregate of all other members taken together.[27] The criticism raised against such a perspective is that

---

25 Capotorti (note 20 above) at 96.

26 See Warren Weinstein 'Africa: Problems Relating to the Conflict Between State and Group' in Robert G. Wirsing *Protection of Ethnic Minorities: Comparative Perspectives* (1981) 213 (noting that definitional problems are especially acute for students of Africa's minorities).

27 See G Alfredsson 'Minority Rights: International Standards and Monitoring Procedures' in N Taku (ed.) *From human wrongs to human rights – Part VII* (2000) 37; J Crawford 'The rights of

'the comparison is between a culturally homogeneous group and an amorphous one (the aggregate of all the rest)'.[28] Most importantly, it defines minority status mainly in terms of size-based inter-group relations rather than in terms of a group's relations to political and socio-economic power.

There are other factors that cast further doubt on the relevance of the numerical factor for determining the status of groups as minority in the African context. Unlike in Europe, in most African countries there is no single group that constitutes a numerical majority. Similarly, unlike the experience in Europe where the majority not only commands numerical and socio-economic dominance, but has also been central in the process of the making of the state, in those African states where there is a group with a numerical majority, despite its numerical strength, the group often possesses none of these attributes. This mainly reflects the difference in the process of the making of European states and the post-colonial African state. Whereas in Europe the state emerged through a long historical and organic process of state building by historically dominant groups, the state in Africa is a product of colonial rule, an externally imposed and artificially constituted entity. Most African states are thus composed of numerous and divergent ethno-cultural groups of which none constitutes a majority nor had any meaningful role in the process of the making of the state.

This difference means that in the context of Europe and similarly situated countries elsewhere in the world, the issue of minorities is about how to protect numerically smaller and ethno-culturally distinct groups from assimilation into and domination by the majority. Although it involves power relations, the issue of minorities has basically been seen as a statistical and cultural issue.[29] The numerical factor has accordingly assumed particular importance in the definition of a minority in the European experience. In Africa, by contrast, the issue of minorities is not a statistical problem involving counter-balancing of the numerical strength of a majority. It is more about the accommodation of population diversity. The central thrust of minority issues in Africa is how to recognise and accommodate in the processes of the state the diverse identities and interests of members of the various ethno-cultural groups constituting the post-colonial African state in a way that provides sufficient structures and processes for the expression and accommodation of those identities and interests as well as for achieving socio-economic justice and equality of opportunities for members of the diverse groups.

---

peoples: "Peoples" or "Governments"?' in J Crawford (ed.) *The Rights of Peoples* (1988) 55, 60–61.

[28] PV Ramaga 'Relativity of the Minority Concept' (1992) 14 *Human Rights Quarterly* 104, 117.

[29] For an analysis of the background to this see Solomon A. Dersso 'The Socio-historical and political processes leading to the emergence and development of norms on minorities' in Solomon A Dersso (ed.) *Perspectives on the Rights of Minorities and Indigenous Peoples in Africa* (2010) Chapter III.

It is clear from all the above that the numerical factor should not generally be seen as essential for the definition of the term minority, particularly as it applies in Africa and is used in this study. This is not entirely a novel approach. Indeed, it is not uncommon that writings on Africa use the term minority along similar lines. The UN Independent Expert on Minority Issues, Gay McDougall, in her report on her mission to Ethiopia adopted a similar approach. As she explained, not only that minority status is not necessarily defined by numerical factors but she also acknowledged that distinct groups that are numerically a minority in society may at the same time have dominance over the economy, political structures, or other sector. Accordingly, in using the term minorities, she 'focuses on ethnic and religious groups of varying sizes in a society of numerous distinct ethnicities.'[30]

However, this does not mean that the numerical factor is totally irrelevant in the discussion on minorities in Africa. It is, for example, one of the considerations in assessing the degree of vulnerability of groups, and in determining the appropriate form that the application of various rights takes and how such rights are tailored to the particular condition and scale of groups. The numerical factor can also play a role in other ways. It is important, for example, to examine the question of the minimum numerical threshold required to qualify for recognition as minority. Clearly, two persons do not form a minority for the purpose of minority rights.[31] It seems however a prerequisite that a group has to be large enough to have a distinct culture that defines the identity of the group and its members. According to Capotorti, '[i]n principle, even quite a small group has the right to claim the protection provided for in Article 27, to the extent to which it seems reasonable to expect the state to introduce special measures of protection.'[32] In the context of Africa, the size of ethnic groups varies from many millions, as in the case of the Hausa-Fulani of Nigeria, to some thousands, as in the case of the Harari of Ethiopia. The application of this rule of reasonable expectation must therefore also be seen in the light of other considerations, particularly marginalisation and the historical inequities suffered by the group, among others.

The numerical factor also becomes particularly important in Africa with respect to the issue of whether the determination of minority status can be made in relation to the population of some internal political unit such as a province or a unit of a federation. Undoubtedly, the expression 'the rest of the population' in Capotorti's definition, is primarily a reference to the total population

---

[30] See Report of the Independent Expert on Minority Issues, Gay McDougall 'Mission to Ethiopia: 28 November – 12 December 2006)' submitted to the Human Rights Council, UN Doc. A/HRC/4/9Add.3 para. 4.

[31] Nowak (note 23 above) 488.

[32] Capotorti (note 20 above) 12.

of a state. At the level of the UN, the UN Human Rights Committee (HRC), the body responsible for supervising the implementation of the ICCPR, held in *Ballantyne, Davidson and McIntyre v Canada* that 'the minorities referred to in Article 27 are minorities within such a state (party to the ICCPR), and not minorities within any province'.[33]

The problem with this approach is that it fails to take account of situations in which a large portion of political power is constitutionally or otherwise vested in provincial or regional government, as is usually the case in federal or federal-like states. In such states, the issue of minorities arises even at the provincial or regional level, particularly where the boundaries of such internal political units coincide with the territorial concentration of particular groups leading to the domination of those units by such groups.[34] In a separate opinion, the minority of the HRC in *Ballantyne, Davidson and McIntyre v Canada* expressed the need to take into account such considerations in the application of Article 27.[35] Some scholars also rightly maintain that the numerical status of the group may be judged by reference to an internal political structure in addition to the whole country, in so far as such entities have certain powers, as federal units do, and this can affect the interest of the population group concerned.[36] This seems to be a reasonable approach in the light of the overall purpose of minority rights and protection. In India, this approach has also been adopted. Accordingly, the Supreme Court of India established that minority status can be determined not only nationally but also within the units of the federation, depending on the matter in question.[37]

At the European level, the Parliamentary Assembly of the Council of Europe has proposed a definition in Recommendation 1201.[38] According to Recom-

---

[33] *John Ballantyne and Elizabeth Davidson, and Gordon Mcintyre v Canada* (Communications Nos. 359/1989 and 385/1989) UN Doc. U.N. Doc. CCPR/C/47/D/359/1989 and 385/1989/Rev.1 (1993) para 11(2).

[34] In his note 44, De Varennes makes the point: '[I]t could be validly maintained that the drafters of Article 27 simply overlooked that in a federal state, even a national majority may find itself subjected to serious mistreatment if it is a numerical minority in one of the federal units and outside the reach of federal (national) protection.' F De Varennes *Language, Minorities and Human Rights* (1996) 143.

[35] The minority members of the HRC disagree with the reasoning that 'because English-speaking Canadians are not a numerical minority in Canada they cannot be a minority for the purposes of Article 27' and with the conclusion that 'persons are necessarily excluded from the protection of Article 27 where their group is an ethnic, linguistic or cultural minority in an autonomous province of a state, but is not clearly a numerical minority in the state itself'. Individual opinion by Mrs Elizabeth Evatt, co-signed by Nisuke Ando, Marco Tulio Bruni Celli and Vojin Dimitrijevic as quoted in De Varennes (as above) 142–143.

[36] See Ramaga (note 28 above) 105–110; K Henrad *Devising an adequate system of minority protection*: Individual *Human Rights, Minority Rights and The right to Self-determination* (2000) 35.

[37] *D.A.V. College, Jullunder v Punjab*, A.I.R. (1971) S. Ct. 1731.

[38] Parliamentary Assembly, Council of Europe, *Recommendation 1201* (1993), 'On an Additional Protocol on the Rights of National minorities to the European Convention on Human Rights', 1993.

mendation 1201's definition of minority, the concept can also include minorities at the regional level in a given state. This recognises that a minority situation can arise not only at the national level but also at provincial or regional levels as long as such structures exercise autonomous governmental authority within their territory.[39] One can rightly say that this is an appropriate approach as it affords protection to groups in a minority situation at various levels and reflects the context specific nature of minority status.

Non-dominance is another defining element of a minority. This element recognises that a minority is most importantly a political and sociological reality. In the light of this, minority status is conceptualised in terms of the relationship of the group in question, primarily, to political power,[40] although the economic, cultural and social standings of the group may also be important indicators of the weak position of that group to qualify it as a minority.[41] Thus, a minority is generally regarded as lacking political and economic clout to influence the decision-making processes of a state. It is this reality of powerlessness that makes minorities vulnerable and constitutes a chief defining element of a minority. And it is from this position of general vulnerability and weakness that the need for minority protection finds one of its justifications.[42] Given the history of the making of the African state, it is, however, important that non-dominance should be seen not just in terms of existing political, cultural and socio-economic marginalisation but also in terms of vulnerability to such marginalisation as well. That is, non-dominance should not necessarily be restricted to the status of being subordinate or oppressed.[43] The effect of this in the African context could be that all groups, large and small, may become minorities. This should not, however, be regrettable. This is because, first, as noted above and as will be further shown in the following chapters, the most important dimension of the issue of minorities in African countries, is the relationship of all constituent ethno-cultural groups to state power. Second, while recognising all constituent groups as minorities, it is also possible to make further differentiations in terms

---

[39] In its Opinion on Finland the Advisory Committee of the Framework Convention for the Protection of National Minorities observes that 'taking into account the level of autonomy enjoyed and/or the nature of the powers exercised by the province of Åland, the Advisory Committee is of the opinion that the Finish-speaking population there could also be given the possibility to rely on the protection provided by the framework Convention as far as the issues concerned are within the competence of the Province of Åland.' ACFC/INF/OP/I (2001)002 para. 17 as quoted in note 18 of M Pentikäinen 'Integration of Minorities into Society' in M Scheinin & R Toivanen (eds.) *Rethinking Non-discrimination and Minority Rights* (2004) 103.

[40] 'In modern times,' writes Ramaga, 'political power is the major instrument of dominance. It may negate the possible influence of the majority by precluding the effect of all other elements of dominance.' Ramaga (note 28 above) 113.

[41] Nowak (note 23 above) 188.

[42] Capotorti (note 20 above) 12.

[43] Henrad (note 36 above) 36.

of the particular form that the application of the rights of minorities takes to different groups, depending on the degree of vulnerability and disadvantage of each group.[44]

Another component of Capotorti's definition is the possession by the group of ethnic, religious or linguistic characteristics that are different from the rest of the population of the state. Accordingly, groups within a state may be considered minorities for the purposes of international law only when they differ from the rest of the population of the state in which they exist by reference to these distinct characteristics.[45] Minority rights as enunciated under Article 27 of the ICCPR or under the 1992 UN Declaration on Minorities provide various minimal guarantees relevant to the cultural, religious or linguistic interests of minorities thus identified. Notwithstanding such a distinction international law makes between language, ethnicity and religion, the discussion on ethnic, religious or linguistic minorities is essentially a discussion about groups with a distinct culture. Culture thus looms large as an important component in the identification of minorities.

Although the meaning of culture is generally contested, in the discussion on minorities it is used to broadly refer to those aspects of the character of the group that its members and others use to identify the group. Culture can accordingly be described in terms of the variables characterising it: '… [C]ulture is distinguished by such characteristics as language, religion, and race'.[46] It can also be described in terms of symbols and patterns of relations or behaviour 'as a coherent self-contained system of values, and symbols as well as a set of practices that a specific cultural group reproduces over time and which provides individuals with the required signposts and meanings for behaviour and social relationships in every day life.'[47]

One question that can be raised with respect to the identification of a minority by reference to such historically constructed characteristics from the perspective of the nature of diversity in Africa is whether inhabitants of a particular region can be taken to constitute a minority on account of their common experience of marginalisation, discrimination or possession of other shared features or historical experience as inhabitants of such a region, despite belonging to

[44] Such an approach is inspired by the difference in reality among minority groups and is not a new one. On the question of whether all minorities should be treated alike see A Eide *Working Paper on the Relationship and Distinction Between Minorities and Indigenous Peoples* UN Doc. E/CN.4/Sub.2/2000/10 para. 26. Also see SJ Anaya 'On Justifying Special Ethnic Group Rights: Comments on Pogge' in I Shapiro & W Kymlicka (eds.) *Ethnicity and Group Rights* (1997) 222, 225 (stating that 'the degree and kind of protection provided diverse minority groups will not in all instances be the same.')

[45] Nowak (note 23 above) 491.

[46] V Dyke *The Cultural Rights of Peoples* (April-June 1980) 2 (2) *Universal Human Rights* 2.

[47] R Stavenhagen 'Cultural Rights: A Social Science Perspective' in A Eide, C Krause & Allan Rosas (eds.) *Economic, Social and Cultural Rights: A Textbook* (2001) 85, 89.

different ethnic groups. Examples that illustrate this include black Muslims of the Darfur region of Sudan, the people of South Sudan, peoples of Cabinda of Angola, the Casamans of Senegal or the people of Northern Uganda or Eritrea before its independence from Ethiopia. In Ethiopia, historically, it is common that people identify themselves mainly by reference to their provincial origin. Accordingly, the Amharic-speaking people of highland Ethiopia have mainly identified themselves as Shewe, Wolloye, Gojame and Gondere. Similarly, Tigrigna speaking people in the north have identified themselves as Tigrayans of various localities, and Oromos as Quotu or Harar Oromo, Arsi Oromo, Shewa Oromo, Jimma Oromo and Wollega Oromo.[48] As the consideration of the complaints from the people of Katanga by the African Commission on Human and Peoples' Rights indicates,[49] it is accordingly plausible in some cases to identify a population group on the basis of its regional origin where regional identity is politically more salient and is used by the inhabitants of the region as well as others in the society as a principal identification marker.[50]

The elements of the definition of a minority analysed above constitute the objective characteristics of a group. The last element of the definition, the collective will of the group to preserve its distinctive features, constitutes the subjective dimension of what distinguishes the group as a minority. This involves the awareness of the group that it differs from others on account of its distinctive features and its willingness to identify itself in terms of its distinct culture. The question that often arises in this regard is how to determine the existence of this subjective dimension. Is it necessary for the group to declare its willingness to preserve its distinctive characteristics or can this be determined in another way?

The most plausible approach to this is expressed by Capotorti. He emphasises the close link between the objective dimension in the possession of distinct ethnic, religious or linguistic (even regional) features and the subjective dimension. Accordingly, he maintains that the subjective element does not need to be expressed; instead, 'the will in question generally emerges from the fact that a given group has kept its distinctive characteristics over a period of time'.[51] Most importantly, this subjective element can be gathered from the fact that members of minorities continue to identify themselves as belonging to a group, to participate in and observe cultural activities, and make use of their language or practise the religion of the group.

[48] See A Habtu 'Ethnic Pluralism as an Organizing Principle of the Ethiopian Federation' (2004) 28 *Dialectical Anthropology* 91, 109–111.

[49] *Katangese People Congress v Zaire* (2000) AHRLR 72 (ACHPR 1995) [Communication 75/92 8th Annual Activity Report, 1994–1995].

[50] See TR Gurr & JR Scarritt 'Minority Rights at Risk: A Global Survey' (1989) 11 *Human Rights Quarterly* 375, 380–81. (Region of residence is identified as one of the many possible bases for separate group identity by reference to which the minority status of a group is determined.)

[51] Capotorti (note 20 above) 28.

For the purposes of this study therefore, a minority is a population group that distinguishes itself and is distinguished by others by reference to ethnicity, language or religion or a combination of any of these, or by reference to regional origin, and suffers political, socio-economic or cultural oppression and/or marginalisation or is vulnerable to such oppression or marginalisation. The term minority can accordingly include groups that are not necessarily a numerical minority but are nevertheless politically, socio-economically or culturally vulnerable to oppression or marginalisation. Hutus in Rwanda are a good example here. This relatively broad definition would treat the groups constituting the majority of African states as minorities. However, since some groups are more marginalised than others, it is further suggested that a distinction be made between highly disadvantaged minorities and others. Such a distinction means that minority rights should be given different forms of application to cater for the interests of these highly disadvantaged minorities. Accordingly, those population groups identified in the literature as indigenous peoples also constitute minorities, albeit a special category of minority.

It is important to emphasise that minorities are not regarded in this study as self-contained and monolithic or internally homogenous entities. As a group, a minority acquires its significance by how its members and others regard and relate to the culture that gives it its identity. This implies that it is not just the cultural features that distinguish minorities that matter by themselves, but the consequence that members and others attach to them.[52] The possibility that members of minorities may abandon or revise their group membership or that they may not necessarily seek to identify themselves or be identified by others as such is accordingly recognised. For the purposes of this study, the communitarian conception of groups as homogenous, static or self-contained entities with identifiable and stable boundaries is also rejected. Instead, it is recognised that different minorities exist in continuous interaction, often sharing and intermixing in the same territory.

Finally, as it is clear from the foregoing discussion the term minorities as used in this book is restricted to groups identified by reference to common culture, language or religion. Hence, it does not include social minorities such as women, the disabled, and those defined by reference to their sexual orientation. This is premised on the fact that in Africa as in many other parts of the world language, culture and religion constitute the major faultlines along which individuals and

---

[52] N Lerner observes that '[g]roups are often the result of complex combinations, and the issues of self-perception and perception by the surrounding community are of great importance.' He goes on to say at note 13 that 'judicial decisions in several countries have stressed that more important than the nature of the group is how they regard themselves and are regarded by others in the community.' N Lerner 'The Evolution of Minority Rights In International Law' in C Brölman, R Lefeber & M Zieck (eds.) *Peoples and Minorities in International Law* (1993)75, 80.

groups are mobilised in the struggle for defining the identity of the state and for controlling political power.

1.3. The Framework of Minority Rights Defended in this Study

An examination of international norms on minorities reveals that there are two related types of guarantees. The first guarantee is what may be referred to as institutional tolerance, which can be expressed as a non-discrimination right.[53] This ensures to minorities that state authorities refrain from engaging in activities that interfere with or unduly restrict minorities from pursuing their cultures, using their languages and practising their religions. It imposes on state authorities a negative obligation by prohibiting them from actions that prevent members of minorities from enjoying their culture. It entitles members of minorities not to be prevented from participating in the cultural life of their group.

Accordingly, members of minorities are free, within certain limits, to use their minority languages, participate in the reproduction and development of the minority culture and practise their religion. It is formulated as a negative right and takes the form of non-discrimination. As a negative right, it entitles members of minorities to remedies when their freedom to participate in the cultural life of their group is curtailed by an action of state authorities.[54] It does not aim at affording any substantive positive guarantees that ensure the survival of minority cultures. In international law, this perspective is represented by the literal and traditional understanding of Article 27 of the ICCPR.[55] This perspective is generally in agreement with the dominant liberal individual rights and nation-state framework: not only that the right guaranteed is individual but also that it is a negative one.

The other guarantee that international norms on minorities provide is what may be referred to as rights of protection (positive right to culture). These are rights whose objective is to make it possible for minorities to preserve their identity, characteristics and cultures, and which are often called special.[56] These

---

[53] See United Nations Human Rights Fact Sheet No. 18 (Rev.1) *Minority Rights* (1998) 2–4.

[54] Like any other right, interference with the right of a person belonging to a minority to participate in the cultural life of the minority would not automatically entitle the person to a remedy. Often, it is generally where such interference is unreasonable and disproportionate that such a person would be granted a remedy. See *Sandra Lovelace v Canada* (Communication No. 24/1977) U.N. Doc. Supp. No. 40 (A/36/40) 166 (1981) (HRC) para. 16; *Ivan Kitok v Sweden* (Communication No. 197/1985) UN Doc. Supp. No. 40 (A/43/40) 221 (1988) (HRC) para. 9.8; *Ilmari Länsman et al. v Finland* (Communication No. 511/1992) UN Doc. Supp. No. 40 (A/50/40) 66 (1992) (HRC) para 9.4; *Jouni E. Länsman et al. v Finland* (Communication 671/1995) UN Doc. Supp. No. 40 (A/52/40) 191 (1996) (HRC) para. 10.3.

[55] GA Res. 2200 A (XXI), 16 Dec. 1966. See note 26 above.

[56] See United Nations Human Rights Fact Sheet No. 18 (Rev.1) *Minority Rights* (1998) 4.

provide certain limited guarantees for minorities, whereby state authorities not only refrain from obstructing the right of members of minorities to participate in the cultural life of their groups, but also provide certain positive or protective measures that are necessary for the enjoyment of that right in certain circumstances. The aim of these guarantees is to protect the culture of minorities in the interest of members of minorities.[57] It is normally formulated as a positive right to culture. In its strong formulation, this right requires state authorities to make provisions that allow the preservation of minority cultures, such as through minority schools and other cultural institutions. Some of the positive guarantees under the 1992 UN Declaration on Minorities[58] include the right of a minority to exist and the right to enjoy its own culture, to profess and practise its own religion, and to use its language.

Although this constitutes significant improvement towards accommodating the interests of minorities, the formulation is largely influenced by the dominant liberal individual rights and nation-state framework. Although positive in their formulation, the rights are often expressed in vague and highly qualified terms. The extent and nature of the state's positive obligations are not sufficiently elaborated either. Most importantly, the reach of these positive minority guarantees, although generally in the right direction, is inadequate to give just satisfaction to minority needs, even with respect to their culture and language, let alone to secure guarantees for their political participation and self-government. Accordingly, they do not offer sufficient guidance in relation to whether and under what circumstances states need to recognise minority languages for public purposes, including in communication between members of minorities and state agencies. Instead, as John McGarry observed, '[i]nternational law ... has been largely integrationist in character, and has usually focused on promoting individual rights and freedoms rather than power-sharing, territorial self-government, or official bilingualism.'[59] Thus, despite the plethora of instruments developed during the post-Cold War period, international law has achieved little in the substantive accommodation of minorities.

As the subsequent chapters of this study show, in order to address adequately the issue of minorities in multi-ethnic societies in general and in Africa in particular, there is a need for further guarantees that go beyond the protection of minority cultures as articulated under the international minority rights regime. Such guarantees help elaborate the necessary institutional framework both for

---

[57] It is maintained that these rights are granted 'to make it possible for minorities to preserve their identity, characteristics and traditions.' Ibid.

[58] UN Declaration on the Rights of Persons Belonging to National or Ethnic, Religious and Linguistic Minorities GA Res. 47/135, 18 Dec. 1992. (hereinafter the UN Declaration on Minorities).

[59] Johan McGarry 'Ethnic-domination in Democracies' in Marc Weller (ed.) *Political Participation of Minorities: A Commentary on International Standards and Practice* (2010) 35, 65.

the institutional expression and affirmation of minority cultures alongside the dominant culture as defining elements of the character of the states to which they belong, and for the inclusion of minorities in the political and socio-economic processes of the state. Accordingly, this study defends a robust and effective system of minority rights as the basis for designing the relevant constitutional structures, norms and processes for accommodating the identities and interests of constituent minorities of the post-colonial African state, and hence for building a legitimate system of governance. As the analysis from normative political theory and the international law framework in Chapter IV shows, such a conception of minority rights consists of three normative pillars. The first is what Kymlicka calls 'the good of cultural membership',[60] whose guaranteed access both ensures 'for minority elements suitable means for the preservation of … their traditions and their national characteristics'[61] and necessitates the institutional expression of minority cultures as important elements of the character of the state.

Multi-ethnic post-colonial societies such as those in Africa face other challenges of group inequality in addition to cultural recognition. These most importantly relate to the discrimination that highly marginalised groups face due to societal prejudice and institutional bias, and the socio-economic disparity affecting significant number of groups and regions. In addition to cultural recognition, there is therefore a need for other forms of recognition that aims at redressing the socio-political and socio-economic injustice and inequalities that affect minorities. The second normative pillar is thus equality, which addresses the question of the relevant institutional and policy arrangements to be made in order to achieve socio-economic and political equality in the context of ethno-cultural diversity and of disparities in the conditions of ethno-cultural groups or ethno-regions.

Given the colonial process of the suppression of the freedom and independence of African societies, which led to the genesis of the issue of minorities in the first place, it is necessary in the African context that minority rights also operate as mechanisms for rectifying the political, socio-economic and cultural maladies that continue to affect minorities as a result of the colonial experience. Accordingly, the third pillar that frames the content of minority rights as defended in this study is self-determination. The importance of the minority rights framework elaborated and presented as such is that it is necessary and serves as comprehensive normative basis in the redefinition of a legitimate system of governance in Africa.

---

[60] See generally W Kymlicka *Liberalism, Community and Culture* (1989).

[61] In its advisory opinion on the Minority Schools in Albania the PCIJ indicated that there are two considerations underlying the minority protection system and one of which is to ensure for the minorities suitable means for the preservation of their linguistic, ethnic, religious and racial characteristics. *Minority Schools in Albania* PCIJ (Ser. A/B) No. 64 (1935) 17.

Against this background, in Chapter V this book elaborates how such a robust minority rights framework should be translated into an effective constitutional design for the accommodation of ethno-cultural diversity and achieving a legitimate system of governance. To illustrate how the relevant constitutional mechanisms, processes or principles and guarantees should be and are actually institutionalised, and how in practice they should and do operate, the study also uses as case studies the constitutional design of South Africa and Ethiopia, in Chapters VI and VII respectively. Within the framework of such a conception of minority rights, it is submitted that the state is best conceived to be multi-ethnic, composed of diverse and overlapping ethno-culturally identifiable groups, rather than a nation-state. This acknowledges not only the existence of ethno-cultural diversity but also its importance in national life, not as a condition of division to be overcome, but as a basis of politically relevant social identity to be accommodated and even celebrated.

This is generally a controversial matter and even more so in the context of Africa. Many people question the need for and the validity of minority rights as a mechanism for addressing issues of ethno-cultural diversity and ethnic conflicts in Africa, as elsewhere. For some, particularly nationalist politicians, ethnicity is a divisive force that must be countered through state-controlled nation-building process. For others, who see the main problem of the post-colonial African state as being a lack of both democracy and respect for human rights, problems of ethno-cultural diversity and conflicts are better addressed through the institutionalisation and effective implementation of liberal democratic processes and individual human rights. In all these cases, problems surrounding ethno-cultural diversity and inequality, such as those referred to above, are treated as being capable of resolution without resorting to group-specific minority rights.

Some of these arguments are rooted in the view widely held during the post-colonial period that ethnic attachment in Africa was a product of colonial invention or a manifestation of tribal differences and that the only legitimate form of social organisation is the nation-state, with its singular national character, an ideal to which the post-colonial African state has actively sought to conform, at least in rhetorically and policy or legal pronouncements.[62] Other arguments are expressions of a liberal view that has been dominant until recent times in Western democracies and in the constitutional systems of Africa as well. While on the one hand this rejects the necessity of minority rights, on the other hand it expresses the fear that minority rights may lead to divisions and fragmentation. These concerns are not all without merit. As subsequent chapters will show, however, neither the post-colonial nation-building process nor the return to democratisation, as well as the constitutional recognition of human rights would

---

[62] See Davidson (note 1 above).

be sufficient to address the issue of minorities in Africa as in other parts of the world. Indeed, state-centred and homogenising nation-building, rather than resolving minority problems, has further entrenched the problem, leading to heightened ethnic rivalry and conflicts. Although fundamental, democratisation and individual human rights would only address the symptoms of the problem and obscure the root of the issue of minorities, ultimately only to postpone its resolution, if not exacerbate it further. While acknowledging the merits of some of the concerns, this book contends that in the post-colonial state, the effective resolution of the issue of minorities demands that democracy be reconceptualised beyond the majoritarian liberal model to accommodate minorities and individual human rights that are complemented by group-specific rights.

1.4. The Implications of a Minority Rights Framework for Democratisation in Africa

This study contends that minority rights understood as such can provide the necessary framework to address the claims of members of various groups for inclusion and accommodation in the political and socio-economic processes of the state, claims which in the African context are central to the issue of minorities. Clearly, these are questions regarding fundamental aspects of democracy, most importantly, the framework of representation of members of society, the process of participation in the political and socio-economic processes of the state, and the character of the basic structure of the state and the mode of organisation and distribution of political power and other resources among members of society. These issues relate to the general question of the form that democracy takes in multicultural and multinational societies, not only in Africa but also in established multi-ethnic democracies such as Canada.[63] There are, however, more factors that make this question particularly critical for Africa. These include illegitimate state formation through the process of colonisation and its continuing effects, the high degree of centralisation of political power, domination of the state machinery by the few, the emergence of patterns of exclusion and marginalisation from the processes of the state, horizontal inequality among groups or ethno-regions in their respective share from political power and socio-economic opportunities and generally, the lack of a democratic culture.

---

[63] According to Plattner and Diamond 'perhaps the most serious challenge both to the consolidation of new democracies and to the health of well-established ones is posed by the problem of ethnic conflict'. M Plattner & L Diamond 'The Challenge of Ethnic Conflict' (1993) 4 (4) *J of Democracy* 17. On the character of democracy and constitutionalism in multinational societies see J Tully 'Introduction' in AG Gagnon & J Tully (eds.) *Multicultural Democracies* (2001) 1; S Tierney *Constitutional Law and National Pluralism* (2004).

Generally speaking, the problem that multiculturalism in general, and in Africa in particular, presents as far as democracy is concerned, relates to the question of whether and in what ways ethno-cultural diversity and inequality should be considered in the political, socio-economic and cultural processes of the state. To put it differently, the question is what account should be given to ethno-cultural membership in the political life of society to achieve a legitimate democratic order.

Broadly speaking, it is possible to identify three strands of democratic systems. The first is majoritarian liberal democracy, which is premised on the centrality of the individual and majoritarian decision-making processes. Its concern is the proper relationship of the individual with the state. As such, it is premised on the understanding of the society as a collection of atomised individuals who share common citizenship but having no subnational attachments. Individual rights, a majoritarian electoral system and generally a unitary or centralised system of organisation of political power, and political pluralism are its main features. It is further characterised by the representation of individual choices or alternating interest groups. In a context of ethno-cultural diversity and inequality majoritarian liberal democracy often leads to undemocratic results as it tends to perpetuate the marginalisation of minorities from decision-making.[64] This is essentially because such a system operates in a way that advantages dominant ethno-cultural groups and disfavours minority groups. Crudely speaking, on the one hand, '[o]ften majoritarian democracy facilitates the domination of majority ethnicity's socio-political and economic interests by guaranteeing its control over the apparatus of the state.' On the other hand, 'it promotes the political (one can add socio-economic and cultural) submergence of the minorities by preventing them from exercising any effective levers ... to empower their special representatives, needs and interests.'[65]

In its republican form, it envisages a membership-blind political system and institutional organisation. Ethno-cultural groups are not recognised as having any political role and hence there is no political space envisaged for minorities with such characteristics. In relation to ethnicity, it is predicated on the unstated principle of separation of state and ethnic identity, although such separation has historically been rare, if at all it existed. Ethnic identity, so the argument goes, is a matter that is left to the private sphere, where the state plays neither a promotional nor inhibitive role.[66] Despite this pretention, the 'liberal insistence

---

[64] See WA Lewis *Politics in West Africa* (1965).

[65] YN Kly 'Democratic Pluralism, the Right to Remedy and National Minorities' in YN Kly (ed.) *A Popular Guide to Minority Rights* (1995) 135.

[66] As Kymlicka put the position of such approach '[E]thnic identity, like religion, is something which people should be free to express in their private life, but which is not the concern of the state. The state does not oppose the freedom of people to express their particular cultural

on the privatisation of culture is better than coercive assimilation'. This is essentially because in a system where governments assume power on the basis of majority vote, ethnic membership serves as one of the basis for mobilisation of political support. Under such circumstances, 'the modern state is not an ethnically neutral actor or a mere arena for political competition, but a central object of and participant in ethno-political power-struggle.'[67] Equally importantly, the state cannot be neutral on issues relating to language and culture, its cohesion and functioning as a modern state requires it to promote majoritarian policies on such subjects.

As will be shown in Chapter III, liberal democracy understood in these terms has not been adequate for addressing the claims of members of minorities for representation and effective participation, and more generally for real socio-economic, cultural and political equality in the multi-ethnic societies of the post-colonial African state. In the African context, as witnessed at the time of and subsequent to independence and during the post-1990 period, democracy in its majoritarian form and without due regard to ethnic diversity is prone to lead to a zero sum game of winner-takes-all, in which the members of many groups, particularly marginalised ones, would continue to be excluded and ethnic rivalry and conflicts are perpetuated. As Claude Ake rightly pointed out, 'we might well consider whether democracy is possible … without ethnicity, without at any rate coming to terms with ethnicity?'[68] It is necessary to add to this the question of what form democracy should take if it should give due regard to ethnic diversity? And in what ways and how far should democracy take account of ethnic diversity?

Beyond majoritarian liberal democracy, which is generally associated with societies with high degree of ethno-cultural cohesion or homogeneity, one can idetify two forms of democracy whose application is associated with ethno-culturally diverse societies. As John McGarry and Brendan O'Leary in a recent study argued, the two forms of democracy that are used in multi-ethnic societies to respond to the demands of diversity are integrationist democracy and consociational democracy.[69] Integrationist democracy, which is often associated with Donald Horowitz,[70] emphasises the need to transcend the

attachments, but nor does it nurture such expression-rather, as Glazer elsewhere put it, the state responds with 'salutary neglect.' W Kymlicka 'Introduction' in Will Kymlicka (eds.) *The Rights of Minority Cultures* (1995) 9.

[67] Andreas Wimmer, Lars-Erik Cederman, and Brian Min 'Ethnic Diversity, Political Exclusion, and Armed Conflict: A quantitative analysis of a global dataset' in Marc Weller (ed.) *Political Participation of Minorities: A Commentary on International Standards and Practice* (2010) 3, 5.

[68] Claude Ake 'What is the Problems of Ethnicity in Africa' 22 *Transformation* 1993 (6).

[69] John McGarry and Brendan O'Leary 'Iraq's Constitution of 2005: Liberal Consociation as Political Prescription' 5 (4) *I.CON* (2007), 670–698.

[70] See Donald Horowitz, *A Democratic South Africa? Constitutional Engineering in a Divided Society* (1991).

ethno-cultural divisions and demand 'a state that is impartial, meritocratic, and that promotes equal citizenship through individual bill of rights'.[71] According to this view, the institutions of a multi-ethnic society should be designed in such a way that political actors are deterred from mobilising support along ethnic lines but are encouraged and induced into seeking support across ethnic divisions. Integrationists thus reject proportional electoral systems. They also 'back executive systems that favour candidates who rise above religious, linguistic, and ethnic factions. They favour a unitary centralised state, or a federation that is constructed on non-ethnic criteria.'[72]

Clearly, integrationist democracy has much more in common with the republican form of liberal democracy most notably in its demand for separating state from ethnicity. In multi-ethnic societies, such a system can be a serious option where there is strong belief in the possibilities of forming and running institutions that are autonomous from and impartial to prevailing ethnic differences in society. It may also best work in societies where ethno-cultural diversity is not politically salient and there is no or very low level of inequality along ethno-cultural lines.

The second form is consociational democracy, which is generally associated with Arend Lijphart,[73] and with specific reference to Africa, W Arthur Lewis.[74] Consociational democracy recognises ethno-cultural divisions in society as politically salient and provides for mechanisms for their accommodation in the public sphere. McGarry and O'Leary aptly summed it, [c]onsociation accommodates groups: (*a*) by involving all sizable communities in executive institutions provided they wish to participate; (*b*) by promoting proportionality throughout the public sector, not just in the executive and legislature but also in the bureaucracy, including the army and the police; (*c*) through autonomy of either the territorial or nonterritorial variety; and (*d*) through minority vetoes, at least in those domains the minority communities consider important.[75] Consociation represents a serious option in societies where ethno-cultural diversity is politically salient. These is also the case where there is high level of group inequality in terms of control over or share of political power and socio-economic opportunities and in terms of representation in the historical and national narratives of the state.

---

[71] McGarry and O'Leary (note 69 above) 670.

[72] Ibid.

[73] See Arend Lijphart, *Democracy in Plural Societies: A Comparative Exploration* (Yale Univ. Press 1977); *Democracies: Patterns Of Majoritarian And Consensus Government In The Twenty-One Century* (1984); 'Self-Determination versus Pre-Determination of Ethnic Minorities in Power-Sharing Systems' in Will Kymlicka (ed.) *The Rights of Minority Cultures* 275 (1995).

[74] .Lewis (note 64 above).

[75] McGarry and O'Leary (note 69), 671.

The framework of minority rights adopted in this study entails and envisages a type of democracy that can be broadly termed as multicultural democracy. In some ways, this is akin to consociational democracy as proposed by scholars such as Arend Lijphart, and W Arthur Lewis. It also draws heavily from multicultural theorists such as Will Kymlicka,[76] Iris Marion Young,[77] James Tully[78] and Monique Deveaux,[79] among others, who maintain that in multicultural societies democracy based on majority rule and individual rights would not offer proper mechanisms to determine just appropriation of societal (constitutional) goods among individuals belonging to different groups. Indeed, many political thinkers concluded that it has led to injustice to members of minority groups.[80] Its reliance on individual rights does not leave space for groups that seek state recognition of their distinct culture and for them to take part and have a say in political decision-making, not just as citizens but as members of particular groups as well.[81] This would mean that democracy based on majority rule or the integrationist model would create a problem in multi-ethnic societies in so far as it fails to accommodate the 'group-specific rights' of minorities. In such societies, strict adherence to individual-centred democracy would in effect mean the perpetuation of the marginalisation of non-dominant groups and of prevailing ethno-cultural inequality.

Like consociationalism, the multicultural model not only recognises diversity, but also requires the provision of mechanisms that facilitate the representation of members of the diverse groups in the political process and the creation of structures for the self-government of territorially concentrated minorities.[82] Accordingly, not only does it seek to treat members of various groups with equal concern and respect regarding their cultural commitments, but it also institutionalises guarantees for their inclusion and effective participation in the political decision-making processes of the state. It operates on the basis of deliberation (in which all interested parties including members of minorities are guaranteed representation and fair hearing), negotiations and reciprocity, thus empowering minorities to have a wider role in the decision-making process, and in the process promoting national cohesion. The specific structures and principles which would underpin this institutional application are outlined in Chapters V, VI and VII.

---

[76] W Kymlicka *Multicultural Citizenship: A Liberal Theory of Minority Rights* (1995).

[77] Iris Marion Young *Justice and the Politics of Difference* (1990).

[78] J Tully *Strange Multiplicity: Constitutionalism in an Age of Diversity* (1995).

[79] M Deveaux *Cultural Pluralism and Dilemmas of Justice* (2000).

[80] Young (note 77 above); Deveaux ibid, J Räikkä 'Is a Membership-Blind Model of Justice False by Definition?' in J Räikkä (ed.) *Do We Need Minority Rights?* (1996) 3–19.

[81] Deveaux (note 79 above) 147.

[82] Young (note 77 above) 185; Tully (as not 78 above) 3–4; Deveaux (note 68 above); Kymlicka (note 76 above).

Unlike consociational democracy, particularly its corporate variant, the model that the minority rights framework elaborated and defended in this book is not premised on the 'assumption that group identities are fixed and that groups are both internally homogeneous and externally bounded'.[83] Given the nature of the issue of minorities in Africa as discussed in Chapter II and to some degree in Chapter IV, the model suggested in this book gives recognition to ethno-cultural diversity to the extent that there is demand for such recognition and hence without necessarily institutionalising all the elements of consociationalism (particularly autonomy and minority veto) in all circumstances. Seen from this perspective multicultural democracy, as used in this book, is more like what McGarry and O'Leary call liberal consociation, which 'rewards whatever salient political identities emerge in democratic elections, whether these are based on ethnic or religious groups, or on subgroup or transgroup identities. Liberal consociations also take care to ensure that the rights of individuals as well as groups are protected.'[84] This is distinguished from corporate consociation, which entitles all ethno-cultural groups to various political rights, despite the fact that some or many of them have shown or show no interest for such rights. Going beyond the institutional focus of liberal consociation, multicultural democracy additionally concerns it self with mechanisms and principles of participation and decision-making such as deliberation, compromise and inclusiveness and with policies relating to language, culture and religion.

The implication of minority rights as defended in this book is therefore that any exercise in democratising the state in Africa must provide sufficient mechanisms for ensuring participation and representation of all minorities, equitable distribution of and access to socio-economic goods and where necessary, for recognising their self-government or autonomy. The nature of ethnic diversity in Africa, as examined in Chapter II and IV, is such that democracy can enable all members of the constituent ethnic groups of the post-colonial African state to feel that they are justly included and accommodated in the political and socio-economic processes of the state, only if it provides specific institutional guarantees to ensure that members of all groups are guaranteed effective opportunity to take part and have their say in political decision-making without discrimination and enjoy a fair share from the socio-economic opportunities of the state, freed from historically inherited cultural and socio-economic disadvantages. Accordingly, the study proposes and employs the framework of minority rights as a foundation in redefining the system of political representation and the internal power structure of the post-colonial African state.

---

[83] McGarry and O'Leary (note 69 above), 675.

[84] Ibid, 675–676.

The argument that supports this proposition is that it is only if members of all the various ethno-cultural groups constituting the post-colonial African state are given representation and inclusion, that they can have just opportunities in the political and socio-economic processes of the state to which they belong. This acknowledges that the recognition and inclusion of members of various groups in the democratic process is a necessary condition for addressing the threat of or marginalisation of some groups and the resultant conflicts, as well as the persistent illegitimacy of the structure of the African state.[85]

This implies two things in relation to the existing basic structure of most post-colonial African states. First, as will be shown in Chapters II, III and IV, the basic structure[86] of the these states lacks legitimacy,[87] and the issue of minorities is a manifestation and product of the crisis of legitimacy of the African state. Secondly, and more importantly, the framework of minority rights as elaborated and defended in this study offers a basis for conceptualising a democratic structure that is capable of accommodating the interests and identities of minorities and thereby reshaping the nature of the post-colonial African state.

Clearly, the issue is the form that democracy should take in Africa. There is no question here that democracy and the institutionalisation of human rights is the proper institutional system to best address the issue of minorities and its various manifestations including 'tribalism', ethnic conflicts and deadly rivalry for control of the state.[88] Democracy cherishes diversity and offers the necessary framework for pursuing issues of equity and social justice.[89] Its provision for realising the enjoyment of human rights by all and the rule of law and constitutionalism is beyond reproach. The importance of democracy as the requisite political system for the protection of minorities is clearly spelt out by the OSCE member states as follows:

---

[85] The form in which such a system is to be devised is a central issue that this study will pursue later on.

[86] This term is used in the sense defined by Rawls as 'a society's main political, social, and economic institutions, and how they fit together into one unified system of social cooperation from one generation to the next.' J Rawls *Political Liberalism* (2005) 11.

[87] See Mutua (note 15 above); OC Okafor *Re-Defining Legitimate Statehood: International Law and State Fragmentation in Africa* (2000); CR Ezetah 'Legitimate Governance and Statehood in Africa: Beyond the Failed State and Colonial-Self-determination' in EK Quashigah & OC Okafor (eds.) *Legitimate Governance in Africa: International and Domestic Legal Perspectives* (1999) 15; Abdulahi (note 15 above).

[88] Writing on human rights and democracy in Africa, Sidgi Kaballo remarked that 'only a democratic order which takes human rights seriously will be capable of avoiding or resolving ethnic conflict' S Kaballo 'Human Rights and Democratization in Africa' in D Beetham (ed.) *Politics and Human Rights* (1995) 189, 192.

[89] What makes democracy instrumental for managing issues involving minorities are its qualities of 'inclusiveness, pluralism and its sensitivity to uniqueness or diversity, along with the bargaining, coalition building, and political learning it spawns.' See PC Aka 'Nigeria: The Need For An Effective Policy of Ethnic Reconciliation in the New Century' 14 *Temp. Int & Comparative LJ* (2000) 351.

> The participating states recognise that the questions relating to national minorities can only be satisfactorily resolved in a democratic political framework based on the rule of law, with a functioning independent judiciary. This framework guarantees full respect for human rights and fundamental freedoms, equal rights and status for all citizens, the free expression of all their legitimate interests and aspirations, political pluralism, social tolerance and the implementation of legal rules that place effective restraints on the abuse of governmental power.[90]

This study fully shares these views. For democracy to work in addressing minority issues it is necessary that it provides institutional mechanisms and measures for the accommodation of minorities.

1.5. Methodology of the Study

Although this is mainly a legal study, its approach is a multidisciplinary one. Accordingly, it relies on more than one method. For the legal component, a legal method is employed. This method relies on analysis and construction of primary sources such as relevant international instruments, cases and national laws. This is supported by secondary sources from published academic and research works. The main purpose of this is to examine how the issue of minorities is addressed in international law and the constitutional practice of states, as well as to identify and elaborate the relevant constitutional guarantees and institutional arrangements necessary for achieving the accommodation of ethno-cultural diversity within the post-colonial African state.

Materials from the social sciences including history, political science, sociology and philosophy are accessed from various secondary sources, including journal articles, books, internet sources and relevant reports. They are used in this study in different ways, both to understand and analyse the problem and to develop the relevant constitutional guarantees and institutional arrangements. Accordingly, the resources from these materials will help to examine the historical and socio-political processes that led to the issue of minorities and to establish the nature of ethno-cultural diversity in Africa. Those resources from political science and philosophy are particularly valuable in discussing the normative bases by reference to which the various dimensions of the issue of minorities can be analysed and the necessary constitutional guarantees and institutional arrangements can be identified and defended. They are also important to help to identify and understand the various political, social and cultural factors that affect the operation of the constitutional guarantees and arrangements defended

---

[90] Copenhagen Meeting as note 81 above para. 30. In his Study for Peaceful and Constructive Solutions to Problems involving Minorities, Special Rapporteur Asbjon Eide indicated that full democracy and the rule of law form the basis of any effort to solve minority problems. U.N Doc. E/CN.4/Sub.2/1991/43 (1991) 6.

in this study as the defining elements of an adequate constitutional design for the accommodation of diversity.

Finally, to illustrate how the proposed constitutional design should be and is actually translated into specific norms, processes and institutions and to exemplify how it should and does operate, the study uses the constitutional models of South Africa and Ethiopia. These two case studies are chosen for different reasons. The first and main reason is that of all the countries that introduced constitutional reform during the so-called second liberation of Africa, these are arguably the only ones that deliberately provided comprehensive mechanisms for the accommodation of diversity. The second reason is that the constitutions of these two countries employ two different approaches, representing two different models of accommodation of diversity. The last reason is personal familiarity with these two countries: Ethiopia being my country of origin and South Africa the place where I have been pursing my postgraduate studies.

1.6. Outline of Chapters

In the following chapter, (Chapter II) two issues are investigated. The first is the historical, socio-economic and political processes that led to the issue of minorities in Africa. In this regard, it will be argued that the issue of minorities is inseparably linked to the making of the African state and the way this has historically defined the relationship of members of various groups with the state. The other issue addressed in this chapter is the question of the nature and types of claims to which the issue of minorities has given rise. Here, the study identifies four types of minority claims. The first is the claim for the recognition and provision of public space for the expression of the culture and language of groups. The second is expressed by the struggle or conflict between various groups in relation to taking part and having a say in the processes of the state. The third is the claim for achieving self-government. Finally, there is also the claim of highly marginalised minorities for the recognition of their distinct identity, for their socio-economic and political inclusion and sometimes for special measures to rectify their historical oppression or marginalisation.

Chapter III deals with the approach of the post-colonial African state to the issue of minorities. The purpose of this is to investigate the limits of first, the nation-state model of post-colonial nation building and second, the dominant liberal nation-state constitutional model to address the issue of minorities in Africa. It is argued that in the particular conditions of ethno-cultural diversity and inequality that is characteristic of the population makeup of the post-colonial African state, the issue of minorities cannot be addressed on the basis of a national project that suppresses the ethno-cultural attachments of people and a difference-blind constitutional system that is inhospitable to group membership claims.

In Chapter IV, the study examines and elaborates a robust minority rights framework by reference to which the mechanisms and guarantees for constitutional accommodation of ethno-cultural diversity are to be identified. It is proposed here that a robust minority rights framework that defines the basis for constitutional recognition and accommodation of diversity in Africa should have three components. The first is culture. The discussion on culture seeks to establish the moral and legal basis for recognising the importance of culture and the particular claims that can be addressed within the framework of culture. The second component of the minority rights framework defended in this study is equality. This helps to identify the conditions that necessitate the recognition of ethnic membership in determining the organisation and distribution of political power and socio-economic goods and opportunities in the multi-ethnic African state. The third and final component is self-determination. Self-determination captures the historical and political processes that led to the issue of minorities and offers a framework for substantiating the institutionalisation of self-government structures and the recognition of the interests of peripheral minorities, such as indigenous peoples, over the land and resources to which they have cultural and socio-economic attachment.

Chapter V seeks to outline the institutional mechanisms and constitutional guarantees through which the minority rights framework elaborated in Chapter IV can be institutionalised. In other words, this chapter elaborates the structures, processes and principles that institutionalise multicultural democracy in Africa. Although the exact form and the particular institutional mechanisms and policy options adopted in a country will be dictated by reference to the specific requirements of the country's ethno-cultural diversity, this chapter identifies the various institutional mechanisms and policy directions that translate the minority rights framework elaborated and identified in the pervious chapter into constitutional design. One of the arguments of this chapter is that the mere institutionalisation of the minority rights framework through appropriate constitutional design by itself alone is not adequate. For such constitutional design to be effective in accommodating ethno-cultural diversity, it has to comply with and operate within the framework of fundamental values and principles. Accordingly, the chapter additionally identifies those values and principles that are of particular importance for the proper functioning of an effective constitutional design for accommodation of ethno-cultural diversity.

Chapters VI and VII consist of the case studies of South Africa and Ethiopia respectively. These case studies are used to exemplify how the institutional arrangements and constitutional guarantees elaborated in Chapter V are, and should be translated into constitutional design for the accommodation of diversity and how they should and actually do operate in practice. They also help to substantiate the argument of the book that addressing the issue of minorities in Africa requires the constitutional recognition and accommodation of ethno-cultural diversity.

Chapter VIII provides some general conclusions and specific observations.

CHAPTER II

THE ISSUE OF MINORITIES IN AFRICA: DESCRIBING ITS CONTEXT AND UNDERSTANDING ITS NATURE

2.1. Introduction

One of the arguments of this book is that the issue of minorities and the nature of ethno-cultural diversity in most, if not all, African states reflects in important ways the political saliency of prevailing ethnic diversity and the particular attachment or regard that individuals ordinarily have for their group membership. This chapter has two objectives. As the introductory chapter of this study indicates, the issue of minorities in Africa is a reflection of the (il)legitimacy of the post-colonial state, its stability, and its level of democratisation. To understand why this issue occupies such a central place in Africa's quest for justice, peace and democracy, one needs to examine the nature of the phenomenon of minorities in Africa, and the political and historical processes and circumstances that led to its genesis. The first aim of this chapter is thus to outline the historical, ethno-cultural and political context of the issue of minorities in Africa. This serves both to show and explain why ethno-cultural diversity is politically salient in most African countries, so much so that in some cases it largely defines the boundaries along which violent conflicts are fought.

The political saliency of ethno-cultural diversity and more generally the issue of minorities does not however have a single manifestation. It rather takes different forms. The determination of the design of the necessary constitutional processes and mechanisms best suited to address the issue of minorities in Africa also largely depends upon an understanding of the nature and various types of claims that minorities make or the ideal form that the issue of minorities take.[1] The other task of this chapter is accordingly to identify and articulate the nature of those claims. In this regard, although it is acknowledged that the issue of minorities varies from country to country and from one group to another, minority claims in many ways share common themes, on the basis of which they are categorised and elaborated in this chapter to illustrate a typology of minority groups/claims in Africa.

[1] As Thio rightly observes, 'The understanding of "minorities" and the nature of minority problems will color a determination of what solutions are appropriate. In this regard, it is important to consider the different situations encountered by minorities.' Li-ann Thio 'Battling Balkanization: Regional Approaches Towards Minority Protection Beyond Europe' (2002) 43 *Harvard Int LJ* 409, 411.

2.2. The Nature and Genesis of Ethno-Cultural Diversity in Africa

One of the features of the state in Africa is its deep ethnic diversity. This is not to say that ethnic diversity is unique to Africa. Indeed, it is a feature common to many countries worldwide.[2] But the state in Africa is unique in both the degree and nature of its diversity. Although the number of ethnic groups in Africa is not exactly known, if the estimated number of languages spoken in Africa is anything to go by, the continent's 54 countries are home to no less than 2,000 distinct ethnic groups.[3] Almost all African states thus exhibit rich linguistic, cultural and religious diversity. Comparatively speaking, African states are home to more ethnic groups than other states in most parts of the world.[4]

Except for Somalia and, to a lesser extent, Lesotho, virtually every African country is composed of more than one ethnic group.[5] Notably, one of the characteristics of the multi-ethnic composition of these states is the presence of a large number of different ethnic groups. Some African states are, however, more diverse than others. Nigeria is composed of more than 250 ethnic groups.[6] Sudan,[7] Chad[8] and Cameroon[9] each reportedly have more than 200 ethnic groups. Many other African states are home to many ethnic groups, ranging from little more than a dozen, as in the case of South Africa,[10] to more than 100, as in the case of Tanzania.[11] Countries with half a dozen or less ethnic groups are in the minority. These include almost all of northern African states, as well as Djibouti,

---

[2] There are about 8,000 distinct cultural groups inhabiting the more than 190 independent countries of the world. See A Addis 'On Human Diversity and the Limits of Toleration' in I Shapiro & W Kymlicka (eds.) *Ethnicity and Group Rights* (1997) 112.

[3] See A Lodhi 'The Language Situation in Africa Today' (1993) 2(1) *Nordic J of African Studies* 79, 81.

[4] See C Legum 'Africa's Quest for Nationhood and Stability' in *Black Africa Twenty-Five Years After Independence: Lessons for the Future* Africa Institute of South Africa, Conference (1985) 17.

[5] Ninety-nine per cent of the population of Lesotho is composed of the Sotho ethnic group. See C Dammers & D Sogge 'Central and Southern Africa' in *World Directory of Minorities* (1997) 494. Although Somalis constitute one ethnic group, they are divided along clan lines. Since 1991 these divisions have led to the collapse of the Somalian state, with inter-clan warfare involving various warlords who have been exercising control over different parts of its territory. For a succinct account of the conflict in Somalia see R Cornwell 'Somalia: Fourteenth Time Lucky?' (April 2004) ISS Occasional Paper 87.

[6] J Maxted & A Zegeye 'North and Central Africa' *World Directory of Minorities* (note 5 above) 405–408.

[7] See RK Hitchcock 'Human Rights and Indigenous Peoples in Africa and Asia' in DP Forsythe & PC McMahon (eds.) *Human Rights and Diversity* (2003) 209.

[8] Maxted & Zegeye (note 6 above).

[9] Dammers & Sogge (note 5 above) 479.

[10] The 11 official languages and the San and Koi languages listed in Section 6 of the Constitution of the Republic of South Africa, 1996 more or less reflect the ethnic makeup of South Africa.

[11] See RE Howard *Human Rights in Common Wealth Africa* (1986) 97.

Rwanda and Burundi. The observation that 'the African states south of the Sahara are more ethnically diverse than those in other regions'[12] reflects this reality.

2.2.1. *The Pre-colonial Background*

The diversity of the modern African state can be traced back to the pre-colonial period. Before the advent of European colonialism in Africa, there were many societies, mostly bound by kinship ties. Although the colonial policy of divide and rule created further divisions or new 'tribes' by merging resembling groups into one for political purposes, there were almost as many traditional societies in Africa as the number of the ethno-cultural groups that inhabit the post-colonial African state today.[13] These were historically evolved societies that possessed their own culture and language. They inhabited smaller territories than most distinguishable groups do today, and had mostly smaller population size. According to Mutua, 'a feature common to all pre-colonial African societies was their ethnic, cultural and linguistic homogeneity – a trait that gave them fundamental cohesion.'[14]

Africa's pre-colonial societies, regarded by many as national societies,[15] had different historical experiences, political traditions and social structures.[16] Following Busia Jr's classification and Wilson's typology of African pre-colonial societies in terms of their socio-political structures and historical experiences, one can identify four patterns of socio-political organisation.[17]

First, there were communities with their own pre-colonial states in the form of empires or kingdoms.[18] These had their own state-like political system centred on a culturally identifiable core group. They possessed centralised political structures involving administration, law-making and enforcement. In these societies, people had a common sense of belonging and of sharing one

---

[12] TR Gurr *Minorities at Risk: A Global View of Ethnopolitical Conflicts* (1993) 225.

[13] See B Davidson *The Black Man's Burden: Africa and the Curse of the Nation-State* (1992) 100–102; On the survival of these identities see Davidson at 99.

[14] MW Mutua 'The Banjul Charter and the African Cultural Fingerprint: An Evaluation of the Language of Duties' (1995) 35 *Virginia J Int L* 339, 347. Some of those with highly centralised political structures were, however, constituted by more than one ethnic community, but possessed a strong core ethnic group or shared a common religion.

[15] For a detailed examination and illustration of this see Davidson (note 13 above) 74–98.

[16] As Wilson pointed out, '[p]recolonial African societies exhibited great diversity, comprising city states and self-governing villages alongside sizable nations with distinctive political structures.' HS Wilson *The Imperial Experience in Sub-Saharan Africa Since 1870* (1977) 24.

[17] For further analysis of the nature of these formations and their human rights implications in present-day Africa see NKA Busia, Jr 'The Status of Human Rights in Pre-Colonial Africa: Implications for Contemporary Practices' in E McCarthy-Arnolds et al. (eds.) *Africa, Human Rights and the Global System: The Political Economy of Human Rights in a Changing World* (1994) 225–250.

[18] Examples of groups in this category include, among others, the Buganda, Ashanti, AmaZulu, Bakongo, Mossi etc. See OC Okafor *Re-Defining Legitimate Statehood: International Law and State Fragmentation in Africa* (2002) 23.

system of government, even if they were not ethno-culturally homogenous. At the advent of colonialism, some were in the process of developing important characteristics to become nation-states.[19] In Wilson's typology, these are referred to as communities with a history of imperial structures of varying durability.[20]

The second category consists of communities of smaller size and territorial jurisdiction. These were more homogenous communities with centralised and hierarchical socio-political structures and traditions. They constituted polities having chiefdoms and kingdoms of various kinds.[21] The socio-political organisation of most groups in this category was centralised and hierarchical, which provided their individual members with a shared sense of belonging.

The third category of groups consists of those with decentralised social and political structures.[22] Their political units constituted no more than loose village alliances.[23] They had egalitarian social formations, where political and social relationships were essentially horizontal, while allowing village elders a degree of leadership. In these societies, age grades were very central to the organisation of society and village elders therefore held the centre stage of political authority.[24]

There are also groups that fall outside of Wilson's typology. These are what Busia Jr called non-settled nomadic polities – hunters and gatherers or cattle herders leading a pre-modern way of life with no identifiable political structure.[25] In these societies, the idea of organised political structure was the least developed, and their members were barely conscious of belonging to a distinct political community.[26]

Apart from differences in their political traditions, these historical communities constituting modern African states additionally differed in their lifestyle and mode of livelihood, as they do today. Whereas some are pastoralists, many

---

19 The case of Ashanti of Ghana aptly illustrates this. According to Davidson, 'it was manifestly a national state on its way towards becoming a nation-state with every attribute ascribed to a west European nation-state' Davidson (note 13 above) 76. The same is true of the Buganda of Uganda and the Bakongo of Angola.

20 See Wilson (note 16 above) 97.

21 Examples in this category include the Ankole and Toro of Uganda, the Hausa and Niger Delta states of what is now Nigeria, the Akan states of Ghana, and the Tswana, Ndebele, Sotho, Xhosa etc. of southern Africa. See CA Diop *Pre-colonial Black Africa* (1987) 89–92; Wilson (note 16 above) 97.

22 These are, according to Davidson, 'segmentary societies' where delegation of power to chiefly persons was limited, minimal or nonexistent. Davidson (note 14 above) 86.

23 Examples include the Lou, Oromo, Igbo, Nuer, Ebrie, Tallensi, Kikuyu, Akamba, Igbo etc. See Busia, Jr (note 17 above) 232. In Wilson's typology these were stateless societies, which were divided into small village units. Wilson (note 16 above) 97.

24 See Busia, Jr (note 17 above) 232–233.

25 Ibid.

26 As one report on the pygmies of central Africa states, '[t]he traditional power structure of representative institutions is entirely foreign to pygmy society, as hierarchy is not necessarily a dominant feature of pygmy clans'. IRIN News In-Depth Report *Minorities under Siege: Pygmies Today in Africa* (April 2006) 12 (hereinafter IRIN In-Depth).

others practise sedentary agriculture. There are also scores of hunter-gatherer groups in many African states.

Irrespective of differences in their level of political organisation, size and way of life, these pre-colonial formations are the foundations for present day ethnic groups constituting the modern African states. According to Davidson, '[m]ost of these precolonial political formations were communities with a venerable past rooted in popular acceptance. In the public mind, they were living realities; they were identities to which people strongly held.'[27] Notwithstanding the legitimacy issues that may arise in relation to the political manipulation of ethnicity, even today, ethnic groups continue to constitute identities to which people strongly held and on which people rely to protect their interests. As Cloud Eke observed '[e]thnic formations are often the most significant countervailing force to state power as well as the best defense of a separate space against the totalising tendencies of the post-colonial state. They have been major contributors to the defense of human rights although they have done so largely within the narrow confines of their membership.'[28]

2.2.2. *Colonialism: The Emergence of New Patterns of Relations*

Colonisation completely changed the map of Africa. One of the lasting legacies of the brutal conquest of Africa by European colonial powers was the partition of the continent into various colonial units. At the notorious Berlin Conference of 1884–1885, the colonial African state was established within borders that were contrived on the basis of a combination of negotiation among colonial powers, reference to geographic features and resort to simple geometrical lines.[29]

One of the most distinctive features of this process of the radical imposition of the colonial state was that many of the various pre-colonial societies were forcibly amalgamated under the same political unit and others were sliced and placed into different units. This totally interrupted the autonomous development of these societies and, depriving them of their independence, subjected them to the authority of an alien political structure: the colonial state. Regarding the nature and effect of the colonial boundaries, Lewis rightly notes that:

> [T]he colonial frontiers rarely followed tribal boundaries; and even when they did, grouped together different tribes and language groups with little regard for ethnographic niceties. Each European Colony was thus typically a mosaic of peoples, many of whom had previously little knowledge of, or contact with those

---

[27] Davidson (note 13 above).

[28] Cloude Ake 'What is the Problems of Ethnicity in Africa' 22 *Transformation* (1993) 7.

[29] See I Brownlie *African Boundaries: Legal and Diplomatic Encyclopedia* (1979) 6.

> other communities with whom they were now inseparably associated under a common destiny.[30]

From the perspective of this study, one important consequence of the making of the African state by colonial fiat is the conglomeration within the same political unit of large numbers of culturally divergent, socio-politically and numerically unequal ethno-cultural communities. This gave the African state what Nwabueze calls 'staggering ethnic plurality'[31] involving in some cases hundreds of communities, some of which had a history of animosity and conflict.[32]

In political terms, the effect of the amalgamation of such numerically and socio-politically unequal groups under the colonial state was unequal patterns of relations between the groups and the state, and among the groups themselves. While some of the groups adapted to the colonial state and were relatively well integrated into it in most cases with active colonial favouritism, others were ignored by the colonial powers and excluded from the process. In the development process, this led to some groups being integrated into, and others marginalised from, the newly introduced economic system of the colonial state. In East Africa, for example, those groups who were mainly cultivators and adopted sedentary agriculture after contact with the colonial powers came to constitute the mainstream population of the post-colonial states of the region.[33] This pattern was directly inherited by the post-colonial states. As the economy of the post-colonial state has invariably been structured in a way that privileges crop production, including cash crops, state development policies have prioritised sedentary agriculture while neglecting other traditional modes of livelihood such as pastoralism, animal herding, hunting and gathering.

The agglomeration of such distinct and unequal groups within the same political unit under the colonial-state system simultaneously forced increased interactions between members of those groups that sought to participate in the processes of the new political order. Not only did this bring ethnic self-consciousness to the fore as a necessary element in the processes of the state, but it also set the stage for post-colonial rivalry and conflicts.[34] The result was

---

[30] IM Lewis 'The Tribal Factor in Contemporary Africa' in C Legum & J Drysdale (eds.) *Africa: Contemporary Record 1969–1970* (1971) A 13.

[31] B Nwabueze *Constitutional Democracy in Africa* Vol. 5 (2004) 298.

[32] Howard (note 11 above) 93; Okafor (note 18 above) 25.

[33] See J Ngugi 'The Decolonization-Modernization Interface and the Plight of Indigenous Peoples in Post-Colonial Development Discourses in Africa' (2002) 20 *Wisconsin Int L J* 279, 324.

[34] As G Selassie argued, this is partly because the 'juxtaposition of two or more ethnic groups in the same political environment often results in each group attempting to disaffirm the other politically'. AG Selassie 'Ethnic Identity and Constitutional Design for Africa' (1992–93) Fall 29 (1) *Stanford J of Int Law* 1, 9. It is not, however, the mere existence of different groups within one political system that produces the rivalry. The problem arises where this is accompanied by the absence of an agreed-upon democratic framework for mutual benefit and coexistence among the constituent groups within a polity, hence opening the state up for grabs by any of the groups. See

'more pronounced cleavages between groups which have given rise to lasting patterns of tension in the postcolonial times.'[35]

It was not merely the amalgamation of culturally distinct and politically and socio-economically unequal groups, and the resultant inequality, that led to the genesis of the issue of minorities in Africa. The colonial state, as part of its system of control known as divide and rule, institutionalised unequal patterns of relations among members of various groups horizontally, and between particular groups and the state vertically. This system ranked members of various groups differently as 'advantaged' or 'disadvantaged' based on their ethnic membership. As L Adel Jinadu puts it:

> This asymmetrical stratification system fractured or differentiated citizenship in many colonial territories, in such a way that it facilitated (for privileged ethnic groups) or constricted (for underprivileged ethnic groups) access to the state and its resources, in the public services, in commerce, trade and industry, in the judicial system and administration of justice ...[36]

Although the colonial process denigrated and deformed traditional institutions and the cultures of various groups, it has in important ways reinforced group or cultural membership to be the dominant marker of individual identification not only horizontally in the social realm but also vertically in the political sphere. In other words, the colonial process assigned ethnic group membership a particular level of political saliency.

The nature of the administration of the colonial state, more particularly its economic processes, also led to the creation of new patterns of inequality among members of the various ethno-cultural groups. This mainly related to the uneven distribution by the colonial state of the goods of modernisation, such as education, jobs in the colonial administration and infrastructure development. As a result, while some enjoyed access to education and employment opportunities, acquired skills in the running of European institutions and hence achieved higher levels of political and socio-economic integration, many others had only limited access, and some were totally excluded.

Moreover, as its main purpose was advancing the economic goals of the relevant colonial power, the state was run in a way that resulted in an uneven distribution of economic advantages. As a result, peoples living in areas that served as centres of economic activity and administration 'were exposed to

---

A Eide 'Minority Situations: In Search of Peaceful and Constructive solutions' 66 *Notre Dame L. Rev.* (1991) 1311, 1321.

[35] D Rothchild 'Reconfiguring State-Ethnic Relations in Africa: Liberalization and the Search for New Routines of Interaction' in P Lewis (ed.) *Africa: Dilemmas of Development and Change* (1998) 215.

[36] LA Jinadu *Explaining and Managing Ethnic Conflict in Africa: Towards a Cultural Theory of Democracy* Claude Ake Memorial Papers No 1 (2007) 15.

greater administrative intensity, more commercial activity, and more active missionary and education presence'[37] than peoples in peripheral areas. Such is the case, for example, with respect to the coastal areas of West Africa and the mining lands of southern Africa and the DRC, as well as the coastal areas and farm lands of East Africa.[38] This resulted in unequal access to economic resources and modern social goods among the various constituent groups and regions of African states, further accentuating the already existing cleavages occasioned by the amalgamation of groups without regard to their historical, cultural and socio-political differences. The effect has been to intensify rivalry and 'tension between ethno-regions that were advantaged by close contact with Western education, infrastructural improvement, and agricultural and industrial development and those in the hinterland that remained neglected.'[39]

The cumulative effects of the imposition of the colonial state on arbitrarily amalgamated diverse and unequal ethno-cultural groups, the manipulation of ethnicity and the uneven distribution of modern goods in the colonial process has been the institutionalisation of ethnic divisions, rendering ethno-cultural diversity politically salient. As the patterns of minority claims identified below in this chapter and the discussions in Chapter III show, the political saliency of ethnicity has further been entrenched in the patterns of governance and state-society relations pursued by post-colonial governments.

2.2.3. *Patterns of Ethno-Cultural Diversity Bequeathed to the Post-colonial State*

2.2.3.1. *States with a Majority Group*

Although there is no up-to-date and reliable official population census on the ethnic composition of most African states, examination of secondary sources suggests that only about one fifth have a *numerically* dominant majority group.[40] In some of these states, the largest group constitutes only a bare majority. This

---

[37] D Welsh 'Ethnicity in Sub-Saharan Africa' (1996) 72 *Int'l Affairs* 479.

[38] See details D Horowitz *Ethnic Groups in Conflict* (1985) 151–156.

[39] Rothchild (note 35 above) 215.

[40] Of these many are northern African states, such as Egypt, Libya, Tunisia, Algeria and Morocco – each of which, except Algeria and Morocco where Berbers constitute twenty one and thirty seven per cent respectively, has a majority group that accounts for more than ninety per cent of the population. In Swaziland and Seychelles, Swazis and Creole respectively account for more than ninety per cent, in Rwanda and Burundi Hutus constitute about eighty five per cent, and in Equatorial Guinea the Fang ethnic group makes up eighty to ninety per cent of the population. In the others the majority fall in a range from a little more than fifty per cent, as in the case of the Hausa of Niger or Issa of Djibouti, to about seventy seven per cent in the case of the Shona of Zimbabwe. Botswana is another country with dominant majority, the Tswana, who comprise more than sixty per cent of the total population. The data employed here is collected from CIA World Fact Book 2005 <http://www.cia.gov/cia/publications/factbook> and the general information available at <http://www.library.uu.nl/wesp/populstat/Africa/algeriag.htm>.

is, for example, the case in Niger and Djibouti.[41] In most cases, the numerically minority groups are numerous and diverse.[42]

There are differences among these states in the nature of the relationship between the majority group and minorities. From this perspective, one can identify two classes of states: those with a single numerically and politically dominant group, and those with two numerically large and politically contending groups. Botswana,[43] Egypt,[44] Algeria and Morocco[45] are among the single-group-dominated states, where the majority group enjoys an established dominant position and hence is generally in effective control of the state. In these states, minority groups are generally in a precarious situation, faced with the danger of discrimination, assimilation and domination.[46]

Zimbabwe, Rwanda and Burundi exemplify states with two large and contending groups, what Ali A. Mazrui termed dual societies.[47] In Zimbabwe, there has been a history of rivalry for political power between the majority Shona and the Ndebele, who constitute the largest minority. Other minorities, including the Shangaan, Venda and Tonga, are 'at the political and geographical margins outside the Shona-Ndebele polarity'.[48] Rwanda and Burundi manifest a history of genocidal strife and deep ethnic animosity between the majority Hutu and the dominant minority Tutsi. The Tua, the smallest minority group in these two countries, are generally outside of the Hutu-Tutsi rivalry and constitute the most marginalised and vulnerable section of society. In these states the majority has not established itself as being in effective control of the state system. As a result, its relationship with the minority is best characterised as having been one of

---

41 In Niger, the majority Housa people form only a little more than half of the total population. See Niger *CIA World Fact Book* 2006 <http://www.cia.gov/cia/publications/factbook>; A Neef 'Ethnic Groups in Niger' in GP Lawrence & M von Oppen (eds.) *Adapted Farming in West Africa: Issues, Potentials and Perspectives* (2000). The Isa of Djibouti account for about sixty per cent of the total population. See PJ Schraeder 'Ethnic Politics in Djibouti: From "Eye of the Hurricane" to "Boiling cauldron"' (1993) 92 *African Affairs* 203.

42 Such is, for example, the case with respect to Zimbabwe, Botswana and Niger.

43 See JS Solway 'Reaching the Limits of Universal Citizenship: "Minority" Struggles in Botswana' in B Berman et al. (eds.) *Ethnicity and Democracy in Africa* (2004) 129–147. In Botswana such minorities as the Kalanga, BaKgalagadi and the Basarwa, comprising seven, five and three per cent respectively, have experienced various degrees of exclusion, the Basarwa being the most disadvantaged of all. See Dammers & Sogge (note 5 above) 474–475.

44 See Maxted & Abebe Zegeye (note 6 above) 405–408.

45 See section on ethno-cultural minorities below.

46 These are groups who are in a similar situation to what Kymlicka calls national minorities. He describes the circumstances underlying their vulnerability: '[T]he viability of their societal cultures may be undermined by economic and political decisions made by the majority. They could be outbid or outvoted on resources and policies that are crucial to the survival of their societal cultures.' W Kymlicka *Multicultural Citizenship: A Liberal Theory of Minority Rights* (1995) 109.

47 Ali A. Mazrui 'Black Berlin and the Curse of Fragmentation: From Bismark to Barak' preface to Adekeye Adebajo's *The Curse of Berlin: Africa after the Cold War* (2010) ix, xv.

48 See Dammers & Sogge (note 5 above) 530; see further M Sithole 'Ethnicity and Democratization in Zimbabwe' in H Glickman (ed.) *Ethnic Conflict and Democratization in Africa* (1995) 121–160.

rivalry for control of the state machinery. However, in Zimbabwe, although it has caused intermittent tensions and violence, this rivalry has not led to the kinds of catastrophic conflicts and civil wars that it induced in Rwanda and Burundi.

2.2.3.2. *States of Minorities*

In most African states, there is no single majority group, in numerical terms. These states are all inhabited by many different groups, each comprising less than half of the total population. These are close to Mazrui's plural societies, societies with multiple groups.[49] There are, however, wide differences among the groups constituting these states in terms of population size and power relations.

The groups constituting these states vary widely in terms of population size. Many of these states are composed of a few numerically dominant groups and numerous other smaller groups. The population sizes range from many millions, as in the cases of the Hausa, the Buganda, the Ashanti and the Oromo, to some thousands, as in the case of the Zemi.[50] While the few large groups account for somewhere in the range of 20 to 45 per cent of the total populations of the states to which they belong, the large number of smaller groups contribute about ten per cent or less each. In Nigeria, the Housa-Fulani, Yoruba and Igbo account for 29, 20 and 17 per cent of the population respectively. Similarly, in Ethiopia, the Amharas, Oromos and Tigreans together form more than 66 per cent of the total population. The Fang in Gabon; the Kongo, Sangha, Mboshi, and Teke in the Republic of Congo; and the Baya, Banda and Mandiji in the Central African Republic enjoy a numerically dominant position. Similar demographic trends exist in other countries, such as Kenya, Angola, Zambia and Malawi.[51]

Most importantly, the various groups differ in terms of political influence and access to resources, and degree of inclusion in the socio-cultural and economic framework of the state. Generally speaking, in these states no one particular group has achieved an established political or socio-economic dominance. With no agreed upon and inclusive political processes, the constituent groups in most of these states have been in constant rivalry for a share of political power and access to resources. In many of these states, such as Nigeria, Kenya, Ethiopia, Angola etc., the larger groups are generally at the centre of this struggle. Often the smaller groups are either drawn into this rivalry or, in most cases, remain at the periphery of the political and economic processes of the state, which are

---

49 Mazrui (note 47 above).

50 JS Wunsch 'Foundations of Centralization: The Colonial Experience and the African Context' in JS Wunsch & D Olowu (eds.) *The Failure of the Centralized State: Institutions and Self-Governance in Africa* (1990) 34.

51 The data employed here is collected from CIA World Factbook 2005 available at <http://www.cia.gov/cia/publications/factbook> and the general information available at <http://www.library.uu.nl/wesp/populstat/Africa/algeriag.htm>.

dominated by the struggle of the large contending groups. Where any one of the contending groups or a coalition of some of them takes power, it puts the machinery of the state to the service of their own interests. Members of other groups are often left out of the political and socio-economic structures. Those that (have been perceived to) pose a threat to the political elite in power, as in Liberia under Samuel Doe, have often been subject to repression through arbitrary arrest, torture and intimidation of their leaders, and, in the worst cases, mass killings and massacres.

2.3. Various Categories of Minorities and the Nature of their Claims

Given the high level of diversity and the demographic, socio-economic and historical inequality of the various communities that form part of the post-colonial African state, the issue of minorities in Africa does not take any one particular form. Rather, the issue of minorities takes different forms. The aim of this section is thus to identify the various kinds of minorities and the nature and types of claims that they make.

As the discussion in the foregoing sections illustrates, the genesis of the issue of minorities (or ethno-cultural diversity) in Africa significantly differs from the historical process that accounts for the issue of minorities in Western democracies. As Kymlicka explains, the issues of minorities in Western democracies arises mainly from the nature of the process of nation-building pursued in these countries over several centuries, and minority rights acquire their moral justification from the injustice that this process caused to minority groups. This difference implies that the classification of minorities into national minorities and ethnic minorities developed by multicultural theorists such as Kymlicka is not adequate to understand and analyse the phenomena of minorities in Africa.[52] Informed by the discussion in the foregoing sections, the classification elaborated in this section illustrates the specific features of minority issues in Africa. Most importantly, this analysis provides the basis for identifying and elaborating the characteristics of a constitutional design that best achieves the accommodation of diversity specific to the African experience.

---

[52] On nation-building as the origin and underlying justification of minority rights in Western democracies see Will Kymlicka 'Nation-building and Minority Rights: Comparing Africa and the West' in Bruce Berman (et al.) *Ethnicity and Democracy in Africa* (2004) 54. It is not uncommon to classify groups for the purpose of understanding minority demands. See Kymlicka (note 46 above) Chapter 2. This analysis is informed by the classification that Ted Robert Gurr makes in his work on minorities at risk, but since that work does not sufficiently capture the nature and situation of groups in Africa, on account of its global orientation, his classification is also not adopted in its entirety in this study. See Gurr (note 12 above).

The typology of minority issues identified in this section does not suggest that there are distinct boundaries in the different forms that the issue of minorities takes in Africa. It acknowledges that in the real world there are overlaps, and circumstances revealing mixed or intermediary cases. Nor does the categories of minorities identified in this section cover all aspects of the manifestations of the phenomenon of minorities in Africa. It recognises the historical and socio-cultural specificity of the various groups falling within the same classification and the diversity in the focus and range of claims they make. The typology is mainly limited to identifying categories of those aspects of Africa's ethno-cultural diversity that mostly define patterns of ethnic-based political contestation, strife, inequality and domination as salient elements of the crisis of legitimate statehood and of nation-building in post-colonial Africa.

2.3.1. *Ethno-Cultural Minorities*

The first category consists of *ethno-cultural minorities*. These are groups that have and seek to maintain and enjoy recognition for their own distinct culture/language which is different from the culture/language of the dominant population, and/or the large ethnic groups in the population. Examples include the Berbers of Morocco and Algeria; the Copts of Egypt; non-Chewa-speaking groups in pre-1994 Malawi; the Wayeyi, Kgalagadi and other non-Tswana groups in Botswana and the various non-Amharic speaking ethnic groups in Ethiopia. These minorities have been disadvantaged by the institutionalisation of the dominant language and other cultural attributes of the mainstream society in the processes of the state, leading to their non-recognition and the marginalisation of their distinct culture. As a result, they face multiple pressures to abandon their culture and assimilate into the mainstream society, or face exclusion and hence relegation to a status of secondary citizenship.

This is as much a result of the making of the African state by colonial fiat that lumped together culturally divergent and unequal historical communities as it is of the failure of the post-colonial state to acknowledge the cultural attachments of its population and integrate them on an equitable basis. The post-colonial nation-building process of some African states has been hegemonic. The dominant culture has been used to create a semblance of national integration by way of a common language, national identity and, in some cases, even religion. In these countries, the language and other cultural attributes of dominant groups have been institutionalised in the processes of the state to the exclusion of other languages and cultures. As a result, minority cultures, having been left unrecognised and subjected to repression, have been exposed to erosion and ruin, and the dignity and sense of equality of members of these groups have consequently also been damaged.

The state employs a variety of approaches to induce the assimilation of minority cultures or their peripheralisation. One can categorise these approaches as taking either of the following forms, or a combination of both: a coercive one, consisting of the restriction or outlawing of a group's language, impositions upon its traditional practices and ways of life, the persecution of cultural leaders and clergy members, and attacks on academics and intellectuals; and an assimilationist one, involving a systematic process of nationalising the dominant culture to the exclusion of others.[53]

A good example of a country that has employed a coercive approach to institutionalise the dominant culture is Algeria.[54] The question of the identity of Algeria has been one of the most contentious issues in the country's post-independence politics. Although Algeria is multicultural, and 27 per cent of its population is composed of the indigenous Amazigh, throughout its post-independence existence Algeria has defined itself as a purely Arab state and pursued a policy of Arabisation. As a result, under Article 3 of Algeria's Constitution, Arabic has been institutionalised as the only Algerian language. Linguistic and cultural expressions of the Amazigh were forbidden and the practice of Amazigh nationalism, labelled 'Berberism', has been outlawed.[55] As part of the policy of Arabisation, in 1998 the government passed a comprehensive law that required the use of Arabic in all spheres of public life.[56] The nationalisation of Arab identity has thus involved, to use Anderson's expression, 'a systematic, even Machiavellian, instilling of nationalist ideology through the mass media, the educational system, administrative regulations and so forth',[57] exclusively on the basis of the cultural attributes of the dominant Arab majority. The Amazigh in Morocco are in a similar situation to their counterparts in Algeria.[58]

This has led to the emergence of an Amazigh ethno-cultural movement demanding equal recognition and protection for their languages and cultural practices.[59] The expression and articulation of their distinct culture and the use of their language in public has frequently resulted in detentions and violent

---

[53] The essence of the assimilationist approach is aptly captured in Adeno Addis's definition of assimilation. See A Addis 'Individualism, Communitarianism, and the Rights of Ethnic Minorities' (1992) 67 *Notre Dame LR* 615, 619–620.

[54] See Jacob Mundi 'The Failure of Transformative Minority Politics in Algeria: The Kabyli Citizen's Movement and the State' in *Minorities and the State in Africa* (2010) 81.

[55] 'From 1980 to 1988, an estimated 300 activists for Amazigh were imprisoned for "Berberism".' ACHPR *Report of the African Commission's Working Group of Experts on Indigenous Populations/Communities* (2005) 43 (hereinafter ACHPR Report).

[56] See UNHRC *Concluding Observations of the Human Rights Committee on the Second Periodic Report of Algeria* UN Doc. CCPR/C/79/ADD. 95 (August 1998) para 15 (hereinafter UNHRC on Algeria).

[57] B Anderson *Imagined Communities: Reflections on the Origin and Spread of Nationalism* (1991) 113–114.

[58] See ACHPR Report (note 49 above) 42–43.

[59] See J McDougal *History and the Culture of Nationalism in Algeria* (2006) 184–216.

repression.[60] Although the Arabic Language Decree of 1998 has been suspended following a recommendation by the UNHRC,[61] and the Algerian Constitution was amended in October 2002 to recognise Tamazight, the Amazigh language, as a national language, there has been no significant change in legislation or practice to reflect this and hence the situation of the Amazigh remains precarious.

The definition of the identity of the state has also been a source of tension between dominant and smaller groups in many other African states. Most notable examples include countries composed of Arab and African-origin population groups such as Sudan, Chad[62] and Mauritania.[63] Much of the post-independence political history of these countries reflects the struggle arising from the attempts of successive governments to impose the dominant Arab culture and Arabic language on African population groups, and the resistance of the latter.[64] Indeed, this is one of several factors which led to the civil war in the Sudan.[65] The approach employed by governments in these states has often been generally repressive, and sometimes violent. Other African states have employed a variation on the coercive approach, in which institutional pressure has been put on certain groups to force them into abandoning their traditional practices and ways of life.[66]

The assimilationist approach is reminiscent of Benedict Anderson's idea of official nationalism.[67] This is a process by which a state institutionalises the culture of the dominant group as a national culture by way of 'stretching the short, tight, skin of the nation over the gigantic body of the empire.'[68] It involved the diffusion of the majority (or dominant) group's language and culture all over

[60] See Maxted & Zegeye (note 6 above) 394.

[61] Practices against the culture of the Amazigh include the prohibition of the registration of children who are given Amazigh names as well as the outlawing of the use of Tamazight in courts. Amazigh are not also allowed to give Amazigh names to their organisations and companies, nor to write in Tifingh. Tamazight is not as yet officially recognised nor is it taught at any level of the education system. UNHRC on Algeria (note 56 above) para 15.

[62] See generally S Decalo 'Chad: The Roots of Centre Periphery Strife' (1980) 79 *African Affairs* 491.

[63] The title of the news item 'Mauritania – Neither Arab nor African' from the Nordic Africa Institute succinctly captures the nature of the problem that characterises much of the post-independence politics of Mauritania. See Gariba Diallo 'Mauritania – Neither Arab nor African' <http://www.nai.uu.se/newsfromnia/arkiv/2000/diallo.html>.

[64] According to Horowitz for these Afro-Arab states the persistent questions have been: is the state to be Arab or African, and its derivative: who would rule it, Arabs or Africans? Horowitz (note 38 above) 189.

[65] For a discussion on the cultural basis of the southern Sudan struggle, see FM Deng 'Sudan's Turbulent Road to Nationhood' in R René Larémont (ed.) *Borders, Nationalism and the African State* (2005) 33, 42–60.

[66] One illustration of this is the attempt of Tanzanian authorities to destroy the cultural identity of the Massai ethnic group, giving the group a choice between 'abandoning the ancestral customs or exclusion from public life.' See ACHPR Report (note 55 above).

[67] See Anderson (note 57 above) particularly 83–112.

[68] Ibid, 86.

the territory of the state through state institutions. The media, the education system and all other public activities reproduce the dominant culture and are conducted in the language of the dominant group. No space is left for expression of other cultures, and those who are not members of the dominant culture have no choice but to assimilate into it or face exclusion.[69] This has been the case, for example, in such countries as Ethiopia,[70] Malawi[71] and Botswana.[72]

It is clear from the foregoing that one of the various forms that the issue of minorities in Africa takes involves situations in which the existence and identity of non-dominant ethnic groups have been denied public expression, either through forced imposition of the dominant culture and the concomitant repression of

---

[69] This happens to be the case even when effective and seemingly 'neutral' individual rights are accorded to all citizens. For further discussion of this see Chapter III.

[70] See C Clapham 'Ethnicity and the National Question in Ethiopia' in P Woodward & M Forsyth (eds.) *Conflict and Peace in the Horn of Africa: Federalism and Its Alternatives* (1994) 27–40; A Fiseha *Federalism and the Accommodation of Diversity in Ethiopia* (2006). The origin of the modern Ethiopian state was what was known as historic Ethiopia. According to Adhana Haile Adhana, '[t]he historic Ethiopian state normally known as Abyssinia had the Tigray (speaking Tigrigna), the Christian Agew (speaking Agewigna) and the Amhara (speaking Amharic) as its core and as components of its nationhood, although the Tigray and the Amhara were preponderant ... *The uniting or core culture consisted of common history and Christianity, not Amharic or the Amhara core culture*' (my emphasis). A Haile Adhana 'Mutation of Statehood and Contemporary Politics' in A Zegeye & S Pausewang (eds.) *Ethiopia in Change: Peasantry, Nationalism and Democracy* (1994) 12, 19. Ethiopia's sovereignty was legally established – after the Battle of Adwa, where Ethiopia defeated the colonial forces of Italy – when Ethiopia signed boundary agreements with France, Great Britain, and Italy between 1898 and 1907. See Brownlie (note 29 above) 775. The process of boundary consolidation that took place during the course of late 19th and early 20th centuries and gave Ethiopia its current demographic and territorial shape involved, to use the words of Anderson, the 'welding of two opposing political orders, one ancient [historic Ethiopia], one quite new [modern Ethiopia]'. Anderson (note 57 above) 86. The imposition of the identity of historic Ethiopia over the gigantic body of the new empire led to the emergence of numerous ethno-national and ethno-cultural movements.

[71] See generally D Kaspin 'Tribes, Regions and Nationalism in Democratic Malawi' in I Shapiro & W Kymlicka (eds.) *Ethnicity and Group Rights* (1997) 464–503. Although Malawi consisted of more than a dozen ethnic groups, its post-independence nation-building process under the one-party rule of Hastings Banda was directed to 'the promotion of one ethnicity – the Chewa – as the national mainstream, and one region – the centre – as Malawi's heartland'. Ibid, 470. This was accompanied by the promotion of Chewa language as the national language and Chewa culture as the cornerstone of nationhood and the source of its political iconography. See ibid; Pascal Kishindo 'The Impact of a National Language on Minority Languages: The Case of Malawi' (1994) 12(2) *J of Contemporary African Studies* 138.

[72] The post-independence constitutional and political order of Botswana was established on the premise of what Richard Werbner called the One-nation Consensus. Richard Werbner 'Introduction: Challenging Minorities, Difference and Tribal Citizenship in Botswana' (2002) 28(4) *J of Southern African Studies* 676. This was an assimilationist and culturally exclusive policy that was directed at the official nationalisation of the Tswana nation with no regard to the cultures and languages of the various other groups. See Solway (note 43 above); *Kamanakao & Others v Attorney-General and Another* (2002) *African Human Rights Law Reports* (AHRLR) (BwHc 2001) 35–58; 'Violations of Linguistic and Cultural Rights of Minority Groups in Botswana': statement of Lydia Ramahobo to the UN Working Group on Minorities (1 March 2004) available at <http://www.unhchr.ch/minorities/statements10/MCB3a.doc> last accessed on 27 September 2006.

minority cultures, or through official nationalisation of the cultural attributes of the dominant society and the promotion of the assimilation of members of other cultures. For groups in this category, their non-recognition has not only undermined their members' identity and self-respect, it has also caused their marginalisation from the political and socio-economic framework of the state in which they live. As an expression of their equal inclusion into society and an affirmation of their equal rights and status as citizens, members of these groups therefore demand not only the recognition of their languages and culture, but also the expression of their linguistic and cultural attributes in the structures and processes of the state, as constituent elements of the national make-up of the state. This entails the re-definition of the state as a multicultural state. Although the detailed institutional and policy arrangements that this entails varies considerably from case to case, the scope of such arrangements ranges from symbolic recognition reflecting the culture, language or religion of the group in the national symbols, institutions and characters to the granting of self-government.

2.3.2. *Ethno-Political Minorities*

The second category of minorities involves those communities whose main concern is to achieve representation and participation in the political process of the state. Their interest is more in gaining a fair share of political power or in having adequate or effective representation or say in the decision-making processes of the state than in the recognition and protection of their cultural identity per se. Being at the centre of competition for political power, the main focus of the demand of groups in this category is the distribution of political power. In other words, their demand requires the formulation of mechanisms that ensure their effective political representation and participation, among other issues. Seen in this light, the term *ethno-political minorities* best describes the nature of such minorities.[73] Arguably, most ethnic groups in most African states are ethno-political.[74]

It is the historical process of the making of the African state, and the inability of the post-colonial state to build legitimate political and constitutional frameworks, that have adversely affected a just distribution of constitutional goods, most particularly political rights (the equitable representation and participation of members of the constituent ethno-cultural groups), in conditions of deep

[73] Such groups are also known in Gurr's typology as communal contenders. Gurr (note 12 above) 18.

[74] This is consistent with the finding in Gurr's study that most groups in sub-Saharan Africa are communal contenders, and account for about eighty per cent of the world's communal contenders. Ibid, 22 & 255.

ethno-cultural diversity and inequality. The colonial origin of the African state affected power relations among various groups and between the groups and the state in two ways. First, it brought together groups with different historical traditions, and unequal political and socio-economic standing, under one political authority with no guarantee of or provision for their equitable integration into the state. This inevitably led to formidable challenges for mutual co-existence as part of one political community and in the organisation and distribution of political power.[75] Secondly, it set the stage for increased interactions between, particularly, those groups that mobilised in the struggle for independence. As previously noted, intensified ethnic self-consciousness and rivalry were the result.[76]

The structure of government introduced by the colonial state was not organised to harness integration and a common political vision in the various African territories on which it was imposed.[77] In the first place, it had no historical or social foundations in those territories. Moreover, the colonial state organised political authority and operated in these territories in a way that entrenched the system of divide and rule,[78] and hence political as well as socio-economic inequality among the various groups. Furthermore, by its nature, it was highly centralised and its authoritarian administrative machinery brought almost all political and military power, as well as economic resources and modern social goods, under centralised control.[79] One of the dominant features of the African political scene during and after formal independence has therefore been the rivalry of the constituent units of society for control of the state.[80]

In most post-colonial African states, during the process of independence and also thereafter, the parties involved did not properly negotiate or establish a workable political and constitutional framework that would have provided

[75] See NKA Busia, Jr 'The Right to Self-Determination, the State and the Quest for Democracy in Africa: An Explanatory Analysis' (1992) *Proceedings of the 4th Annual Conference of African Society of Int and Comparative Law* 24.

[76] See Seilassie (note 34 above) 9; Eide (note 34 above) 1321.

[77] See A Rivkin *Nation-Building in Africa: Problems and Prospects* (1969) 1; see also Davidson (note 13 above) 184–185.

[78] See JO Ihonvbere 'The State and Ethnicity in Africa' in E Ike Udogu (ed.) *The Issue of Political Ethnicity in Africa* (2001) 59, 70; see also MW Mutua 'Putting Humpty Dumpty Back Together: The Dilemmas of the Post-colonial African State' (1995) 21 *Brooklyn J of Int Law* 505, 520–522.

[79] J Wilson 'Ethnic Groups and the Right to Self-Determination' (Spring 1996) 11 *Connecticut J of Int L* 433, 441 (stating that during the colonial period, colonial powers had exclusive control over the political and economic resources of their colonies).

[80] Exceptions to this include, most importantly, Botswana and Tanzania. On Botswana, see J Reader *Africa: A Biography of the Continent* (1998) 665. For Tanzania, the use of Swahili as a common language and the particularly small size of all of the 125 ethnic groups, together with their mostly non-hierarchical traditional political structure, has made ethnic mobilisation for control of state power unworkable. Since the institutionalisation of multiparty democracy, however, the country has witnessed Christian-Muslim tensions and rising secessionist sentiments in offshore Zanzibar. See H Glickman 'The Management of Ethnic Politics and Democratization in Tanzania' in Glickman (note 48 above) 289, 291–297.

sufficient guarantees of equitable representation and effective participation for the members of various groups. As a result, in the run-up to independence and subsequently (such as most notably when the wind of democratic change blew over Africa in the 1990s), political power has been contested among political movements that mainly mobilised their support from members of particular ethnic groups.[81] Such has been the case, for example, in Nigeria,[82] Angola,[83] the DRC (former Zaire),[84] Mauritius,[85] Kenya,[86] Uganda,[87] Zambia,[88] Zimbabwe,[89] Ghana,[90] Sierra Leone,[91] Sudan,[92] Chad,[93] Rwanda,[94] and Burundi.[95] The nature of the competition has been a zero-sum game, with each group seeking to dominate the political environment. Thus, in the cases of Rwanda and Burundi,

---

[81] See S Adejumobi 'Citizenship, Rights, the Problem of Conflicts and Civil Wars in Africa' (2001) 23 *Human Rights Quarterly* 148, 159.

[82] See John Reader *Africa: A Biography of the Continent* (1997) 660–665.

[83] AV Malaquias 'The Political Economy of Angola's Ethnic Conflict' in S MacLean et al. (eds.) *The Crises of Governance in Asia And Africa* (2001) 207–226; See A Pitsch 'Ovimbundu of Angola: A Case from University of Maryland's Minorities at Risk Project' (1995) <http://www.bsos.umd.edu./cidcm/mar/angovim.htm.>.

[84] See A Heraclides *Self-Determination of Minorities in International Politics* (1991) 58.

[85] See D Kadima & R Kasenally 'The Formation, Collapse and Revival of Political Party Coalitions in Mauritius: Ethnic Logic and Calculation at Play' in D Kadima (ed.) *The Politics of Party Coalitions in Africa* (2006) 73–110, 74–76.

[86] See the case study on Kenya, J Scarrit 'Communal Conflict and Contention for Power in Africa South of the Sahara' in Gurr (note 12 above) 270–277; see also G Muigai 'Jomo Kenyatta and the Rise of the Ethno-Nationalist State in Kenya' in Berman et al. (note 40 above) 200–217. For a discussion on current communal rivalry in Kenya see A Pitsch 'Political Rivalries and Communal Vengeance in Kenya' in TR Gurr *Peoples Versus States: Minorities at Risk in the New Century* (2000) 261–265.

[87] See N Kasfir 'Cultural Sub-nationalism in Uganda' in VA Olorunsola (ed.) *The Politics of Cultural Sub-nationalism in Africa* (1972) 51–148; P Mbabazi 'Ethnicities in Crises of Governance in Africa: The Case of Uganda in the Great Lakes Region' in S MacLean et al. (note 77 above) 227–244.

[88] See generally DN Posner *Institutions and Ethnic Politics in Africa* (2005); Also on Zambia see J Scarrit in Gurr (note 12 above) 264–279.

[89] See Sithole (note 44 above) 132–145.

[90] According to Howard, before independence, the Ashanti-based National Liberation Movement was the chief opponent of Kwame Nkrumah's Convention Peoples Party. Howard (note 11 above), 92–93.

[91] The conflict that ended in 1999 started as rebellion by the Revolutionary United Front (RUF) which drew its main support from the Tamne ethnic group. According to Gurr, the rebellion that led to the conflict was an outgrowth of long-standing communal rivalries over access to official positions and largesse. He further added that one of the justifications offered by the RUF leader was to eliminate the 'hegemony of the Mende' in Sierra Leone's government. See Guru (note 80 above) 54. See S Rein 'Sierra Leone: Between the Prison Houses of Nationalism and Transnationalism' in MS Smith (ed.) *Globalizing Africa* (2003) 127, 131.

[92] See Rivkin (note 77) 35–37.

[93] Decalo (note 62 above) 497–506.

[94] See Reader (note 82 above) 665–672.

[95] Although it did not have a political-party framework as in the case of Rwanda, the rivalry for political power took an ethnic dimension, pitting Hutus against Tutsis. See R Lemarchand 'Burundi in Comparative Perspective: Dimensions of Ethnic Strife' in J McGarry & Brendan O'Leary (eds.) *The Politics of Ethnic Conflict Regulation: Case Studies of Protracted Ethnic Conflicts* (1993) 151–171.

one group rose to political dominance to the exclusion of the contending group, leaving the countries in cyclic genocidal conflict.[96] The disagreement between the highly federalist group in Katanga, Confédération des Associations Tribales de Katanga (CONAKAT), and Patrice Lumumba's radical and pro-unionist movement pitched independent Congo into a crisis that led to international intervention.[97] In other cases, such as Kenya, Zambia and Zimbabwe, unstable coalitions emerged in which one or some groups dominated.[98] In Ghana and Uganda, the struggle took the form of a rivalry between traditional centripetal forces and modern nationalist centrifugal forces.[99] In the case of Angola, the struggle of the various political forces led to almost three decades of civil war.[100] Nigeria suffered a brutal civil war for the same reason.[101]

The rivalry over political power and eventually access to and control over socio-economic opportunities in many of these countries led, during late 1960s and the 1970s, to the emergence of one-party regimes, military dictatorships or the despotism of 'charismatic' or 'revolutionary' leaders. Constitutions were written, rewritten and reconfigured to entrench the control of those in power and restrict all avenues of political and ethno-cultural pluralism.[102] Although some of these constitutions guaranteed certain human rights to varying degrees, political pluralism and dissent were nevertheless barred. As Chapter III further shows, ethnic claims were brutally suppressed by force or silenced through the co-option of ethnic elites. Minority guarantees and federal arrangements incorporated in some of the independence constitutions were removed. At the same time, while some groups and regions dominated the state machinery and disproportionately controlled and exploited resources, others were systematically marginalised and even subject to repression.[103] This situation was sustained until the end of the Cold War, largely with the support of the superpowers, whose rivalry played itself out on the continent.

---

96 See Reader (note 82 above) 665–672; M Dravis 'Burundi in the 1990s – From Democratization to Communal War' in Gurr (note 86 above) 188–194,189.

97 See HF Weiss & T Carayannis 'The Enduring Idea of the Congo' in Ricardo René Larémont (ed.) *Borders, Nationalism and the African State* (2005) 135, 138–142; Heraclides (note 78 above) 60–62.

98 See Gurr (note 12 above) 264–277; also Sithole (note 48 above) 142–148.

99 See Davidson (note 13) 32–36; C Boon *Political Topographies of the African State: Territorial Authority and Institutional Choice* (2003) 144–146; Kasfir (note 87 above) 89–94, 109–119.

100 Malaquias (note 83 above); A Rozès 'Angolan Deadlock, Chronicle of a War with No Solution' (2001) 10 *African Security Review* available at <http://www.issafrica.org/Pubs/ASR/10No3/Rozes.html>.

101 See, for example, Karl Maier *This House has Fallen* (2000) 7–14; Reader (note 82 above) 660–665; Howard (note 11 above) 94–95; Okafor (note 18 above) 24, 99.

102 See VT Le Vine 'The Fall and Rise of Constitutionalism in West Africa' (1997) 35(2) *The J of Modern African Studies* 181–206.

103 See AM Abdullahi 'The Refugee Crisis in Africa as a Crisis of the Institution of the State' (1994) 6(4) *Int J of Refugee L* 562, 567.

With the end of the Cold War and the subsequent process of democratisation witnessed in many African states, the problems of ethnic inequality and rivalry that had been sidelined by the rivalry of the superpowers and the rise of authoritarian regimes across the continent came into the open. Groups that have hitherto been ruthlessly suppressed have started to assert their claims against their states and even challenge its authority. Many African countries have, as a result, experienced political upheavals of various proportions. In many African states violent conflicts have erupted, and in others, such as Sudan, Burundi and Angola, existing ones have acquired further impetus. In some cases, this has led to the explosion of the state – Liberia, Somalia, former Zaire and Rwanda being examples. Other states, such as Kenya and Senegal, have also witnessed identity-based tensions which have triggered intermittent or short-lived violence. Still others, such as Malawi, Zambia and even Botswana, have witnessed either the emergence of political parties that drew their support from particular groups or regions, or the rise of organisations claiming equal rights for minority groups and the recognition and protection of their identity.

The political scene in these countries has therefore been dominated by rivalry among ethno-political or ethno-regional forces for either control of the state or regional autonomy and a share of political power and resources. Since hegemonic control by the state as a mechanism of management of the ensuing conflicts has failed and is in any case no longer legitimate in the post-Cold War international order, it is becoming increasingly clear that the legally and politically sustainable way to overcome the dangers that minority claims entail is to negotiate mechanisms of just and democratic accommodation.

From a legal point of view, the problem of ethno-political minorities raises a number of crucial questions, including: In what ways can minority-specific norms and other norms of international law, such as the right to self-determination, be articulated to meet group demands for a share of political power and socio-economic resources? What kind of policy approaches and legal methods or institutions are appropriate to realise the potential of these norms for addressing such tensions? What guidance do constitutional/political theory and the constitutional practice of states offer in this regard?

These are the questions that subsequent chapters will address as part of the central problem that this book investigates and to which it addresses itself. Nevertheless, it is possible at this point to conclude that the response to the situation of ethno-political minorities needs to involve the formulation of institutional devices and socio-economic policies that ensure the equitable representation and participation of, and distribution of resources to, various sections of society.

2.3.3. *Ethno-National Minorities*

Although the demand for a share in the control and exercise of state power is therefore an overriding feature of the issue of minorities in Africa, this is by no means the only form that the phenomenon takes. No less important is the demand of some minorities in many African states for regional autonomy, self-government and even secession from the existing state. That significant numbers of African conflicts have been ethno-regional or ethno-national in nature clearly demonstrates this.[104] The third type of minority encompasses those that are referred to, in Gurr's global classification of ethnic political movements as ethno-nationalist groups.[105] These are large minority groups associated with a particular territory whose main claim revolves around self-determination. Minorities in this category can further be divided into two. The first subdivision can be labelled *ethno-regional groups* and includes ethnic groups that are known for their predisposition to maintain their distinct culture, and seek to have their identity and interests recognised through self-government or territorial autonomy.

The second subdivision is composed of what can be referred to as *ethno-national groups*. What distinguishes them from ethno-regional groups is the intensity of their sense of separateness from the dominant population and/or other ethnic groups in the mainstream population, and, most importantly, on account of their quest, in the past or currently, to achieve independent statehood of their own. The distinction between ethno-regional groups and ethno-national groups is therefore that between those who claim autonomy or internal self-government, and secessionists.

Since the independence period in the 1960s, ethno-regional or ethno-national conflicts or movements have arisen in various African states at various times. The most famous historical attempts at secession in Africa include those of Katanga (1960–1963)[106] and Biafra (1967–1970).[107] Ever since Angola gained its independence in 1975, Cabinda has been attempting to secede from it (having fought earlier, from 1965, for independence from Portugal).[108] The various regions of Ethiopia have, since the 1970s, fought against the successive governments of that country

[104] According to some studies, out of more than 40 internal armed conflicts that took place in Africa during 1946–2001, ethno-regional or ethno-national conflicts account for thirty five per cent. See details in *Armed Conflict 1946–2001* at <http://www.pcr.uu.se/publications/ucdp_pub/conflict_list_1946-2005.pdf >.

[105] Gurr (note 12 above) 18.

[106] See R Lemarchand 'The Limits of Self-Determination: The Case of the Katanga Secession' (1962) 56(2) *American Political Science Review* 404–416.

[107] Of the various secessionist conflicts in Africa, this was unmatched for the level of its human casualties. In this war, regarded by some as genocide, between 600,000 and 1,000,000 persons are said to have died from the fighting, starvation or disease. See L Kuper 'Genocide and Mass Killings: Illusion and Reality' in BJ Ramacharan (ed.) *The Right to Life in International Law* (1985) 117, 118.

[108] See further JG Porto *Cabinda, Notes on a Soon-to-be-Forgotten War* (2003) ISS Occasional Paper 77 (2003).

– in this case, with the exception of Eritrea,[109] more for regional autonomy than secession.[110] The same is true of the Southern Sudan conflict that began in 1956. The Movement of the Democratic Forces of the Casamance has been fighting for the independence of Casamance from Senegal since 1983.[111] In 1999, a bloody attempt to sever the Caprivi Strip from Namibia took place.[112] Since 1997, the secessionist Anjouan People's Movement which controls the Island of Anjouan has defied the rule of the government of Comoros.[113] In Mali, the period 1990–1994 saw the Azawad Peoples' Movement and the Islamic Arab Front of Azawad begin fighting for Tuareg separatism.[114] Similarly, Tuareg secessionism emerged as a violent ethno-national movement in Niger in the 1990s.[115] In Eritrea, the Afar Revolutionary Democratic Union, representing the indigenous Afar people, has called for the autonomy of the Danakil region from the Asmara government.[116]

Demands for regional autonomy and/or issues of self-determination have been at the centre of contemporary political/constitutional debates and conflicts in many African states. They feature prominently in the peace negotiations on Darfur, in the constitutional review process in Kenya and the political crisis that unfolded in that country, and in the Comprehensive Peace Agreement between the Sudan People's Liberation Movement/Army (SPLM/A) and the government of Sudan. One of the thorny issues in the constitution-making process in South Africa was the degree to which the post-apartheid state would accommodate regional autonomy or self-government.[117] It is also the main question to which the Ethiopian Constitution of 1994 addresses itself.

At least three factors underlie the claims of ethno-regional and ethno-national minorities in Africa. These are the legacy of colonial rule, the possession of distinct cultures and political histories, and inherited and continuing patterns of socio-economic inequality and discrimination among groups and regions.[118]

The colonial origin of the state plays a pivotal role in African ethno-regional/national movements. One of the developments in the decolonisation process of

---

[109] See J Klabbers & R Lefeber 'Africa: Lost Between Self-Determination and Uti Possidetis' in C Brölmann, R Leteber & M Zieck (eds.) *Peoples and Minorities in International Law* (1993) 37, 70–74.

[110] See Fiseha (note 70 above) 60–79.

[111] See B Sonko 'The Casamance Conflict: A Forgotten Civil War?' (2004) 3&4 *CODESRIA Bulletin* 30–33.

[112] See further IRIN News *Namibia: Caprivi Political Party Declared Illegal* <http://www.irinnews.org/report.asp?ReportID=55509&SelectRegion=Southern_Africa&SelectCountry=NAMIBIA>.

[113] See C Ayangafac *Situation Critical: The Anjouan Political Crisis* (5 March 2008) ISS Situation Report <http://www.iss.org.za>.

[114] Gurr (note 86 above) 53–54.

[115] Ibid.

[116] See the Minorities at Risk project website of the University of Maryland at <http://www.cidcm.umd.edu/mar/assessment.asp?groupId=53101>.

[117] See B de Villiers 'A Constitutional Scenario for Regional Government in South Africa: The Debate Continues' (1993) 18 *SA Public L* 86–101. Also see Chapter VI.

[118] See Gurr (note 12 above) 261.

Africa has been the convergence of, on the one hand, the colonial practice that imposed the colonial state, and, on the other, rules of international law, as international law was subsequently called upon to validate colonially defined entities. It was on the basis of colonial administration, rather than the self-determination of pre-colonial states and peoples, that the decolonisation process under the UN was designed and implemented.[119] This can be contrasted with Wilsonian self-determination, which assigned the right to self-determination to peoples and nations of eastern and southern Europe on the basis of a common cultural tradition, language, territory and shared history as a people.[120] What determined the 'self' of decolonising self-determination was not peoplehood in the Wilsonian sense. It was rather the administrative territories of the various colonial powers, which were almost invariably inhabited by a multitude of diverse groups, that constituted the unit for self-determination.[121] Political self-determination was therefore guaranteed, and sovereign statehood achieved, in Africa on the basis of territorial units that were defined by colonial powers. The result was the emergence of independent African states which incorporated within their territories many 'selves' which 'have never had the time nor the opportunity to integrate into one "self" which would become the nation.'[122]

After independence, the absence of agreed-upon mechanisms for mutual accommodation has also engendered fertile ground for the birth of ethno-regional and ethno-national movements.[123] As Jackson puts it, '[s]ince most of the new states ... do not provide minority rights and internal autonomies to compensate ethno-nationalists and indeed often deliberately withhold them, they tend to provoke civil discord along ethnic lines as did the old multinational empires of Europe.'[124] The case of the Igbo of Nigeria in the Biafra war is a good example of this.[125] Other examples include Ewe of Ghana, the Tuareg in Niger and Mali,

---

119 See RB Neuberger *National Self-Determination in Post Colonial Africa* (1986) 21.

120 On the distinction between Wilsonian self-determination and decolonising self-determination, see J Castellino 'Order and Justice: National Minorities and the Right to Secession' (1999) 6 *Int J on Minority and Group Rights* 389–415. Davidson makes a very interesting comparison between the redefinition of the map of Europe that took place after World War I on the basis of Wilsonian self-determination and the map of Africa that resulted from decolonisation. See Davidson (note 13 above) 187–188.

121 According to Mutua, '[i]nternational law only seemed to contemplate the right of the territorial unit as a whole to choose to become free as one entity or to associate with another state; the birth of many new states from one territorial unit, based on pre-colonial political identities, seems to be out of the question'. MW Mutua 'Why Redraw the Map of Africa: A Moral and Legal Inquiry' (1995) 16 *Michigan J of Int L* 1113, 1141.

122 CC Mojekwu 'Self-Determination: The African Perspective' in Y Alexander & RA Friedlander (eds.) *Self-Determination: National, Regional, and Global Dimensions* (1980) 221, 234.

123 Ibid, 235.

124 RH Jackson *Quasi-States: Sovereignty, International Relations and the Third World* (1990) 78.

125 For a discussion on the attempted secession of Biafra, see generally RC Njoku 'An Endless Cycle of Secessionism – Intellectuals and Separatist Movements in Nigeria' in B Coppieters & M Huysseune (eds.) *Secession, History and the Social Sciences* (2002) 249–274.

and Casamance of Senegal. This is also true of Kenya, which has in recent years witnessed the resurgence of demands for regional autonomy or 'Majimboism'.[126]

In some states, the demand for self-determination or territorial autonomy is aggravated by the political importance that ethnic-based territories acquired during the colonial period. This is particularly the case in those states in which political and administrative units, which sometimes enjoyed varying forms of autonomy, as in Nigeria, Sudan and Uganda, were established on the basis of ethnic units.[127] Other notable examples are Kenya, Malawi, Zambia and the DRC.

A strong sense of a distinct culture and long political tradition or history also explains some of the movements for self-determination. This is an important, although not the only, factor for movements such as the Inkatha Freedom Party[128] in South Africa and that of the Buganda of Uganda.[129] The secessionist movement in the Cabinda region of Angola also has its origin in the pre-colonial history of Cabinda, which is linked to the historically powerful kingdom of the Bakongo, and the sense of ethno-cultural separateness of the people.[130] Accordingly, their claim for self-determination is a manifestation of a tension between the Angolan identity of Cabinda and the sense of ethno-cultural and territorial distinctness felt by the region's people.[131] The coupling of ethno-cultural differences with perceived or real socio-economic and political marginalisation accounts for the demands of Afars in Eritrea and black Muslims in Darfur for autonomy and of the Tuareg in Mali and Niger, the Somalis in the Ogaden region of Ethiopia and the people of South Sudan for self-determination.

Apart from historical factors, colonial or otherwise, and cultural factors, prevailing and continuing regional economic disparities strongly explain many of the ethno-regional and ethno-national claims in Africa. According to Horowitz, it is the 'relative group' position combined with the 'relative regional' position that determines the conditions for secessionist movements.[132] In other words, one of the most important factors leading to such claims is economic discrimination, which involves the systematic exclusion of members of a group from access to desirable economic goods, conditions, or positions, which are to a large extent

[126] See B Wainaina 'Majimbo Mania in Kenyan poll' (5 November 2007) *Mail and Guardian*; L Juma 'Ethnic Politics and the Constitutional Review Process in Kenya' (2002) 9 *Tulsa J of Comparative and Int L* 471.

[127] EE Osaghae *Ethnicity and the State in Africa* (2006) Afrasian Centre for Peace and Development Studies Working Paper Series No 7 7.

[128] See Wilson (note 79 above) 442–456.

[129] See generally J Oloka-Onyango 'The Question of Buganda in Ugandan Contemporary Politics' (1997) 15(2) *J of Contemporary African Studies* 173–179; C Johannesen *Kingship in Uganda: The Role of the Buganda Kingdom in Ugandan Politics* (2006) CMI Working Papers 8.

[130] See Porto (note 108 above).

[131] Ibid.

[132] Horowitz (note 38 above) 235.

monopolised by other groups in society.[133] This view suggests that secessionist movements are triggered or exacerbated by the regional dynamics of different groups in relation to the state, and that, among other things, poor groups in underdeveloped regions are the most prone to secessionist movements. The southern Sudan case[134] and the political movements of various communities in the Niger Delta of Nigeria, particularly the Ogoni, the Tourug rebellion in Niger and Mali, the armed rebel groups that fought the Emperor and the military regime in Ethiopia sufficiently illustrate this point.[135]

It is clear from the foregoing that the needs of ethno-national minorities is best addressed through constitutional arrangements involving some level of self-government guarantees to such groups. Depending on the specific political and historical circumstance of each case, such guarantees may range from self-government confined to the cultural sphere to a full measure of self-government involving political and economic powers.

2.3.4. *Peripheral Minorities*

Finally, there are minorities who are at the periphery of the dominant or mainstream society. They are referred to as *peripheral groups* and largely live outside the socio-economic and political processes of the state to which they nominally belong. The conditions of these minorities raise the issue of redressing past and continuing exclusions, and creating conditions for their empowerment and substantive inclusion in the various processes of the state. Examples include the black Muslims in Darfur; some of the communities in the Niger Delta region of Nigeria; the communities in northern and north-eastern Kenya, particularly the Somalis; the various groups in the western and eastern lowlands of Ethiopia, such as the Agnuak, Nuer, Berta, Afar and Somali; and the Nubians in Egypt.

Peripheral groups often live in remote and socio-economically marginalised areas.[136] These are territories in which the institutions and operations of the state have often had very little presence.[137] They were mostly left out from the colonial

---

[133] Gurr (note 12 above) 43. One manifestation of this, particularly in Africa, is the existence of substantial material deprivation (inequality) affecting the group or groups in question. This is a result of the uneven distribution of economic goods by colonial powers and the indifference of the post-colonial state to rectifying this situation.

[134] Heraclides (note 78 above) 110; see also Horowitz (note 38 above) 239; See H Hannum *Autonomy, Sovereignty and Self-Determination – The Accommodation of Conflicting Rights* (1990) 309–311.

[135] CR Ezetah 'International Law of Self-Determination and the Ogoni Question: Mirroring Africa's Post-Colonial Dilemma' (1997) 19 *Loyola of Los Angeles Int and Comparative L* 814. EE Osaghae 'The Ogoni Uprising: Oil Politics, Minority Agitation and the Future of the Nigerian State' (1995) 94 *African Affairs* 325.

[136] Ngugi (note 33 above) 322.

[137] Since the colonial period, peripheral communities have come into contact with the state only where the state required the land they inhabited for development projects because of its

processes of integration into the economy and the political processes of the colonial state, a situation that has continued in the post-colonial period. Thus, most of the areas they occupy are impoverished and have poor infrastructure. There is little or no access to health services and appropriate education systems. They also have limited or no meaningful political participation. Peripheral groups have, as a result, been at the fringes of the political, economic, social and cultural processes of the states into which they were incorporated.[138]

Within the category of peripheral minorities, certain groups constitute a special category. These are those who, in recent works of the African Commission on Human and Peoples' Rights (ACHPR), are referred to as indigenous populations/communities.[139] These groups have largely remained outside of the political and socio-economic systems of the states in which they now live. One distinguishing feature of indigenous groups is also the distinctness of their culture from other groups in society.[140] Most of them live in peripheral and forest lands, leading a pre-modern way of life based on hunting, gathering and herding or pastoralism. Their claims raise the seemingly paradoxical issue of how to ensure their political, economic and social well-being on an equal basis with other members of society while at the same time recognising and respecting their cultural distinctness and their traditional way of life and mode of livelihood.

They possess their own cultures, significantly distinct from other ethic groups that form part of the mainstream society, which are in some cases in a state of ruin and near-extinction. This is one but not the exclusive defining element of indigenous peoples in Africa.

Indigenous peoples exhibit additional characteristics to those that they share with other peripheral groups. One of these distinguishing features is a strong sense of attachment to their ancestral land. Not only their livelihood, but their culture, beliefs and medicine depend on the land they inherited since time immemorial. For them, their ancestral land is worth far more than the economic value that may be attributed to it by other members of society. For example, the pygmies of central Africa sustain themselves through a symbiotic relationship with the forest which is the source of all their basic needs and their socio-cultural well-being. The forest is the basis for their distinct livelihood. It is also their home and their spiritual centre, where they communicate with

---

location, fertility or rich resources. Whenever that happened, the communities ended up being removed from their land. During British colonial rule in Kenya, the Massai were dispossessed of their grazing grounds in the Central Rift Valley and pushed to the periphery. Since independence, little attempt has been made to reinstate the Massai in their land.

138 This is partly explained by their pre-modern way of life and partly a result of the failure of the colonial state to include them in the state system. See Busia, Jr (note 17) 239.

139 See generally ACHPR Report (note 55 above).

140 Gurr (note 12) 20.

their ancestors and carry out their religious rituals and practices. Moreover, it is a source of medicine.[141]

What seems to distinguish the attachment of indigenous peoples in Africa[142] to their land from that of other African ethnic groups is not their spiritual and cultural association to their land. It is the combination of this association with the livelihood purpose for which the land is used, namely hunting and gathering, cattle herding, pastoralism or traditional agro-pastoralism. Once again, the pygmies of central Africa serve as good examples. They live in dense tropical rainforest across central Africa, and obtain their livelihood by hunting and gathering forest resources. Essential aspects of their culture and traditional religious practices are also closely linked with the practices of hunting and gathering. It is clear from this that not only the forest, but also the practice of hunting and gathering which depends on the land and the forest, have fundamental importance for their collective existence and cultural survival as distinct peoples.

There are two types of communities in Africa that possess most of these characteristics. Hunters and gatherers, such as the pygmies of the central African region,[143] comprise the one type, and pastoralists, animal herders or nomads and agro-pastoralists the other. Apart from the pygmies, other examples of hunters and gatherers include the San of southern Africa, the Hadzabe of Tanzania, and the Ogiek of Kenya.[144] The Maasai, Pokot, Barbaig, Borena and Afar of the Horn of Africa and other eastern African territories; the Tuareg in west and north Africa; and the Mbororo of west and central Africa are examples of pastoralist or agro-pastoralist indigenous peoples.[145] Berbers in North Africa are also regarded as indigenous peoples, mainly on the bases of self-identification and their historically distinct culture and languages.[146]

Like other peripheral groups, since they live outside of the socio-economic processes of their state, indigenous peoples 'operate within their own cultural

---

[141] See IRIN In-Depth (note 26).

[142] In its original understanding, 'the term indigenous peoples,' according to José Bengoa, 'had been attributed to the first nations existing there prior to transatlantic colonization'. And hence the term recognises that these peoples had, prior to colonisation and domination by European settlement, a history of independent political systems. In the African context, the communities regarded as indigenous peoples did not have any history of having autonomous political organisation, nor can they be regarded, unless except in very exceptional cases, as the original inhabitants of a particular country. See *Report on the Second Workshop on Multiculturalism in Africa* UN Doc. E/CN.4/Sub.2/AC.5/2001/3 para. 48.

[143] See IRIN In-Depth (note 26 above) 7; ACHPR Report (note 55 above) 15–16.

[144] The San of Southern Africa are spread in most countries of southern Africa, such as Botswana, Namibia, South Africa, Zimbabwe, Angola and Zambia. Their population is estimated at 107,071. See ACHPR Report (note 55 above)16–17.

[145] For more on the characters of these communities see ACHPR Report (note 55 above) 16–18; A Said 'Afar Ethnicity in Ethiopian Politics' in Mohamed Salih and John Markakis (eds.) *Ethnicity and the State in Eastern Africa* (1998) 108–115.

[146] ACHPR Report (note 55 above) 18–19.

enclaves, ignoring [I prefer having been ignored by] modern state institutions and lacking the necessary human or other resources to enable their people to participate in the political or economic life of a modern complex society'.[147] With minimal economic influence,[148] they often remain effectively outside of the economic life of the society.[149] Following the internationally legalised colonial differentiation between the 'primitive' and the 'modern', the general perception so far held among members of mainstream social groups is that indigenous peoples (not necessarily other peripheral groups) are 'backward' or 'primitive'.[150] All these factors have made these communities vulnerable to being neglected and even victimised by the dominant development paradigms and socio-economic perspectives pursued by mainstream social groups at the behest of state institutions.

In most cases, being the least represented and politically mobilised sections of society, like other peripheral groups, indigenous peoples have virtually no voice. As one report revealed with regard to the pygmies, for example, they 'do not benefit from any form of political representation and also lack institutions able to directly defend their rights.'[151] As a result, they have no participation, nor do they have any one to speak on their behalf, in the decision-making processes of the state, even on matters directly affecting them. As Ngugi rightly states:

> Untutored in the ways employed by a new intrusive and ubiquitous State manned by an elite with everything to gain from their unheralded assimilation, the indigenous peoples could only lose the battle that pitted them against the post-colonial State. National interests meant uniform 'development' policies that further disempowered the indigenous peoples in their attempts to protect their lands and natural resources in a system unknown to them.[152]

This generally marginal status of indigenous communities in Africa has meant their virtual absence from the imagination of mainstream society in the formulation and implementation of national policies. Apart from non-recognition of their way of life as legitimate, certain policies have brought about consequences that endanger their very survival as peoples. The most important of these concern the use of land and resources and development policies, which are in many ways interrelated. Since the way of life of indigenous peoples is not recognised as legitimate, the use to which they put their land is also not recognised as worthy of legal protection. As a result, their interest in the land they inhabited has not been protected. The development policies of post-colonial African states

---

147 Busia Jr (note 17 above) 239.
148 IRIN In-Depth (note 26 above) 11.
149 Ibid.
150 See Ngugi (note 33 above) 326-328.
151 IRIN In-Depth (note 26 above) 12.
152 Ngugi (note 33 above) 326.

have been not only assimilationist in their orientation but have also involved, for their implementation, the dispossession of indigenous peoples' land and exploitation of its resources, with no regard to the interests of the indigenous peoples themselves.[153]

The situation of peripheral minorities touches on a range of institutional and policy dimensions. The adequate accommodation of their situation thus requires a mix of legal and policy measures including special protection to their distinct culture, affirmative action, land rights, representation in the politics and institutions of the state, and where circumstances warrant some measure of self-government.

2.4. Conclusion

This chapter has addressed two important issues. The first is the genesis and nature of ethnic diversity and its political saliency in the post-colonial African state, which forms the context for the issue of minorities in Africa. It has been shown that ethnic diversity is characterised by the presence of large numbers of groups with unequal population size and socio-political conditions, and divergent cultures and histories, and having attachment to a specific territory and a strong sense of identity. The genesis of these features of ethnic diversity in Africa is located in the pre-colonial socio-economic conditions and political traditions of many of the groups, and most significantly in the colonial and post-colonial socio-economic and political developments. Of these, the forcible and arbitrary amalgamation of numerous, distinct and in many ways unequal ethnic groups into a single political unit by colonial fiat left by far the most enduring influence in shaping the nature and political saliency of ethnic diversity in Africa.

Unlike the experience in Western democracies where the issue of minorities is a result of majoritarian nation-building process, in Africa it is attributable to the ahistoric colonial making of the African state, the resultant staggering level of diversity, and colonial and post-colonial patterns of uneven power relations and mismanagement. The result is that the typology of minority issues developed by multicultural theorists based on the experience of Western democracies does not apply to the African context. Accordingly, the second issue dealt with in this chapter is the nature and types of minority groups and the various claims that are characteristic of the issue of minorities in Africa. In this regard, four types of minority groups have typically been identified and the genesis and nature

[153] See ACHPR Report (note 55 above) 21-34. The colonial dispossession of the Massai was legitimised and the further alienation of their land justified based on arguments that their use of land was wasteful and the land should be used for mainstream development purposes. See Ngugi (note 33 above) 339-341.

of the claims of these minorities have been analysed in some detail. It clearly emerges from this analysis that the issue of minorities in Africa goes beyond and above cultural recognition, albeit that is fundamental in many ways. Other than cultural recognition, two additional areas are also equally relevant for effective group recognition. The first relates to representation and participation in the political processes of the state. This is about 'having a say'. The second is about socio-economic justice. This directs attention to the historically created and politically perpetuated socio-economic disparities and disadvantages that characterises ethno-cultural and regional diversity in Africa.

The chapter argued that the issue of minorities is a product and manifestation of the historical and socio-political processes of the construction and (mis)management of the African state. It logically follows from the specific features of ethno-cultural diversity in the post-colonial African state that the resolution of the issue of minorities in Africa requires the existence of a constitutional structure that is commonly accepted by members of the constituent minorities to be just and inclusive for accommodating their identities and interests, thus rendering it capable of nurturing a shared sense of inclusion and belonging as well as stability and social co-operation. The following chapter accordingly examines the nature of the basic structure of the post-colonial African state, as inherited from the colonial state and further redefined by post-colonial constitutions and nation-building processes, and how and why it has failed to receive the acceptance of members of all the constituent ethno-cultural groups, and therefore has engendered conflicts instead of serving as a basis for social co-operation and national integration.

CHAPTER III

THE ISSUE OF MINORITIES IN THE POLITICAL AND CONSTITUTIONAL DISCOURSE AND PRACTICE OF POST-COLONIAL AFRICA

> In three or four years, no one will remember the tribal, ethnic or religious rivalries which, in the recent past, caused so much damage to our country and its population.[1]

3.1. Introduction

As the previous chapter showed, the proper resolution of the issue of minorities is fundamental to building cohesive and just societies in Africa, founded on a sustainable democratic system. To borrow from G Selassie, nothing is more perplexing or critical to African states than how to address this issue.[2] The object of this chapter is accordingly to investigate the nature of the constitutional and politico-legal approaches employed by post-colonial African states to the issue of minorities, with the aim of demonstrating their limits and explaining their ultimate failure. It further discusses the relationship of this question to the wider debate on the inadequacy of the nation-state model of nation-building and universal individual rights (common citizenship) to achieve equality and justice for minorities in multi-ethnic societies in general, and especially in Africa. The chapter also defends the need to embrace a multi-ethnic process of national integration and democratisation and go beyond majoritarian democratic structures and processes, as well as individual rights, in order to address adequately the issue of minorities in Africa.

3.2. The Imperative of Nation-Building

One of the most fundamental constitutional problems African states were faced with at independence was how to address the demands of their diverse constituent communities, forcibly brought under the arbitrarily contrived colonial boundaries and structures of the post-colonial state. What made this problem

---

[1] S Touré *Toward Full Reafricanisation* (1959) 28.

[2] AG Selassie 'Ethnic Identity and Constitutional Design For Africa' (Fall 1992–1993) 29(1) *Stanford J of Int L* 1, 5.

particularly formidable is that almost all African states, as the product of the colonial process and its system of divide and rule, lack national cohesion. Not only did their populations lack any shared consciousness of belonging to one country, but they were also ethno-culturally divided and socio-economically and politically unequal. The fragility of the post-colonial states was further compounded by the weak institutional foundation and capacity of the independent governments,[3] a situation exacerbated by extremely underdeveloped and fragmented economies.[4] Nation-building thus rightly topped the agenda of the post-colonial African states.[5] As David Welsh has noted, 'in the heydays of independence, [beginning] in Ghana in 1957 and accelerating in the 1960s and beyond, "nation building" was assumed to be the priority of all the newly emerging [African] states.'[6]

Given the colonial origin of the African state as a political unit constituted by an amalgamation of various communities of different histories, political traditions and cultures, the independent governments had two options in their endeavour to achieve nation-building. The first was based on the hitherto dominant model of the nation-state. The other was what may be referred to as a multicultural model of nation-building, exemplified by Switzerland and, probably of more relevance to Africa, India. The nation-state approach tends to ignore and even combat expressions of ethno-cultural diversity, with its strong assimilationist features emphasising national unity. Central to it is the idea that somehow there has to be coincidence between the nation, as a culturally and linguistically homogenous entity, and the state. Accordingly, the dominant view of the 20th century was that a state should have a homogenous national identity, and this feature forms an important defining element of the modern constitutional state.[7]

---

[3] Despite the deceivingly authoritarian structure and centralised power of the state inherited from colonial powers, the state was also described as the 'soft state'. Rothchild and Olorunsola explain: 'In Africa, the soft state is marked by fragile institutions; not only are these institutions constrained by the ineffectiveness of linkages and the unavailability of human, material and fiscal resources, but the presence of domestic and international demands.' D Rothchild & VA Olorunsola 'Managing competing state and ethnic claims' in D Rothchild & VA Olorunsola (eds.) *State Versus Ethnic Claims: African Policy Dilemmas* (1983) 1, 7.

[4] Nwabueze puts it in vivid terms: in these countries 'even those basic necessities for human existence are either non-existent or minimal for the vast majority of the population, for whom poverty, illiteracy, disease and apathy are inescapable conditions, hovering over the community like plague'. BO Nwabueze *Constitutionalism in the Emergent States* (1973) 164.

[5] 'The fundamental political problem,' as W Arthur Lewis aptly noted in 1965, 'is neither economic policy nor foreign policy, but the creation of nations out of heterogeneous peoples.' WA Lewis *Politics in West Africa* (1965) 49–50. See B Davidson *The Black Man's Burden: Africa and the Curse of the Nation-State* (1992) Chapters VI & VII.

[6] D Welsh 'Ethnicity in Sub-Saharan Africa' (1996) 72 *Int Affairs* 477, 477.

[7] James Tully notes that one of the characteristic features of the constitutional state following the French and American revolutions has been that it 'possesses an individual identity as a "nation"'. J Tully *Strange Multiplicity: Constitutionalism in an Age of Diversity* (1995) 68.

The multicultural model, and largely minority approach throughout the 20th century, by contrast recognises the reality of ethno-cultural diversity. It institutionalises mechanisms to accommodate the interests of diverse groups, and thereby actively nurtures a sense of allegiance to the state among the individual members of the different groups. Under this system of nation-building, as in Switzerland and India, ethnic identity is given recognition both for cultural and socio-economic justice through institutions and policies that provide public space for its expression and for addressing the demands of justice it gives rise to, while national identity is simultaneously fostered through common institutions, shared values and a shared historical past as well. Although not widely accepted in post-colonial states at independence, this has increasingly become a common mode of nation-building in multi-ethnic states in recent times.[8]

Almost all African states chose the first option on the basis of various constitutional models inherited at independence.[9] Various arguments rooted in the liberal tradition presented, at that time and for most of the 20th century, the nation-state model as the dominant and only legitimate form of political organisation both normatively and for the particular context of Africa. Firstly, the possession of a single homogenous national identity was seen as a condition necessary to the generation of the sense of common purpose required for democratic government.[10] For influential 19th-century liberals such as John Stuart Mill, a democratic system of government is possible only where the people of a country share a common sense of nationhood. Mill put it thus:

> Free institutions are next to impossible in a country made up of different nationalities. Among a people without fellow-feeling, especially if they read and speak different languages, the united public opinion necessary to the working of representative government, cannot exist.

According to him, therefore, it is 'a necessary condition of free institutions that the boundaries of government should coincide in the main with those of nationalities.'[11]

Prior to this period, French philosopher Rousseau expounded an equally, if not more, powerful argument on the need for homogeneity as a condition necessary for popular sovereignty or the general will, which is the basis for the legitimacy of the modern nation-state. Writing elsewhere, I have presented the

[8] See AG Gagnon & J Tully (eds.) *Multicultural Democracies* (2001).

[9] See B Neuberger 'State and Nation in African Thought' in J Huchinson & AD Smith (eds.) *Nationalism* (1994) 231–235.

[10] For a discussion on this, see W Kymlicka *Multicultural Citizenship: A Liberal Theory of Minority Rights* (1995) 50–57.

[11] JS Mill 'Considerations on Representative Government' in H Acton (ed.) *Utilitarianism, liberty, representative government* (1972) 230, 233.

essence and implications of this argument.[12] Rousseau envisaged the difficulties of forming the general will where in a society 'factions arise and partial associations are formed'. Thus he saw the cohesion and homogeneity of citizens as a necessary condition for the formation of the general will as an expression of popular sovereignty. As he put it, '[T]he greater harmony that reigns in public assemblies, the more, in other words, that public opinion approaches unanimity, the more the general will is dominant.' In what seems to suggest the centrality of this, Rousseau went as far as saying that a state needs a religion, the religion of the citizen, which is

> [t]he religion established in a single country; it gives that country its gods and its special tutelary deities; it has its dogmas, its rituals, its external forms of worship laid down by law; and to the one nation which practices this religion, everything outside is infidel, alien, barbarous; it extends the rights and duties of man only so far as it extends its altars.[13]

This favours not only majoritarian system of government but insists on the necessity for a state of achieving socio-cultural and linguistic homogeneity. It offered the philosophical foundation for countries such as France to pursue a homogenising nation-building process that turned peasants and distinct communities in the country into French men and women.

Secondly, the possession of a commonly shared identity by a state and its nationals was also seen as necessary to the unity and political stability of a modern constitutional state. Thus, it was suggested that the nation must generally be the basis of the state. This is because, as Ernest Barker argued:

> There must be a general social cohesion which serves, as it were, as a matrix, before the seal of legal association can be effectively imposed on a population. If the seal of the State is stamped on a population which is not held together in the matrix of a common tradition and sentiment, there is likely to be a cracking and splitting, as there was in Austria-Hungary.[14]

The third argument is based on a functional requirement of the modern society. The modern state requires, it is argued, a culturally homogenous society for its effective running.[15] Members of society must conduct transactions with each other, run the bureaucracy, operate the same court system and the like. This is possible, the argument goes, only where there is a standardised language and where people share common cultural attributes and historical symbols. Thus, the constitutional state has enforced 'a kind of homogeneity of language and

---

[12] Solomon A. Dersso 'The Socio-Historical and Political Processes Leading to the Emergence and Development of Norms on Minorities' in Solomon Dersso (ed.) *Perspectives on the Rights of Minorities and Indigenous Peoples in Africa* (Pretoria: Pretoria University Law Press, 2010) Chapter 3.

[13] J J Rousseau *The Social Contract* trans M Cranston (1968) 181.

[14] E Barker *Principles of Social and Political Theory* (1951) 3, 42.

[15] E Gellner *Nations and Nationalism* (1983) 39.

culture, both designedly, as through the education system', and by the very way it operates, as through the media.[16]

This perspective, dominant particularly at the time of the independence of the post-colonial African states, was fully appropriated by the post-colonial African elite. There were also particularly African conditions and arguments that led to the wholesale adoption of the nation-state model of nation-building. The first of these was the deep ethno-cultural division of the post-colonial state's population and their lack of a shared political history. The other was the widely held view at the time that African ethnicity, dubbed tribalism, was an impediment to modernisation and the achievement of national unity. Accordingly, these states adopted assimilationist and integrationist nation-building processes, within the framework of the constitutions inherited at independence and further revised subsequent to independence to suit the objectives of state-centred nation-building.

More specifically, post-colonial nation-building has taken two forms. The first is what Kymlicka calls a 'pan-ethnic' nation-building, which was aimed at developing pan-ethnic bases of identification with the state through common supra-ethnic institutions and symbols.[17] This was the declared aim in many African states.[18] The second is what may be called majority nation-building, which involves, as we observed in Chapter II, building the state around the language, culture and history of the dominant ethno-national group.[19]

Notwithstanding these differences, the post-independence constitutional systems and nation-building policies of the majority of African countries have conceived of national unity in terms of homogeneity and oneness.[20] The prevailing ethno-cultural diversity has generally been seen as reflecting some weakness in the character of the African state, or as being antithetical to the process of nationalisation of the dominant culture or the creation of a common national

---

[16] C Taylor 'Nationalism and Modernity' in JA Hall (ed.) *The State of the Nation: Ernest Gellner and the Theory of Nationalism* (1998) 191, 193.

[17] W Kymlicka 'Nation-Building and Minority Rights: Comparing Africa and the West' in B Berman, D Eyoh & W Kymlicka (eds.) *Ethnicity and Democracy in Africa* (2004) 54, 65. As E Gellner observed, such types of nation-building projects 'neither perpetuate nor invent a local high culture … nor do they often elevate an erstwhile native culture into new, politically sanctioned literate culture, as European nationalisms had often done'. They rather allowed the perpetuation and even active promotion of European languages and political culture inherited from the colonial state to be the basis of their rule. E Gellner *Nations and Nationalisms: New Perspectives on the Past* (1983) 9.

[18] Mauritius is probably the only country that genuinely deployed this approach without attacking the particular attachments of its people to their groups, but rather by cultivating the development of overlapping identification with one's cultural group and with the state.

[19] Kymlicka (note 17 above) 64.

[20] See IJ Wani 'Cultural Preservation and the Challenges of Diversity and Nationhood: The Dilemmas of Indigenous Cultures in Africa' (1991) 59 *UMKC LR* 611, 630–636; NJ Udombana 'The Unfinished Business: Conflicts, the African Union and the New Partnership For Africa's Development' (2003) 35 *Geo. Wash Int LR* 55, 93–94.

identity. As Davidson summed it, '[f]or post-colonial nation-statism in policy and rhetoric has preferred to talk down 'ethnic survivals' like the Soninke ... as deplorably illegitimate and best forgotten, because, not having formed nation-states and therefore not being admitted to be nations, they have no right or reason to remain alive'.[21] Accordingly, the constitutions, laws and development policies of these states have all been used as instruments in a highly centralised, unitarist and homogenising nation-building process. In the constitutional and political discourse of the post-colonial state, as Francis Deng observed, '[u]nity was postulated in a way that assumed a mythical homogeneity amidst diversity.'[22]

This has been expressed in the principles that their constitutions proclaimed. For example, the 1975 Constitution of Angola provides that '[t]he People's Republic of Angola shall be a unitary and indivisible state ... and any attempt at separatism or dismemberment of its territory shall be vigorously combated.'[23] Similarly, the independent constitutions of almost all of the ex-French colonial countries declared, in typical Jacobian style, and frequently in the very first article, the national unity, indivisibility and sovereignty of the state. A representative formulation of this can be found in the 1960 Constitution of Ivory Coast.[24] According to Article 2, '[t]he Republic of the Ivory Cost is *one and indivisible*, secular, democratic and social.'[25] Many of the countries 'have tried to pursue a top-down Jacobian nation-building strategy'.[26] Although the independent constitutions of some anglophone countries incorporated some institutional guarantees, such as federalism or regionalism, in an attempt to accommodate diversity and as a mechanism for the protection of minorities, most were subsequently amended to give way to a highly centralised unitary political system.[27] A typical example here is the declaration in the 1960 Constitution of the Republic of Ghana that 'Ghana is a sovereign unitary state.'[28]

'Too often,' observed former UN Secretary-General Kofi Annan, '... the necessity of building national unity was pursued through the heavy centralization

[21] Davidson (note 5 above) 97–98.

[22] FM Deng 'Ethnicity: An African Predicament' (Summer 1997) 15 (3) *The Bookings Review* 28–31, 28.

[23] Constitution of Angola of 1975, Article 4.

[24] Constitution of Ivory Coast of 3 November 1960 as amended 11 January 1963 reprinted in A Peaslee (ed.) *Constitutions of Nations* Vol 1 Africa (1965) 242–253. A common theme in the mottos of many of the constitutions of the ex-French colonies is 'unity'. The Constitution of the Republic of Mali of 1960 as amended in 1961 thus provides in its Article 1 that '[t]he motto is "one people, one purpose, one faith"'. Reprinted in ibid, 535–545, 535.

[25] Constitution of Ivory Coast Ibid, 242 (my emphasis).

[26] On the nature of this approach see B Berman et al. 'Introduction: Ethnicity and the Politics of Democratic Nation-Building in Africa' in Berman et al. (note 17 above) 17–18.

[27] See below, notes 34–47 and accompanying text.

[28] Article 4(1) reprinted in Peaslee (note 24 above) 213–228, 214.

of political and economic power and the suppression of political pluralism.'[29] The homogenisation impulse of the mottos of national unity in the rhetoric and practice of post-colonial nation-building has thus also been seen as requiring the restriction of political and most importantly ethno-cultural pluralism. The predication of the nation-building project on the emphatic premise of creating a singular national identity and oneness, as a precondition for development and national unity, was translated into a requirement that the various ethno-political communities be moulded into an artificially constructed state identity or assimilated into the nationalised identity of the dominant ethnic group.[30]

The constituent ethnic groups, branded as atavistic 'tribal' remains of a primitive past, thus soon became the main targets of the nation-building project.[31] Accordingly, consistent with the nation-state model, one common theme running through almost all the constitutions of these countries has been the refusal to give any legal or political recognition and institutional expression to the various distinct groups constituting the state. The belief that ethnicity is divisive and undermines national unity informs the constitutional and political discourse of many African states throughout the post-colonial period.[32] In almost all the multinational countries of Africa, the expression of ethnic solidarity and the mobilisation of people on the basis of group identity have therefore been proscribed in various ways or else discouraged. For instance, following the Jacobian tradition of the French, almost all of the constitutions of francophone countries prohibit the expression of any particularist propaganda of a racial or ethnic character.[33] In other countries, such as Ghana, laws were enacted to proscribe the establishment of organisations on the basis of group membership

[29] *The Causes of Conflict and the Promotion of Durable Peace and Sustainable Development in Africa* Report of Secretary General Kofi Annan to the Security Council April 16, 1998 para 8.

[30] See Wani (note 20 above) 630–636. 'The assimilationist tendency,' notes Shivji, 'which in practice usually translates itself into oppression of other nations/nationalities by dominant nations/nationalities, has been so strong in Africa that even in situations of "voluntary" union like that of Zanzibar and Tanganyika, it has found some ugly expressions.' IG Shivji 'State and Constitutionalism: A New Democratic Perspective' in IG Shivji (ed.) *State and Constitutionalism: An African Debate on Democracy* (1991) 27, 34.

[31] FRELIMO, the Mozambican ruling party, solemnly pledged in the 1970s 'to kill the tribe to build the nation'. M Cheg 'Remembering Africa' (1992) 71 *Foreign Affairs* 146. The reasoning for such a conception of national unity is that 'since the nation-state must be seen as an integral part of modernity, and sub-state groups must be seen as existing in competition with the nation-state, the fragmentation of states must, invariably, be undesirable, a disintegrating factor, an obstacle to be overcome'. OC Okafor *Re-Defining Legitimate Statehood: International Law and State Fragmentation in Africa* (2000) 93.

[32] See G Selassie (note 2 above) 11–21; Deng (note 22 above); Wani (note 20 above) 633–636.

[33] For example, see Article 4 of the 1963 Constitution of Togo which provides that 'any regionalist propaganda which might threaten the internal security of the state, national unity or the integrity of the territory, shall be punished by law'. As reprinted in Peaslee (note 24 above) 890–905, 891.

along ethnic, regional or religious lines.[34] Colonial languages were adopted as national languages and their use has been aggressively promoted.[35] Children were to be taught in English or French, and the teaching of local languages was abolished.[36]

Another logical consequence of building a singular national identity that supplants local ethnic affiliations was a process of centralising political power, involving the elimination of institutional guarantees for minorities, such as territorial autonomy, from the independent constitutions.[37] Thus, although various kinds of federal arrangements were incorporated into the constitutions of many countries, including Kenya, Uganda, the DRC, Nigeria, Ethiopia, Sudan and Cameroon, these federal experiments were abandoned as divisive and obstructive of national unity in all but Nigeria.[38]

The 1963 'Majimbo Constitution' of Kenya established a quasi-federal arrangement that divided legislative and executive powers among the central government and the seven regions.[39] Not only did it seek to create a framework for a just distribution of political power, but it aimed in particular to safeguard the interest of smaller ethnic groups from marginalisation and domination by larger ethnic groups. It did not last very long. Neuberger summarises this short-lived federal experiment succinctly:

> In Kenya the quasi-federal 'Majimbo Constitution', which divided the country into regions with their regional Assemblies, Regional Civil Service and regional powers, was designed to protect the small backward ethnic groups from the Kikuyu-Luo alliance. It had strong support in Kadu, which represented the Coastal, Baluhya and Kalenjin tribes. One of its leaders, Masinde Muliro, saw in federalism the ideal solution for Africa … because it provides for 'free association' and prevents 'imposed unity'. The dominant Kenyan African National Union opposed federalism,

[34] SKB Asante 'Nation Building and Human Rights in Emergent African Nations' (1969) 2 *Cornell Int LJ* 83, 93–96. As Asante puts it, the 'Ghanaian Act did more than merely ban political organisations using or engaging in tribal, racial or religious propaganda to the detriment of any other community; it also forbade the election of persons on account of their tribal or religious affiliation – in my view an unwarrantable fetter on the principle of free elections'. Ibid, 95.

[35] See D Smock & K Bentsi-Enchill (eds.) *The Search for National Integration in Africa* (1976) 161–167.

[36] Wani (note 20 above) 633.

[37] Welsh (note 6 above) 483. This led, as we have noted in Chapter II, to struggles for regional power, local autonomy and decentralisation, which in some cases escalated into violent conflicts. Okafor (note 31 above) 103.

[38] Many of the leading African nationalist leaders of the post-independence era, including Kwame Nkrumah, Milton Obote, Jomo Kenyatta, and Patrice Lumumba, saw federalism as an external plot by Western countries to weaken the newly independent African states by further balkanisation. According to them, federalism was inefficient, an invitation to 'tribalism, and a waste of resources'. MW Mutua 'Why Redraw the Map of Africa: A Moral and Legal Inquiry' (1995) 16 *Michigan J Int L* 1113, 1169.

[39] The names of the seven regions, their organisations and powers are provided for in Chapter VI of the Constitution, reprinted in Peaslee (note 24 above) 257–418, 313–322.

> which it regarded as a colonial device to strengthen those tribes which did not participate in the anticolonial national movement, and to weaken the position of the 'radical' Kikuyu. KANU accepted the 'Majimbo Constitution' because that was the British condition for independence. It very soon eroded and then abolished the federal system, and imposed a unitary regime strongly dominated by the Kikuyu bureaucracy.[40]

The emergence of a unitary system of governance led to the domination of the machinery of the state by particular groups and the consequent political and socio-economic disparities among regions and members of various groups. This has led to a call for Majimbo in recent years, and lies at the root of the crisis that unfolded in Kenya following the December 2007 elections.

The independent constitution of Uganda had similarly introduced a form of asymmetrical federal system, recognising self-government for some of the pre-colonial ethnic-based states, particularly the Buganda. Accordingly, its Article 2(1) stipulated that 'Uganda consists of Federal States, Districts and the territory of Mbale.'[41] Although the influential Ugandan People's Congress, under the leadership of Milton Obote, initially accepted this arrangement for fear of the secession of Buganda and to take control of state power, four years after independence it abrogated the federal structure, violently destroyed the Buganda Kingdom, and centralised power under a unitary system.[42] Although the asymmetrical features of the independent constitution's regionalism were problematic, its total repudiation by Milton Obote and the concomitant centralisation of power without alternative institutional mechanisms for accommodating some of the interests of the country's diverse groups created resentment on the part of Buganda and various groups from western Uganda. This ultimately led to the various conflicts fought in that country.

The 1960 Constitution of the DRC similarly provided that '[t]he Democratic Republic of the Congo is composed of the city of Leopoldville and the autonomous provinces.'[43] Interestingly enough, its Article 5 stipulated that the provinces should be autonomous and each should have separate judicial personality.[44] This system did not get the opportunity to be tested as the DRC sank into a

---

[40] B Neuberger 'Federalism in Africa: Experience and Prospects' in DJ Elazar (ed.) *Federalism and Political Integration* (1985) as quoted in Mutua (note 38 above) 1154.

[41] See the Constitution of Uganda of 2 October 1962, as amended 30 September 1963, reprinted in Peaslee (note 24 above) 921–987, 921.

[42] The constitution was suspended in February 1966 and in April that year a new one was promulgated abolishing the federal status of Buganda. Under the 1967 constitution, Uganda became a unitary republic and all the traditional kingdoms were abolished. See DP Xydis (ed.) *Constitutions of the World* (1974) 999–1000, 1000.

[43] Article 4 Constitution of the Congo (Leopoldville) of 30 May 1960 reprinted in Peaslee (note 24 above) 102–147, 103.

[44] Ibid. The organisation and powers of the provinces are stipulated under Title V of the Constitution, 125–130.

crisis following the conflict between the unionist party, Mouvement National Congolais of Lumumba, and the leaders of the Kongo people and Katanga, Joseph Kasavubu and Moise Tshombe. After Mobutu took power in a military coup in 1965, the provincial federal arrangement was set aside. Under the 1967 Constitution, the DRC was named Zaire and became a unitary state.[45] This has not, however, totally diminished the independence movements of Katanga or Kasai, although the last, failed, attempt to control Katanga was in the late 1970s.[46]

The federal constitutions of Cameroon[47] and Ethiopia[48] were replaced by unitary ones in 1972 and 1962 respectively. Other attempted federal arrangements include Sudan,[49] the union of Tanganyika and Zanzibar that created the United Republic of Tanzania,[50] the Mali Federation, the Federation of French West Africa and the Federation of French Equatorial Africa.

Another development in the undemocratic nation-building processes of the post-colonial African state has been the rejection of multiparty politics, leading to either de jure or de facto single-party authoritarianism or military dictatorship in one country after the other.[51] What informed this development initially was the same reasoning that motivated post-colonial governments to proscribe ethnic-based movements and defy any institutional guarantees aimed at recognising the constituent ethnic communities.[52] President Ahmadou Ahidjo of Cameroon expressed the prevailing view in an interview as follows:

---

45 See Constitution of the Republic of Zaire of 1967 in Xydis (note 42 above) 1028–1146, 1029.

46 See Minorities at Risk data of the University of Maryland on the Lunda and Yeke of the DRC, available at <http://www.cidcm.umd.edu/mar/assessment.asp?groupId=49005>.

47 See AN Fru 'The Reunification Question in Cameroon History: Was the Bride an Enthusiastic or a Reluctant One' (Spring 2000) 47(2) *Africa Today* 91–119; MW DeLancey 'The Construction of the Cameroon Political System: The Ahidjo Years 1958–1982' (April 1987) 6 *J of Contemporary African Studies* 3–24.

48 E Gayim 'The Autonomy of Eritrea (1952–62): Learning from the Failed Experience' in ZA Skurbaty (ed.) *Beyond a One Dimensional State: An Emerging Rights to Autonomy* (2005) 401–419.

49 Under the Addis Ababa Peace Accord of 1972, South Sudan achieved regional autonomy, leading to the emergence of a federal form of state structure in the Sudan by virtue of the Self-Government Act of 1972. See DM Wai 'Geoethnicity and the Margin of Autonomy in the Sudan' in Rothchild and Olorunsola (note 3 above) 304ff.

50 See Article 2 Interim Constitution of Tanzania of 11 July 1965 in Xydis (note 42 above) 926–982, 926. Regarding the union between Tanganika and Zanzibar, Shivji states that due to the assimilationist tendency of mainland authorities, the question of the union has become one of the most explosive political issues in the country. See Shivji (note 30 above) 34.

51 ML Kilson 'Authoritarian and Single-Party Tendencies in African Politics' (January 1963) 15 *World Politics* 262–294.

52 'Political plurality and ethnic diversity,' maintains Hameso, 'were decried as bottlenecks for the project of "nation-building" and national unity.' S Hameso 'Issues and Dilemmas of Multi-Party Democracy in Africa' (2002) *West Africa Review* ISSN:1525–4488. Similarly, Crawford Young pointed out that '[t]he urgency of containing cultural pluralism was not the only argument marshaled, but it was nonetheless a leading plank in the single party platform'. C Young 'Competing Images of Africa: Democratization and its Challenges' in O Akiba (ed.) *Constitutionalism and Society in Africa* (2004) 141, 145.

> For me, the one party structure is the only way to escape this demagogy ['appeals to tribal, ethnic and religious differences in politics'], the only means to forge national unity.[53]

Many post-colonial African leaders, as well as several scholars, were convinced that one-party rule would provide the best framework for successful nation-building, the rationale being that it would put politics beyond the reach of the prevailing ethnic cleavages and thus enhance unity.

One of the advocates of a one-party state was Kwame Nkrumah of Ghana. Under his leadership, the Ghanian Avoidance of Discrimination Act was passed 'to prohibit organizations using or engaging in tribal, regional, racial or religious propaganda to the detriment of any other community, or securing the elections of persons on account of their tribal, regional or religious affiliation and for other purposes connected therewith.'[54] With its 1960 Constitution, Ghana became a one-party state, under the presidency of Kwame Nkrumah. This soon became a general trend. By the end of the 1970s most African countries had either adopted a one-party system or descended into military dictatorship or autocracy.

The natural fate of opposition and dissent under such circumstances was punishment and repression. As Hameso notes, '[i]n some cases, opposition met out with physical elimination and liquidation as in Ethiopia of the 1970s and 1980s, the period also known by White and Red Terror.'[55] The only countries that have continued to practise multipartism throughout all or most of their post-colonial history have been the Gambia in West Africa, Botswana in Southern Africa and Mauritius in East Africa.[56]

3.2.1. *The Flaws and Ultimate Failure of Post-colonial Nation-Building in Africa*

Although some of the post-colonial elites followed the homogenising nation-building process with good intentions, not only did this policy ultimately fail, with disastrous consequences, but it was also fatally flawed from inception. First, underlying the post-colonial nation-building process in Africa was the wrong assumption that ethnic identity and one's identity as a national of a state are mutually exclusive. Indeed, in most cases, not only can these two identities go together, but they can also reinforce each other, particularly where ethnic diversity is valued as an integral part of national identity. Moreover, this misconception overlooks the fact that people can and do live with multiple

---

[53] As quoted in A Rivkin *Nation-Building in Africa: Problems and Prospects* (1969) 48–49.
[54] Asante (note 34 above) 93.
[55] Hameso (note 52 above).
[56] M Owusu 'Domesticating Democracy: Culture, Civil Society and Constitutionalism in Africa' (January 1997) 39(1) *Comparative Studies in Society and History* 120, 123.

identities simultaneously without those identities necessarily conflicting with or undermining each other.

Generally, it is also only where their ethnic identity is recognised and protected that people with deep commitment to their ethnic identity can develop strong attachment to a state.[57] As Kymlicka puts it, although the existence of shared values and inspiring history are important to sustain solidarity in multinational states, '[p]eople from different national groups will only share an allegiance to the larger polity if they see it as the context within which their national identity is nurtured, rather than subordinated'.[58] Similarly, Lewis rightly argues with respect to Africa that

> [a]ny idea that one can make different peoples into a nation by suppressing the religious, tribal or regional or other affiliations to which they themselves attach the highest political significance is simply a non-starter. National loyalty cannot immediately supplant tribal loyalty; it has to be built on top of tribal loyalty by creating a system in which all the tribes feel that there is room for self-expression.'[59]

Secondly, the existence of different ethno-cultural groups in the same country does not in itself lead to political instability and conflicts.[60] As elsewhere, many of the conflicts that occurred in Africa are not the product of ethno-cultural differences per se. They are rather, as argued and shown in Chapter II, a result of the political and socio-economic processes of the state which have continuously created uneven material, cultural and political conditions among ethno-culturally different groups and their members. As many have argued and the case studies in this work will show, the provision of mechanisms to accommodate minority claims helps to address these conflicts through the democratic process and creates the conditions for advancing national integration.

Thirdly, and most importantly, since the state cannot be, and has not been, neutral with respect to members of different and unequal ethno-cultural groups, the homogenising nation-building process often exacerbated the crisis of the

---

[57] With respect to minorities, Timo Makkonen rightly observes that 'the extent to which members of minorities feel accepted, through the accommodation of their specific needs, affects positively their ability to see the society as a common project. On the other hand, if people feel that society does not respect their particular identities and needs, they will feel harmed, and indeed are harmed, and will be less keen to participate in common affairs'. T Makkonen 'Is Multiculturalism Bad for the Fight against Discrimination?' in M Scheinin & R Toivanen (eds.) *Rethinking Non-Discrimination and Minority Rights* (2004) 155, 173.

[58] Kymlicka (note 10 above) 189.

[59] Lewis (note 5 above) 68. This view is shared by others. KA Busia, for example, posited that '[t]he African situation ... calls for the concept of a nation of different tribes, possessing a diversity of traditions and even cultures, inhabiting a common territory, bounded together by the common desire to preserve their newly won independence and unity, and by the goals of economic, social, cultural and political progress which they share in common, and which they can see can be realized only if they stay together as a nation'. KA Busia *Africa in Search of Democracy* (1976) 116–117.

[60] See ibid, 120; *Cultural Liberty in Today's Diverse World* UNDP Human Development Report 2004 Chapter II.

legitimacy of the state and frustrated the possibility of national integration. This is attributable to two factors. The first is that, given the prevailing deep ethno-cultural diversity and inequality, not only has such neutrality become unattainable, but the lack of it has invariably also engendered political and socio-economic inequality and contestation between the members of the various groups. Secondly, in many of the countries concerned, little attempt was made in practice to observe state neutrality. Instead, contrary to the principle of neutrality, in many African countries, '[p]ost-colonial attempts at nation-building were overlaid on top of ethnically defined patronage politics, which rapidly reproduced itself within national institutions of states and parties.'[61]

Indeed, among the many consequences of the homogenising nation-building process, in the context of the authoritarianism and specific features of diversity in African states the most catastrophic was its inherent tendency to foster the co-option of the institutional apparatus of the state by one or more dominant groups to the relative exclusion of others.[62] Post-colonial political developments in many African countries have abundantly attested that state power has often been employed to the benefit of relatively strong communities and to the disadvantage of others.[63] Paradoxically enough, '[m]any African one party and military regimes, in spite of their supposed aversion to ethnicity … rested on distinctly ethnic political foundations and reproduced themselves on the basis of definable, in most cases, narrow ethnic alliances.'[64] And when some groups are found in control of the state apparatus, as shown in Chapter II, the repression of other groups takes, among other things, the 'form of state sanctioned imposition of cultural or political motifs of one or more groups on the rest of the population'.[65] The excluded groups have often been either co-opted or silenced,

---

[61] Berman et al. (note 26 above) 8.

[62] See Okafor (note 31 above) 102; Donald R Horowitz *Ethnic Groups in Conflict* (1985) 193–194; Alemante (note 2 above) 17; AM Abdullahi 'The Refugee Crisis in Africa as the Crisis of the Institution of the State' (1994) 6(4) Int J Refuge L 562, 567 & 570–578. In Kenya, it led to the domination of the state by the Kikuyu, and, when Arap Moi became president, mostly by Kelengi. In Liberia, the state was dominated by Samuel Doe's Kore ethnic group, in Malawi by the Chewa, in Zaire by Mobutu's Ngbandi ethnic group, in Sudan by northerners and Arabs, in Rwanda by Hutus until 1994, in Burundi by Tutsis, in Djibouti by Isa, in Ivory Coast by southern ethnic groups and in Mozambique by southerners. Similar patterns prevailed in many other African countries.

[63] On how non-dominant groups felt excluded from the homogenising conception of national unity and resisted their resultant marginalisation, see the contributions of Cheryl Hendricks (on South Africa) Jacqueline S Solway (on Botswana), Githu Mugai (on Kenya), Mamadou Diouf (on Senegal), Dickson Eyoh (on Cameroon) and Falola (on Nigeria) in Berman et al. (note 17 above) (arguing that the state in Africa has lacked the appropriate power configuration and institutional structure to deter the predisposition of particular groups to control it to their benefit to the exclusion of others).

[64] L Laakso & A Olukoshi 'The Crisis of the Post-colonial Nation-State Project in Africa' in A Olukoshi & L Laakso (eds.) *Challenges to the Nation-State in Africa* (1996) 15.

[65] See EE Osaghae 'Ethnicity, the State and Constitutionalism in Africa: Preliminary Observations' in O Akiba (ed.) *Constitutionalism and Society in Africa* (2004) 95, 96–97.

and when they have protested against discrimination and marginalisation they have been subjected to repression.[66] The overall effect of these post-colonial developments in African states has been that both authoritarianism of the state and opposition to it tended to rely on ethnic formations.

Political power has been organised and distributed within the state in such a way that the African state has not been a neutral arbiter of the competing interests of its diverse constituent groups. In the post-colonial African state, political power took a unitary and highly centralised form. Since control or domination of this power by members of one group leaves others on the political and socio-economic margins, this has often led to a Hobbesian-like rivalry between the constituent groups, which usually degenerates into violent conflict.[67] Yet, the domination of the state by relatively stronger communities often means that the state itself becomes involved in the struggle. This has predisposed the state to advance the interests of some ethnic groups while neglecting those of others.[68] In most instances, opposition and armed rebellion have invariably been organised along ethnic lines and directed against the state.

The attempted institutionalisation of a unitary political order and centralisation of power amid the prevailing ethno-cultural inequality have also furthered ethno-culturally unequal patterns of relations between members of various groups and the state. Not only have the constituent groups been unequally represented in the decision-making framework of the state, as well as in the bureaucracy and other state organs, but societal resources have often also been disproportionately controlled by and distributed in favour of dominant groups, further entrenching the inequality and the marginalisation of others. With the resultant marginalisation of certain sections of society from the state machinery and the spoils of economic development, the ethnic fragmentation inherited from colonial rule was further accentuated or otherwise given a new dimension. In such political context, ethnic rivalry and conflict tends to be unavoidable and prevalent.

It is clear today that the homogenising, state-centric and authoritarian nation-building policies of African states have utterly failed.[69] As Berman et al. noted, 'the level of identification with the state remains very low, the strategy

---

[66] See Abdullahi (note 62 above) 567. Okafor observes that '[s]ocio-cultural groups have, in some cases such as the case of the Ogoni, Katafa and Bajju of Nigeria, been brutally suppressed in the drive to impose the power of the central authority on them'. Okafor (note 31 above) 72.

[67] See Chapter II.

[68] Okafor (note 31 above) 95.

[69] To be exact, what it resulted in was the further alienation of the state from society, the deterioration of the capacity of the state, and ultimately the very disintegration of the state itself. It is in this context that it became common in the literature to speak of collapsed states, failed states etc. See IW Zartman (ed.) *Collapsed States: The Disintegration and Restoration of Legitimate Authority* (1995); MW Mutua 'Putting Humpty Dumpty Back Together Again: The Dilemmas of the Post-Colonial African State' (1995) 21 *Brooklyn J of Int L* 505; K Mengisteab 'New Approaches

has simply not worked, and in many cases has backfired, by fuelling fear and resentment amongst groups who feel excluded.'[70] After more than four decades of nation-building efforts, almost all of these states are still faced with two challenges inherited from their colonial past: the urgent need to integrate their nations and to accommodate the claims of their constituent sub-national groups democratically.

3.3. The Influence of the Dominant Constitutional Paradigm of the Nation-State

As indicated above, a characteristic of post-colonial African constitutions is that they were much influenced by the dominant liberal constitutional paradigm (mainly based on the Westminster or the French republican model). Despite the fact that along the way some constitutions have incorporated influences from socialist traditions or African socialism, and many others have also been scrupulously violated, these constitutions contained some of the important elements of the dominant nation-state constitutional paradigm which are inhospitable to ethno-cultural accommodation. The most important aspects of this paradigm discussed here are the idea of national or popular sovereignty, and the definition of state-society relations in terms of individual rights and the related idea of common citizenship.

3.3.1. *National (Popular) Sovereignty*

One of the achievements of the modern constitutional state is the shift in the locus of sovereignty from the divine right of kings to that of the people. Popular sovereignty came to be the very basis on which the edifice of the modern constitutional state was erected. In modern constitutionalism, following the American and French Revolutions, popular sovereignty has been articulated as a politico-legal expression of the self-image of the state as a nation-state. According to this perspective, the state is imagined and portrayed as being made up of one people, or a single 'demos'.[71] Indeed, this is formally expressed in the

---

to State Building in Africa: the Case of Ethiopia's Ethnic-Based Federalism' (1997) 40(3) *African Studies Review* 111–132, 116–119.

[70] Berman et al. (note 17 above) 18.

[71] James Tully identifies as the first feature of modern constitutionalism three concepts of popular sovereignty that preclude cultural diversity as a constitutive aspect of politics. (Tully note 7 above) 63–64. 'The people are sovereign and culturally homogenous in the sense that culture is irrelevant, capable of transcended, or uniform.' Ibid, 63. In the first conception of popular sovereignty 'the people are taken to be a society of equal individuals'. The second aspect is that 'the people are taken to be a society of equal individuals who exist at a "modern" level of historical development and recognise as authoritative a set of threshold, European institutions, manners and traditions of interpretation'. Ibid. Finally, 'the people are seen as a community bound together

very first words with which modern constitutions following the United States Constitution open: 'We the People ....'

One of the most important features of the modern constitutional paradigm is this narration of the unity and singularity of the sovereign people. This is meant to imagine the homogeneity of the people, and seeks to attribute to the population of the state a common identity. As Nergis Canefe has observed, '[i]n the European nation-state model, homogeneity rather than heterogeneity of the social texture was the foundation for the legitimating of self-determination and sovereignty.'[72] Such projection or characterisation of the population of the modern state as one people or one nation provided the basis on which the state is attributed with an individual identity as a 'nation', which is one of the features of the modern constitutional state.[73] This individual identity of the state as a 'nation' also encapsulates the unity of the sovereign people and their constitutional characterisation as a homogenous unit. This is the common identity that is constitutionally given to the citizens of the state by virtue of which the bond between the populace and the institutions of the state is engraved in law.

It is this feature of modern constitutionalism that European states employed to achieve the processes of nationalising themselves. Similarly, this dominant paradigm, bequeathed to Africa as part of the legacy of European colonial rule, has been religiously pursued in the discourse and formal structures of the post-colonial African state, to facilitate and legitimise a homogenising nation-building process. Rather than building nationhood on the basis of the indigenous ethno-political communities forming the African state, as argued by Arthur Lewis, it was the European experience of constructing relatively homogenous nation-states, culminating in the modern constitutional state, that controlled the imagination of post-colonial African constitutionalists and policy-makers. As this dominant paradigm admits of only one people and a constitutionally sanctioned common identity, it tends not only to overlook societal plurality, but also to encourage its assimilation into the common national identity, even if such identity is based on the language and cultural attributes of a dominant culture.[74] As Julius O Ihonvbere notes, 'most first generation constitutions in

by an implicit and substantive common good and a shared set of European institutions, manners and traditions of interpretation.' Ibid, 64.

[72] N Canefe 'Sovereignty Without Nationalism? A Critical Assessment of Minority Rights Beyond the Sovereign Nation-State Model' in M Sellers (ed.) *The New World Order Sovereignty, Human Rights, and the Self-Determination of Peoples* (1996) 91, 107.

[73] See Tully (note 7 above); Taylor (note 16 above); SA Dersso 'The Socio-Historical and Political Processes Leading to the Emergence of the Discourse on Minorities' in Solomon Dersso et al. (eds.) *Perspectives on Minority and Indigenous Rights in Africa* (2010).

[74] Tully states that '[t]he requirements of one sovereign people ...one nation and one uniform order of modern legal and political institutions make the recognition and accommodation of diversity impossible.' Tully (note 7 above) 140.

the continent pretended that ethnicity, cultural and religious diversity did not exist and that what was important was the so-called quest for nationhood.'[75]

It has been within this constitutional framework that post-colonial African states have pursued their mission of nation-building, aiming at the removal of what they called 'tribal divisions' and identities and the sanctioning of the state-chosen identity. And this state-chosen identity has either been artificially constructed or created by nationalising the cultural attributes of the dominant group, to the exclusion of all others.[76] Indeed, almost all the constitutions of post-colonial Africa speak of 'We the people ...'. The implication is that there is only one demos, constituted by individual members (as opposed to the various constituent groups by which the African state is constituted), and the individual members share a *collective character* (to use Frank Michelman's term)[77] as a people. Accordingly, in constitutional terms, the post-colonial state imagines itself and is therefore portrayed, at least in legal and political discourse, as the political and institutional expression of a single community of individuals as 'people', without regard to the histories, political traditions and cultures of the constituent communities.[78]

The unitary conception of sovereignty of the people is also given constitutional expression in the nature of the organisation of the internal sovereignty (political power) of the state.[79] 'In terms of classical illustrations of constitutional theory of the nation-state,' writes Tierney, 'sovereignty as a legal concept is conceived of in unitary terms.'[80] What James Tully refers to as 'political and legal monism' captures the way in which this is expressed in modern constitutions. Accordingly, internal sovereignty is expressed through, among other things, 'one national

[75] JO Ihonvbere 'Politics of Constitutional Reforms and Democratization in Africa' (2000) XLI *IJCS* 1, 22.

[76] As Wani notes, '[t]he conception of nationhood embraced by Africans at independence was of an homogenous society, speaking the same language and bearing the same basic attitudes and habits. Tribalism, or pluralism for that matter, was perceived to be inconsistent with this conception of nationhood.' (Wani note 20 above) 634.

[77] FI Michelman 'Constitutional Authorship' in Larry Alexander (ed.) *Constitutionalism: Philosophical Foundations* (1998) 64, 80.

[78] This has acquired particular attention in countries that were under French colonial rule. In all but one of the constitutions of these countries, the state has been portrayed as being constituted by one people. The exception is the 1979 Constitution of Benin which amended the independence constitution, although the guarantees stipulated have in the end been empty. See Selassie (note 2 above) at his note 69.

[79] As Macklem has it, 'constitutional law comprehends sovereignty as referring to political and legal authority within states'. P Macklem *Indigenous Difference and the Constitution of Canada* (2001) 109. Also see IDetter de Lupis *International Law and the Independent State* 2 ed (1987) 3; S Assefa 'Two Concepts of Sovereignty' paper prepared for a symposium held in Mekelle on the occasion of the twenty-fifth anniversary of the TPLF (24 February 2000) in *Addis Tribune* <http://www.addistribune.com/Archives/2000/03/24-03-00/Two.htm> .

[80] S Tierney *Constitutional Law and National Pluralism* (2004) 102–103.

system of institutionalised legal and political authority rather than many'.[81] This implies that within the dominant constitutional paradigm there can only be a single locus of authority within a state and sovereign power is undivided, and in the post-colonial African state neither was it sought to be limited. In terms of the internal power arrangement of the state, sovereign power is thus centrally controlled and organised in a unitary form. This is the only aspect of the constitutional framework that African states have further strengthened and jealously guarded, as John Stone observes.[82]

The constitutional revisions made in many African states subsequent to the departure of the colonial powers were meant further to accentuate the unitaristic power structure already established under the independent constitutions, and led to a high degree of centralisation of power.[83] Subsequent constitutional changes involving the removal of forms of decentralisation and constitutional limitations aggravated this by creating unlimited governments.[84] This has made it possible for many African governments not only to repress demands for dispersion of sovereign power among the constituent communities – as, among others, in the Sudan, Ghana, Ethiopia, Senegal, Algeria, Chad, Nigeria, and Mozambique – but also to abrogate constitutionally entrenched autonomy regimes as well as any form of group rights – as in Kenya,[85] Uganda,[86] the DRC,[87] Cameroon[88] and Tanzania.[89]

---

[81] Tully (note 7 above) 66.

[82] J Stone 'Ethnicity versus the State: The Dual Claims of State Coherence and Ethnic Self-Determination' in Rothchild and Olorunsola (note 3 above) 85, 89.

[83] See VT Le Vine 'The Fall and Rise of Constitutionalism in West Africa' 35(2) *The J of Modern African Studies* (1997) 181–206, 188–198.

[84] Ibid, 188–189. See also F Reyntjens 'Authoritarianism for Francophone Africa from the Colonial to the Post-Colonial State' (1988) *Third World Legal Studies* 59; 'Recent Developments in Public Law of Francophone African States' (1986) 30 (2) *The J of Modern African Studies* 75–90. AS Alexander Jr., 'The Ivory Coast Constitution: An Accelerator, not a Brake' (1963) 3(1) *The J of Modern African Studies*' 293–311.

[85] See notes 39–40 above and accompanying text.

[86] See notes 41–42 above and accompanying text.

[87] See notes 43–46 above accompanying text.

[88] See note 47 above.

[89] The 1965 Constitution of Tanzania provided for some form of federal union between Zanzibar and Tanganyika, leading to the establishment of Tanzania. Shivji observes: '[t]he articles of the union between Zanzibar and Tanganyika provided for some form of federation. The attitudes and expressions of the Zanzibari people since have clearly demonstrated their preference for a loose federation with substantial autonomy for Zanzibar. Yet, mainland authorities have been pushing for greater integration – or as it has been put "consolidation of the union". Every opportunity has been taken to *further* integration, at least constitutionally, even though in practice it has been found difficult to effect such integration due to the resistance of Zanzibaris. The result is that the question of the union has become one of the most explosive political issues in the country.' IG Shivji 'State and Constitutionalism: A New Democratic Perspective' in IG Shivji *State and Constitutionalism an African Debate* (1991) 27–54, 34.

3.3.2. *The Limits of the Unitarist Conception of National Sovereignty*

The unitary conception of popular (national) sovereignty and the nature of the political organisation it engendered are problematic in multi-ethnic societies in general, and in Africa in particular, on several counts. In the first place, it does not cohere with the prevailing ethno-cultural diversity that is characteristic of the African state. Writing on Nigeria, Kelechi A Kalu states that '[a]s a product of [this] European intellectual tradition [of the constitutional state with a homogenous and singular popular sovereignty], the Nigerian state is assumed to possess one identity'.[90] He argues with insight that '[s]uch fallacy of a single alternative is not only ignorant of the history of Nigeria's state formation, but when superimposed on existing conflictual identities makes Nigeria prone to self-implosion.'[91] Moreover, it has not only justified the process of homogenisation and coercive national unity, but also contributed to the neglect of the existing inequalities among members of various groups. This has had the effect of integrating members of these groups into the state on an unequal basis, leading to the inevitable relegation of members of disadvantaged groups to the status of second- or third-class citizenship. In the particular circumstances of African states, it also invites the explosive question of who should control political power, often leading to the kind of ethnic antagonism and violent conflicts witnessed in many African states, including relatively stable ones, as the 2007 post-election election crisis in Kenya attests.

Probably the most serious flaw of the unitary conception of popular sovereignty in the context of the colonial origin of the state and its deep ethno-cultural diversity and inequality is the nature of the internal organisation of political power it entrenched. This structural flaw defines the essence of the institutional or legitimacy crisis of the post-colonial state, and constitutes the root basis of the issue of minorities in Africa. From the perspective of this study, there are two particularly important aspects to this crisis. The first is that the state is 'a generally unalloyed external imposition rather than … a largely organic entity created through an internal process of consensus-building.'[92] Moreover, its unitarist and highly centralised organisation of political power generally tends to induce ethnic rivalry and conflict rather than accommodation and peaceful coexistence. Most importantly, it failed, as discussed in Chapter II and is further shown in the next chapter, to create just and democratic political and

[90] KA Kalu 'Constitutionalism in Nigeria: A Conceptual Analysis of Ethnicity and Politics' (2004) 6 *West Africa Review*.

[91] Ibid.

[92] OC Okafor '"Righting", Restructuring, and Rejuvenating the Postcolonial African State: The Case for the Establishment of an AU Special Commission on National Minorities' (2007) 13 *African Yearbook of Int L* 2005 43, 49–50.

socio-economic processes that guarantee and enhance genuine equality for members of different groups in all aspects of public life.

The second and related issue that forms an important aspect of the institutional crisis of the post-colonial African state has been the absence of 'fit' between the institutions of the state and the indigenous social structures and values of the constituent ethno-cultural communities. This has caused what Mutua called 'a crisis of cultural and philosophical identity'[93] and has also led to the alienation of the citizenry from the processes of the state. The devaluation and suppression of indigenous languages, cultures and traditions within the framework of the unitary and homogenous conception and application of sovereignty has further accentuated this disconnection.[94]

Another problem of the unitarist conception of sovereignty, at least in the context of Africa, has been its tendency to encourage concentration of power at the centre. As already noted, one of the developments witnessed during the post-colonial period in tandem with the homogenising nation-building process has been a centralisation of power. This has had the effect of narrowing the political space and making the central government a seat of fierce rivalry among various groups for its control or domination, which, as discussed earlier, in many countries degenerated into violent conflicts.

3.3.3. *The Individual-Rights-Based Conception of the State-Society Relationship*

The development of the modern constitutional state additionally involved the transformation of the basic unit of society from hierarchically organised social groups to the individual.[95] Against the background of this transformation and under the influence of the political thought of the Enlightenment, starting with Hobbes, who began the analysis of political society from an individualist perspective, the individual and the state became the only relevant actors in terms

---

[93] This crisis is expressed in terms of the non-recognition, marginalisation and 'delegitimation of values, notions, philosophies about the individual, society, politics, and nature developed over centuries'. MW Mutua 'The Banjul Charter and the African Cultural Fingerprint: An Evaluation of the Language of Duties' (1995) 35 *Virginia J Int L* 339, 343.

[94] As Abdullahi observes, '[t]he absence of ethnically based values in both the formation and management of African States and the exclusion of ethnicity as a component in political management accentuate the … crisis of the State'. Abdullahi (note 62 above) 567. See also DW Nabudere 'Traditional and Modern Political Systems in Contemporary Governance in Africa' (2004) 3 (1) *J of African Elections* 13.

[95] As Charles Taylor's analysis aptly demonstrates, this transformation corresponds with the rejection of honour as determining the status of individuals in the ancien régime, and its replacement by the notion of dignity, which has become the basis of the modern democratic state. Charles Taylor 'The Politics of Recognition' in Amy Gutman (ed.) *Multiculturalism: Examining the Politics of Recognition* (1994) 25–73, 26–27.

of which modern constitutionalism defines the state-society relationship.[96] In Hobbes and Locke it is individuals in the state of nature that come together to form the political community. Hobbes speaks of the agreement of 'a multitude of men';[97] Locke talks of 'any number of men'.[98] In contemporary contractarian theories, such as that of John Rawls, those who negotiate the principles of justice behind the veil of ignorance are also individuals.[99] This theoretical understanding is reproduced in the way by which the state-society relationship is imagined and formulated in modern constitutional law. Accordingly, the people or the nation that constitutes the modern constitutional state 'are taken to be a society of equal individuals'.[100] This tendency of modern constitutionalism to define the nature of the state-society relationship on the basis of the duality of the individual, on the one hand, and the state, on the other, fails to have 'any regard for any other actors on the social and political stage.'[101]

Two devices are used in the modern constitutional state to define the boundaries of the state-society relationship on such terms. The first is the distinction often made between the public or the political and the social or the private. John Rawls, for example, distinguishes the political from the associational, which is voluntary in ways that the political is not; and from the personal and the familial, which are affectional domains, in ways that the political is not.[102] This distinction identifies certain matters as falling within the public domain, and hence as matters which the state can legitimately regulate. On the other hand, it relegates other matters to the private sphere, which the state cannot regulate by its laws and institutions. One such matter is ethnic membership. This is a matter with respect to which the constitutional state should be neutral, according to mainstream liberal thinking.[103] Properly understood, this entails not only that the state should not be biased against any particular group, but also that it is 'supposed to be free of all identifying characteristics or associations with particular

---

[96] For a detailed analysis of this and its implications for the recognition of ethnic groups as relevant entities see V van Dyke 'The Individual, the State and Ethnic Communities in Political Theory' in W Kymlicka (ed.) *The Rights of Minority Cultures* (1995) 31–56; see also RN Clinton 'The Rights of Indigenous Peoples as Collective Group Rights' (1990) 32 *Arizona LR* 739, 740; Tully (note 7 above) 63.

[97] See T Hobbes *Leviathan* (1651) (CB Macpherson ed., 1968).

[98] See J Locke *Two Treatises of Government* (1690) (ed Peter Laslett 1960, 1992) 330–331.

[99] See Johan Rawls *A Theory of Justice* (1971).

[100] Tully (note 7 above) 63.

[101] G Selassie (note 2 above) 16; see also RR Garet 'Community and Existence: The Rights of Groups' (1983) 56 *South Carolina LR* 1001, 1013–1014; N Glazer 'Individual Rights against Group Rights' in Kymlicka (note 96 above) 125–126.

[102] J Rawls *Political Liberalism* (2005) 137.

[103] According to Nathan Glazer, for example, in a liberal society the constitutional state 'set before itself the model that group membership is purely private, a shifting matter of personal choice and degree, something that may be weakened and dismissed as other identities takeover'. Note 101 above,134.

groups or individuals.'[104] 'This separation of state and ethnicity', as Kymlicka terms it, 'precludes any legal or governmental recognition of ethnic groups, or any use of ethnic criteria in the distribution of rights, resources, and duties.'[105]

'This vision of constitutionalism,' maintains Selassie, 'animated African states at the time of independence and has since remained the dominant vision.'[106] As the state should be identified as embodying no cultural attribute particular to any group, but rather as a supra-ethnic construction possessing some abstract identity, what many post-colonial governments sought to achieve through nation-building was the creation of states based upon a nationalism transcending the existing ethnic cleavages characterising their states. This has often denied the various groups lumped together under the unitary state any legal and political space. It has rather served to the advantage of those post-colonial governments which rejected ethno-cultural diversity as divisive and backward.[107] Preoccupied with unitary nation-building, the framers of the post-colonial constitutions did not concern themselves with the dangers of unchecked political power, nor with the threat that failing to address these dangers posed to the hopes and ambitions of peoples for a peaceful and prosperous statehood. As the quotation at the beginning of this chapter illustrates, many African governments believed that they would achieve nationhood as a society of individual citizens with equal individual rights, without regard to, and by transcending, existing ethno-cultural identifications. This vision was eloquently summed up by Kwame Nkrumah of Ghana:

> We must insist that in Ghana, in the higher reaches of our national life, there should be no reference to Fantes, Ashantis, Ewes, fas, dagombas, 'starangers', and so further, but we should call ourselves Ghanians – all brothers and sisters, members of the same community – the state of Ghana.[108]

In many post-colonial African countries the private-public distinction was taken to the extreme. As noted above, in some cases the establishment of any form of association or movement on the basis of ethnic membership was banned.[109] After Nkrumah was ousted from power by a coup in 1966, a law was enacted allowing the establishment of political parties,[110] but it prohibited the establishment of

---

[104] Y Tamir *Liberal Nationalism* (1993) 141.

[105] Kymlicka (note 10 above) 4.

[106] G Selassie (note 2 above) 16. Similarly Shivji argues that the 'liberal perspective was part of the heritage left by the colonial power in the form of independence constitutions'. Shivji (note 30 above) 28.

[107] '[A]s soon as the conception of an independent nationhood subsuming tribal divisions was born,' IM Lewis noted, 'tribalism was relegated to the status of a dangerous, subversive factionalism'. IM Lewis in C Legum and J Drysdale (eds.) *Africa: Contemporary Record 1969–1970* (1971) A13.

[108] K Nkrumah, *I Speak of Freedom* (1961) 212.

[109] See JW Clay 'Nation, Tribe and Ethnic Group in Africa' (1985) 9 *Cultural Survival Quarterly* 2 (discussing the various efforts of African states to 'eliminate' ethnic identity).

[110] Political Parties Decree issued by the Government of Ghana on 28 April 1969.

political parties on an ethnic or religious basis, and even the use by any political party of names, words or symbols intended by such party to arouse tribal or religious feelings.[111] This has been the dominant feature of African statecraft throughout the post-colonial period and beyond. In Kenya, President Daniel Arap Moi 'startled his country in July 1986 by securing the party's elite's support for a resolution calling for the "wind up" of all tribal associations.'[112] In Burundi, the government of Albin Nyamoya 'went as far as declaring that ethnic names should not be used any longer'.[113]

In this way, the private-public distinction that modern constitutionalism has envisaged has been stretched to its limits as a means to forge national unity, usually against and at the expense of ethnic identity – all that, however, to end up achieving anything but national integration. In the first place, it is not possible to maintain that distinction. This is because '[g]overnment decisions on languages, internal boundaries, public holidays, and state symbols unavoidably involve recognising, accommodating, and supporting the needs and identities of particular ethnic and national groups.'[114] Moreover, as we have seen above, in the practice of the post-colonial African state this distinction has not in any case been followed.

The other device employed in the definition of the state-society relationship in modern constitutional law is the protection of the rights and liberties of the individual. Since in modern constitutional thought the individual is often imagined as standing in opposition to the state, modern constitutionalism defines the free domain of the individual, which the state is required to respect and protect, through the idea of individual rights and liberties. Premised on the Lockean and Jeffersonian view that the principal purpose of the state is to ensure the preservation of individual rights, modern constitutionalism demands that the state guarantee those rights and liberties to the individuals forming part of it.[115]

The language of individual rights is also meant to define state-society relations in other ways. Members of society are seen to relate to the state as individual citizens, not as members of particular groups.[116] And through these rights and liberties, the state defines the status of members of its population as equal citizens. A characteristic of the modern constitutional state is accordingly the attribution of common (universal) citizenship to its people(s) on an individual basis. This

---

[111] Asante (note 34 above) 96.

[112] Rothchild and Olorunsola (note 3 above) 7.

[113] JB Ejobowah 'The Limits and Possibilities of Conflict-Reduction Strategies in Africa's Polyethnic States' in EI Udogu (eds.) *The Issue of Political Ethnicity in Africa* (2001) 149, 177.

[114] Kymlicka (note 10 above) 108. See also see Berman et al. (note 26 above) 16.

[115] Ronald Dworkin thus held that constitutionalism is 'a system that establishes individual legal rights that the dominant legislature does not have the power to override or compromise'. R Dworkin 'Constitutionalism and Democracy' (1995) 3 *European J of Philosophy* 2.

[116] See Glazer (note 101 above) 125.

entails that there has to be one package of individual rights and liberties that apply commonly and equally to all individuals, and that all citizens, as equals qua citizen, should be treated in the same way before the law.

Despite the ambivalence that many African governments have shown to the protection of individual rights for political reasons, the constitutions they received and designed enshrined these rights, albeit with varying degrees of emphasis and form, and of course with little respect and application. Accordingly, the constitutional systems of most, if not all, African countries have been framed and operated in such a way that individual rights can be guaranteed and enforced, notwithstanding rampant rights violations and the authoritarian nature of the post-colonial state. Many of the constitutions of anglophone countries accordingly retain an elaborate bill of rights. They also expressly empower courts to enforce such rights. Francophone countries likewise give recognition to individual rights in their constitutions. Unlike anglophone countries, however, they recognised individual rights in the preambles to their constitutions. For example, the Preamble of the Constitution of Chad of 1962 declares its commitment to the principles set forth in the Declaration of the Rights of Man of 1789, and the Universal Declaration of Human Rights (UDHR) of 1948. It elaborates this further by listing the individual rights recognised. According to Asante, unlike the constitutions of anglophone countries, these constitutions have provided for 'these rights in categorical terms, but in the form of general directive principles rather than precise legal rights.'[117] All the same, the constitutional systems of these countries have also been hospitable to claims of individual rights and operated on the basis of common citizenship.

Consistent with the liberal constitutional tradition, a common feature of many of the African constitutions was accordingly that they did not provide for group-specific rights. Shivji notes that '[t]he approach in African Constitutions … to the nationality question … is total silence on nationality rights even where the constitution has elaborate provisions on individual rights and freedoms.' He further says that '[w]here the constitution does avert to the issue of nationalities … as in Nigeria, it subtly reflects assimilationist tendency.'[118] So, following the dominant modern constitutional paradigm, in the constitutions of African countries only individual rights have been recognised.

Of course, most have provided for rights of non-discrimination on the basis of various group characteristics, including race and ethnic origin. This indirect acknowledgement is, however, as close as they have come to guaranteeing rights on the basis of group membership. Even then, the aims were, at least on paper, to ensure that the state remains neutral on matters such as ethnicity, or to

[117] Asante (note 34 above) 75.
[118] Shivji (note 30 above) 35.

promote unity. The logical consequence of this is the exclusion of constitutional or legislative designs involving the granting of rights or distribution of benefits on the basis of ethnic membership. This sought to dictate that all the citizens of the state relate and interact with the state as individuals only, without due regard to the impact of ethno-cultural membership on citizenship.

The problem is not merely that the constitutions of African countries have failed to incorporate any guarantees that accommodate diversity and justly resolve group-based claims. These constitutions, and the legal systems they instituted, have been inhospitable to claims other than those formulated in individual terms. The net effect of this hostility has been to preclude – not just the articulation of group claims, which has often been prohibited – but even the formulation of ethnic-based claims as individual-rights claims, such as on the basis of freedom of expression and freedom of association, individual liberties that could advance group interests. In many of these countries *any* expression of ethnic nationalism has been prohibited, and it has been 'an invective to be referred to as a tribalist'.[119]

The difficulty with the definition of state-society relations in terms of individual rights is not limited to the African state, but applies to all multi-ethnic societies generally. Vernon van Dyke, for example, argues: 'It is not enough to think in terms of a two level relationship, with the individual at one level and the state at another .... Considering the heterogeneity of ... the population of virtually every existing state, it is also necessary to think of ethnic communities ... and to include them among the kinds of right-and-duty bearing units'.[120] In the African context, it is generally believed that the exclusive focus of the discourse on individual human rights is limited, as it ignores and leaves no space for group identity and the group-based rights embedded in African cultures and traditions. It runs in the face of the particular importance attached to group membership by many communities in the continent.[121] The recognition and elaboration of peoples' rights under the African Charter on Human and Peoples' Rights in part sought to rectify this omission and complement individual rights by recognising communities in the domain of the state-society relationship and in rights discourse.

The validity of universal citizenship has also been challenged in recent years, particularly from the vantage point of minorities and other similar historically non-recognised groups. Many have argued that it has the tendency to enforce homogeneity of citizens.[122] It denies recognition to and public space for the

---

[119] Wani (note 20 above) 633.
[120] Van Dyke (note 96) 31–56, 31.
[121] See Chapters II & IV.
[122] IM Young 'Polity and Group Difference: A Critique of the Ideal of Universal Citizenship' in RE Goodin & P Pettit (eds.) *Contemporary Political Philosophy: An Anthology* (1997) 256–272,

expression of the cultural distinctness of minorities, and hence is assimilationist in its operation and discriminatory in its effect.[123] It is further argued that in the context of ethno-cultural diversity and socio-economic and political inequality among members of different groups, the principle of common citizenship tends to perpetuate oppression or disadvantage.[124] This is partly because universal citizenship assumes that cultural membership has no effect on the enjoyment of equal rights, or else its operation assumes the cultural equality, if not homogeneity, of citizens belonging to different ethno-cultural groups.

In the African context, the possibility and validity of maintaining universal citizenship without regard to factual differences, including those based on ethnic membership, has been and continues to be highly questionable, to say the least. Speaking in particular on the right to participation, Ben Nwabueze argues that in states composed of diverse and unequal ethnic groups who compete for control or a share of political power, as is the case in most African countries, 'a right to ... participate in government based solely on individual merit (common citizenship) is no less unacceptable than based on birth or wealth.' He continues: '[T]he problem of social justice and democracy in a multi-racial or multi-ethnic society is about how to give all the component groups the opportunity to participate in both the elective and non-elective organs, arms and agencies of government, since only thus can each feel that it is a full member of the nation.'[125] Because it is generally indifferent to the situation of disadvantaged groups, universal citizenship can also lead to instability and conflicts as it has no effective framework to address group-based demands for inclusion and recognition.

L Adele Jinadu writes:

> The inclusivist notion of common citizenship, based on individual rights, that has tended to underline this (Africa's) state formation process, has been problematic in Africa not only because virtually all the countries on the continent are 'ethnically split' ... but also because the political economy of colonial rule, and the state formation process that went *pari passu* with it encouraged and deepened intense ethnic conflict on the continent, differentiating citizens into stratified aggregations of first-class, second-class and third-class citizens.[126]

Under such circumstances, the claim of the state that it guarantees equal rights for all on the basis of universal citizenship can only obscure the problem of

---

257; C Taylor 'The Politics of Recognition' in A Gutmann (ed.) *Multiculturalism: Examining the Politics of Recognition* (1994) 25.

[123] See Taylor (ibid); Tully (note 7 above) Chapter 1; Canefe (note 69 above) 103–109.

[124] See Young (note 122 above); Tully (note 7 above); Kymlicka (note 10 above); M Freeman *Human Rights: An Interdisciplinary Approach* (2002) 117.

[125] B Nwabueze *Constitutional Democracy in Africa* Vol 1 (2003) 55–56.

[126] LA Jinadu *Explaining and Managing Ethnic Conflict in Africa: Towards a Cultural Theory of Democracy* Claude Ake Memorial Papers No 1 (2007) 10.

group inequality and claims for recognition.[127] It cannot meet the interests of minorities to have their languages, cultures, histories and traditions are given due recognition and guarantee.[128] Worse still, as the experience of many African countries shows, the attempt to enforce universal citizenship and nation-building has led to and often precipitates 'ethnic resentment, disaffection, resistance, and political disorder'[129] and, in extreme cases, violent conflicts. This is essentially because, being difference-blind in its conception and operation, it ignores and even gives a semblance of legitimacy to the continuing socio-economic, cultural and political inequalities, and hence to the second- or third-class status of disadvantaged groups, albeit the skewed relationship of the state with different groups is also in part to blame. It is clear from this that universal citizenship is not only inadequate to resolve ethno-cultural conflicts, but it even tends to exacerbate them. The unavoidable conclusion is that although universal citizenship, defined in terms of individual rights, is a crucial component of any democratic society, it must be complemented by group-specific rights or arrangements.

3.4. The 'Second African Independence' and the Neglect of the Issue of Minorities

As a result of the above developments in the three decades since independence, almost all African states witnessed ethnic rivalries which led to not only social divisions and conflicts, but also a weakening of democratic institutions and an attendant rise of authoritarianism. Under the domination of one-party, military or no-party regimes, and with support from either of the two blocs in the Cold War, most African states came to have all-powerful presidents with unchecked executive powers and domination over legislatures, reminiscent of the absolute monarchs of 17th-century Europe.[130] Democratic rights such as the right to political participation (including through voting and the formation and running of political parties) and freedoms of the press, expression, association and assembly, among others, were all curtailed or systematically made inoperative. Rule of law, the independence of the judiciary and constitutionalism were all abused or else rendered useless. Human rights were either suspended or routinely violated. Corruption, nepotism, incompetence and gross misgovernance

[127] Ibid.
[128] G Selassie (note 2 above) 27.
[129] Ibid, 28, 29.
[130] According to Samuel Huntington, the majority of African countries were either 'personal dictatorship, military regimes, one party authoritarian systems or a combination of these three'. S Huntington *The Third Wave of Democratization in the Late Twentieth Century* (1991) 295. The list of tyrants include Idi Amin of Uganda, Mengistu Hailemariam of Ethiopia, Daniel Arap Moi of Kenya, Kamuzu Banda of Malawi, Mobutu Seseseko of former Zaire, etc.

prevailed. Economic growth has also generally been declining, with governments failing to meet the basic needs of their people such as food, shelter, drinking water, schooling etc., leading some scholars to refer to the post-colonial state as the 'irrelevant state'.[131]

As alluded to above, apart from the internal conditions of these states, most importantly, the superpower ideological struggle and imperial rivalry that played itself out in the politics of many African countries during the first three decades of the post-colonial period cultivated many of these ailments. Many analysts agree that almost all of the post-independence regimes actively solicited support from either the former USSR or the United States to sustain their grip on power.[132] This is one of the most significant factors that explains the long duration of authoritarian rule by the likes of Arap Moi of Kenya, Mobutu of former Zaire, and Banda of Malawi.[133]

With the unceremonious end of the Cold War in 1989, the authoritarian rulers and the highly weakened (but highly centralised and authoritarian) post-colonial states were left exposed. The door was wide open for the expression of hitherto suppressed political dissent and societal grievances. Almost everywhere on the continent, people rose up – in most cases spontaneously and without clearly organised and historically established political leadership – to demand long-overdue political and socio-economic changes. The post-1990 period has therefore been characterised by a wave of political turbulence sweeping through Africa. Described by many as the 'second African independence or liberation',[134] this has brought about a process of constitutional change and political reform in many countries.

3.4.1. *The Nature of Post-1990 Constitutional Reform*

Although very broad in aspiration, this new wave of democratic change was largely limited to addressing certain aspects of the problems of the post-colonial African state. The issues that this democratic and constitutional reform process focussed on were authoritarianism, unlimited government, human-rights

---

[131] See J Ihonbvere 'The "irrelevant" State, Ethnicity and the Quest for Nationhood in Africa' (1994) 17 *Ethnic and Racial Studies* 42–60.

[132] As Edward Jaycox puts it, during the Cold War, 'there was practically no African state that was not propped up by the East or West for its legitimacy'. Quoted in M Owusu 'Domesticating Democracy: Culture, Civil Society and Constitutionalism in Africa' (January 1997) 39(1) *Comparative Studies in Society and History* 120–152, 130.

[133] According to a 1990 survey of African heads of state since independence, of the 22 longest-serving African heads of state then in power, one was a president for life, three had been in office for 30 to 31 years, seven for 22 to 29 years, eight for 11 to 20 years, and four for 10 years. As quoted in Owusu (ibid) 142.

[134] See R Joseph 'Democratization in Africa after 1989: Comparative and Theoretical Perspectives' (April 1997) 29(3) *Comparative Politics* 363- 382.

violations and the lack of a human-rights culture, and the restriction of political rights, including the formation and running of political parties, and multiparty elections.

As can be gathered from the previous sections in this chapter, the post-colonial African state inherited and further perfected the use of violence and repression as a mode of governance.[135] Dissent was not tolerated, and almost any form of political opposition was severely punished. African governments have in many ways been tyrannical, with no respect for the interests and wishes of their people. The rise of authoritarianism in post-colonial Africa involved a centralisation of power and the progressive removal of various institutional limits established under the early independence constitutions. This led to the emergence of unlimited governments, leaving no place, in practice, for the rule of law and constitutionalism.[136] Moreover, unlimited government, with all its failures to deliver on the promises of economic progress and political liberties, soon became a source of ethnic clientelism and repression.[137]

Related to the problem of authoritarian rule and centralisation of power have been the prohibition of political pluralism and the curtailment of citizens' political liberties. It has been noted above that the one-party system became an African political orthodoxy, such that 'in almost all the independent countries of sub-Saharan Africa free political competition was eliminated either by the establishment of the one-party state or the complete replacement of civilian politicians by military rulers.'[138] Political liberties such as the freedoms listed above were, for all practical purposes, disallowed.[139] Those who dared to practise them did so on pain of imprisonment, torture and even death. People were effectively denied, as in colonial times, any possibility of exercising their right to self-determination through participation in the management of public affairs. As multiparty politics gave way to one-party rule, political liberties were lost to allow despotism and repression to reign.

The liberation struggle for which Africans laid down their lives was expected to bring freedom from not only colonial rule but also from the attendant violations of the rights and dignity of colonial peoples. The struggle was undoubtedly

---

[135] See, for more, M Meredith *The State of Africa: A History of Fifty Years of Independence* (2005, 2006) Chapter 13 'The Coming of Tyrants' & Chapter 23 'The Struggle for Democracy'; J Reader *Africa: A Biography of the Continent* (1997,1998) Chapter 55; Davidson (note 5 above) Chapter 7 & Chapter 8.

[136] See B Obi Nwabueze *Constitutionalism in the Emergent States* (1973) 155–170; AA An-Na'im 'Introduction: Expanding Legal Protection of Human Rights in African Countries' in AA An-Na'im (ed.) *Human Rights Under African Constitutions* (2003) 1, 14.

[137] Davidson (note 5 above); EE Osagehe *Ethnicity and the State in Africa* Working Paper Series No 7 Afrasian Centre for Peace and Development (2006).

[138] P Slinn 'A Fresh Start for Africa? New African Constitutional Perspectives for the 1990s' (1991) 35 *J of African L* 1–7, 1.

[139] Nwabueze (note 136 above) 150–153.

as much for self-rule as for the achievement of economic development and for the rights and liberties of individuals as well as communities. However, within a few years these promises of independence were betrayed in almost all African countries. Human-rights guarantees were honoured more in their breach and violation than in their respect and protection. '[T]he idea that government must be in accordance with the rule of law in ways that uphold the fundamental individual and collective rights of all citizens has not been observed by the post-colonial states.'[140] As Osaghe has observed, it is only logical that '[o]ne of the areas of national life where (post-1990) democracy is expected to make a major difference and facilitate development is the enjoyment and protection of human rights.'[141]

These were also regimes that squandered the meagre resources of their countries and allowed the embezzlement of state money and rampant corruption, leaving the state without the means to provide for basic services such as health, sanitation, justice, water and education.

There is no doubt that all these are among the most serious democratic deficiencies of Africa's post-colonial political order. Post-1990 democratic and constitutional reforms in Africa have legitimately sought to address them. The problem with this diagnosis is, however, that it does not identify all the problems of democratic governance and legitimate statehood in Africa, but deals largely with the symptoms alone. The various ailments of the post-colonial order identified for resolution by post-1990 democratisation processes are in reality attributable to the institutional crisis of the state. This is an area that has not been sufficiently problematised and articulated in the post-1990 constitutional changes and political reforms adopted by the majority of African countries. The issue of minorities, which is the product and an important manifestation of the crisis, has not also figured as a critical issue that has to be addressed by the new democratic and constitutional reforms.

3.4.2. *The Nature of Post-1990 Constitutional Changes and Democracy in Africa and their Limitations*

Clearly, the problem with the post-Cold War constitutional reforms and processes of democratisation in Africa relates as much to the gap in the nature of the proposed reforms as to the diagnosis of the problems sought to be addressed. The constitutional changes and the nature of democratic change embraced by African states during this period are largely confined to addressing authoritarianism, unlimited government and the absence of political pluralism.

---

[140] An-Na'im (note 136 above) 14.

[141] EE Osaghae 'Making Democracy Work in Africa' (2004) 3(1) *J of African Elections* 1, 6.

The first change introduced by this wave of reforms has been the institutionalisation of limited government. The new constitutions express commitment to constitutionalism and the rule of law. Some, such as the Benin Constitution, go as far as expressly rejecting government 'founded on arbitrariness, dictatorship, injustice, corruption, misappropriation of public funds, regionalism, nepotism, confiscation of power, and personal power.'[142] As part of this commitment, many of these constitutions declared the supremacy of the constitution and instituted a constitutional court to oversee its implementation and enforcement. Most of the newly made or amended constitutions also adopted presidential term limits, although some of these were later tampered with.[143]

Similarly, to address the problem of concentration of power in the executive, the reformers sought to establish the constitutional separation of powers as well as checks and balances. Accordingly, not only were the executive, legislative and judicial organs assigned their respective powers, but an attempt was also made to define their relationship in such a way that the legislature and the judiciary exercise some effective control over government. In the new constitutions, therefore, parliament is vested with the power to oversee the activities of the government and have it account for its actions. Nevertheless, the dominance of the presidency and the struggle for its control continues to be a feature of the political order of many African countries.

Another important part of the new constitutional reform process has been the reintroduction of multiparty politics and the establishment and changing of governments by elections. Most African states have held multiparty elections for the first time in their post-colonial history. By the early 1990s, Africa had 20 elected governments. In 1996 alone, there were 18 multiparty elections, the most ever held in post-colonial Africa in a single year.[144] Not only has this enabled most African countries to institutionalise multiparty politics and elect their governments, but it has also led to the removal of long-serving dictators. Notably, in many of these countries, constitutional reform has also led to the emergence of vibrant independent media, the widening of the democratic space with mushrooming civil society organisations, increasing enjoyment of civil and political rights by citizens, and a relative expansion of political participation.[145]

---

142 See Preamble to the Constitution of the Republic of Benin of 2 December 1990.

143 According to Njunga M Mulikita, of the 37 African constitutions in force by 1994, all but four contained provisions for term limits. NM Mulikita 'A False Dawn? Africa's Post-1990 Democratization Waves' (2003) 12(4) *African Security Review* 105, 107.

144 See *New York Times* (11 January 1997) 3.

145 In terms of the regulation of political rights, particularly freedom of association, in many of the constitutions there are as many continuities as changes. Following the post-colonial trend, the constitutions of 21 African states proscribe the establishment of parties on the basis of group membership. See C Heyns and W Kaguongo 'Constitutional Human Rights Law in Africa' (2006) 22(4) *SAJHR* 673, 694.

Finally, all the constitutions incorporated a catalogue of human rights and freedoms.[146] The human rights defined by these constitutions are individual rights, largely those traditionally known as civil and political rights.[147] The lists of rights are generally accompanied by guarantees for their respect and protection. Accordingly, many of the constitutions, in addition to the ordinary mechanism of judicial enforcement, introduced national human-rights institutions charged with the responsibility of promoting the implementation and protection of the rights guaranteed.[148] Like the post-independence constitutions, most of the new constitutions do not recognise, or only marginally recognise, minority rights.[149]

These are undoubtedly all very crucial changes and constitute important manifestations of democratisation on the continent. They have not, however, addressed the structural dilemma of the post-colonial African state. Notwithstanding these changes, the problems of political rivalry along ethnic lines and the disconnection between the state and the majority of the population have continued to plague many of these states. Some countries, including Uganda, Angola, Burundi, Sierra Leone, Kenya, Côte d'Ivoire, Senegal, and Niger, have experienced varying levels of conflict.[150]

As this brief exploration of the nature of the reforms instituted shows, the model of democracy embraced in Africa is generally the conventional model of majoritarian liberal democracy. Indeed, the most widely held conception of democracy in theory and in the practice of many states on the continent is associated with one important aspect of this type of democracy: elections. In political theory, this conception of democracy is intimately associated with Schumpeter, for whom democracy merely meant 'that institutional arrangement for arriving at political decisions in which individuals acquire the power to decide by means of a competitive struggle for the people's vote.'[151] From this perspective, democracy is understood as a basis for control of political power by shifting political parties

[146] For a review of the nature and type of rights guaranteed by these Constitutions, see Heyns and Kaguongo, ibid.

[147] Ibid, 677.

[148] According to the above study, 12 African constitutions provide for national human-rights institutions, and 19 provide for an ombudsman or public protector. Ibid, 678.

[149] The above study, for example, shows that the constitutions of only three African states recognise some minority rights, making direct reference to minorities, although this number omits the Ethiopian Constitution of 1994 and even South Africa, which provide for community rights without making specific use of the phrase 'minority rights'. Ibid, 711. But in addition to South Africa and Ethiopia, which institutionalised different but sufficiently sophisticated minority rights guarantees, the constitutions of a few other African states give recognition to certain aspects of minority rights related to culture and language. These are Ghana, Uganda, Benin, The Gambia, Malawi, Namibia, Sudan and Zambia. Ibid.

[150] See Crawford Young 'Democratization in Africa: The Contradictions of a Political Imperative' in JA Widner (ed.) *Economic Change And Political Liberalization in Sub-Saharan Africa* (1994) 230–250.

[151] JA Schumpeter *Capitalism, Socialism and Democracy* (1943, reprinted 1996) 269.

formed by self-interested individuals or socio-economic classes. The focus of this model is accordingly on multiparty political and electoral processes. It is a thin conception that reduces democracy to competition between parties for control of power.

From the perspective of this study, the problem with this model is more fundamental than its thinness. The model is, in fact, fraught with multiple problems. Firstly, as Nergis Canefe has pointed out, 'as long as the central state is perceived and functionalised as the basis for shifting coalitions between self-interested individuals and/or socio-economic classes, there is no room left for the instrumental inclusion of minority communities as actors in state-building processes or state and civil society relations.'[152] Secondly, even if minority communities get some representation, they generally run the risk of being outvoted on important issues.[153]

In the context of Africa's ethno-cultural diversity and patterns of rivalry among ethnic or ethno-regional groups, such a thin conception of democracy tends to produce governments that draw electoral support from particular ethnic groups or, in ideal situations, coalitions of such groups. In this winner-takes-all style of politics, while members of some groups win, others 'face a grim prospect of permanent exclusion from political power and the resources that emanate from therein.'[154] In conditions of inequality of access to political power and resources, and historical rivalry for power, this inevitably leads, as the experience of many African countries has shown, to ethnic or ethno-regional conflicts as those in power seek to retain power and others try to displace them.[155] This is exactly the underlying factor which accounts for the post-election violence in Kenya in 2008 and in Cote d'Ivoire during late 2010 and early 2011. For the highly disadvantaged minorities, referred to in this study as peripheral minorities such as indigenous peoples, Schumpeterian democracy tends to entrench their marginalisation.[156] This leads to what Horowitz calls 'the injustice of procedural democracy.'[157] Generally, Schumpeterian liberal democracy not only lacks the required framework to address political inequalities among members of various groups and minorities' fears of exclusion, but may also be 'destructive of any

[152] Canefe (note 72 above) 106.

[153] G Selassie (note 2 above) 27–28; A Eide 'Minority Protection and World Order: Towards a Framework for Law and Policy' in A Philips & A Rosas (eds.) *Universal Minority Rights* (1995) 87, 105; Kymlicka (note 10 above) 109.

[154] Hameso (note 52 above) 13.

[155] A recent illustration of this is the political crisis that engulfed Kenya following the controversial December 2007 elections. See G Prunier 'Kenya: Roots of Crisis'; R Southall 'South African Lessons for Kenya' both available at <http://www.opendemocracy.com> accessed on January 28, 2008.

[156] As Eide rightly observed, '[b]eing in the position of a disadvantaged minority means, in fact, that one's interests can be neglected even within a democratic order.' Eide (note 153 above) 105.

[157] See DC Horowitz 'The Challenge of Ethnic Conflict: Democracy in Divided Societies' *J of Democracy* (1993) 18–37.

prospect of building a nation in which different peoples might live together in harmony.'[158] This model of democracy also entails the continuation of the winner-takes-all pattern of politics that ultimately leads to rivalry and conflicts.

Democracy can be just and legitimate in the particular context of Africa only if it provides mechanisms to manage the issue of minorities, what Arthur Lewis called the democratic problem in a plural society – that is, if it establishes 'political institutions which give all the various groups the opportunity to participate in decision-making, since only thus can they feel that they are full members of a nation, respected by their numerous brethren, and owing equal respect to the national bond which holds them together.'[159] There is, in other words, a need for ethno-culturally inclusive and deliberative democracy.[160] Seen in this light, of the countries that have adopted new constitutions or constitutional reforms, the most exemplary and probably the only states whose constitutions are deliberately designed to provide for comprehensive institutional mechanisms for accommodating ethno-cultural diversity are South Africa and Ethiopia. They are accordingly given particular attention in Chapters VI and VII.

3.5. Conclusion

This chapter has examined the nature and limits of the approach of the post-colonial African state to the issue of minorities. Within the framework of the homogenising nation-building process in post-colonial Africa, ethno-cultural diversity has been treated as obstacle to the quest for national integration. As a result, far from developing mechanisms for its accommodation, African states did not even think it appropriate to tolerate this diversity. Instead they actively sought to forge a single national identity that would ultimately eliminate peoples' ethnic attachments. Following the framework of the dominant liberal nation-state constitutional model, the tendency has also been to maintain difference-blind legal and institutional structures, common universal citizenship and individual rights. Both politically and constitutionally, the post-colonial African state has therefore been inhospitable to ethno-cultural diversity and the claims to which it gives rise. The chapter has demonstrated the limits of these approaches and their eventual failure to achieve stability, justice and national integration. The chapter clearly illustrated Ake's view that 'the democratisation of Africa, and indeed every aspect of social transformation has to come to terms with ethnicity. No project of social transformation can succeed by ignoring it'.[161] It is therefore

[158] Lewis (note 5 above) 66; G Selassie (note 2 above) 28–29.

[159] Lewis (note 5 above) 66–67.

[160] The foundations of this are discussed in Chapter IV and its structures and principles are outlined in Chapter V below.

[161] Claud Ake 'What is the Problem of Ethicity in Africa' 22 *Transformation* (1993) 8–9.

suggested that addressing the issue of minorities requires changes to the existing structure and composition of representative political institutions, so as to allow all ethno-national groups, particularly the historically disadvantaged, a greater voice in the political and economic processes of the country. This analysis also suggests the need for constitutional reform in the form of a state structure that allows, where necessary, devolution of power through federalism, regionalism or autonomy.

CHAPTER IV

THE NORMATIVE BASES FOR CONSTITUTIONAL ACCOMMODATION OF ETHNO-CULTURAL DIVERSITY IN AFRICA: THE THREE COMPONENTS OF THE MINORITY RIGHTS FRAMEWORK

4.1. Introduction

This chapter opens the discussion on the examination and elaboration of a robust minority rights framework on the basis of which the relevant constitutional guarantees and institutional arrangements for the accommodation of ethno-cultural diversity within the post-colonial African states are to be identified and elaborated. Taking into account the historical and socio-political contexts that define the particular characters of ethno-cultural diversity in Africa, and drawing from relevant norms of international law and constitutional theory on multiculturalism, the chapter contends that there are three elements that constitute such a robust minority rights framework. These are cultural identity, equality and self-determination.

4.2. Cultural Identity

4.2.1. *The Theoretical Framework*

In Africa, as in other parts of the world, the issue of minorities relates in significant ways to cultural identity and its recognition.[1] To the extent that the claims of minorities in Africa are about the recognition and protection of their identity and interest as belonging to cultural groups, they are intertwined with the importance of membership in one's ethnic group. The importance of cultural membership in Africa is expressed, for example, by its relation to the understanding of the essence of a person and human dignity in African thought.[2] Individuals are conceived as being part, rather than independent of or prior to,

[1] See AG Selassie 'Ethnic Identity and Constitutional Design for Africa' (Fall 1992–1993) 29 *Stanford J of Int L* 1; IJ Wani 'Cultural Preservation and the Challenges of Diversity and Nationhood: The Dilemmas of Indigenous Cultures in Africa' (1990–1991) 59 *UMKC LR* 612.

[2] See JAM Cobbah 'African Values and the Human Rights Debate: An African Perspective' (1987) 9 *Human Rights Quarterly* 309–331, 320–325; MW Mutua 'The Banjul Charter and the African Cultural Fingerprint: An Evaluation of the Language of Duties' (1995) 35 *Virginia J Int L* 339, 346–359.

and in harmony rather than in conflict with, their community.[3] It is within a communal context and through culture that individuals become persons. The philosophical expression 'I am because we are, and because we are therefore I am' aptly captures this.[4] As Chief Justice Pius Langa of the South African Constitutional Court has put it, in the tradition of many African cultures this 'is often expressed in the phrase *umuntu ngumuntu ngabantu*[5] which emphasises "communality and the inter-dependence of the members of a community"[6] and that every individual is an extension of others'.[7] The community is the locus by reference to which the identity and place of a person in the world is defined and given meaning. Membership in a community (culture) for peoples in Africa is a fundamental framework that defines 'the most important parts of a person's identity'.[8] Claude Ake puts this when he noted that in the traditional African context 'persons have identity only because they are part of a community, their freedom lies in the concrete capabilities, privileges and immunities which arise from communal life. Integrity is embedded in one's location in a community and the ways in which one manages the entitlements and obligations of community membership.'[9]

The importance that is given to cultural membership in Africa is not substantively unique to groups in Africa. In multicultural liberal theory, there is increasing support for and acknowledgement of the importance of culture as a basis for the personal identity of individuals. Kymlicka, who has offered one of the most influential theories of minority rights,[10] maintains that 'cultural membership affects our sense of personal identity and capacity'.[11] This view is shared by many others.[12]

---

[3] BO Okere 'The Protection of Human Rights in Africa and the African Charter on Human Rights and Peoples' Rights: A Comparative Analysis with the European and American Systems' (1984) 6 *Human Rights Quarterly* 141, 148 (indicating that the 'African conception of man is not that of an isolated and abstract individual, but an integral member of a group animated by a spirit of solidarity'). Also see Mutua (note 2 above) 376; R Kiwanuka 'The Meaning of "People" in the African Charter on Human and Peoples' Rights' (1988) 82 *American J Int L* 80, 82.

[4] JS Mbiti *African Religions and Philosophy* (1970) 141.

[5] This translates literally as 'a person is a person through other people'.

[6] *Bhe and Others v Magistrate, Khayelitsha, and Others (Commission for Gender Equality as* Amicus Curiae*); Shibi v Sithole and Others; South African Human Rights Commission and Another v President of the Republic of South Africa and Another* 2005 (1) SA 580 (CC); 2005 (1) BCLR 1 (CC) at para 163.

[7] *MEC for Education, KwaZuu-Natal & Others v Pillay* 2008 (1) SA 474 (CC) para. 53. [Pillay Case]

[8] Pillay case (ibid).

[9] Claude Ake 'What is the Problem of Ethnicity in Africa?' 22 *Transformation* (1993) 10.

[10] See W Kymlicka *Liberalism, Community and Culture* (1989); *Multicultural Citizenship: A Liberal Theory of Minority Rights* (1995).

[11] Ibid, 175.

[12] See A Margalit & J Raz 'National Self-Determination' in W Kymlicka (ed.) *The Rights of Minority Cultures* (1995) 79, 85–88; C Taylor 'The Politics of Recognition' in A Guitmann (ed.) *Multiculturalism: Examining the Politics of Recognition* (1994); A Addis 'Individualism,

As the quote above from Claude Ake suggests, cultural membership is also more than an identity marker. G Sellasie observes that '[i]n much of Africa, ethnicity is the hub around which life revolves'.[13] It is a source of peoples' sense of belongingness, self-worth and security, and of feeling at home in the world. Francis Deng writes: 'Ethnicity is more than skin colour or physical characteristics, more than language, song, and dance. It is the embodiment of values, institutions, and patterns of behaviour, a composite whole representing a people's historical experience, aspirations, and world view.'[14] Accordingly, not only people's sense of identity but also their self-respect and dignity are in deep ways tied with and structured by cultural membership. Treating people seriously, wholistically and with mutual concern thus requires due recognition of their cultural membership. In Africa, culture additionally has significant spiritual value, akin to religion. It offers a framework through which persons not only identify themselves and associate with others and the world, but also communicate with the dead, the living, those yet to be born and, ultimately, God.[15] In short, *for many* in Africa, culture expresses a way of life as well as a world-view.[16] Clearly, depriving a people of their ethnicity, their culture, is to deprive them of their sense of identity and direction or purpose.[17] It is not uncommon to come across an argument that accords priority to cultural membership in the Rawlsian sense as is the case when Hannah Arendt posited, '[s]omething much more than freedom and justice ... is at stake when belonging to the community into which one is born is no longer a matter of course and not belonging a matter of choice'.[18]

In addition to satisfying the human desire of belonging and due recognition, the value of cultural membership also relates to the role of culture as a context of choice, the framework that renders the choices we make meaningful. This is one of the foundations of Kymlicka's influential liberal theory of minority rights. According to him, individual freedom in the sense of the ability of individuals to define and choose among different conceptions of the good is tied to cultural membership. He emphasises that, '[p]ut simply, freedom involves making choices amongst various options, and our societal culture not only provides these options, but also makes them meaningful to us'.[19] Although he does not articulate the consequence that must follow from people's deep attachment to their culture, Dworkin maintains in no less emphatic terms:

Communitarianism, and the Rights of Ethnic Minorities' (1992) 67 *Notre Dame LR* 615; Y Tamir *Liberal Nationalism* (1993).

[13] G Selassie (note 1 above) 12.

[14] FM Deng 'Ethnicity: An African Predicament' (Summer 1997) 15 (3) *The Brookings Review* 28.

[15] See GBN Ayittey *Indigenous African Institutions* (1991) 14–20; Mbiti (note 4 above).

[16] Cobbah (note 2 above) 320–323.

[17] Deng (note 14 above) 28.

[18] H Arendt *The Origins of Totalitarianism* (1972) 296.

[19] Kymlicka (1995) (note 10 above) 83.

> They [people] need a common culture and particularly a common language even to have personalities, and culture and language are social phenomena. We can have only the thought, and ambitions, and convictions that are possible within the vocabulary that language and culture provide, so we are all, in a patent and deep way, the creatures of the community as a whole.[20]

In the African context, as in other parts of the world that suffered the brutalities of colonial rule, the claim for the recognition of minority cultures additionally manifests a resistance to the colonial and post-colonial denigration, devaluation, marginalisation and suppression of indigenous African cultures and the resultant sense of alienation and dispossession.[21] Seen in this light, the claim for recognition of cultural identity partly represents an attempt on the part of members of the various cultures to have the dignity of their culture and identity restored as a means to regain their self-respect and dignity as members of those particular cultures. As many people in Africa continue to draw meaning from and define their life goals by reference to their cultural dispositions, the quest for recognition of cultural pluralism in Africa is also meant to prevent the further erosion of indigenous cultures and languages, and the resultant loss of identity that members of these cultures would face. The recognition of cultural diversity in the public sphere also reduces the experience by many of the state as alien and imposed entity and facilitate the connection of the state with the indigenous plural public. This is fundamentally important in Africanising the state and establishing its legitimacy. Moreover, for many people in Africa one of the barriers to active participation in the processes of the state is that the state and its institutions operate on the basis of languages and other cultural forms which are alien to them. Cultural rights, particularly the recognition of indigenous languages, thus additionally serve to end this alienation of people from the state and facilitate their integration into its processes by enhancing linguistically unrestricted participation in the management of public affairs. So, the argument for cultural recognition goes further than the idea that cultural membership is the main marker of the identity of most Africans, as for others, and provides the context for defining their life goals and relations to the world. It also draws from the need to redress the pain suffered by members of indigenous cultures due to the denigration, non-recognition and marginalisation of their cultures and languages under the colonial state and its successor. The question that arises is how to protect minority cultures and eliminate the disadvantages that often result from membership in a minority culture.

Although individual rights such as freedom of expression, religion and association offer a valuable framework for the protection of minority cultures, many

---

[20] R Dworkin 'Liberal Community' (1989) 77 *California LR* 479–504.

[21] See Wani (note 1 above); Mutua (note 2 above) 343; Ayittey (note 14 above); B Nwabueze *Constitutional Democracy in Africa* Vol 5 (2004) 271–277.

have rightly argued and demonstrated that they are nevertheless inadequate.[22] The main reason for this is that these rights do not regulate important aspects of public life that directly impact upon the cultural identity of minorities. As Kymlicka indicates, these traditional human rights standards

> are simply unable to resolve some of the most important and controversial questions relating to cultural minorities: which languages should be recognised in the parliaments, bureaucracy, and courts? Should each ethnic or national group have publicly funded education in its mother tongue? Should internal boundaries (legislative districts, provinces, states) be drawn so that cultural minorities form a majority within a local region? ... Should political offices be distributed in accordance with a principle of national or ethnic proportionality?[23]

And, needless to say, supplementing them with affirmative action measures would not be enough to ensure the equality of members of minorities in having secure access to their culture.[24] As we have seen in Chapter II, in the multi-ethnic African state, arguably more than in other multi-ethnic societies, different groups are situated in unequal political, socio-economic and cultural circumstances and therefore are placed unequally within the processes of the state, in a way disadvantageous to the equal enjoyment of political rights and socio-economic opportunities and the cultural identity of many groups. There is therefore a need for affirmative support to members of disadvantaged cultures. However, '[s]ince this inequality would remain even if individual members of (minority or disadvantaged) communities no longer suffered from any deprivation of material resources, temporary affirmative action programmes are not sufficient to ensure genuine equality'.[25] Accordingly, in multicultural societies, real equality and the need to treat members of different groups with equal respect

---

[22] After examining the jurisprudence on the European Convention on Human Rights regarding the potential and actual capacity of non-discrimination and individual rights to address minority issues, Kristin Henrard concluded that 'approaching the minority issue merely through the prohibition of non-discrimination and individual human rights is rather unsatisfactory'. K Henrard *Devising an Adequate System of Minority Protection: Individual Human Rights, Minority Rights and the Right to Self-Determination* (2000) 141–142. See also G Gilbert 'The Legal Protection Accorded to Minority Groups in Europe' *Netherlands Yearbook of Int L* (1992) 67–104, 90.

[23] Kymlicka (1995) (note 9 above) 4–5.

[24] Addis (note 12 above) 659.

[25] Kymlicka (1989) (note 10 above) 191. In Africa a very good example of the inadequacy of the equalisation of the material conditions of members of minorities for securing the equal enjoyment of their culture is Botswana. As Jacquelin S Solway's study of the struggle of minorities in Botswana shows, the fact that non-Tswana-speaking groups other than the San are in a position of relative material equality with members of the dominant Tswana people did not help them to achieve cultural equality in public life. Accordingly, their main claim is the political and institutional recognition of their cultures and languages, which is necessary for achieving cultural equality in the public sphere. See JS Solway 'Reaching the Limits of Universal Citizenship: "Minority" Struggles in Botswana' in B Berman, D Eyoh & W Kymlicka (eds.) *Ethnicity and Democracy in Africa* (2004) 129.

and concern[26] may entail that individual human rights are supplemented with not only affirmative action measures, but also rights relevant to the situation of minorities.[27] These rights relate to language, including in communication with public authorities; religion; education in minority languages; recognition of customary or religious law; communal land; access to media and other means of reproducing and transmitting culture; and exemptions from general rules.[28] The foregoing strongly establishes that the African state – as part of the process of building national integration and reinstating the dignity of African cultures and traditions, and treating them with equal seriousness – must recognise and give public expression to the culture and identity of members of the various groups that constitute it through culturally inclusive and just language, cultural and educational policies. These should include, among others, guarantees for the use of indigenous African languages in the public sphere, including in communication with public authorities where practicable and necessary; education in these languages as necessary; and recognition of customary laws.

4.2.2. *The International Law Framework*

In international human rights, cultural rights are addressed in a wide range of ways.[29] Of particular interest for purposes of this study are the cultural rights of groups. With respect to minorities, international human rights law provides certain guarantees of culture, language and religion, albeit in modest terms that do not define in sufficient detail the content of those rights and the obligations of states. During the time of the League of Nations, the European minority protection system was essentially designed to afford protection to the cultural identity of minority groups. In its advisory opinion on *Minority Schools in Albania*, the Permanent Court of International Justice (PCIJ) elaborated the rationale for minority protection in a frequently quoted passage:

---

[26] Adeno Addis rightly points out that '[t]o treat individuals with "equal respect" entails, at least partly, respecting their traditions and cultures, the forms of life which give depth and coherence to their identities'. A Addis 'On Human Diversity and the Limits of Toleration' in I Shapiro & W Kymlicka (eds.) *Ethnicity and Group Rights* (1997) 112, 121. See also D Miller 'Liberalism, Equal Opportunities and Cultural Commitments' in P Kelly (ed.) *Multiculturalism Reconsidered: Culture and Equality and its Critiques* (2002) 45, 48.

[27] Kymlicka (1989) (note 10 above) 162. See J Anaya 'On Justifying Special Ethnic Group Rights: Comments on Pogge' in Shapiro & Kymlicka (note 25 above) 222, 223; Addis (note 12 above) 659–660.

[28] For a useful identification and analysis of these various forms of rights see JT Levy 'Classifying Cultural Rights' in Shapiro and Kymlicka (note 25 above) 22–67.

[29] See A Eide 'Cultural Rights and Minorities: Essay in Honour of Erica-Irene Daes' in G Alfredson & M Stavropoulou (eds.) *Justice Pending: Indigenous Peoples and Other Good Causes: Essays in Honour of Erica-Irene A. Daes* (2002) 83, 84–88; E Stamatopoulou *Cultural Rights in International Law: Article 27 of the Universal Declaration of Human Rights and Beyond* (2007); YM Donders *Towards a Right to Cultural Identity?* (2002).

> The idea underlying the treaties for the protection of minorities is to secure for certain elements incorporated in a state, the population of which differs from them in race, language or religion, the possibility of living peacefully alongside that population and co-operating amicably with it, *while at the same time preserving the characteristics which distinguish them from the majority, and satisfying the ensuing special needs.*

According to the Court, this objective requires states to ensure that minorities (a) are placed on a footing of perfect equality with others in the society, and (b) have '*suitable means for the preservation of racial peculiarities, their traditions and their national characteristics*'.[30] It is on this foundation that the edifice of contemporary international norms on minority rights is constructed. The second of the two aspects that underlie this legal regime establishes the cultural rights of minorities and forms part of what is known in international legal parlance as the 'special rights of minorities'.[31]

These rights are generally defended and articulated using more or less the same line of reasoning that is used in normative political theory, discussed above. Eide, for example, maintains: 'The basic source of identity for human beings is often found in the cultural traditions into which he or she is born and brought up. The preservation of that identity can be of crucial importance to well-being and self-respect.'[32] He accordingly concludes that '"*cultural rights*" *should give priority to access to, and education of, one's own culture as well as the right to participate in the reproduction and further development of that culture*'.[33] This essentially entails that minorities are provided with special rights or protection mechanisms, since without such mechanisms 'cultural rights will not be fully enjoyed and guaranteed for everybody, notwithstanding the principles of equality and non-discrimination'.[34] The reason why such rights or guarantees are called special is what the PCIJ calls the 'special needs' of these groups, arising from their minority status.[35] They are special in the sense 'that certain kinds of rights are of direct interest to or addressed to, ethnic, religious or linguistic groups in order to defend their cultures, the practice of their religion and the use of minority languages'.[36]

Although international law has not fully elaborated the content and reach of such cultural rights of minorities qua minorities, as noted in Chapter I it

30 *Minority Schools in Albania* PCIJ (Ser. A/B) No 64 (1935) 17 (my emphasis).
31 See UN *Minority Rights* Human Rights Fact Sheet No 18 Rev 1 (1998) 4–7.
32 Eide (note 29 above) 85.
33 Ibid, 85–86 (my emphasis).
34 R Stavenhagen 'Cultural Rights: A Social Science Perspective' in A Eide, C Krause, & A Rosas (eds.) *Economic, Social and Cultural Rights: A Textbook* (2001) 92.
35 Minority Schools in Albania (note 30 above).
36 P Thornberry 'Is There a Phoenix in the Ashes? International Law and Minority Rights' (1980) 15 *Texas Int L J* 421, 440.

nevertheless provides certain guarantees to members of minorities for the protection of their culture. Built on the minority rights regime of the League of Nations, these rights, apart from equality and non-discrimination, include the right to existence and identity, language rights and some rights relating to education.

4.2.2.1. *Identity and Existence*

Article 27 of the ICCPR is by far the most important provision on minority rights, as the only legally binding provision at the international level. Notwithstanding its negative formulation, it is regarded as positively guaranteeing the right of minorities to identity.[37] The HRC, the body responsible for supervising and enforcing the ICCPR, has accordingly asserted that Article 27 'is directed towards ensuring the survival and continued development of the cultural, religious, and social identity of the minorities concerned'.[38] According to the HRC, the effective protection of this right may require the provision of positive measures 'necessary *to protect the identity of a minority and the rights of its members to enjoy and develop their culture and language and to practice their religion*, in community with other members of the group'.[39] It is, however, clear that this extended elaboration of Article 27 does not give sufficient guidance for resolving some of the most important issues, such as how to determine the use of languages for government purposes, in education and in the media, as well as the form of the electoral system.

The 1948 Convention on the Prevention and Punishment of the Crime of Genocide prohibits the physical or biological destruction of national, ethnic, religious or racial *groups*.[40] According to Buergenthal, by outlawing the destruction of national, ethnic, racial or religious groups, the Genocide Convention formally recognises the right of these groups to exist as groups, which surely must be considered as the most fundamental of all cultural rights.[41]

These rights are guaranteed more extensively in Article 1 of the 1992 UN Declaration on the Rights of Persons Belonging to National or Ethnic, Religious

---

[37] See F Capotorti *Study on the Rights of Persons Belonging to Ethnic, Religious and Linguistic Minorities* (1979) Sales No. E.78XIV. 1 37.

[38] Human Rights Committee, General Comment 23, Article 27 (fifth Session, 1994) UN Doc. HRI/GEN/1/Rev.1 at 38 (1994) para. 9.

[39] Ibid, para 6(2) (my emphasis).

[40] Genocide Convention Article 2 provides: 'In the present Convention, genocide means any of the following *acts committed with intent to destroy, in whole or in part, a national, ethnical, racial or religious group...*' (my emphasis).

[41] T Buergenthal *International Human Rights in a Nutshell* (1988) 49. Also see Y Dinstein 'Collective Human Rights of Peoples and Minorities' (1976) 25 *Int and Comparative L Quarterly* 102, 105–106, 118.

and Linguistic Minorities.[42] Thornberry asserts that this transcends the tentative phrasing of Article 27 (of the ICCPR) and proposes identity and existence as fundamental attributes of groups. He goes on to say that '[t]he "group protection" nature of the Declaration is very evident from this provision and the obligation to protect existence and identity is mandatory as evidenced by the use of "shall"'.[43]

As Thornberry points out, under the 1992 Declaration on Minorities the existence and identity of minorities is to be protected not only by outlawing the physical destruction of the group, as done by the 1958 Convention against Genocide, but also through other positive provisions, including basic subsistence rights and cultural and spiritual protection, including protection against forced assimilation, ethnocide, and forced population transfer.[44] Here the state is also under obligation to provide security to minorities to ensure that they are not subjected to attacks and abuses by members of dominant groups or others. Under Article 4(2) of the UN Declaration on Minorities, this is given further elaboration by the requirement that states 'take measures to create favourable conditions to enable persons belonging to minorities to express their characteristics and to develop their culture, language, religion, traditions and customs'. Most importantly, this declaration calls upon states to promote cultural diversity through, among other measures, encouraging knowledge of the history, traditions, language and culture of the minorities within their territory.[45] Other international instruments that recognise the right to cultural identity include the Convention on the Rights of the Child,[46] the 2007 UN Declaration on the Rights of Indigenous Peoples,[47] the UN Convention on the Elimination of All Forms of Racial Discrimination[48] and the UN Educational, Scientific, and Cultural Organisation (UNESCO) Declaration on Race and Racial Prejudice.[49] Taken together, these instruments require states not only to tolerate minority cultures and their observance or expression by their members, even in the public sphere, but also to 'encourage conditions for their promotion'. Clearly, this is best achieved if states accord legal recognition to the existence of minority cultures and institutionalise mechanisms for their accommodation in the processes of the state.

---

42 GA Res. 47/135 adopted 18 December 1992, UN Doc. A/RES/47/137. (Declaration on Minorities).

43 P Thornberry 'The UN Declaration on the Rights of Persons Belonging to National or Ethnic, Religious and Linguistic Minorities: Background, Analysis, Observation, and an Update' in A Philips & Allan Rosas (eds.) *Universal Minority Rights* (1995) 13, 39.

44 Ibid, 40.

45 Article 4 (4) Declaration on Minorities (note 42 above).

46 Art. 30 GA Res. 44/25 adopted 20 Nov. 1989, entered into force 2 Sept. 1990.

47 See GA Res. 61/295 adopted on 13 September 2007.

48 See GA Res. 2106 A (XX) adopted 21 December 1965.

49 See Article 9 (2).

4.2.2.2. *Rights Relating to Language and Education*

With respect to language rights, Article 1(1) of the 1992 Declaration on Minorities affirms the right of minorities to their linguistic identity, which was not explicitly recognised under Article 27 of the ICCPR.[50] Most importantly, notwithstanding its vague formulation, Article 4(2) provides that states shall take measures to create favourable conditions to enable members of minorities to develop their language. Depending on the particular context of each society and the needs of minorities, this may include the provision of various forms of assistance that facilitate the use of their languages. Apparently, this is merely related to the right of members of minorities to speak their languages, and does not involve a right to use such languages in communication with public authorities. The two most important European instruments provide better guarantees in this area.[51] Article 10 of the Framework Convention on the Protection of National Minorities recognises the right to use a minority language. This includes a qualified right to use the language in communications with public authorities where the group speaking the language is of a sufficiently large size and territorially concentrated.[52] More specifically, the European Charter for Regional or Minority Languages enjoins states to protect and promote the use of regional or minority languages in the field of education,[53] among judicial[54] and administrative authorities and public services,[55] in access to media[56] and in the spheres of cultural, economic and social activities.[57] These are the kind of guarantees whose national implementation can give optimal satisfaction to the interests of minorities in this area.

With respect to education, Article 4(3) of the 1992 Declaration on Minorities enjoins states to provide minorities 'adequate opportunities to learn their mother tongue or have instruction in their mother tongue'. This provision, although formulated in such open terms, clearly recognises that it is just for minorities to receive education in their own language at least at the level of primary school and, where circumstances do not warrant that, to learn their language as a subject. Moreover, it calls upon states to promote multicultural education through taking measures that encourage knowledge of the history, traditions,

---

[50] This article stipulates: 'In those states in which ethnic, religious or linguistic minorities exist, persons belonging to such minorities shall not be denied the right, in community with the other members of their group, to enjoy their own culture, to profess and practice their own religion, or to use their own language.'

[51] See K Henrard *Devising an Adequate System of Minority Protection: Individual Human Rights, Minority Rights and the Right to Self-determination* (2000) 210–217.

[52] Article 10.

[53] Article 8.

[54] Article 9.

[55] Article 10.

[56] Article 11.

[57] Article 12 & 13.

language and culture of minorities.[58] Minorities also have the right, subject to national regulations on quality standards, to establish and maintain their own educational institutions. Other instruments guaranteeing such rights at the international level include the UNESCO Convention against Discrimination in Education.[59]

4.2.3. *The African Human Rights System*

In Africa there are several regional instruments that articulate the right to culture in various ways. The first and most important of such instruments is the African Charter itself.[60] Article 17 of the African Charter provides for the right to cultural identity. This right is given further protection under Article 22(1), which specifically guarantees the right to cultural development and identity. The right of peoples to existence is also one of the cultural rights guaranteed by the Charter, under Article 20.[61] With respect to language, the African Commission held that the right to culture under Article 17 extends to language as necessary for the identity and personality of individuals. The Commission states:

> Language is an integral part of the structure of culture; it in fact constitutes its pillar and means of expression par excellence. Its usage enriches the individual and enables him to take active part in the community and its activities. To deprive a man of such participation amounts to depriving him of his identity.[62]

Broader language guarantees are envisaged elsewhere. Under the African Cultural Charter,[63] the importance of the various cultures of African peoples and the need for their protection are also extensively articulated, although the process for the application of measures to this end and mechanisms for their enforcement are not clearly spelt out.[64] The Declaration of Principles of Freedom of Expression in Africa, a non-binding instrument developed by the African Commission, calls upon states to take positive measures to promote diversity, including through 'the promotion of the use of local languages in public affairs, including in the courts'.[65] Notwithstanding its non-binding status, this clearly

---

58 Article 4 (4).

59 See Articles 2 & 5.

60 The African Charter on Human and Peoples' Rights adopted 27 June 1981, entered into force 21 October 1986 OAU Doc. CAB/LEG/67/3/Rev. 5. [the African Charter]

61 See F Ouguergouz *The African Charter on Human and Peoples' Rights: A Comprehensive Agenda for Human Dignity and Sustainable Democracy in Africa* (2003) 217–227.

62 See *Malawi African Association, Amnesty International, Ms. Sarr Diop, Union Interafricaine des droit de l'Homme and RADDHO, Collectif des Veuves et Ayants-droit & Association Mauritanienne des Droits de l'Homme v Mauritania* (2000) AHRLR 149 (ACHPR 2000) Communications 54/91, 61/91, 98/93, 164/97, 196/97 & 210/98 (13th Annual Activity Report ACHPR,1999–2000) para. 137.

63 Adopted 5 July 1976 and entered into force on 19 September 1990.

64 See Part V.

65 See Principle III Resolution on the Adoption of the Declaration on Principles of Freedom of Expression in Africa, adopted by the ACHPR at its 32nd ordinary session held in Banjul,

goes beyond what is provided in most international instruments in addressing the most controversial component of minority language claims. It expresses an acknowledgement that without the promotion of the use of these languages in public affairs, most people cannot adequately participate in public life as they are not generally well versed in the official European languages.

Generally, although the formulation of some of the guarantees recognising the cultural rights of minorities are terse, weak and qualified, and enunciated in legally non-binding instruments, they nevertheless establish a growing normative recognition that the adoption of linguistic, cultural and educational policies that give public space to, and embrace the full diversity of, the cultural and linguistic components of societies, with particular attention to the cultures of non-dominant and marginalised sections of society, is a necessary aspect of effective minority protection.[66] In this age of multiculturalism, this is becoming part of the standard of measurement of the commitment of states to ensure that members of all groups are taken equally seriously and treated fairly and with equal concern.

In this context, the importance of the theory of multiculturalism (or minority rights) lies both in providing the theoretical underpinnings of these international legal norms, and in giving meaningful interpretation and content to them in a way that spells out the form that their institutionalisation within states has to take to address the issue of minorities adequately, and ultimately contributes to a just democratic order in multi-ethnic societies. This, according to the 1992 UN Declaration on Minorities, is the ultimate aim of minority rights.[67]

4.3. Equality

4.3.1. *Theoretical Framework*

Although the international legal framework on the rights of minorities to cultural membership addresses important aspects of concern to minorities, particularly vis-à-vis the good of cultural membership, it does not tell us why minorities should also have further guarantees pertaining to the political and socio-economic spheres of public life. Even when it addresses this question, it defends such other guarantees only instrumentally. For example, it is argued, of course rightly, that the cultural rights of minorities cannot be fully secure

the Gambia on 17–23 October 2002 available at <http://www.achpr.org/english/declarations/declaration_freedom_exp_en.html>.

[66] See M Koenig & P de Guchteneir 'Political Governance of Cultural Diversity' in M Koenig & P de Guchteneir (eds.) *Democracy and Human Rights in Multicultural Societies* (2007) 3, 7 (indicating the effect of these developments in delegitimising the nation-state model and requiring new public policies of governing diversity).

[67] See Preamble 1992 Declaration on Minorities (note 42 above).

unless they are accorded effective participation in the formulation of the rules, or the making of public decisions, that affect their enjoyment of cultural rights, and have access to the resources necessary for participation in their culture. Although this is a powerful and very important argument, as far as minority guarantees in the political and socio-economic spheres of public life is concerned, it is nevertheless only a secondary argument.

It is true that these guarantees enable members of minorities to defend their cultural rights by making them direct participants in the political and socio-economic processes of the state, not just as citizens, but most importantly as members of their respective cultures. But primarily they are expressions of recognition that the limitations or disadvantages that minorities suffer due to their minority status are not limited to the security of cultural membership. As the discussions in previous chapters show, minorities also suffer disadvantages in terms of the exercise and enjoyment of other goods, including political and socio-economic equality.[68] Indeed, in the context of Africa, minority claims are more strongly expressed with respect to these disadvantages than those in the cultural sphere. The main issue here is thus the achievement of equality in the political and socio-economic spheres rather than secure access to one's cultural membership alone.

Indeed, in addition to, or even more than, cultural identity, what gives the claims of ethnic groups in Africa, as in almost all post-colonial societies in other parts of the world, a powerful moral, legal and political force is their grounding in problems of socio-economic and political inequality. In order to understand and identify these issues of equality that underlie most ethnic claims in Africa, it is necessary in the first place to identify their context.[69]

As can be gathered from the previous two chapters, the historical, political and socio-economic processes of the African state have fundamentally shaped the relative position of groups and patterns of power relations. Historically, this relates in the first instance to the incorporation of unequal and culturally distinct groups within the unitary political structures of the colonial state, the

---

[68] Political equality refers to that which affects the access to or control of and exercising of public powers in society. By economic equality, we mean that which makes reference to the equitable distribution of burdens and benefit that members of a community support or obtain from public powers. These equalities are not separate, but mostly converge and influence each other. See A Phillips *Which Equalities Matter?* (1999) 74–79.

[69] C Albertyn & B Goldblatt 'Equality' in S Woolman et al. (eds.) *Constitutional Law of South Africa* 2nd edition OS (2007) Chapter 35, 35-3 (stating that the meaning of equality is context specific in that it is influenced by the historical, socio-political and legal conditions of the society concerned). This is particularly true if one is looking at substantive equality. Patrick Macklem thus holds that '[a] commitment to substantive equality mandates an examination of the concrete material conditions of individuals and groups in society and the ways in which state structuring can ameliorate adverse social and economic circumstances'. P Macklem *Indigenous Difference and the Constitution in Canada* (2001) 126.

precursor to the modern African state. The uneven distribution of political and economic goods (such as education, jobs, administrative posts, access to land etc.) as well as infrastructures of political and economic opportunities (roads, schools, hospitals, industrial and commercial centres etc.) among groups and/or ethno-regions have created further disparities and inequalities in terms of participation in the political and economic processes of the state during and after colonialism. Discriminatory political and socio-economic structures, as well as colonially and historically induced relationships of animosity and conflict, have further reinforced deeply unequal patterns of political and socio-economic development and relationships among constituent groups. The post-colonial state inherited distinct ethno-cultural groups with disproportionately unequal political, economic and numerical circumstances as well as distinct cultural and socio-political traditions.[70]

Post-colonial political and economic developments (the enhancement of centralised organisation of political power; the process of concentration of political power and socio-economic resources away from the local to the centre; the rise of ethnic clientelism, leading to disproportionate control of political and economic resources by one or more dominant groups; inefficient and corrupt systems of governance; and other similar patterns of discriminatory and authoritarian tendencies targetting groups other than the ethnic group(s) that constitute the power base of the regime), rather than rectifying these disparities, have in many ways further entrenched them, and in some cases created additional dimensions of imbalance.[71] The post-colonial period has also witnessed in many African countries not only unequal patterns of representation in and control of the political process, but also unbalanced development among different ethno-regions. Moreover, as noted in the previous chapter, the nation-building process of the post-colonial state, based on the nation-state paradigm, denied the various constituent groups due recognition in the political processes of the state (while favouring the group(s) that form the power base of the regime) and failed terribly in almost all African states, unleashing violent civil wars and ethnic conflicts.

These historical, political and socio-economic developments have led to group and ethno-regional disparities and inequalities in almost all African countries, with the consequence of creating patterns of domination and subordination, inclusion and marginalisation, and non/misrecognition.[72] Although most

[70] Mutau (note 2 above) 342–343, 365; Nwabueze (note 21 above); B Berman, D Eyoh & W Kymlicka 'Introduction: Ethnicity and the Politics of Democratic Nation-Building in Africa' in Berman et al. (note 25 above) 1–21.

[71] See Chapter III above.

[72] Clearly, within the various disadvantaged communities some are worse off than others. The case of women is a good example of this. Minority women generally suffer double disadvantage: on

minorities have suffered these discriminatory patterns, some, such as peripheral minorities, and more particularly indigenous peoples, are more seriously affected than others. The inequalities and patterns of disadvantages (discrimination) that affect such minorities are expressed not only in socio-economic terms, involving high levels of illiteracy or lack of access to education and basic services, including water, health and sanitation,[73] but also in political terms, such as weak or no representation of minorities in policy-making bodies, as well as in the public services.[74] The specific conditions of groups, such as their numerical size, the size and resource endowment of their territories, and the nature of their political and socio-economic traditions, are additional factors that often put some groups at a disadvantage.[75] Additionally, members of some groups suffer certain disadvantages due to societal prejudices, stereotypes and negative attitudes towards their distinct way of life and culture.[76] It is this context that informs the nature of equality issues that lie beneath many of the claims of the minorities constituting African states. If a just and democratic solution is to be found to minority issues in this context, it is therefore important that equality is achieved among the members of various groups in terms of political representation and participation, distribution of and access to socio-economic goods, and recognition of their identities.

In the light of this, it is clear that minority claims for equality in Africa are claims for achieving substantive inclusion and participation in the political and socio-economic life of the society to which they belong. This can be achieved only if the state provides for institutions or guarantees that ensure that members of minorities are able to enjoy their rights and are treated with equal concern and respect, not only as citizens, but also as members of particular groups. It is also important that there exists a socio-economic regime that rectifies past patterns of socio-economic marginalisation or deprivations, and institutionalises a fair system of distribution of the burdens and benefits of living under a common government. This implies that the idea of equality among members of various

---

account of both their ethnic membership and their gender. See, for more, F Banda & C Chinkin *Gender, Minorities & Indigenous Peoples* (2004).

[73] P Justino & J Litchfield *Economic Exclusion and Discrimination: The Experience of Minorities and Indigenous Peoples* (2003); Report of the African Commission's Working Group of Experts on Indigenous Populations/Communities (2005) (ACHPR Report) Chapter II.

[74] Ibid, 45–49. As we have noted in Chapter II, however, the main site of minority contention in Africa relates to the issue of political equality and affects all constituent minorities of the post-colonial African state.

[75] This and the account given in Chapter II regarding the process of the making of the African state and the unequal conditions of members of the various groups brought under the colonially contrived state clearly show that the disadvantages suffered by such groups are not a product of the free choice their members. They are rather products of circumstances over which they have had no control. On the distinctions between chosen disadvantages and disadvantages that are product of unequal circumstances see Kymlicka (1989) (note 10 above) 185–190.

[76] See ACHPR Report (note 73 above) 34–38.

groups referrs not only to the provision of the same rights, in those respects that people are the same or equal, but also to the provision of differential rights or guarantees in those relevant respects that people are different or unequal.[77] The latter aspect suggests the provision of political and socio-economic as well as cultural guarantees relevant to the needs and circumstances of members of different groups.

One should accordingly distinguish between universal (formal) equality, on the one hand, and substantive equality and/with equality in difference, on the other. Universal equality involves the provision of the same rights, privileges and powers to all individuals and their identical treatment by institutions of the state, without regard to their particular differences. Substantive equality, on the other hand, involves the provision of different rights, privileges and powers with regard to the relevant matters in respect of which people are different or, more accurately, unequal.[78] Equality in difference, which is a narrow form of substantive equality, is specific to the recognition of and provision for the security of the cultural identity of individuals and groups.[79]

In his widely acknowledged work, *The Politics of Recognition*, Charles Taylor locates the origin of universal equality in the emergence of the politics of the equal dignity of all citizens, which he associates with Rousseau and Kant.[80] '[T]he content of this politics,' Taylor states, 'has been the equalisation of rights and entitlements. What is to be avoided at all costs is the existence of "first-class" and "second-class" citizens.'[81] The basis for this is 'the idea that all humans are equally worthy of respect'.[82] This 'fundamental intuition', he explains, 'focuses on what is the same in all'.[83] Laurie WH Ackermann, Emeritus Justice of the Constitutional Court South Africa, similarly locates the basis of universal equality in what makes all human beings common.[84] He says: '[T]he *attribute* in respect of which all humans are equal, must be treated equally and may not be discriminated against, is their common and immeasurable human worth (dignity).'[85]

---

[77] For an apt elaboration of the difference between the two see B Parekh *Rethinking Multiculturalism: Cultural Diversity and Political Theory* (2000) 239–242. See also I Brownlie 'The Rights of Peoples in Modern International Law' in J Crawford (ed.) *The Rights of Peoples* (1992) 1, 7–11.

[78] See Kymlicka (1989) (note 10 above), 190–191; Parekh ibid, 240.

[79] The idea of equality in difference as it pertains to culture was fully articulated as part of the politics of difference for the first time by Charles Taylor in 'The Politics of Recognition' (note 11 above).

[80] Ibid, 44–57.

[81] Ibid, 37.

[82] Ibid, 41.

[83] Ibid, 43.

[84] LWH Ackermann 'Equality and Non-Discrimination: Some Analytical Thoughts' (2006) 22 (4) *SAJHR* 597–612.

[85] Ibid, 611 (emphasis in the original).

It is important to note that universal equality, in some circumstances, most specifically in cases of past discrimination, allows what Charles Taylor calls reverse discrimination, which is also what Justice Ackermann calls remedial or restitutionary equality.[86] As Charles Taylor points out, the aim of this is, however, to level the playing field and allow the old blind 'rules' to come back into force in a way that does not disadvantage any one.[87] As Adeno Addis aptly puts it, in this instance the reality of groups is being acknowledged so as ultimately to remove the conditions for their existence and thereby transcend them.[88] In effect, reverse discrimination is an application of the principle of universal equality to extraordinary situations.

As the basis of universal equality is what Justice Ackermann called the 'common and immeasurable human worth (dignity)' of individuals, it ultimately aims at 'treating people in a difference-blind fashion'.[89] It is ordinarily made operational by anti-discrimination norms 'that seek to ensure that decision-making is, as a default position, colour and culture blind: people are to be treated as if there was no such thing as ethnic origin'.[90]

Although universal equality is absolutely fundamental, it is not enough to achieve equality among members of various ethno-cultural groups in the political, socio-economic and cultural life of multi-ethnic societies in general, and the post-colonial African state in particular. Its inadequacy mainly pertains to its being difference-blind and its inattention to circumstantial inequality. In other words, as Iris Marion Young and Melissa S Williams, among others, have shown, it does not recognise systematic inequality rooted in the existence of group-based marginalisation and subordination, and in the non/misrecognition of the identity of members of some groups in society as constituting discrimination or second-class citizenship.[91]

In multicultural societies, particularly of the kind in Africa, as argued in Chapter III, this has at least two adverse effects. The first is that the application of such a conception of equality has discriminatory results. It preserves the unequal power relations in society among members of different groups, as well as the non-recognition of minorities. The effect is to condemn minorities,

---

86 Ibid, 605.

87 Taylor (note 12) 40.

88 Addis (note 12 above) 639. According to Addis, 'this was the guiding principle of the United States Supreme Court in the 60s and 70s when dealing with race conscious remedies. Perhaps Justice Blackmun expressed that view most eloquently in Bakke when he observed, "In order to get beyond racism, we must first take account of race. There is no other way."' Ibid, 632.

89 Ackermann (note 79 above) 90.

90 T Makkonen 'Is Multiculturalism Bad for the Fight against Multiculturalism?' in M Scheinin & R Toivanen (eds.) *Rethinking Non-discrimination and Minority Rights* (2004) 155, 158.

91 See IM Young *Justice and the Politics of Difference* (1990) 164–165; MS Williams 'Memory, History and Membership: The Moral Claims of Marginalized Groups in Political Representation' in J Raikka (ed.) *Do We Need Minority Rights?* (1996) 85–119, 105, 110; Phillips (note 68 above) 90–98.

particularly the most vulnerable ones, to perpetual political and socio-economic marginalisation.[92] Secondly, it is also assimilationist in its effect. It recognises only what is the same in all (dignity) and hence is inhospitable, or gives no public space, to identity differences and the issues of equality to which these differences give rise.[93] Given the unequal position of various groups, such assimilationism means an inequitable treatment of minority cultures that may eventually result in the demise of their cultural integrity.[94]

It is in response to these drawbacks of universal equality that substantive equality, which also involves equality in difference have been elaborated.[95] These dimensions of equality extend the understanding of discrimination and second-class citizenship to issues of power relations in society and to assimilation, uniformity and the neglect of the distinctness of peoples' identity. Substantive equality and equality in difference broaden the principle of equality to involve not only the provision of the same rights and guarantees to all without distinction, but also the provision of group-specific minority rights both to offset their political and socio-economic vulnerabilities and prevent their future exclusion, and to recognise and affirm their particularity or cultural distinctness (which is covered by what Albertyn and Goldblatt call 'social equality')[96] as additional, but equally important, dimensions of equality.[97]

Substantive equality in the context of ethno-cultural diversity and inequality thus calls for measures and institutional arrangements necessary to improve the material conditions of minorities and to guarantee them increased voice in politics.[98] As Monique Deveaux accurately pointed out, this entails, even in established democratic states, 'either the reform of certain political institutions so as to secure permanent representation for national minorities (for example, through the introduction of group-based cultural rights) or a realignment of the state's internal power relationships (for example, by devolution of power or greater self-government for certain groups)'.[99] Such measures that are meant to institutionalise substantive equality should be seen as forming part of the

---

[92] See IM Young 'Polity and Group Difference: A Critique of the Ideal of Universal Citizenship' in RE Goodin & P Pettit *Contemporary Political Philosophy: An Anthology* (1997) 256–272; Williams (note 90 above) (rejecting the idea of universal equality in situations of 'group-structured inequality' saying that ignoring social difference by strict adherence to difference-blind equality will only serve to perpetuate such inequality). Also see Phillips (note 68 above) 25.

[93] Taylor (note 12); Phillips (note 68); C Albertyn 'Equality' in E Bonthuys & C Albertyn (eds.) *Gender, Law & Justice* (2007) 87 (arguing that formal equality cannot tolerate differences on grounds such as race or gender, even if they promote equality).

[94] Taylor (note 12); Phillips (note 68 above) 25.

[95] Taylor (note 12 above); Phillips (note 68 above) Chapter 4.

[96] Note 68 above.

[97] Kymlicka (1989) note 9 above, 190–194; Young (note 91 above).

[98] Macklem (note 69 above) 126.

[99] M Deveaux *Cultural Pluralism and Dilemmas of Justice* (2000) 3 & Chapters 5 & 6.

general scheme of rights necessary for the enjoyment of freedom and equality by minorities.[100] The objective is not necessarily to bring about equality of result, although that may be a preferred outcome. These measures rather serve to ensure that members of minorities have the necessary guarantees for full and equal participation in the political and economic processes of the state.[101]

4.3.2. *The International Law Framework*

The arguments made on the basis of various dimensions of equality find modest, though inadequate, articulation in international law as well. Universal equality is enunciated in general terms in Articles 1 and 55 of the UN Charter; Article 2 of the UDHR; Articles 2 and 26 of the ICCPR; and Article 2 of the International Covenant on Economic, Social and Cultural Rights (ICESCR). These guarantees, although general in their formulations, deal with situations in which minorities and their individual members may be denied equality of treatment and non-discrimination as they insist on equal enjoyment of rights without distinction on grounds of group membership of various kinds.

The principle of non-discrimination, an essential element of equality of dignity, is also guaranteed in various specialised instruments, including: the International Convention on the Elimination of All Forms of Racial Discrimination of 1965;[102] UNESCO Convention Against Discrimination in Education of 1960;[103] UNESCO Declaration on Race and Racial Prejudice of 1978;[104] Declaration on the Elimination of All Forms of Intolerance and of Discrimination Based on Religion or Belief

---

[100] This is because, as Kymlicka argues, 'it must be recognized that the members of minority cultures can face inequalities which are the product of their circumstances or endowment, not their choices or ambitions'. Kymlicka (1989) note 9 above 190. See also Addis (note 12 above) 659.

[101] Kymlicka (note 10 above, 1995) 109; S James Anaya *Indigenous Peoples in International Law* (1996) 110–111.

[102] Under Article 2 racial discrimination is defined as 'any distinction, exclusion, restriction or preference based on race, colour, descent, or national or ethnic origin which has the purpose or effect of nullifying or impairing the recognition, enjoyment or exercise, on an equal footing, of human rights and fundamental freedoms in the political, economic, social, cultural or any other field of public life'.

[103] Article 1 defines the term 'discrimination' to include 'any distinction, exclusion, limitation or preference which, being based on race, colour, sex, language, religion, political or other opinion, national or social origin, economic condition or birth, has the purpose or effect of nullifying or impairing equality of treatment in education'.

[104] Article 3 in its relevant part provides: 'Any distinction, exclusion, restriction or preference based on race, colour, ethnic or national origin or religious intolerance motivated by racist considerations … is incompatible with the requirements of an international order which is just and guarantees respect for human rights.'

of 1981[105] and the Convention on the Rights of the Child.[106] The guarantees that these instruments provide are of direct importance to minorities.[107]

Affirmative action (reverse discrimination) is increasingly being articulated as an important aspect of non-discrimination. In consequence, there is a trend in contemporary international law and legal analysis 'to emphasise that non-discrimination not only allows, but also in some situations *requires*' treating individuals differently on the basis of having regard to their ethnic origin or religious conviction.[108] Accordingly, the Committee on the Elimination of Racial Discrimination (CERD) mandates affirmative measures directed towards achieving substantive equality among racial and ethnic groups.[109] Similarly, the HRC, in its General Comment 18(37), stated that 'the principle of equality sometimes requires States parties to take affirmative action in order to diminish or eliminate conditions which cause or help to perpetuate discrimination prohibited by the covenant'.[110] As already alluded to above, such measures are, in the words of McKean, 'strictly compensatory'.[111] Affirmative action can be given application in various forms, including quota or other similar mechanisms that accord preferential treatment to minorities in various spheres of public life, most particularly access to education and other basic amenities, and public as well as private employment.

Beyond such temporary measures, other measures that may be taken to ensure equal access to opportunities in the political and socio-economic spheres of public life need not necessarily be temporary.[112] When measures that states need to adopt take such form, they constitute aspects of substantive equality, which has found some articulation in various instruments, albeit in a weak or indirect and not sufficiently detailed form. Rights that are of particular importance in this regard include those relating to participation and representation.[113]

---

[105] The expression 'intolerance and discrimination based on religion or belief' is understood in Article 2 of the Convention to mean 'any distinction, exclusion, restriction or preference based on religion or belief and having as its purpose or as its effect nullification or impairment of the recognition, enjoyment or exercise of human rights and fundamental freedoms on an equal basis'.

[106] In Article 2 States Parties undertake to 'take all appropriate measures to ensure that the child is protected against all forms of discrimination or punishment on the basis of the status, activities, expressed opinions, or beliefs of the child's parents, legal guardians, or family members'.

[107] See Henrard (note 51 above) 193–205.

[108] Makkonen, (note 90 above) 158–159.

[109] Accordingly, under Article 2(2) States Parties are required, when circumstance warrant, to take in the social, economic, cultural and other fields 'special and concrete measures to ensure the adequate development and protection of certain racial groups or individuals belonging to them'.

[110] Para 10.

[111] W McKean *Equality and Discrimination under International Law* (1983) 288.

[112] See *General Comment No 25*, Committee on the Elimination of Discrimination against Women, para 19.

[113] See, on such rights, V van Dyke *Human Rights, Ethnicity and Discrimination* (1985) 36–37.

The 1992 Declaration on Minorities, in addition to elaborating the rights under Article 27,[114] enunciates additional rights that aim to ensure substantive equality for minorities. The most important is the right 'to participate effectively in cultural, religious, social, economic and public life'.[115] Effective participation is further elaborated in Article 2(3) which provides for

> the right to participate effectively in decisions on the national and, where appropriate, regional level concerning the minority to which they belong or the regions in which they live, in a manner not incompatible with national legislation.

Although the right to effective participation as provided in this declaration does not specify the form that the right takes and its specific institutional implications, it is only logical to regard its reach as extending beyond Article 25 of the ICCPR, which guarantees the right of individuals to participation. The implication of this is that, beyond and above individual participation, effective participation of minorities requires states to adopt various arrangements, such as power-sharing political processes or electoral schemes, which facilitate the representation and participation of minorities.[116]

In the socio-economic sphere, Article 5(1) provides for the obligation of states to plan and implement national policies and programmes with 'due regard for the legitimate interests of persons belonging to minorities'. States are also required to 'consider appropriate measures so that persons belonging to minorities may participate fully'.[117] Elaborating on this, Asbjorn Eide states:

> Members of the different ethnic, religious, linguistic groups should on the basis of equality participate in, contribute to and benefit from the right to development. Consequently, development policies should be conducted in ways which decrease the disparities that might exist between different groups. Groups living compactly together should always be fully consulted with regard to development projects affecting the regions in which they live.[118]

---

[114] See the Declaration on the Rights of Minorities Articles 2(1) and 4(2).

[115] See the Declaration on the Rights of Minorities Article 2.

[116] See Lund Recommendations on the Effective Participation of National Minorities in Public Life principle 1.1; F De Varennes *Towards Effective Political Participation and Representation of Minorities* E/CN.4/Sub.2/AC.5/1998/WP.5; A Eide *Commentary to the Declaration on the Rights of Persons Belonging to National or Ethnic, Religious or Linguistic Minorities* Working Paper, Working Group on Minorities (6th Session) E/CN.4/Sub.2/AC.5/2000/WP.1. (Commentary to the Declaration).

[117] The Declaration on the Rights of Minorities Article 4(5). See also UN *Manual on Human Rights Reporting* (1997) (HR/PUB/91/1 (Rev.1)), 277 (where specific indication was made to the effect that attention be paid to the socio-economic and political situation of minorities to ensure that their development in the social, economic, and cultural spheres takes place on an equal footing with that of the general population).

[118] *Possible Ways and Means of Facilitating the Peaceful and Constructive Solution of Problems Involving Minorities* Report submitted by Special Rapporteur Asbjørn Eide Addendum 4, Recommendations UN Doc. E/CN.4/Sub.2/1993/34/Add.4, 11 August 1993 11 August 1993 para 16.

In more concrete terms, the Committee on Economic, Social and Cultural (CESC) Rights has highlighted the obligation to ensure equal opportunities for minorities in several fields, but especially in relation to employment, housing, health and education.[119] Rights to land and natural resources are guaranteed, particularly with respect to peripheral minorities.[120]

4.3.3. *The African Human Rights System*

The right to equality in its universal form is provided for under Article 3 of the African Charter. Under Article 2 of the Charter, the non-discrimination clause also provides that

> [e]very individual shall be entitled to the enjoyment of the rights and freedoms recognized and guaranteed in the present Charter without distinction of any kind such as race, ethnic group, color, sex, language, religion, political or any other opinion, national and social origin, fortune, birth or other status.

This provision is mainly an expression of universal equality and as such is understood to require states to ensure that all individuals, including members of minorities, enjoy rights guaranteed in the Charter without discrimination. Additionally, however, given the pervasive inequality among members of different groups in many African states, this provision can also be understood as requiring states to take affirmative measures in favour of disadvantaged minorities.[121] Accordingly, it also has aspects of substantive equality.

The enunciation of socio-economic rights under Articles 14–17 of the African Charter, although formulated as individual rights, must, in the particular circumstances of many African states, enjoin the state to develop policies that are not only capable of being directed towards improving the socio-economic conditions of citizens generally, but also both remedial (of the socio-economic marginalisation of disadvantaged groups and regions) and distributive in their effect.[122] As the decision of the African Commission in the Ogoni case also shows,[123] these rights, despite their formulation as individual rights, may be used to safeguard the socio-economic needs of minorities who are subject to particular

---

[119] W VandenHole *Non -Discrimination and Equality in the View of the UN Human Rights Treaty Bodies* (2005) 234.

[120] See Declaration on Indigenous Peoples Article 8 (2) (*b*).

[121] See KA Acheampong 'The African Charter and the Equalization of Human Rights' (1994) 12 *Scandinavian Human Rights J* 168.

[122] See SA Dersso *Promotion of Human Security in Africa: The Role of African Human Rights Institutions* ISS Monograph Series No 145 (June 2008) 12, 24–30; see also the Guidelines for National Periodic Reports in Second Activity Report of the African Commission as adopted in June 1989 annex XII, reprinted in C Heyns (ed.) *Human Rights Law in Africa* Vol I (2004) 507, Guidelines II, 47, 515 & 55, 516–517, which make direct reference to minorities.

[123] See *SERAC & CESR v Nigeria* Communication No. 155/96 decided at ACHPR's 30th Ordinary Session held in Banjul, The Gambia from 13–27 October 2001.

socio-economic disadvantages and, at a minimum, to guarantee, together with the right of peoples to dispose of their natural wealth under Article 21, that such groups are not deprived of their means of subsistence.

One of the unique features of the African Charter is that it guarantees the rights of peoples. Although the position of minorities as beneficiaries of peoples' rights under the Charter has been a subject of controversy, it is now established that minorities are indeed among the beneficiaries of peoples' rights.[124] One of these set of rights is the right of peoples to equality. Article 19 stipulates:

> All peoples shall be equal. They shall enjoy the same respect and shall have the same rights. Nothing shall justify the domination of a people by another.

This provision strengthens the protection envisaged under Article 2 for members of minorities by specifically recognising the importance of inter-group equality, particularly in the prevailing context of Africa, for achieving substantive equality. The inter-group equality that it guarantees covers all aspects of public life: political, social and economic. Other guarantees that are of particular importance for minorities generally, and for indigenous peoples in particular, are the rights of peoples to their natural resources and to development, guaranteed under Articles 21 and 22 respectively.[125]

It is clear from the foregoing that there is sufficient evidence in international law of the recognition of group-specific rights as a necessary component for ensuring the genuine equality of minorities. This implies the emergence of an evolving international legal expectation that states, having regard to their historical and socio-political conditions and the needs and interests of minorities, should adopt relevant institutional arrangements and socio-economic regimes that give optimal effect to these rights.[126]

4.4. Self-Determination

Equality is undoubtedly a powerful normative framework for elaborating and defending minority rights, not only as they relate to the good of cultural membership but also in terms of political participation and representation, as well

---

[124] See SA Dersso 'The Jurisprudence of the African Commission on Human and Peoples' Rights With Respect to Peoples' Rights' (2006) 6 (2) *African Human Rights J* 358.

[125] See, for example, Report of the African Commission's Working Group of Experts on Indigenous Populations/Communities (2005) 75–76. On the importance of Article 21, see J Oloka-Onyango 'Reinforcing Marginalized Rights in an Age of Globalization: International Mechanisms, Non-State Actors, and the Struggle for Peoples' Rights in Africa' (2003) 18 *American University Int LR* 851, 889–893.

[126] These are generally regarded as offering an institutional framework for conflict management in various parts of the world and as producing positive results. See TR Gurr *Peoples Versus States: Minorities at Risk in the New Century* (2000) Chapter 8.

as socio-economic needs. However, some of these rights can find stronger and more direct support on another basis, namely, the right to self-determination. Given that the issue of minorities in Africa is also a product of the suppression of the autonomous political development of diverse pre-colonial ethno-cultural communities, and their forcible amalgamation under the colonially contrived state structure,[127] the defence and articulation of minority rights within the post-colonial African state cannot be separated from but rest on and draw from self-determination. In other words, it is only if minority rights are robustly defended as forms of the application of self-determination required to rectify these violations, which continue to affect many communities to this day, that they can capture the full scope of the historical and political dimensions of Africa's ethno-cultural diversity. The following section accordingly investigates and defends this possibility.

4.4.1. *The Dominant Perspective and its Limits*

The Charter of the United Nations Organisation[128] is the first modern international legal instrument to enunciate self-determination as a principle of international law.[129] Previously, during the League of Nations, this only had the status of a political idea. Under the 1960 UN Declaration for the Granting of Independence to Colonial Countries and Peoples,[130] self-determination was elevated to the status of a *right* of peoples, albeit that the reference to people was confined to those in 'territories which have not attained independence'.[131] Although this has been a very important development, as Umozurike maintains, 'the resolution does not offer false hope to minorities within states, for it expressly refers to "alien subjugation" as an essential qualification to "peoples" in "all peoples have the right to self-determination"'.[132]

Under the UN, as under the Organisation of African Unity (OAU), decolonisation in Africa and Asia has been the most important development with respect to the articulation of self-determination as the right of peoples. The effect, however, has been the tendency under international law to equate the right to self-determination with independence. As Thornberry puts it, the logic of the 1960 Declaration is that 'peoples hold the right to self-determination; a

[127] See Chapter II.
[128] See Charter of the United Nations of June 26, 1945 *UNTS* No. 993, 3 (hereinafter the UN Charter) Article 1 (2) & Article 55. Its enunciation in this text is generally associated with independence or the freedom of *a people* from external domination or interference.
[129] See A Cassese *Self-Determination of Peoples: A Legal Reappraisal* (1995) 19–33.
[130] UN GA Res. 1514 (XV) of 14 Dec. 1960 15 *United Nations General Assembly Official Records*, Supp. (No. 16) 66, UN Doc. A/4684 (1961).
[131] See para 5 & principle I.
[132] UO Umozurike *Self-Determination in International L* (1972) 72.

people is the whole people of a territory; a people exercises its right through the achievement of independence'.[133] As a result, the right to self-determination has been limited to, firstly, peoples of a particular territory under colonial rule or alien subjugation and, secondly, independence.

This inevitably linked self-determination with territory and sovereignty, leading to the rise of a tension between self-determination and the principles of the sovereignty and territorial integrity of states, principles on which the international system is founded. According to Hannum, in order to reconcile this tension self-determination is formulated, in the practice of the UN, as the right to freedom for a colonial people, or *external* self-determination, and the independence of a state's population from foreign intervention, or *internal* self-determination.[134]

There is the additional problem of the definition of the term 'peoples'. In international law, consistent with the dominant perspective, the term 'peoples' as subject of the right to self-determination has generally been considered to signify either people under colonial rule or alien subjugation, or the whole people of a state.[135] Other groups, such as minorities, including indigenous peoples, have not been regarded, at least until recently, as having the attributes of 'peoples' as a subject of self-determination.

In Africa, the effect of this is the restriction of the application of self-determination to the removal of the colonial authority (independence) and the corresponding legal sanctification of everything else, including the highly contrived borders and state structures.[136] As noted in Chapter II, the post-colonial African state is, in terms both of its conception and making, a product of colonial rule. It 'was so created by forcibly merging together various groups of different cultures'.[137] The members of these hitherto independent groups forming the colonial state

[133] P Thornberry *International Law and the Rights of Minorities* (1991) 18.

[134] H Hannum *Autonomy, Sovereignty, and Self-Determination* 49. Here, the internal and external aspects of self-determination are actually expressions of self-determination as independence. The second aspect, although labelled external, in actual fact constitutes the principle of sovereignty of states. As will be shown below, the internal aspect of the right to self-determination, rather than being an expression of the international-law principle of sovereignty, refers to the institutions and norms that define the internal political structures and processes of the state.

[135] See R Higgins 'Post-Modern Tribalism and the Right to Secession, Comments' in C Brölmann et al. (eds.) *Peoples and Minorities in International Law* (1993) 29, 32; J Dugard 'A Legal Basis for Secession – Relevant Principles and Rules' in Julie Dahlitz (ed.) *Secession and International Law* (2003) 92.

[136] CC Mojekwu 'Self-determination: The African Perspective' in Y Alexander & RA Friedlander (eds.) *Self-Determination: National, Regional & Global Dimensions* (1980); A Xnathaki 'The Right to Self-determination: Meaning and Scope' in N Ghanea & A Xanthaki (eds.) *Minorities, Peoples & Self-Determination: Essays in Honour of Patrick Thornberry* (2005) 15, 22–24; B Neuberger *National Self-Determination in Postcolonial Africa* (1986).

[137] Nwabueze (note 21 above) 296.

had no say at all in the process of its making.[138] During decolonisation, while the colonial territory achieved independence, the diverse ethno-cultural groups forcibly included in it did not regain their freedom.[139] The process did not allow for negotiations and deliberations among the members of the constituent groups to determine, by themselves, the unit within which they should attain their independence.[140] Ben Nwabueze comments: 'Africa's independence has operated, not to liberate the ethnic nationalities by restoring to them their pre-colonial autonomy, but *rather to continue the denial of that autonomy and to heighten their continued alienation from the state*.'[141] It is only logical to conclude with Mutua that 'the right to self-determination was exercised not by the victims of colonisation but by their victimisers'.[142]

The constitutional configuration of the states was devoid of any popular consensus and cultural and historical foundation. On top of that, however, it also lacked the kind of institutional and normative framework (basic structure) that is necessary to effect a just organisation, distribution and sharing of political power, relevant to the deep ethno-cultural diversity and political and socio-economic asymmetry that characterises the situation of so many groups and ethno-regions.[143] Moreover, the institutions and processes of the state had no affinity with the social structures and values with which the life of members of the various communities is intimately connected.[144] The continuation of the respective colonial language as the officially sanctioned medium of public communication 'deprives the majority of Africans of access to knowledge, and hinders them from participating in national politics and the decision making processes' and 'creates insecurity and feelings of inferiority among those who have to operate in the foreign language of the ruling elite'.[145] As a result, many

---

[138] See B Davidson *The Black Man's Burden: The Curse of the Nation-state* (1992); OC Okafor *Redefining Legitimate Statehood: International Law and State Fragmentation in Africa* (2000), particularly Chapter 2; MW Mutua 'Why Redraw the Map of Africa: A Moral and Legal Inquiry' (1995) 16 *Michigan J Int L* 1113, 1122–1141.

[139] As Mojekwu aptly puts it: 'It is a simpler matter for a given colonial territory to be independent. It is a much more involved affair for the same territory to be self-determined.' Mojekwu (note 136 above) 234.

[140] As Davidson pointed out, 'the leading nationalists found themselves obliged by imperialist policies, fashioned in London and Paris, "to seek independence within the existing power unit" of their colony, rather than in any more rational or historically logical territorial unit'. Davidson (note 138 above) 183; AA An-N'im 'Introduction: Expanding Legal Protection of Human Rights in African Context' in AA An-N'im (ed.) *Human Rights Under African Constitutions* (2003) 1, 12.

[141] Nwabueze (note 21 above) 309.

[142] Mutua (note 138 above) 1117.

[143] AM Abdullahi 'The Refugee Crisis in Africa as a Crisis of the Institution of the State' (1994) 6 (4) *International J of Refugee L* 562–580, 566 (arguing that the African state failed to construct an institution of the state that not only looks viable, but also functions and accommodates the diverging and often conflicting interests of the diverse ethnic nationalities within its borders).

[144] See B Nwabueze *Constitutionalism in the Emergent States* (1973) 24; Davidson (note 138).

[145] A Lodhi 'The Language Situation in Africa Today' (1993) 2 (1) *Nordic J of African Studies* 81.

members of the population of the newly independent African states have been alienated from the process of the state, and hence continued to be excluded from exercising their basic freedom of self-rule.

So peoples in Africa were deprived not only, by colonial conquest, of their inherent right to determine their own political, economic and social organisation, but also, during and subsequent to 'decolonisation', of any meaningful say in respect of that process and the running of the formally independent African state. Moreover, the state continued to operate as an alien and abusive imposition, detached from the social structures and historical and cultural values, as well as the lived experiences, of the diverse people constituting it. This has often led, Shivji observed, to 'internal oppression and discrimination of nations and nationalities within state borders'.[146] The issue of minorities as examined in Chapter II is a direct manifestation of this crisis of the legitimacy of the African state.[147]

The correction of this structural crisis requires the application of the right to self-determination in a form that both reinstates the freedom that the diverse peoples constituting the African state lost due to colonialism and ends its continuing violation under the post-colonial state. Similarly, it is necessary that not only peripheral minorities, but also minorities generally, are regarded as groups to which the term 'peoples' – as a subject of the right to self-determination – applies. Nevertheless, given that there have been relevant intervening factors since the colonial period, such a formulation and application should necessarily be flexible enough not only to achieve the above ends, but also to address conflicting claims and reflect the interdependencies developed among peoples within the modern African state, and allay the fear of disrupting the sovereignty and territorial integrity of states. This leads us to examine James Anaya's analysis of the content and application of self-determination and the emerging recognition in international law of internal self-determination, which seeks to address all these intricacies.

4.4.2. *Anaya on Self-Determination*

As Anaya's very insightful study shows, the dominant perspective of self-determination associated with UN practice is very restrictive and fails to capture the essence of self-determination. Based on the textual conceptualisation of the right or principle of self-determination and the relevant practice, Anaya

---

[146] IG Shivji 'State and Constitutionalism: A New Democratic Perspective' in IG Shivji *State and Constitutionalism: An African Debate* (1991) 27–54, 33.

[147] On the crisis of the legitimacy of the African state, along the same lines, see Okafor (note 138); JP Pham 'African Constitutionalism: Forging New Models for Multiethnic Governance and Self-determination' in JI Levitt (ed.) *Africa: New Boundaries in International Law* (2008) 183, 184–188.

establishes that self-determination is constituted by a set of universal values that 'are grounded in the idea that all segments of humanity, individually and as groups, have the right to pursue their own destinies in freedom and under conditions of equality'.[148] The essential mark of these common sets of values underlying self-determination is that they define the minimum conditions of human freedom and equality for the constitution and functioning of legitimate government. Anaya thus concludes that self-determination 'comprises a standard of governmental legitimacy within the modern human rights frame'.[149] According to Anaya, the substance of self-determination, which applies to all segments of humanity, lies in what he calls a more or less identifiable 'nexus of opinion about the minimum conditions for legitimate government' shared by relevant international actors at any given time within the modern era of human rights.[150]

The substance of self-determination does not mean that for the institution of government to be legitimate it has to uphold any conception of the good. Substantive self-determination is rather about the procedural aspects of the constitution of the institutions of government and the manner of their operation, particularly in terms of the fairness of the distribution of constitutional goods as well as the burdens and benefits of social co-operation. Accordingly, substantive self-determination is formulated as consisting of two normative aspects: a constitutive aspect and an ongoing aspect. In its constitutive aspect, substantive self-determination entails that 'the governing institutional order be substantially the creation of processes guided by the will of the people, or peoples, governed'.[151] This applies to the process of the formation of or change in the governing structures or institutional order of a society, such as the making or changing of constitutions. Substantive self-determination dictates that there be meaningful participation and consent by the people or peoples concerned to such occasional or episodic procedures. Ongoing self-determination, on the other hand, applies to any governing institutional order and 'continuously enjoins the form and functioning of the governing institutional order'. This requires the existence of 'a governing order under which individuals and groups are able to make meaningful choices in matters touching upon all spheres of life on a continuous basis'.[152] These two aspects of substantive self-determination require that the governing institutional order of a society be one that is, in the first place, a product of the equal and free participation and consent of

[148] See J Anaya 'Self-determination as a Collective Human Right under International Law' in P Aiko & M Scheinin (eds.) *Operationalizing the Right of Indigenous Peoples to Self-Determination* (2000) 3–18, 8.

[149] See J Anaya *Indigenous Peoples in International Law* (1996) 81.

[150] Ibid.

[151] Anaya (note 148 above) 9.

[152] Anaya (note 149 above) 82.

individuals and groups constituting the society, and secondly managed on an ongoing basis through the participation and freely and equally expressed will of the people/peoples.

The violation of self-determination in both its constitutive and ongoing aspects gives rise to contextually applicable remedies. This remedial aspect of self-determination must be distinguished from its substantive aspect. This distinction entails that '"all peoples", not just the aggregate populations of states and colonial territories, but other spheres of community that define human existence and place in the world, including indigenous peoples as well as other groups',[153] such as minorities, have the right to self-determination. But when the right to self-determination is invoked by any one of these groups, its application to them operates as remedy for the particular violations (of substantive self-determination) they suffered under the governing institutional order to which they belong. Given that not all violations of substantive self-determination need to be remedied by the grant of independence, the application of self-determination can and often does take other forms, including representation and participation, self-government or territorial autonomy, language rights, rights to land and resources, and cultural rights, including recognition of customary law.[154]

The treatment to which the diverse ethno-cultural groups making up the post-colonial African state were subjected, as discussed above in this section and in the previous two chapters, clearly violates their right to substantive self-determination, in both its constitutive and ongoing aspects. This necessarily entitles them to remedial self-determination. Generally, this can be achieved through institutionalising relevant structures that guarantee minority representation and participation and self-government; language and cultural rights, including the recognition and enforcement of customary laws; and rights to land and resources. The redefinition of the structures and processes of the state that this necessitates essentially affects the legitimisation of the African state, or, in the words of Okafor, the 'righting', restructuring and rejuvenating of the post-colonial African state.[155]

4.4.3. *Emerging Trends in International Law and the African Human Rights System*

Significant developments in international law are slowly leading to the acceptance of a flexible formulation of self-determination which can be understood

---

[153] J Anaya *Indigenous Peoples In International Law* (2004) 193.

[154] See Anaya (note 149 above) Chapter 4.

[155] See OC Okafor '"Righting," Restructuring, and Rejuvenating the Post-Colonial African State: The Case for the Establishment of an AU Special Commission on National Minorities' (2007) 13 *African Yearbook of Int L* 2005 43, 50–56.

as allowing self-determination in its application to take the above forms. These developments also recognise minorities, and particularly indigenous peoples, as having some of the attributes of 'peoples', and hence as being among the beneficiaries of the right to self-determination in a form relevant to their specific conditions, which are defined by the violations they suffered. In this context, the inclusion of the right to self-determination under the two UN Covenants is of particular importance.[156] These Covenants – the ICCPR and the ICESCR – both accorded the right to self-determination a prime place as Article 1. In the language of the two Covenants, self-determination is a right of *all peoples*. Although the subject 'peoples' is left undefined, in this context it is understood to mean not only those in colonial territories but also identifiable groups within independent states.[157]

Within this human rights framework, probably the most important development is the trend towards recognising and articulating internal self-determination, which embraces a variety of institutional arrangements and entitlements that regulate the relationship between states and sub-national groups.[158] According to Cassese, this was enunciated for the first time at the international level with the adoption of the Helsinki Final Act of 1975.[159] Here, Principle VIII of the Decalogue provides that

> By virtue of the principle of equal rights and self-determination of peoples, all peoples always have the right, in full freedom, to determine, when and as they wish, *their internal and external political status*, without external interference, and to pursue as they wish their political, economic and cultural development. (my emphasis)

Unlike other international pronouncements on the right to self-determination, the express reference to internal political status introduced into international

---

[156] See A Rosas 'Internal Self-Determination' in C Tomuschat (ed.) *Modern Law of Self-Determination* (1993) 225–252.

[157] In its General Comment on the right to self-determination, the UNHRC stated that Article 1 'imposes specific obligations on States parties, not only in relation to their *own peoples* but vis-à-vis all peoples which have not been able to exercise or have been deprived of the possibility of exercising their right to self-determination'. (my emphasis) HRC, *The right to self-determination of peoples (Art. 1) : 13/04/84. CCPR General comment 12,* 1984, at (1984) para 6.

[158] See CERD General Recommendation No. 21: Right to Self-determination adopted on 23 August 1996, para 4. For details on internal self-determination see Tomuschat (ed.) (note 155 above), particularly the contributions by O Kimminich, P Thornberry, A Eide, P Allot, A Rosas and J Salmon; see also L Hannikainen 'Self-Determination and Autonomy in International Law' in M Suksi (ed.) *Autonomy: Applications and Implications* (1998) 97–124; more specifically with respect to minorities see Cassese (note 128 above) 350–359; Henrard (note 51 above) 306–314; G Pentassuglia 'State Sovereignty, Minorities and Self-Determination: A Comprehensive Legal View' (2002) 9 *Int J on Minority and Group Rights* 303–324, 313; SC Roach 'Minority Rights and an Emergent International Right to Autonomy: A Historical and Normative Assessment' (2004) 11 *Int J on Minority and Group Rights* 411–432.

[159] Cassese (note 129 above) 277–312.

legal discourse the notion of internal self-determination as an exercise of political decision-making through which peoples establish a new constitutional order and 'adapt existing social or political structures to meet new demands'.[160] Although less direct, another instrument that makes reference to internal self-determination is the Vienna Declaration and Programme of Action of 1993, which requires governments to be representative of the 'whole people', not just the majority.[161] Recently, internal self-determination for groups within states has been given clearer enunciation as part of international law under the 2007 UN Declaration on the Rights of Indigenous Peoples.[162]

Although self-government or territorial autonomy, which forms part of the right to self-determination, is not expressly recognised in the leading international minority rights standard setting document, the 1992 Declaration on Minority Rights, it is nevertheless taken as one mechanism for giving substantive application to certain minority guarantees, particularly the right to effective participation.[163] As Thornberry puts it, '[t]here is no specific right to autonomy in the Declaration (1992), but "effective" participation through local and national organisations may necessitate the creation of autonomies to achieve the Declaration's standard'.[164] At the European level, there is specific recognition that self-government gives effective protection to minorities. Section IV (35) of the OSCE's Copenhagen Document (1990), for example, recommends 'appropriate local or autonomous administrations corresponding to the specific historical and territorial circumstances of … minorities'.

In Africa as well, the right to self-determination as enshrined under the African Charter on Human and Peoples' Rights embodies the idea of internal self-determination.[165] In the *Katangese Peoples Congress v Zaire* case,[166] the African Commission, the body charged with monitoring compliance with the African Charter, expressly recognised internal self-determination, and held that

> Self-determination may be exercised in any of the following ways independence, self-government, local government, federalism, confederalism, unitarism or any

---

160 Ibid, 287.

161 See Vienna Declaration and Programme of Action of 1993 UN Doc A/CONF.157/23 Part 1.2.

162 See UN Declaration on the Rights of Indigenous Peoples Articles 3 & 4.

163 See A Eide 'In Search of Constructive Alternatives to Secession' in Tomschat (note 155 above) 139–176; The Lund Recommendations of 1999, drafted by international experts for the OSCE High Commissioner on National Minorities, similarly provide that 'effective participation of minorities in public life may call for non-territorial or territorial arrangements of self-governance or a combination thereof'.

164 Thornberry (note 43 above) 43.

165 See Article 20 of the Charter. See F Ouguergouz *The African Charter on Human and Peoples' Rights: A Comprehensive Agenda for Human Dignity and Sustainable Democracy in Africa* (2003) 249–269.

166 (2000) AHRLR 72 (ACHPR 1995) Communication 75/92 8th Annual Activity Report (1994–1995) (Hereinafter the Katanga Case).

> other form of relations that accords the wishes of the people but fully cognizant of other recognized principles such as sovereignty and territorial integrity.[167]

Self-determination formulated in this way relates, particularly in societies with ethno-cultural diversity, to 'the internal state structure as well as to certain legal regulations to accommodate the population diversity of a state in a (more) optimal way'.[168] These structures and legal regulations may include self-government arrangements in the form of federalism or autonomy, and rights of representation and effective participation, as well as various cultural rights.[169] They also include rights to land, the peoples' rights to dispose freely of their natural wealth and resources, and not to be deprived of their own means of subsistence.[170] Taken together, the effect of the above developments is an emerging recognition, rather than denial, of the entitlement of minorities to self-determination, understood as a right to various forms of arrangements that guarantee self-government and participation.

In the particular history of the post-colonial state and the situation of minorities in Africa, the application of internal self-determination in such forms essentially operates much like Anaya's remedial self-determination. It remedies the violations that various minorities suffered by fully embracing and institutionally accommodating their identities and hitherto suppressed group interests. It also empowers members of the constituent minorities and guarantees them fair participation in shaping the political, economic and socio-cultural process of the state, thereby ending what Shivji calls 'national oppression' or what Nwabueze terms 'alienation' from the state.[171] Moreover, as indicated above, such constitutional application of the right to self-determination 'rights', to use Okafor's powerful term,[172] the post-colonial African state, and thereby rectify its inherited and continuing illegitimacy. This approach generally builds upon the jurisprudence of the African Commission and constitutes an elaboration of the direction it should take.[173]

---

[167] Ibid, para 6.

[168] C Tomuschat 'Self-Determination in a Post-Colonial World' in Tomuschat (note 156 above) 129.

[169] See Cassese (note 129 above) 350–359. Fawcett also characterises self-determination as capable of being 'invoked by a whole people as a right of independence … or *by a religious, ethnic, cultural or linguistic group within the state* as *a right to effective representation* in government or *to organisation as a separate political or social unit*' (my emphasis) J Fawcett *The Law of Nations* (1971) 39.

[170] See HRC Concluding Observations on The Periodic Report of Canada (April 1999) para. 8.

[171] Shivji (note 146 above); Nwabueze (note 21 above).

[172] See Okafor (note 155 above).

[173] See Dersso (note 124 above).

4.5. Conclusion

This chapter has identified and elaborated the legal and normative bases for the recognition and accommodation of ethno-cultural diversity in Africa. The foregoing discussion has shown that arguments supporting such accommodation can be drawn from cultural identity, equality and self-determination. Although each of these three elements provides its own basis for addressing the issue of minorities, as shown in this chapter, no one or two of them alone would be enough to constitute a minority rights framework sufficiently robust for designing an adequate constitutional mechanism for accommodation of diversity in Africa. They are also elaborated as complementing each other to offer a comprehensive legal and normative framework, not only to justify the recognition and accommodation of ethno-cultural diversity, but also to identify the mechanisms (the institutions and constitutional principles) for institutionalising such recognition and accommodation.

CHAPTER V

TOWARDS A MULTICULTURAL CONSTITUTIONAL FRAMEWORK: THE INSTITUTIONAL DIMENSIONS OF THE MINORITY RIGHTS FRAMEWORK

5.1. Introduction

The approach to minority rights defended in this study is built on three pillars – access to cultural membership, equality and self-determination – which in turn depend on two frameworks: a theoretical framework and the international law framework. Combining these two, this chapter outlines the specific institutional arrangements and minority guarantees that optimally translate the three pillars of minority rights into an adequate constitutional design for accommodation of ethno-cultural diversity in Africa. Due to space limitations, the following pages offer only a general outline. Apart from the choice of institutions and policy guarantees, the success of a constitutional design in adequately accommodating ethno-cultural diversity requires the existence of and wide political and public commitment for certain fundamental values and principles. As Amartya Sen convincingly argued in his *The Idea of Justice* the choice of institutions by itself alone is not adequate in delivering justice. He thus suggests that 'a realistic reading of behavioural norms and regularities becomes important for the choice of institutions and the pursuit of justice'.[1] These are similar to what Ali Mazrui calls 'the values, beliefs and attitudes of the people that orient their political behavior', which he considers to be 'fundamental in determining the prospects for democratic change in a particular society'.[2] This chapter additionally identifies those values and principles that create the cultural and social foundations necessary for the legitimate operation of an adequate constitutional design for accommodation of ethno-cultural diversity.

5.2. Self-Government and/or Territorial Autonomy

Structures of self-government and/or territorial autonomy constitute by far the most important institutional arrangements and minority guarantees that together translate the three pillars of minority rights into an adequate multicultural

[1] Amartya Sen *The Idea of Justice* (London: Penguin Books, 2009) 81.

[2] Ali A Mazrui & Alamin M. Mazrui *The Power of Babel: Language and Governance in the African Experience* (1998) 98.

constitutional design. They not only satisfy the rights of minorities to internal and/or remedial self-determination, but also provide the strongest institutional framework for the protection of the culture of minorities.

Self-government can be institutionalised within states in various ways.[3] One such important mechanism, increasingly being used in many parts of the world, is federalism.[4] This term signifies some level of normative position about how a polity should organise its power structures.[5] As an ideology about organisation of power, federalism 'holds that the ideal organization of human affairs is best reflected in the celebration of diversity through unity'.[6] As Andreas Eshete points out, however, federalism is not 'a necessary part of an ideal conception or theory of a democratic society'.[7] This means that federalism, unlike public ideals of universal reach such as human rights or justice, would not be applicable to all societies.[8] Accordingly, 'it is difficult to defend federalism as a free-standing ideology comparable to or separate from liberalism or socialism'.[9] Rather, federalism is a situation-dependent theory, if it is to be taken as such, which draws its support from existing ideals of universal reach and the particular circumstances of specific societies. It expresses the idea that political organisation should seek to achieve political union and autonomy by combining shared rule on common matters and self-rule on other aspects of public life.[10]

From the perspective of this study, what makes federalism attractive is its capacity to provide a flexible framework for balancing the demands of unity and diversity by allowing members of various groups to participate at the centre in relation to common concerns through shared rule, while leaving autonomous space for minorities to conduct their affairs through self-rule. The principle of federalism, according to the Supreme Court of Canada, 'recognises the diversity of the component parts of confederation or a federation and the autonomy of the provincial governments to develop their societies within their respective

---

[3] Devolution of power is one means of institutionalising self-government. But such devolution does not have to be and generally is not a constitutionally entrenched mechanism. It is rather a result of political bargaining whose legal basis is generally an act of parliament, which has less durability and a lower level of protection. Preference is therefore given to arrangements, like federalism, that are constitutionally entrenched.

[4] RL Watts 'Federalism, Federal Political Systems, and Federations' (1998) 1 *Annual Review of Political Science* 117–137, 117–120.

[5] For details on this and further references see ibid, 120.

[6] G Smith 'Mapping the Federal Condition: Ideology, Political Practice and Social Justice' in G Smith (ed.) *Federalism: The Multiethnic Challenge* (1995) 4.

[7] A Eshete 'Ethnic Federalism: New Frontiers in Ethiopian Politics' in *First National Conference on Federalism, Conflict and Peace Building* (2003) 142–172, 145.

[8] As Eshete observes, 'Violation of human rights justifies condemnation or even coercive intervention. In contrast, rejection of federalism by a regime does not demonstrate imperfection, much less, wrongdoing in the regime.' Ibid.

[9] Smith (note 6 above) 4.

[10] See R Watts *Comparing Federal Systems* (1999) 9.

sphere of jurisdiction'.[11] It is, however, important to note that whether federalism serves to accommodate the interests of minorities depends on the resolution of two questions.[12] The first is whether, and the extent to which, the boundaries of federal units are defined to allow minorities to exercise some degree of self-government within those units. The other is the degree of autonomy that the division of sovereign powers leaves to the federal units to accommodate self-rule for the minorities concerned.

Federation expresses a particular form of institutional and structural arrangement by which federalism is given institutional application. It refers to a political community in which power is constitutionally divided and shared between a central government, having nationwide responsibility, and constituent governments, having local responsibility.[13] A federation can be created on the basis of either administrative/territorial boundaries or ethnic, religious and linguistic considerations. A distinction can therefore be made between territorial or administrative federalism and multinational federalism.[14] The first of these is institutionalised merely on the basis of historic internal boundaries and administrative considerations. American federalism is the first example of territorial federalism. Others include Germany, Brazil, Mexico and Australia. But as Kymlicka observes, '[f]or a federal system to qualify as genuinely multinational, decisions about boundaries and powers must consciously reflect the needs and aspirations of minority groups'.[15] Examples of such federal systems include Canada, Belgium and Spain.

From the perspective of this study, the problem with territorial federation is that it would not address the claims of minorities for self-government, or for participation through self-government, as internal boundaries are not generally drawn in a way that allows them to form a majority within the federal units.[16] There is also evidence that territorial and unitarist federalism is falling out of favour even in unitarist states such as United Kingdom and France, who are now more disposed towards decentralised autonomy regimes. On the other hand, multicultural federation aims exactly at providing self-government to minorities. In this case, the boundaries of federal units are drawn in a way that allows territorial minorities to be self-governing.[17]

---

[11] *Reference re the Secession of Quebec* (1998) 2 SCR 217 para 58 [*Re Secession of Quebec*].

[12] See W Kymlicka 'Federalism, Nationalism and Multiculturalism' in D Karmis & W Norman (eds.) *Theories of Federalism: A Reader* (2005) 269.

[13] Watts (note 4 above) 121; *Re Secession of Quebec* (note 9 above) para 56.

[14] Kymlicka (note 12 above) 273–277.

[15] Ibid, 276.

[16] Kymlicka (note 12 above) 276; W Kymlicka *Multicultural Citizenship: A Liberal Theory of Minority Rights* (1995) 29.

[17] Ibid. According to the Supreme Court of Canada federalism accordingly 'facilitates the pursuit of collective goals by cultural and linguistic minorities which form the majority within a particular province'. *Re Secession of Quebec* (note 11 above) para 59.

In terms of potential for accommodation of ethno-cultural divisions and respond to the issue of minorities, multinational federalism has received quite a considerable support in the academia[18] and increasingly in practice. The trouble with multicultural federalism is the problem of how to meet the interests of minorities with regard to self-government without compromising democratic ideals of universal reach. There is a danger of fragmenting state institutions and further accentuating the ethnic divisions that federalism is meant to regulate, particularly if the system leads to the emergence of 'exclusive' or 'mono-national' home republics.[19] In the context of this study, it is imperative to underline that the deployment of federalism is only meant to recognise and promote the interest of minorities in self-government and effective participation in the processes of the state of which they form a part.[20] Accordingly, its legitimacy should also ultimately be judged in terms of its ability, not only to accommodate diversity, but also to subject it to universal ideals of constitutional democracy, including non-discrimination, rule of law and the principles of democracy.[21]

There is no hard and fast rule about the degree of authority to be constitutionally vested in federal units; it is a matter to be determined according to the specific circumstances of each society and the nature of the issues affecting the minorities concerned. In the case of multicultural federations, it is important that federal units are assigned the powers necessary for the community or communities constituting the self-governing units to exercise effective self-government over local matters, issues of particular concern for minorities. According to the Lund Recommendations, 'the functions over which such administrations [federal units] have successfully assumed primary or significant authority include education, culture, use of minority language, environment, local planning, natural resources, economic development, local policing functions, and housing, health, and other social services'.[22] They further state that taxation, administration of justice, tourism, and transport are functions shared by central and regional authorities.

---

[18] See M Keating *Plurinational Democracy: Stateless Nations in a Post-Sovereignty Era* (Oxford: Oxford University Press, 2001); Kymlicka (1995); McGarry, J. and B. O'Leary 'The Macro-Political Regulation of Ethnic Conflict' in J. McGarry and B. O'Leary eds., *The Politics of Ethnic Conflict Regulation*. London: Routledge, (1993) 1–40; 1999. 'Federalism and Democracy: Beyond the U.S. Model' 10(4) Journal of Democracy (October 1999) 19–34.

[19] See *Cultural Liberty in Today's Diverse World* Human Development Report (2004) 52; A G Selassie 'Ethnic Federalism: Its Promise and Pitfalls for Africa' (Winter 2003) 28 *Yale J of Int L* 51.

[20] As Elazar puts it, federal principles are said to work if they can 'combine kinship (the basis of ethnicity), and consent (the basis of democratic government) into politically viable, constitutionally protected, arrangements involving territorial and non-territorial polities'. D Elazar *Federalism and the Way to Peace* (1994) 23–24.

[21] See The Lund Recommendations on the Effective Participation of National Minorities in Public Life (1999) prepared by international experts for OSCE High Commissioner on National Minorities, principles 16 and 21. See further below on principles that regulate the application of minority rights.

[22] Ibid, principle 20.

This does not, however, mean that there has to be a watertight division of power between the centre and the federal units. This is neither necessary nor practically possible. Accordingly, while the respective spheres of competence of the two domains have to be constitutionally defined as clearly as possible, and guarantees provided against either level of government encroaching upon the powers of the other, there has to be flexibility and co-ordination between the two levels for the effective and efficient exercise of their respective powers. It is also more important in the context of developing multi-ethnic societies, such as those in Africa, that such autonomy is not of such a nature that it frustrates national cohesion or undermines the emergence of effective national government necessary to advance the countries' socio-economic development.

Federalism also enhances the participation of minorities in public life by creating different levels of policy making.[23] In a federal system, minorities can effectively take part in and influence the decision-making processes through representation and participation in national as well as regional policy making.[24] The system creates this possibility by providing for institutions of both self-rule and shared rule. In federal systems, parliament is thus organised in such a way that the interests of both unity and diversity have representation and voice in the national law-making process.[25] 'In federations,' writes Preston King, 'the people are taken as a single entity, in one sense, but as a plurality in another. The people are represented *as whole* and *as parts*.'[26] The lower house of parliament in a federation is constituted on the basis of universal elections and represents the interest of the whole, while the upper house is constituted on the basis of federal units, and represents the interests of those units or the relevant differences in society.[27] Minorities can have representation in the national law-making process directly through the lower house, but mainly on the basis of citizenship and through the upper house, by being part of the federal units represented in it mainly on the basis of their group membership. They can thus ventilate their group interests in the national policymaking processes. This clearly assumes and

[23] C Young 'Ethnic Diversity and Public Policy: An Overview' in C Young (ed.) *Ethnic Diversity and Public Policy: A Comparative Inquiry* (1998) 1, 11.

[24] This is the essence of the definition of a federation by James Tully. According to him a federation is a society in which democratic self-government is distributed in such a way that citizens participate concurrently in different collectivities – in the democratic institutions of the society as a whole and of the federated members, such as provinces, states, nations or first nations. J Tully 'Introduction' in AG Gagnon & J Tully (eds.) *Multicultural Democracies* (2001) 1, 10. Also see *Re Secession of Quebec* (note 11 above) para 59.

[25] See ibid (where the Supreme Court of Canada held that federalism allows minorities to form majorities within particular provinces and made provision for their representation in the federal parliament).

[26] P King 'Federation and Representation' in M Burgess & A Gagnon (eds.) *Comparative Federalism and Federation* (1993) 95, 95–96.

[27] On the organisation of upper house of parliaments see A Fiseha *Federalism and the Accommodation of Diversity in Ethiopia* (2005/2006) Chapter 3.

requires that adequate provisions are made in the federal design for effective (not merely descriptive) representation of minorities in institutions and processes of shared rule at the centre. This also helps in tampering the centripetal tendencies that may emerge at the level of federal units.

In Africa, as noted in Chapter III, federalism has not had a good history. Consequently, many query its workability.[28] But, as Ladipo Adamolekun and John Kincaid observe, 'the failures of federalism in Africa are not peculiar to federalism; they are part of the general failure of democratic governance on the continent'.[29] Even in the case of Nigeria, federalism has had only limited success not because it is not workable, but because of the particular characteristics of the design of the federation, such as concentration of power at the centre, and the particular political, demographic and socio-economic context in which it is made to work.[30] What this says is not that federalism cannot accommodate diversity in Africa, but that its workability depends on the way it is institutionalised and the particular political and socio-economic context as well as patterns of public behaviour of the country within which it operates.[31] In this study, as well, federalism is seen only as a necessary mechanism whose efficacy depends on the political, social and legal context of particular societies.[32]

5.3. Institutionalising Effective Representation and Participation of Minorities

The institutionalisation of self-government or territorial autonomy through federalism to address minority claims is not without its limits. It can be a more effective instrument in countries where minorities are territorially concentrated. Where minorities are dispersed it may be of very limited use, although not necessarily irrelevant. Besides, the circumstances of some societies and their minorities may not require the institutionalisation of self-government structures. In that case, federalism may not provide the answer. In the context of this study, for example, such is the case with respect to groups identified as ethno-cultural minorities, as well as many ethno-political minorities in Africa. Under such

---

[28] See, for example, MW Mutua 'Why Redraw the Map of Africa: A Moral and Legal Inquiry' (1995) 16 *Michigan J Int L* 1113, 1152–1160.

[29] L Adamolekun & J Kincaid 'The Federal Solution: Assessment and Prognosis for Nigeria and Africa' 21 (1991) *Publius: The J of Federalism* 173, 174.

[30] See O Nnoli *Ethnicity and Development in Nigeria* (1995) 95.

[31] As Young pointed out, and as the case studies particularly on Ethiopia (Chapter VII below) would show, probably the strongest argument for federalism is that in large and culturally complex societies no other formula may work. Note 20 above, 11.

[32] See DJ Elazar 'International and Comparative Federalism' (June 1993) 26 (2) *Political Science and Politics* 190–195; RL Watts 'Federalism and Diversity in Canada' in Y Ghai (ed.) *Autonomy and Ethnicity: Negotiating Competing Claims in Multi-ethnic Societies* (2000) 29, 49.

circumstances, participation rights and the manner of their institutionalisation become avenues for increased minority representation and participation. Finally, even when federalism is an option, states must still make provision for minority representation and participation.

Probably the most effective, though not uncontroversial, way for achieving the effective participation of minorities is group representation.[33] As Iris Marion Young argues, this is because '[g]roup representation provides the opportunity for some to express their needs or interests who would not likely be heard without that representation'.[34] It thus enables marginalised groups to voice their interests directly and articulate the ways by which those interests can be accommodated in the process of national policy making.[35] Yash Ghai comments: 'Representation is an emphatic recognition of a positive right of the minority – to take part in the state's political processes and to influence state policies.'[36] Without such participation, members of such groups cannot fully enjoy free and equal status, nor can their marginalisation and subordination be dismantled.[37] Group representation is also the best way to ensure the recognition and institutional expression of the ethno-cultural diversity of society in the decision-making structures of the state. It is therefore necessary to provide for arrangements that secure the representation of minorities in the process of national policy making on the basis of their group characters, although the arrangements must be flexible enough not to force people into identifying themselves with particular groups and to avoid tightly institutionalised divisions.

The most important level for minority representation is the legislative process.[38] As we have seen above, in federations parliaments can be designed with two houses, with the upper house facilitating the representation of groups exercising self-government as units of federation. Another, and probably the most important, mechanism for achieving minority representation in the legislative process is the electoral system. As Steiner points out, 'the electoral structure selected for choosing a legislature ... will significantly influence the degree of representation

[33] On group representation see MS Williams 'Memory, History and Membership: The Moral Claims of Marginalized Groups in Political Representation' in J Raikka (ed.) *Do we need minority rights?* 85–119, 104–109; Kymlicka (note 10 above) Chapter 7; IM Young 'Differing Group Representation' in I Shapiro & W Kymlicka (eds.) *NOMOS XXXIX Ethnicity and group rights* (1997) 349–376.

[34] IM Young 'Polity and Group Difference: A Critique of the Ideal of Universal Citizenship' in RE Goodin & P Pettit *Contemporary Political Philosophy: An Anthology* (1997) 256, 264.

[35] See, for more, IM Young *Justice and the Politics of Difference* (1990) 184–186.

[36] Y Ghai 'Public Participation, Autonomy and Minorities' in ZA Skurbaty (eds.) *Beyond a One Dimensional State: An Emerging Right to Autonomy?* (2005) 3, 19.

[37] Williams (note 33 above) 107.

[38] See S Wheatley 'Deliberative Democracy and Minorities' (2003) 14 (3) *European J of Int L* 507, 514–518.

and power of many minority groups in society'.[39] From the perspective of the normative framework discussed above for the constitutional accommodation of diversity in multi-ethnic societies, preference should be given to an electoral system that can, in the particular circumstances of the particular country, secure both a high level of representation of members of minorities and their effective participation, without institutionalising group differences. The forms that an electoral system may take can be broadly divided into plurality or majority systems, and proportional representation (PR) and/or mixed systems.[40]

Many argue, appropriately in my view, that PR is the preferred electoral system for the just representation of minorities and their effective participation.[41] The essence of this electoral system is that votes cast are translated into a proportional number of seats for each party, and it is thus credited with fairness and inclusivity. According to Lewis, 'in a plural society, proportional representation with a few large several-member constituencies is better than electoral systems with many single-member constituencies not only because it gives more satisfaction to the minorities, but also because it reduces the geographical conflict, and the racial or other differences which go with geography'.[42] Many agree that PR better ensures fair representation of minorities in multi-ethnic societies.[43] It also does not force people to identify with particular groups.

---

[39] HJ Steiner 'Political Participation as a Human Right' in *Harvard Human Rights Yearbook* (1998) 77, 107.

[40] See generally A Reynolds, B Reilly & A Ellis with JA Chebub et al. *Electoral System Design: The New International IDEA Handbook* (2005) (hereinafter *Handbook*); A Lijphart *Electoral Systems and Party Systems: A Study of Twenty-Seven Democracies, 1945–1990* (1994).

[41] There are, however, scholars who reject PR on the ground that instead of dampening divisions it leads to their institutional entrenchment. Thus, Donald L Horowitz, for example, proposes as an alternative to PR the 'Alternative Vote' electoral system. DL Horowitz *A Democratic South Africa? Constitutional Engineering in a Divided Society* (1991) 188–203; DL Horowitz 'Electoral Systems: A Primer for Decision Makers' (October 2003) 14 *J of Democracy* 122–123. In such a system voters cast their votes by ranking their preferred candidates. If a candidate receives an absolute majority of first preferences, he or she is elected; if not, the weakest candidate is eliminated, and the ballots are redistributed according to second preferences until one of the candidates receives a majority of the votes. The aim is to ensure the election of moderate representatives. The problem with this system is that it leads to a difference-blind system of representation, and as a result would not satisfy the needs of minorities that seek fair representation and participation for their members. For further criticisms of this system, see Arend Liphart 'The Alternative Vote: A Realistic Alternative for South Africa?' (June 1991) 18 *Politikon* 9.

[42] WA Lewis *Politics in West Africa* (1965) 72.

[43] A Reynolds 'Constitutional Engineering in Southern Africa' (April 1995) 6(2) *J of Democracy* 86; A Reynolds 'The Case for Proportionality' (October 1995) 6 (4) *J of Democracy* 117; A Reynolds *Report: Electoral System and the Protection and Participation of Minorities* (2006) 11; AL 'Self-Determination Versus Pre-determination of Ethnic Minorities in Power-sharing Systems' in W Kymlicka (ed.) *The Rights of Minority Cultures* (1995) 275, 281; N Topperwien 'Participation in the Decision-Making Process as a Means of Group Accommodation' in GA Tar, RF Williams & J Marko (eds.) *Federalism, Subnational Constitutions and Minority Rights* (2004) 41–52, 47; Ghai (note 36 above) 23; A Reynolds 'The Case for Proportionality' (October 1995) 6(4) *J of Democracy* 117.

As W Arthur Lewis argued in 1965, and others have argued since then, in African plural societies electoral systems that yield governments based on a simple aggregation of votes and majority rule are not to be preferred over those that deliver an inclusive or power-sharing government. PR systems are better suited to deliver such inclusive government. It makes the opportunity to participate in the political processes of the state available to all minorities who seek representation and participation, and thereby minimises the pattern of ethnic rivalry for control or a share of state power that the winner-takes-all system tends to produce.[44]

The PR system, however, is defended here only as a basic institutional design feature for facilitating minority representation. Effective minority representation may in particular situations call for additional arrangements.[45] Accordingly, to accommodate the situation of highly marginalised sections of society, such as the San in Botswana or South Africa, and other peripheral minorities whose representation may not be secured through the mere application of a PR system, states may have to complement it with other methods, such as reserved seats or quotas.[46] The constitutional approach that India adopted vis-à-vis the untouchables or the scheduled castes is a good example that illustrates the need for and the practical application of measures to redress exclusions suffered by highly disadvantaged communities. Once such highly marginalised minorities achieve a degree of socio-economic, cultural and political inclusion sufficient to mitigate their marginalisation, these special arrangements may be removed. '[I]n so far as these rights are seen as a response to oppression or systematic disadvantage,' writes Kymlicka, 'they are most probably seen as a temporary measure on the way to a society where the need for special representation no longer exists.' He adds that 'society should seek to remove the oppression and disadvantage, thereby eliminating the need for these rights'.[47]

The representation of minorities does not necessarily guarantee their effective participation. Once represented in the law-making structures of a state, they need to be given opportunities to contribute to the legislative process. It is important in this regard that minorities are also allowed representation in the various committees, hearings and processes of legislative bodies. Additionally, the promotion and affirmation of diversity in the legislative process can ensure that minority representatives get the opportunity to represent, sufficiently articulate, and defend the interests of minorities.

---

[44] See UNDP Human Development Report 2004 (note 19 above) 54.

[45] Young (note 35 above) 187–188.

[46] Ghai (note 36 above). This is done in many countries, such as Venezuela, Romania, India, Jordan, Niger, Slovenia, Colombia, Croatia and Burundi. See, for example, Human Development Report 2004 (note 19 above) 54.

[47] Kymlicka (note 12 above) 32.

Most importantly, minority representation can be translated into effective participation in countries with a deliberative and participatory democratic process.[48] As many scholars of deliberative democracy argue,[49] and the South African case study in Chapter VI shows, such a system guarantees that minorities are given the opportunity, notwithstanding their representation in the legislature, to have their say and to have their views accommodated, particularly on matters that are of direct concern to them. It affords an opportunity to examine national policies and laws and their impacts through the prism of the interests and needs of minority groups. This approach is capable of transforming post-colonial African politics from a zero-sum game of 'winner takes all' into an all-inclusive process of participatory decision-making. It would also lead, it is hoped, to greater unity and solidarity in society:

> For one thing, political decision making would be seen as more legitimate since every one would have a fair chance to have their views heard and considered. Moreover, the very fact that people share the experience of deliberating in common provides a tangible bond that connects citizens and encourages greater mutual understanding and empathy.[50]

This view emphasises the existence of adequate mechanisms and opportunities to facilitate direct public participation of minorities in decision-making processes, as envisaged in Articles 2(2) and (3) of the 1992 Declaration on Minority Rights. These may include special procedures and arrangements through which minorities can bring relevant facts to decision-makers, articulate and defend their views, propose alternative courses of action, and generally get the opportunity to be heard or become co-decision makers. It is accordingly maintained here that combining PR with such robust forms of participatory/deliberative democratic processes would give minorities adequate voice or influence in the processes of the state.

Minority representation and participation should not be limited to the law-making process alone.[51] They should cover the whole range of the conduct of public affairs. According to General Comment 25 of the UN HRC:

---

[48] See MS Williams 'The Uneasy Alliance of Group Representation and Deliberative Democracy' in W Kymlicka & W Norman (eds.) *Citizenship in Diverse Societies* (2000) 124–152; Wheatley (note 38 above) 509–514.

[49] See Williams (as above); Monique Deveaux *Cultural Pluralism and Dilemmas of Justice* (2000); Anne Phillips *Which Equalities Matter?* (1999) Chapters 4 & 5.

[50] A Patten & W Kymlicka 'Introduction: Language Rights and Political Theory: Context, Issues, and Approaches' in A Patten & W Kymlicka (eds.) *Language Rights and Political Theory* (2003) 1, 1. See also M Deveaux *Cultural Pluralism and Dilemmas of Justice* (2000) 5 & Chapter 5–6; *Democratic Alliance & Another v Masondo NO & Another* 2003 (2) SA 413 (CC) 2006, (12) BCLR 1399 (CC) para. 115.

[51] See Wheatley (note 38 above) 515.

> Conduct of public affairs … is a broad concept which relates to the exercise of political power, in particular the exercise of legislative, executive and administrative powers … covering *all aspects of public administration*, and the formulation and *implementation of policy* at international, national, regional and local levels.[52]

It is therefore important that minorities are represented in executive, administrative and judicial institutions as well. Yash Ghai rightly points out that there are many good reasons for this. 'A great deal of state policy and regulation are made by public servants, and it is appropriate that officials of minorities should be able to participate in those processes.'[53] Moreover, '[d]ecisions on policy and implementation are better informed and improved through the input of minorities'. This broader representation also enhances the identification of minorities with the state and its institutions, and hence nurtures national integration. 'The access of minorities to the public service and their relations with state services are greatly facilitated and improved if they can deal with officials from their community.'[54] The quota system is one possible mechanism for effecting such representation, but such a rigid mechanism may be necessary only in sharply divided societies such as Burundi, and, as the Indian experience shows, for fast-tracking the inclusion of highly marginalised groups. It may therefore be more relevant in the African context in countries with peripheral minorities ro comunities with similar level of marginalisation and disadvantage. Otherwise, greater minority participation can also be effected through a constitutional provision that requires institutions of government to be representative of the diversity of the society and by implementing policies that incrementally guarantee the representation of minorities in the structures of state institutions.

5.4. Language and Cultural Policies, and Guarantees for Cultural, Religious and Linguistic Rights

With respect to language, the most important issues to be addressed include the use of minority languages in communication with public authorities, including courts, and the use of minority languages in public media and in education. To the extent that the language situation of different countries and groups are different, the determination of the appropriate language policy and minority-language guarantees should be decided contextually. The most important thing is that – in order to give optimal constitutional application to the value of cultural identity, the need to revitalise African languages hitherto neglected and suppressed, and

---

[52] UN Human Rights Committee General Comment 25 (57) UN Doc. CCPR/C/21/Rev.1/Add.7 (1996) para. 5.

[53] Y Ghai *Public Participation and Minorities* MRG Report (2003) 12.

[54] Ibid.

to give equality of opportunity in access to public sphere, as discussed above – consideration has to be given to guarantee the use of minority languages in various spheres of public life, including in communication with state authorities.

Given the multiplicity of languages spoken in most African states, as in other multilingual countries such as India, states cannot be said to have the obligation to provide all public services in every language that members of the public might speak. Accordingly, the determination of whether public authorities should use minority languages in their dealings with members of such language groups depends on a number of factors. The 'sliding-scale' approach offers an important standard in this regard.[55] According to this approach, the right of minorities to use their language in communication with public authorities depends upon the size of their population, their territorial concentration, the capacity of the state, and the nature of the service in question.[56] Of course, to this one can add the expressed or manifest need of minorities. This is important particularly with respect to numerically small groups, for whom the use of their own language may have the undesirable consequence of marginalising them from the mainstream political and economic processes.

This clearly acknowledges that in multilingual societies, such as those in most African states, neither justice nor equality demands that all languages be given equal legal status, other than at a normative level, in terms of their use for public purposes. The implication of this is that in such societies states are expected to provide public services and communication in minority languages in places where speakers of those languages are found in significant numbers, the public services in question are of a very important nature, and the resources required to provide the public services can be made available without unduly compromising the distribution of resources in other areas of public demand as well.[57] In the African context, since most groups are territorially concentrated and most social and economic affairs are conducted at local levels in the regional or local vernacular, the recognition and use of minority languages in the conduct of public affairs can best be institutionalised at the regional or local levels. Within the limits of the above considerations, African states should accordingly recognise, for government purposes, the use of local vernaculars at the regional or local levels. At the national level, however, the most widely spoken language/s can be designated as (the) official language/s, as the common

---

[55] F de Varennes *Language, Minorities & Human Rights* (1996) 177.

[56] See F de Varennes 'A Guide to the Rights of Minorities and Language' COLPI Paper No 4 (2001) 30. These various considerations are spelt out in the Oslo Recommendations of the OSCE HCNM Regarding the Linguistic Rights of National Minorities particularly principles 13–15.

[57] De Varennes (note 55 above) 177–178. Also see J Packer's formula of expressed desires + genuine needs against real possibilities. J Packer 'On the Content of Minority Rights' in J Räikkaä (ed.) *Do We Need Minority Rights?* (1996) 121–178, 143–144.

medium of communication necessary for the proper functioning of a modern society particularly where these languages are spoken by individuals belonging to different language groups.[58] Since states should facilitate the learning of such official language/s by members of minorities without depriving them of the freedom to choose the language they wish to use, the national official language/s should be made to operate alongside the regional languages where the latter are official at regional or local levels. This balances the interest of having a common national language with the need to recognise local languages to empower their hitherto neglected speakers. A practical example for such an approach relevant for the African context can be found from the experience of post-colonial India.[59]

The use of minority languages in the conduct of public affairs covers, and is also particularly important in, education and the media.[60] These are important tools for the reproduction and maintenance of not only the cultures of groups, but also their languages. As Adeno Addis has argued, they are also instrumental in nurturing genuine dialogue across difference and developing a strong sense of pluralistic solidarity in multi-ethnic societies.[61] Issues of particular importance with respect to the use of minority languages in education include the provision of public education in minority languages, the establishment of private educational institutions, and the content of curricula.

The concern with cultural identity and equality in access to education, as per the discussion on the normative framework, entails that minorities are guaranteed the right to receive education in their languages, but, once again, subject to the considerations of the sliding-scale approach. Accordingly, 'a state would only be expected to provide education in a certain language if the linguistic group concerned is of a certain size and only in areas where the group reaches a certain concentration'.[62] Nevertheless, as De Varennes argues, '[m]embers of a minority have, at minimum, the right to be taught their language in public schools (as a subject) where practical and justified, even if their numbers are not sufficient for the use of their language as the medium of instruction in public schools'.[63] The qualification 'where practical and justified' mainly relates to, among other

---

[58] See 'Ali A Mazrui and Alamin M. Mazrui *The Power of Babel: Language and Governance in the African Experience* (1998) Chapter 7.

[59] Vasuki Nesiah 'Federalism and Diversity in India' in Yash Ghai (ed.) *Autonomy and Ethnicity; Negotiating Competing Claims in Multiethnic States* (2000) 53, 55.

[60] See Oslo Recommendations (note 56 above).

[61] See A Addis 'On Human Diversity and the Limits of Toleration' in Shapiro and Kymlicka (note 33 above) 112.

[62] K Henrard *Devising an Adequate System of Minority Protection: Individual Human Rights, Minority Rights and the Right to Self-Determination* (2000) 260–261.

[63] De Varennes (note 55 above) 33. Henrard similarly argues that partial satisfaction can be given to the right to education in minority languages in the context of developing multi-ethnic societies through multilingual education, whereby the various languages spoken by students are used as medium of instruction for certain courses or during certain time blocks. Note 57 above, 261.

things, factors such as the number of minority students seeking education in their language and the extent of the burden this puts on public resources. Where resource limitations mean that minority children are not taught in their languages, it may be necessary to make adequate provision to assist them in learning in the official language.

As already observed, education in minority languages is also given effect through the right of linguistic minorities to establish their own educational institutions subject to national standards of quality education. Although generally it is for the group members to bear the costs of such institutions, in certain circumstances the state may bear the costs or provide subsidies. In the light of Article 5(1)(*c*) of the UNESCO Convention on the Elimination of Discrimination in Education and the requirements of substantive equality as discussed above, the state bears such costs where the minority lacks sufficient financial resources and where public schools are not sufficiently pluralistic to give satisfaction to minority-language education.[64]

As far as the content of education curricula is concerned, the normative framework discussed above enjoins states to adopt a multicultural approach.[65] The education curricula should reflect, to the extent possible, in an objective and non-pejorative way, the culture, history, language and traditions of all ethno-cultural groups within states, particularly those of historically disadvantaged or marginalised groups.[66] Ideally, the text materials to be used should also be representative of the perspectives of members of different sections of society.

The most important aspects of the use of minority languages in the media relate to the establishment of print or electronic media in minority languages, and support for printing in minority languages and provision of access to public broadcasting. The first aspect is guaranteed in international instruments as part of the right of minorities to establish their own institutions, which includes media.[67] With respect to state support for printing and broadcasting, it is reasonable to argue that the full realisation of the rights of minorities, particularly those concerning participation and recognition as well as equality, can be understood as entailing that states provide meaningful support for printing in minority languages and, most importantly, access to minority-language broadcasting, particularly the allocation of frequencies for the purpose.[68] It is only where minorities are supplied with the information they need that they can meaningfully

[64] Henrard (note 62 above) 267.

[65] See Article 4 of the 1992 UN Declaration on the Rights of Minorities and Article 12 of the Framework Convention.

[66] Henrard (note 62 above) 262–265.

[67] See De Varennes (note 55 above) 217–225.

[68] Ibid, 223. Also see principle III Resolution on the Adoption of the Declaration on Principles of Freedom of Expression in Africa; principles 9 & 10 of the Oslo Recommendations Regarding the Linguistic Rights of National Minorities.

participate in and engage with the political process, and achieve the substantive equality that affirms the equal worth of individuals, not just as citizens, but as members of particular cultures. Language is the vehicle through which these aims are achieved. Once again the sliding-scale approach applies in determining the extent of state obligation in this area. Accordingly, the size and geographical concentration of the minority population, the capacity of the state concerned, and the needs and interests of minorities should be taken into account.

In the area of cultural rights, an important area in the African context relates to the recognition of customary law. In many African countries, most people continue to regulate their lives and their relationships on the basis of customary law. It accordingly also serves for many minorities as an important institution for the development and preservation of their cultures and traditions. The recognition of the right to cultural identity can therefore be given application through legal recognition of customary law.[69] This allows members of particular cultures or religions to regulate some aspects of their life and relationships on the basis of their traditional or religious norms, and thereby participate in the enjoyment or practice of their culture or religion.[70]

As indicated in the discussion on culture, another dimension of the cultural rights of minorities is exemption rights. These rights relieve members of minorities from complying with otherwise legitimate rules in order to enable them observe their cultural or religious commitments.[71] This forms part of what Kymlicka calls 'polyethnic rights', which 'are intended to help ethnic groups and religious minorities express their cultural particularity and pride without it hampering their success in the economic and political institutions of the dominant society'.[72] Underlying exemption rights is the recognition that ostensibly neutral laws that require citizens to comply with standard norms of behaviour as a condition for public opportunities impose an undue or disproportionate burden on those whose culture requires them to behave in ways that do not conform to such norms. The equal treatment of these minorities therefore entails, within the bounds of limitations that are reasonable and rational in democratic societies, that they be exempted from the requirements of such general norms. There are some who consider exemptions as giving minorities advantages that are not

[69] It is what Levy calls the 'recognition' or 'enforcement' right. See JT Levy 'Classifying Group Rights' in Shapiro & Kymlicka (note 33 above) 36–40.

[70] On the most preferred form that such regulatory power by religious or traditional authorities can take, with due regard to the individual rights of members, particularly women, see A Shachar 'Should Church and State be Joined at the Altar? Women's Rights and the Multicultural Dilemma' in Kymlicka & Norman (note 48 above) 199–223. On various models of customary law see JT Levy 'Three Methods of Incorporating Indigenous Law' in Kymlicka & Norman (ibid) 297–325.

[71] See Levy (note 69) 25–29.

[72] Kymlicka (note 12 above) 31.

available to others and hence contrary to the requirements of equality itself.[73] This is attributable partly to the view that cultural or religious commitments are like expensive tests and partly to the view that somehow those who are not exempted are as a result disadvantaged. The first view fails to recognise properly the extent to which our culture or religion defines the way we relate to the world in general and hence is not something that can be abandoned by choice. The second is also flawed, in the sense that giving exemption to those with certain cultural or religious commitments would not in any way affect others, since the law does not share the burden that it imposes on those who ask for exemptions on account of their religion or culture.

5.5. Socio-economic Guarantees, Including Positive Measures

A characteristic of ethnic diversity in Africa, as in many multi-ethnic societies, is unequal patterns of distribution of socio-economic benefits and opportunities among ethnic groups and regions. These manifest not only in educational, economic, and social inequalities among groups but also in political and bureaucratic inequalities. The institutional and normative arrangements for accommodating diversity accordingly require, for their success, socio-economic policies that redress past discrimination and current patterns of inequalities, and guarantee future equality.[74]

To this end it is imperative that socio-economic rights, including the right of peoples to development and to dispose of their natural resources as enunciated under the International Covenant on Economic, Social, Cultural Rights and the African Charter on Human and Peoples' Rights, are constitutionally guaranteed. Although many of these rights are generally expressed as individual rights to the benefit of 'everyone', in their application they can be used to benefit minorities in two ways. First, they can operate to allow the provision of special measures to remedy the socio-economic disadvantages of minorities, expressed in part by their material deprivation and their extremely low level of access to education, health and public employment.[75] As noted above, international human rights norms both support and require that states adopt positive measures necessary

---

[73] See B Barry *Culture and Equality: An Egalitarian Critique of Multiculturalism* (2001) 40–50. For a response to Barry's critique of multicultural accommodation see P Kelly (ed.) *Multiculturalism Reconsidered: Culture and Equality and its Critiques* (2002).

[74] See Ghai (note 53 above) 11. Young in this regard says that 'no one disputes the importance of overall economic growth as one key policy objective; there is some truth in the adage that a rising tide lifts all boats. But metaphorical reasoning has its limits; some ethnic vessels may be stranded as the tide of prosperity rises, and compensatory measures are indispensable to sustain ethnic accommodation.' Young (note 23 above) 23.

[75] See P Justino & J Litchfield *Economic Exclusion and Discrimination: The Experiences of Minorities and Indigenous Peoples* MRG Issue Paper (2003).

to minimise or eliminate socio-economic disparities among groups. The Special Rapporteur on Minorities, Asbjorn Eide, states in his report 'Possible Ways and Means of Facilitating the Peaceful and Constructive Solution of Problems Involving Minorities':

> In those situations where *members of particular minorities* are economically in a weaker position than members of majorities, measures of affirmative action should be adopted on a transitional basis to redress the inequality. In that respect specific policies should be formulated in cooperation with the members of vulnerable groups to achieve equality of opportunity and access.[76]

The aim of these measures is not just to redress past inequities suffered by ethnic minorities. Such measures are also necessary 'in order to avoid relegation (of minorities) to an economic and social backwater, excluded from mainstream improvements'.[77] This invariably means that a wide range of specially tailored measures will also be required in various areas of the socio-economic life of society, including access to health, education and public-service recruitment. Generally, however, states have to adopt socio-economic regimes that fairly distribute the benefits and burdens of living under a common government among members of society, and group membership may accordingly be a factor in such a regime.

The design of positive measures to rectify past discrimination and reduce existing inequalities must ensure that they offer various opportunities and benefits not only to members of minorities that are well off but also, and most importantly, to poor members of such minorities. Moreover, special measures will fail to attract wide societal support and will be less effective if they simply focus on shifting opportunities and benefits from one section of society to another without expanding them and creating new ones. It is therefore important that special measures are designed and implemented within the framework of economic policies that invest in job creation and new development initiatives and socio-economic opportunities.[78]

With respect to groups regarded in this study as peripheral minorities, such as indigenous peoples who depend for their socio-economic and cultural survival

---

[76] A Eide *Possible Ways and Means of Facilitating the Peaceful and Constructive Solution of Problems Involving Minorities* Addendum 4, Recommendations, E/C.4/Sub.2/1993/34/Add.4, para 14 (my emphasis).

[77] P Thornberry 'The UN Declaration on the Rights of Persons Belonging to National or Ethnic, Religious and Linguistic Minorities: Background, Analysis, Observation, and an Update' in A Philips & A Rosas (eds.) *Universal Minority Rights* (1995) 13, 49.

[78] A special-measure regime that is widely acknowledged for its success is the one adopted by Malaysia. This Malaysian experience shows the importance of such approaches for the success and society-wide legitimacy of special measures. See DR Snodgrass *Successful Economic Development in a Multiethnic Society: The Malaysian Experience* <http://www.earth.columbia.edu/sitefiles/File/about/director/pubs/503.pdf>.

on land and natural resources, socio-economic guarantees are best formulated to include rights to land and resources. These include, in particular, access to and control over land, including security of occupation of the land the minority has historically inhabited and the utilisation of its resources, as well as the right to a share of the proceeds of the exploitation of resources from the land that they inhabit. Given the special attachment that such groups have to their land and the use of its resources, and the importance thereof to their survival, when state authorities venture into using these territories and the resources in them for public purposes special attention should be given not to dislocate them entirely and deny their means of survival.[79]

5.6. The Nature and Limits of Minority Rights and the Principles Regulating Them

In any discussion on minority rights one of the most contentious issues is their nature. The controversy often centres on whether the subjects of the rights are individuals or groups. I argue, following Kymlicka, that the determinant of the character of the right as a group right is not necessarily tied to the question of who holds the right.[80] Indeed, it can be said that that question is irrelevant. The most important determinant is the interest that is protected by those rights. The discussions in this chapter and in Chapter I reveal that minority rights are essentially group rights. Their essence as such is that they protect, firstly, the identity and other interests (socio-economic and political) of individuals *as members of minorities* and, secondly, the linguistic or cultural attributes of the group whose protection is necessary for the identity, self-respect and personal development of its members. It is clear that what minority rights protect is an interest that is shared by, or common to, the members of the minority on account of their membership, and hence is, by its character, a group interest.

Another related characteristic of minority rights that signifies their nature as group rights is that, unlike individual human rights, they depend upon group membership. As Charles Taylor shows, universal human rights are based on what all human beings have in common: their equal worth or dignity. Being human is the basis for entitlement to universal human rights, and therefore whether one is black or white, Amhara or Oromo is irrelevant. But group membership is the basis for the recognition of minority rights, hence the reference to them as group rights.

---

[79] See *Ilmari Länsman et al. v Finland* (Communication No. 511/1992) UN Doc. Supp. No. 40 (A/50/40) 66 (1992) (HRC); *Jouni E. Länsman et al. v Finland* (Communication 671/1995) UN Doc. Supp. No. 40 (A/52/40) 191 (1996) (HRC).

[80] See Kymlicka (note 12 above) Chapter 3.

Notwithstanding that they are essentially group rights, minority rights can be exercised by individual members of the group or by the group as a whole, or in a federation by the federal state or province within which the minority forms a majority.[81] One objection that is often raised to minority rights is their frequently assumed problematic relationship to individual human rights. Some critics of minority rights tend to conceive of them as a threat to individual human rights.[82] This conception wrongly depicts minority rights and universal human rights as essentially irreconcilable. This is partly attributable to the possible tension that may arise between minority rights as group rights and the individual rights of members of minorities. Partly, it is based on the fear that accepting minority rights suggests prioritising the group over the individual. All these are pertinent issues that should not be dismissed out of hand. But to a large extent they are a result of a misconception of the nature of minority rights.

It is true that conflicts can arise between minority and individual human rights. This nevertheless does not necessarily suggest that the former are invalid. As Akermark argues, the rejection of such rights

> on the basis of risks to individual rights ignores the fact that conflicts of rights are common also as regards individual rights, thus leading to a debate about priorities. In other words, the existence of conflicts calls for a balancing of the underlying interests. If one accepts the recognition of collective rights this does not imply automatically that those rights should always be given priority.[83]

Therefore, the recognition of minority rights does not imply the communitarian logic that group rights take precedence over individual rights.[84] It is also clear that conflicts that may arise in particular circumstances between minority and individual rights are not, and should not necessarily be seen, as being significantly any different from conflicts between different individual rights.[85] Accordingly,

---

[81] Ibid, 45.

[82] N Glazer 'Individual Rights against Group Rights' in Kymlicka (note 43 above) 123;

[83] AS Akermark *Justification of Minority Protection in International Law* (1996) 44–45.

[84] The fear that minority rights may lead to the precedence of the community over the individual is a result of the association of minority rights with communitarianism and individual rights with liberalism. As Casalas observes, it is this association that often leads to the unfortunate depiction of group rights as being incompatible with individual rights. See NT Casalas *Group Rights as Human Rights: A Liberal Approach to Multiculturalism* (2006) Chapter I. Casalas effectively demonstrates in Chapter II of this work that group rights need not be seen as conflicting with individual rights in that way.

[85] Charles Taylor maintains that the difficulties faced as a result of the tension or conflict that may arise between the two categories of rights 'are not in principle greater than those encountered by any liberal society that has to combine, for example, liberty and equality, or prosperity and justice'. C Taylor 'The Politics of Recognition' in A Gutmann (ed.) *Multiculturalism: Examining the Politics of Recognition* (1994) 59–60. Similarly, Gillian Triggs maintains that 'individual rights are frequently balanced both with other individual rights and with the interests of a democratic society (the latter a collective interest)'. G Triggs 'The Rights of "Peoples" and Individual Rights: Conflict or Harmony?' in J Crawford (ed.) *The Rights of Peoples* (1992) 141, 144.

the resolution of a conflict that may arise should be determined on a case by case basis rather than by applying prior principles.[86]

There is, however, a need for a certain caveat here. It is important to note that there are certain rights that should not be limited on account of minority rights. As many scholars have argued, this leads to making a distinction between rights that should be observed at all times and others whose limitation on account of minority rights can be defended. Thus, for example, Charles Taylor speaks of the distinction between

> fundamental liberties, those that should never be infringed and therefore ought to be unassailably entrenched, on the one hand, from privileges and immunities that are important, but that can be revoked or restricted for reasons of public policy – although one needs a strong reason to do this – on the other.[87]

Within the international human rights framework, such a distinction can be gathered from the differentiation between derogable and non-derogable rights. Triggs observes: 'Most human rights instruments permit derogation from at least some of the rights they define, giving a temporary priority to the state in public emergencies "threatening the life of the nation".'[88] At the same time, these instruments exclude any derogation from certain fundamental rights even in situations of emergency.

Following almost the same line of analysis, Martin Scheinin identifies what he calls 'a tentative list of human rights that must enjoy absolute protection in relation to the regulatory authority of a minority community'.[89] These include the right to life (in all its dimensions); the prohibition against torture and inhuman, degrading or cruel treatment; the prohibition against all slavery-like practices; the prohibition against deprivation of liberty, save for cases where legislation explicitly prescribes powers of detention and they are subject to appropriate safeguards, including court review; and the prohibition against grave forms of discrimination.[90]

---

[86] This can also be gathered from the jurisprudence of the UNHRC with respect to Article 27 of the ICCPR. Whereas in the *Lovelace* case it found that the way the group sought to secure its right was contrary to the individual right of Lovelace, who as a result was excluded from membership; in *Kitok* it did not hold such exclusion to be a violation of the right of the individual. See *Sandra Lovelace v Canada* (Communication No. 24/1977) U.N. Doc. Supp. No. 40 (A/36/40) 166 (1981) (HRC) [Hereinafter Lovelace]; *Ivan Kitok v Sweden* (Communication No. 197/1985) UN Doc. Supp. No. 40 (A/43/40) 221 (1988) (HRC).

[87] Taylor (note 85 above) 59.

[88] Triggs (note 85 above) 144.

[89] M Scheinin 'How to Resolve Conflicts Between Individual and Collective Rights' in M Scheinin & R Toivanen (eds.) *Rethinking Non-Discrimination and Minority Rights* (2004) 233–234.

[90] As Scheinin points out, inasmuch as they relate to the very core of the group's identity and hence are based on objective and reasonable grounds in specific situations, distinctions based on group membership or other grounds cannot be presumed to constitute discrimination and hence can be justified as the necessary consequence of the rights of the group to practice its culture or religion. Ibid, 234.

The normative defence of minority rights in the form elaborated in this book and the identification of the relevant institutional and policy arrangements necessary for accommodating ethno-cultural diversity is no guarantee of success in addressing the issue of minorities. The success of the institutional and policy arrangements and the specific minority rights guarantees depends on the political and socio-cultural context defined by the values, beliefs, and attitudes of a people which orient their political behaviour. In addition to a brief descriptive analysis of the nature of minority rights as defended in this book, the other purpose of this section is accordingly to identify those socio-political and legal values and principles the adherence to which facilitates success for minority rights.

Minority rights, like individual rights, are also subject to various other limitations and regulated by principles of constitutional democracy. As the jurisprudence of the HRC shows, the exercise of some of these rights is subject to considerations of the interests of other members of society or public policy, where the latter has a reasonable and objective justification.[91] Moreover, the exercise of minority rights is also subject to the regulation of certain important principles of democracy and constitutionalism. In the context of multi-ethnic democracies, one such principle is that of mutual recognition or reciprocity.[92] According to this principle, the recognition of the rights of minorities entails that minorities (a) respect the rights and interests of internal minorities, including those individuals residing in a federal unit controlled by a minority, and (b) accept the authority of the state to enforce the rights of such internal minorities or common citizenship rights in general.[93] From the perspective of international law, this latter aspect of the principle can be taken as an expression of the obligation of the state to maintain and enforce internationally recognised human rights, which is an aspect of common citizenship.[94] It is also an embodiment of the principles of equality and non-discrimination.[95] As Asbjørn Eide puts it, '[w]here pluralist arrangements are contemplated, they should ideally be limited in such a way as not to prevent the state from being able to ensure,

---

91 See, for example, *Lovelace* (note 86 above) para. 16.

92 See J Tully *Strange Multiplicity: Constitutionalism in an Age of Diversity* (1995) 165–176, particularly at 167. Also see Also see Case U 5/98, Request for Evaluation of Constitutionality of Certain Provisions of the Constitution of Republika Srpska and the Constitution of the Federation of BiH, Partial Decision (Constitutional Ct. Bosn. & Herze. July 1, 2000), available at <http:// ccbh.ba/ decisions> (last accessed June 4, 2008).

93 See L Green 'Internal Minorities and their Rights' in Kymlicka (note 43 above) 256.

94 See A Eide 'Minority Protection and World Order: Towards a Framework for Law and Policy' in Phillips and Rosas (note 77 above) 99.

95 See, for example, Article 20 of the Framework Convention for the Protection of National Minorities.

without discrimination, the enjoyment of human rights to everyone under their jurisdiction'.[96]

The implication of this is that minority rights should operate alongside universal human rights. As Charles Taylor puts it, a society committed to collective goals can be liberal not only where 'it is capable of respecting diversity' but also where 'it can offer adequate safeguards for fundamental rights'.[97] The relationship between the two can *generally* be one of complementarity and interdependence. The guarantee of human rights to all individuals ensures that a common civic bond pervades the whole political community, a bond that coexists, without mutual conflict, alongside each individual's particularist attachments and loyalties specific to group membership and a particular territory or jurisdiction.[98] To the extent that these are rights that define the status of all individuals, including members of minorities, as citizens, respect for these rights by minorities is also respect for their own rights of citizenship. On the other hand, minority rights give substantive recognition and protection to the interests of individuals as members of minority groups.

In the context of multi-ethnic federations, this principle entails that federal units, which serve as the structure of self-government for minorities that form majorities within such units, should not be institutionalised and operate as the exclusive possession of such minorities.[99] If such units are meant to give institutional expression to the distinct characters of such minorities within the national population, the same logic dictates that they should reflect in their structures the diversity of their territory.[100] Rainer Baubock argues that 'even with regard to national cultural matters the (regional) majority cannot legitimately govern in a way that exclusively promotes its own interests … claiming for itself a federal privilege to establish its own regional cultural hegemony obliges it to honour similar claims by cultural minorities living in its own territory … it must provide

---

[96] Eide (note 94 above) 102.

[97] Taylor (note 92 above) 59.

[98] S Assefa 'Of Federalism and Secession' in *Constitutionalism: Reflections and Recommendations, Symposium on the Making of the New Ethiopian Constitution* (1993) 113, 118.

[99] A G Selassie 'Ethnic Identity and Constitutional Design for Africa' (Fall 1992–1993) 29 (1) *Stanford J of Int L* 1, 50; See para 33 of the Copenhagen Document, according to which measures that states adopt should be 'in conformity with the principles of equality and non-discrimination with respect to other citizens'. *The Document of the Copenhagen Meeting of the Conference on the Human Dimension of the Conference on Security and Cooperation in Europe (CSCE)* (29 June 1990) reprinted in (1990) 29 ILM 1305. The explanatory note to the Lund Recommendations provides in its para 21 that '[w]here powers may be devolved on a territorial basis to improve the effective participation of minorities, these powers must be exercised with due account for the minorities within these jurisdictions. Administrative and executive authorities must be accountable to the whole population of the territory.' Note 18 above, 31.

[100] See Tully (note 92 above) 167.

opportunities for a public representation of minority cultures'.[101] This dictates that there shall be avenues for effective participation of regional minorities at the regional level as well through various mechanisms. In developing multi-ethnic societies, where democratic institutions and practices are weak, particularly at sub-national/regional levels, federal arrangements should institutionalise some form of power-sharing arrangements for minorities within federal units.[102] At a minimum, there should be guarantees of non-discrimination and cultural rights specific to regional minorities.[103]

The other related principle is that of stability.[104] This principle recognises that the institutionalisation of mechanisms for the accommodation of diversity can have adverse effects on stability or national cohesion of a society. For this reason, it is generally regarded that, in giving expression to minority rights, a balance should be struck between stability and unity, on the one hand, and multi-cultural accommodation and diversity, on the other.[105] This may not be achieved by constitutional design alone. The point is that in institutionalising mechanisms for accommodation of diversity, sufficient attention must be paid to the requirements of stability and unity. Related to this is the principle of common national identity. The recognition and institutionalisation of membership-based rights and institutions should not obstruct the achievement of a common national identity.[106] In other words, mechanisms should be provided to meet both the interests of particularity and the need for nurturing and maintaining a common national identity. The common national identity envisaged is not the nation-state model of a homogenous national identity. It is rather what Patten calls multinational identity, which is expressed in terms of a 'commitment to the ideal of making a social order in which different national groups have different objects of identification and different modes of belonging but share willingness to live together under arrangements which reflect and endorse the pluralistic

[101] R Baubock 'Why Stay Together? A Pluralist Approach to Secession and Federation' in Kymlicka and Norman (note 45 above) 366, 386.

[102] See Y Ghai 'Ethnicity and Autonomy: A Framework for Analysis' in Ghai (note 32 above) 1, 22.

[103] Ibid; Watts (note 32 above) 41. See also, on language rights of regional minorities, A Patten 'The Rights of Internal Linguistic Minorities' in A Eisenberg & J Spinner-Halv (eds.) *Minorities within Minorities: Equality, Rights and Diversity* (2005) 135–154.

[104] See W Norman 'Justice and Stability in Multinational Societies' in Gagnon & Tully (note 24 above) 90.

[105] Justice Albie Sachs of the Constitutional Court of South Africa in this regard held that any open and democratic society based on human dignity, equality and freedom in which conscientious and religious freedom has to be regarded with appropriate seriousness can cohere only if all its participants accept that certain basic norms and standards are binding. See *Christian Education South Africa v Minister of Education* 2000 (4) SA 757 (CC), 2000 (10) BCLR 1051 (CC) para 35.

[106] See Kymlicka (note 12 above) Chapter 9 ; A Patten 'Liberal Citizenship in Multicultural Societies' in Gagnon & Tully (note 24 above) 279.

character of their society'.[107] A country that best exemplifies the pursuit of national cohesion while respecting and giving due recognition to ethno-cultural plurality is India. In the historical narrative, political discourse and constitutional vision of India, national cohesion draws from shared history, long established political tradition of tolerance, and a constitutional and political commitment for equality, mutual recognition and peaceful coexistence.

Another important principle is that of democracy.[108] This principle insists that the exercise of minority rights, like the exercise of individual rights, should be on the basis of, and abide by, democratic processes. In part, this is very much related to the point made above with respect to the rights of individual members of minorities, as it underscores individual freedom. Accordingly, while operating within the framework of their culture or religion, minorities are expected to respect the freedom of their individual members.[109] On the other hand, minorities should also respect the democratic processes and values of the national community of which they form a part. This in particular means that in the exercise of their rights, members of minorities have to abide by the requirements of respect for the interests and identity of others, and of dialogue.[110]

The adherence of the institutions of the state and large segments of the society with the principle of democracy is also of particular importance in terms of establishing the conditions necessary for the optimal operation and success of the appropriate constitutional design defended and elaborated in this book for accommodation of the identities and interests of members of diverse groups. In other words, it is only where there is both constitutional and actual commitment to the ideals of democracy that such a constitutional design can genuinely and legitimately accommodate group identities and interests.

Finally, minority rights are also informed by the principle of constitutionalism and rule of law. This entails that the enforcement or exercise of minority rights has to comply with the processes laid down under the constitution and such other relevant laws that are made following due procedure, including the participation of minorities.[111] Important aspects of this are the requirements of equality and non-discrimination. These are expressed, among other things, by the principle of proportionality. As Brownlie puts it, 'the modalities of the

---

[107] Patten (ibid) 295. Also see Kymlicka (note 12 above) 190 (speaking of the need to have 'deep diversity' as a basis for social unity in multi-ethnic societies, in the sense of not only respect for diversity but also respect for a diversity of approaches to diversity); D Miller *On Nationality* (1995).

[108] See principle 16 of the Lund Recommendations (note 18 above); *Re Secession of Quebec* (note 11 above) para 80, indicating that three constitutional principles (federalism, democracy and constitutionalism) and rule of law inform the scope and operation of specific provisions that protect the right of minorities. Also see Ghai (note 53 above) 16.

[109] *Christian Education* (note 105 above) para 26.

[110] See *Re Secession of Quebec* (note 11 above) para. 61–68, particularly 68.

[111] Ibid.

different treatment (group-specific minority rights) must not be disproportionate in effect or involve unfairness to other racial groups'.[112] As noted above, this is one of the various considerations that should inform the institutionalisation of minority guarantees in such areas as language use in communication with public authorities, education in minority languages and the media.

5.7. Conclusion

Against the background of the minority rights framework examined in the previous chapter, this chapter has identified and elaborated the constitutional guarantees and institutional mechanisms through which the minority rights framework defended in this study can be translated into a democratic constitutional design for accommodating ethno-cultural diversity in Africa. It has also examined the nature and the form that these guarantees and institutional arrangements take. The nature, limitations and principles that regulate the operation of these mechanisms and constitutional guarantees were also identified and examined.

The analysis clearly reveals that the particular form that the constitutional design for accommodation of ethno-cultural diversity in a particular society takes depends on the particular circumstances and features of diversity of the society concerned. Accordingly it may involve the combination of all or only some of the institutional arrangements and rights guarantees identified here. It also emerges that the choice of the right constitutional design, although important, is not by itself alone adequate. Its contribution in achieving social justice and equality as well as adequate accommodation of diversity is contingent on adherence to certain patterns of institutional and public behaviour consistent with principles of mutual respect and recognition, human rights, democracy, rule of law and constitutionalism. It is thus clear that for countries with limited institutional and societal history and culture that is respectful of human rights and the principles of democracy multicultural constitutionalism faces serious challenges of successful application. In addition to institutional and policy engineering, in such societies there is thus a need for a systematic transformational campaign to nurture and inculcate the ethos and values of tolerance, democracy, human rights and rule of law at all levels of society and structures of the state. This can be channelled through education, the media, civil society, the legal system and the legislative processes of the societies concerned.

---

[112] I Brownlie 'The Rights of Peoples in Modern International Law' in J Crawford (ed.) *The Rights of Peoples* (1998) 1, 10.

CHAPTER VI

SOUTH AFRICA'S CONSTITUTIONAL DESIGN FOR THE ACCOMMODATION OF DIVERSITY

6.1. Introduction

Thus far we have examined and elaborated the form and content of the constitutional minority rights regime defended in this study. Against the background of the arguments made in the last chapter about an ideal constitutional design for the accommodation of diversity, this chapter and the next examine the form and nature of South Africa's and Ethiopia's constitutional designs for the accommodation of their diverse populations. Although these countries have had a relatively short experience with their new constitutions and hence it is not possible to assess their successes or failures conclusively, their experience can help to exemplify how the minority rights regime defended in this study is and should be translated into a constitutional design for accommodation of diversity, and to draw some conclusions regarding its actual operation once institutionalised.

These chapters contend that the constitutional application of the minority rights framework in African countries, as defended in this study, is necessary to address the issue of minorities and establish a just and democratic framework. It is further argued that the success or efficacy of such a constitutional framework depends both on the form and nature of its institutionalisation and on the particular political, socio-economic and ethno-cultural context within which it operates. Accordingly, the chapters examine not only the nature of the constitutional accommodation of diversity in these two countries, but also the extent to which the respective constitutional designs offer the necessary framework to address the issue of minorities as discussed in Chapter II, and thereby contribute to national integration, stability and social equality and justice.

6.2. The Context: The Nature of Minority Issues in South Africa

South Africa is by any standard a multicultural country. It is inhabited by people of different racial, ethno-linguistic and religious groups. Racially the population is divided into four groups: Africans (79.7 per cent), whites (9.1 per cent), coloured (8.8 per cent) and people of Indian and Asian origin (2.4 per cent).[1] Due to the history of apartheid, there is high degree of division and socio-economic inequality between members of the different race groups. As a result, race is most salient in political and social terms. From the perspective of this study, however, the most important dimension of South Africa's diversity is ethno-cultural which more often than not converge with racial division. This is mainly expressed in terms of linguistic differences. There are 11 significant languages in South Africa that are spoken by more than 99 percent of the population.[2] In addition to these, there are also many religious communities.

During the negotiations for the making of South Africa's democratic constitution, the most debated and time-consuming issue was the question of how to accommodate these various dimensions of South Africa's population diversity. This was very controversial for at least two reasons. The first was the history of divisions and manipulation of group membership during the apartheid years. All aspects of public life were organised in a way that accorded different treatment to members of the different race groups. Further to that, Africans were divided into different homelands on the basis of their ethno-linguistic membership. This presented the challenge of overcoming the divisions and inequalities that this had entrenched in society. As a result, claims for accommodation of diversity were viewed with a lot of suspicion and anxiety.

The second reason for controversy was that there was no agreement about the nature of South Africa's ethno-cultural diversity among either the contending parties or the constitutional experts. For the African National Congress (ANC), '[e]thnic divisions were real, but they were essentially the creations of apartheid and once that was abolished then a democracy based on neither race nor ethnicity would be able to emerge'.[3] The party therefore advocated for a unitary state structure and a Westminster-style majoritarian democracy that could ensure social transformation, economic empowerment and nation-building.[4] Others, notably Inkatha Freedom Party (IFP) and the National Party (NP), emphasised the country's ethno-cultural diversity and the need for institutional accommodation of the identities and interests of the various constituent groups.[5] Accordingly, they advocated for power-sharing structures and a federal form of state structure.

---

1 See Statistics South Africa, Mid-year estimates for South Africa by population group and sex, 2007 <http://www.statssa.gov.za/PublicationsHTML/P03022007/html/P03022007.html>.

2 See Statistics South Africa, Census 2001 (2001) <http://www.statssa.gov.za/census01/html/Key%20results_files/Key%20results.pdf>.

3 C Murray & R Simeon 'Recognition Without Empowerment: Minorities in a Democratic South Africa' (2007) 5 (4) *I.CON* 699–729, 711.

4 See H Klug 'How the Centre Holds: Managing Claims for Regional and Ethnic Autonomy in a Democratic South Africa' in Y Ghai *Autonomy and Ethnicity: Negotiating Competing Claims in Multi-ethnic Societies* (2000).

5 See H Ebrahim *The Soul of a Nation: Constitution-Making in South Africa* (1998); Murray & Simeon (note 3 above) 708–713; Klug (ibid) 104–107.

The final constitutional settlement, as set out in the 1996 Constitution, reflects a compromise between these positions but is skewed more in favour of the first.[6] Although the final Constitution (FC) rejects executive consociationalism and group membership as a basis of political participation and representation,[7] the political system that it instituted is founded on the principle of PR. In practice as well, particular regard is taken to generally reflect the racial, religious and ethnic diversity of the society in the distribution of portfolios in the executive branch of government. Similarly, even if a fully-fledged multicultural federalism was not adopted, the FC establishes a federal-like state structure with a system of provincial government. Once again, while rejecting race and ethnicity as relevant identity marker to be formally accommodated institutionally, the FC at the same time provides guarantees and institutional arrangements that not only tolerate, but also ensure respect for, and accommodate and even promote, the various languages, cultures and religions which give meaning and purpose to the life of many South Africans. It is fair to say from this that the 1996 Constitution provides a reasonably sophisticated design for the accommodation of diversity specific to the South African historical and socio-political context, and that this design largely reflects the framework developed and defended in this study but tailored to the particular realities of South Africa. The design articulated under the 1996 South African Constitution aims at addressing the twin demands or needs of recognition and substantive equality. Accordingly, the various institutional arrangements such as the system of proportional representation, provincial system of government and the constitutional guarantees on language, religion and culture are meant to meet not only expectations of recognition of difference and hence the just inclusion all sections of society but also the urgent need for overcoming historical inequalities affecting certain racial groups. The constitutional requirements for transformation of the public service to ensure representativity of the diverse makeup of the South African public or the constitutional guarantee relating to language policy and the rights of linguistic, religious and cultural rights must accordingly be understood as institutional mechanisms necessary for the achievement of substantive equality.

---

[6] The ANC conceded to the demand for regional autonomy by proposing a constitutional principle for a multi-level government structure. As Ebrahim pointed out this had two significant dimensions. 'First, the ANC agreed to accord regions significant legislative and executive powers which would be entrenched in the interim constitution. Secondly, the proposal effectively cast regional powers in stone, denying the constitutional assembly the power to change them.' Ebrahim (ibid) 155.

[7] The CC has affirmed the rejection under the FC of consociational democracy involving executive power-sharing through minority representation in the executive. According to the court, this is because the primary purpose of the executive body 'is to ensure effective and efficient government and service delivery'. *Democratic Alliance & Another v Masondo NO & Another* 2003 (2) SA 413 (CC), para. 18. [Masondo]

6.3. Indirect Accommodation in the Political Processes and the Structures of the State

The FC provides three devices that facilitate, albeit indirectly, the accommodation of members of different groups in South Africa. These are (a) the principle of PR, (b) participatory and deliberative policy-making processes and (c) the system of multilevel government. An outline of how this is institutionalised in the Constitution, how it fares in accommodating diversity and has been applied in practice, follows below.

6.3.1. *Representation and Participation*

The process of South African constitution-making had two stages.[8] The first phase involved the making of the Interim Constitution (IC) that established the Government of National Unity. The second phase involved the drafting and adoption of the final Constitution of 1996.[9] One of the most important outcomes of the first phase of the constitution-making process was the adoption of the 34 Constitutional Principles (CPs).[10] These principles set out in general terms the fundamental items that should be included when the final constitution was drafted by the Constitutional Assembly (CA).[11] One of these CPs that was written into the final constitution was the principle of PR.[12]

This led, among other developments, to the adoption of a PR electoral system. Accordingly, FC s 46(1)(*d*) and s 105(1)(*d*) stipulate elections 'in terms of an electoral system that ... results, in general terms, in proportional representation'. This is further elaborated under the Electoral Law Act 73 of 1998 as amended by the Electoral Laws Amendment Act 34 of 2004 in which Schedule 1 stipulates the design of the electoral system of South Africa to be a closed-list PR system.[13] Under this system, the nine provinces serve as multi-member constituencies

---

[8] See Klug (note 4 above); K Henrard *Minority Protection in Post-Apartheid South Africa: Human Rights, Minority Rights and Self-determination* (2002) Chapters 3 & 4; Ebrahim (note 5 above); S Gloppen *South Africa: The Battle over the Constitution* (1997) Chapter 9; P Andrews & S Ellmann (eds.) *The Post-Apartheid Constitutions: Perspectives on South Africa's Basic Law* (2001); J Robinson 'Federalism and the Transformation of the South African State' in Graham Smith *Federalism: The Multiethnic Challenge* (1995) 255.

[9] The *Constitution of the Republic of South Africa* Act 108 of 1996. [FC]

[10] See Schedule 4 to the Interim Constitution of 1993. [IC]

[11] S 71 of the IC stipulated that a new constitution or any part of a new constitution shall become operational only once the CC has ratified that it complies with the constitutional principles. See for more B de Villiers 'The Constitutional Principles: Content and Significance' in B de Villiers *Birth of a Constitution* (1994) 41–42.

[12] CP VIII stipulated that '[t]here shall be representative government embracing multi-party democracy, regular elections, universal adult suffrage, a common voters' roll, and in general, *proportional representation*.' (my emphasis).

[13] For details on this see G Fick 'Elections' in S Woolman et al. *Constitutional Law of South Africa* (2007) 2nd ed.Chapter 29.

from which half (200) of the representatives for the National Assembly (NA) are elected and the remaining half are elected from a national closed list. According to the Constitutional Court of South Africa (CC), this closed PR electoral system is 'designed to promote optimal proportionality' between votes cast and seats won.[14]

From the perspective of this study, the importance of this system lies, firstly, in the fact that it has made it possible for even minority parties with small electoral support to secure representation that otherwise would not have been possible.[15] Thus, in the 2004 elections wide range of small parties including those that seek group representation such as the Minority Front and United Christian Democratic Party gained seats in the NA. Had it not been for the use of PR electoral system, such parties would have very minimal chance of getting any seat in the NA.[16] Secondly, it encourages parties to list ethnically diverse candidates as a means to secure wide votes and hence enhance minority representation through party structures.[17] Accordingly, the system tends to produce a legislature that largely reflects the diverse makeup of the South African public. Thirdly, this high degree of representation and participation of minorities serves to enhance the legitimacy of South Africa's democracy and national cohesion, and to promote inclusion, mutual respect and tolerance.[18]

This national representation and participation is channelled in two ways, thus multiplying the dimensions of the inclusion and participation of minorities. Firstly, members of various groups get representation through the parties who win seats in the NA in proportion to the votes cast for them nationally. According to FC s 46 (1) (*d*), the NA shall consist of no less than 350 and no more than 400 members elected by an electoral system based on a national common voters' roll and producing, in general, PR. Although this system has not resulted in a coalition government due to ANC's predominant electoral

---

[14] *Ex Parte Speaker of the Western Cape Provincial Legislature: In Re First Certification of the Constitution of the Province of the Western Cape* (1997) (1997) (4) SA 795 (CC), 1997 (9) BCLR 1167 (CC) para. 45.

[15] W James & A Hadland 'Shared Aspirations: The Imperative of Accountability in South Africa's Electoral System' in *Electoral Models for South Africa: Reflections and Options* Electoral Task Team Review Roundtable Konrad-Adenaur-Stiftung Seminar Report No 18 (2007) (2nd ed.) 15, 20. As Reynolds observed 'even with their geographical pockets of electoral support, the Freedom Front, the Democratic Party, the PAC and the African Christian Democratic Party would have failed to win a single parliamentary seat if the elections had been held under a single-member district FPTP [first past the post] electoral system.' A Reynolds 'South Africa: Electoral System, Conflict Management and Inclusion' <http://aceproject.org/ace-en/topics/es/esy/esy_za>.

[16] See *United Democratic Movement v President of the Republic of South Africa* 2002 11 BCLR 1179 (CC) para. 47.

[17] Reynolds (note 15 above).

[18] 'The fundamental constitutional purpose is,' wrote O'Regan J, 'to undo the separation, exclusion and inequality of the past by ensuring that there is shared involvement in deliberation subject, of course, to the right of the majority to make decisions.' *Masondo* (note 7 above) para. 72.

support, it has nevertheless facilitated the representation of significant groups through the various parties that have won seats in the NA.[19]

Secondly, minorities also get indirect representation in the national legislative process through the second house of parliament, the National Council of Provinces (NCOP).[20] FC s 42 (4) provides that the NCOP represents provinces to ensure that provincial interests are taken into account in the national sphere of government.[21] What makes the potential of the NCOP particularly suited for mirroring the diverse ethnic composition of the South African population in the national legislative process, and hence for the accommodation of minorities at the political level, is its composition. The NCOP consists of nine provincial delegations of ten members each.[22] The delegation of each province has to be composed in a manner that enables parties to be represented in the delegation proportionately to their support in the provincial legislature.[23] As one of the characteristics of the provinces is relative concentrations of particular population groups, the national representation of provinces through the NCOP might mean the channelling of the representation of diverse sections of society into national policy making.[24] The role of the NCOP in accommodating minorities is also of particular importance as it is a critical institution responsible for facilitating public participation in national policy making.[25] Not all these potentials of the NCOP have, however, been put into reality as it has yet to establish its influence and gain political recognition as one of South Africa's mainstream political structures.

The constitutional requirement of proportional representation applies to the provincial level of the state system as well. Consistent with the framework adopted in this study, FC s 105(1)(*d*) accordingly provides for a provincial legislature that consists of members elected by an electoral system that results, in general, *in*

---

19 Murray & Simeon (note 3 above) 714–715; Reynolds (note 15 above).

20 In pointing out this role of the NCOP, former President Nelson Mandela stated that it is uniquely placed to reflect the diversity of South African society and to contribute to the project of nation building. President Nelson Mandela, Address to the National Council of Provinces 7 August 1998, Cape Town. See also Henrard (note 8 above)113.

21 See also *Ex Parte Chairperson of the Constitutional Assembly: In Re Certification of the Constitution of the Republic of South Africa* 1996 (4) SA 744 (CC), 1996 (10) BCLR 1253 (CC) 325–30. [First Certification Judgement]

22 FC s 60.

23 See FC s 61 (1) & First Certification Judgement (note 20 above) para. 325. Since it enjoys wide powers with respect to Schedule 4 matters, the NCOP offers minorities an important additional avenue to have a meaningful say in the national legislative process. Siri Gloppen argues that '[t]his is a potentially important source of minority influence'. This is because, Gloppen explains, 'Schedule 4 includes vital matters such as education, health, welfare services, housing, cultural matters, agriculture, environment, tourism, trade and development.' Gloppen (note 8 above) 220.

24 Henrard (note 8 above) 113.

25 For details on this see *Doctors for Life International v Speaker of the National Assembly* 2006 (6) SA 416 (CC), 2006 (12) BCLR 1399 (CC) particularly paras. 79–134. [Doctors for Life]

proportional representation.[26] Thus, even at the regional level the winner-takes-all system does not apply. As is the case at the national level, the application of the requirement of proportional representation to provincial government can be seen as offering a mechanism for ensuring representation and accommodation of the diversity that is characteristic of the various provinces.

The FC renders the representation of various parties espousing the interests of various sections of society more meaningful with the high degree of significance that it attaches to a strong participatory and deliberative system of legislative processes with respect to all the three levels of government.[27] FC s 57(2)(*b*) requires that the rules and orders of the NA provide for 'the participation in the proceedings of the Assembly and its committees of minority parties represented in the national assembly, in a manner consistent with democracy'. The reading of FC s 70(2)(*c*) together with s 70(2)(*b*) and s 61(3) also entails that minority parties are able to participate in the proceedings and the committees of NCOP.[28] Similarly, FC s 116(2)(*b*) stipulates that the rules and orders of a provincial legislature must provide for the participation of minority parties represented in the legislature in the proceedings and committees of the legislature. At the local level, s 160(8)(*a*) guarantees participation in the proceedings and committees of municipal councils in a manner that 'allows parties and interests reflected in the council to be fairly represented'.[29]

Moreover, the articulation of a very strong right of public participation under FC ss 19, 59(1), 59(2), 72(1) and 118(1)[30] is also meant to ensure that the different levels of government sufficiently consult and accommodate the views and concerns of members of various communities on all matters, but particularly on those that are of concern to their rights and interests.[31] Indeed, according to Sachs J, '[t]he principle of consultation and (public) involvement has become a distinctive part of our national ethos'.[32] From the perspective of this study, this constitutional requirement of 'active and on going public involvement' has at least three important elements. Firstly, as Sachs J puts it, the importance that majoritarian democracy has for transformation 'in no way implies that only

---

[26] See T Madlingozi & S Woolman 'Provincial legislative authority' in Woolman et al. (note 13 above) Chapter 19, 19-1 – 19-2.

[27] For a robust analysis of this see T Roux 'Democracy' in Woolman et al. (note 13 above) Chapter 10, 10-37 – 10-43.

[28] Ibid, 10-39.

[29] Note however that in *Masondo* (note 7 above) the CC held that the principle of fair representation does not apply to the mayoral committee of the municipal council. For more discussion on this see Roux (note 27 above) 10-40 – 10-43.

[30] The right to public participation is given its most robust articulation by the CC in *Doctors for Life* (note 25 above).

[31] For details on public participation in deliberative legislative bodies see J Brickhill & R Babiuch 'Political Rights' in Woolman et al. (note 13 above) Chapter 45.

[32] *Doctors for Life* (note 25 above) para. 227.

the most numerous and politically influential voices of our diverse society are entitled to be heard'.[33] As he further explains, since 'public involvement may be of special importance for those whose strongly held views have to cede to majority opinion in the legislature', minorities and historically marginalised groups should have not only a chance to have their say but also the assurance that they will be listened to.[34] Secondly, it expresses a constitutional commitment that all members of society, particularly minorities, 'should feel that they have been given a real opportunity to have their say, that they are taken seriously as citizens, that their views matter and will receive due consideration'.[35] Finally, by making the democratic process sensitive to and accommodative of the voices of minorities, public involvement will 'enrich the quality of our democracy, help sustain its robust deliberative character and, by promoting a sense of inclusion in the national polity, promote the achievement of the goals of transformation'.[36]

It is clear from the above that although the FC upholds majoritarian democracy, the constitutional enunciation of the principle of proportionality as well as robust forms of public participation entails that 'the constitution does not envisage a mathematical form of democracy, where the winner takes all'.[37] It is rather a pluralistic and participatory democracy that is based on the representation of minorities in deliberative decision-making processes (albeit indirectly, through parties) and 'the rights of all to be heard and have their views considered'.[38] Such a system of democracy does not aim only at offering minorities representation and the opportunity to have their say to allow them contribute in shaping public policy.[39] In providing for the representation of the diverse groups constituting South Africa in the deliberative organs of the state and guaranteeing their right to have their say, the principles of proportional representation and public participation also offer a framework for meaningful interaction and constructive engagement among members of various groups, which is the basis on which 'a genuine sense of shared identity, social integration, in multicultural and multiethnic societies' may be developed.[40] Accordingly, South Africa's inclusive and participatory democracy, based on respect for and representation of diversity, has the additional aim of 'achieving

[33] Ibid, para. 233.
[34] Ibid, para. 234.
[35] Ibid, para. 235.
[36] Ibid.
[37] *Masondo* (note 7 above) para. 42.
[38] Ibid.
[39] See Chapter V.
[40] A Addis 'On Human Diversity and the Limits of Toleration' in I Shapiro & W Kymlicka (eds.) *Nomos XXXIX: Ethnicity and Group Rights* (1997) 112, 128.

a just society where, in the words of the Preamble, "South Africa belongs to all who live in it…"'.[41]

As we have seen in Chapter IV, the principle of proportional representation is important not only in deliberative elected bodies of the state, but also in the public service and the executive branch of government. This is also provided for in the FC. The FC has rendered proportional representation one of the principles that govern public administration. FC s 195(1)(*i*) stipulates:

> Public administration must be governed by the democratic values and principles enshrined in the constitution, including the following principles: …(i) Public administration must be *broadly representative of the South African people*, with employment and personnel management practices based on ability, objectivity, fairness, and *the need to redress the imbalances of the past to achieve broad representation* (my emphasis).

This principle has also been given application, not only in the public sector, but in the private sector as well, through such measures as the Employment Equity Act of 2000, the Broad Based Black Empowerment Act of 2003 and the Promotion of Equality and Prevention of Unfair Discrimination Act of 2000. In order to diminish the socio-economic inequalities along racial lines and achieve a workforce that reflects the composition of the whole population in racial terms, the Employment Equity Act requires employers to devise equity strategies and to report on them annually to the Department of Labour.

Once again this expresses the commitment of the Final Constitution to promoting equality among different sections of the population by creating structures of government and public administration that are representative of the South African people. There is no doubt that this brings inclusivity and enhances the sense of identification of members of different racial and ethnic groups with the state and its institutions. In other words, it has the multiple effects of promoting diversity and nurturing peaceful coexistence, social harmony, and mutual respect and understanding. From the perspective of this study, it also has the additional value of contributing to the constitutional aim of 'healing the divisions of the past' and achieving a society where 'South Africa belongs to all living in it, united in our diversity'.[42]

At the level of the national executive, there is no particular constitutional requirement of representativity of diversity. Nevertheless, the practice shows that active effort is made on the part of the governing party that the national executive is representative of various sections of society. The same arithmetic of represenativeness is applied at the province level. Accordingly, the government both at the national and provincial levels has a diverse composition generally

---

[41] *Masondo* (note 7 above) para. 43.

[42] Preamble Constitution of South Africa Act 108 1996.

reflective of the racial, ethnic and religious diversity of the country and the provinces. Irrespective of its efficacy in effectively channelling the interests of different groups, this promotes citizens sense of identification with the government and thus some level of representation. As developments leading to ANC's 52nd National Conference in Plolokwane and the bitter struggle between Thabo Mbeki and Jacob Zuma illustrated, both the electorate and ANC members are sensitive about ethnic (Xhosa to which both Mandela and Mbeki belong) domination of the leadership of the ANC and hence the country. The appointment of Jacob Zuma as the leader of the ANC in 2007 and subsequently as President of the country thus fares very well in terms of countering fears of domination of the executive by one ethnic group.

6.3.2. *Achievements and Limitations*

The application of the principle of proportional representation in the choice of the electoral system as well as in the structures and operations of the national and provincial legislatures has been successful in various ways. It has enabled significant groups and minority parties such as the DA and the IFP to achieve representation and participation in the political processes. It is also one of the important dimensions of the constitutional design that delivered South Africa's peaceful transition to democracy.[43] As Simon Bekker and Anne Leildé observe, '[w]hat has been proclaimed to be the South African miracle is due in no small part to the nature and outcome of this multi-party electoral system which clearly identified the winning party while facilitating the emergence of minority party rule in a number of provinces, and minority party representation in a number of "governments-of-unity"'.[44]

The inclusivity that this principle creates also underlies and nurtures public support across ethnic and racial lines for the central values that underpin South Africa's democracy.[45] People across racial and ethnic lines have come to identify themselves with the Constitution and the institutions of the state that it has established. The various initiatives taken to achieve representation in the economic and social spheres have also served to contribute to the process of

---

[43] As Reynolds rightly observes, '[t]he PR system ... was crucial to creating the atmosphere of inclusiveness and reconciliation which precipitated the decline of the worst political violence and has made post-apartheid South Africa something of a beacon of hope and stability to the rest of troubled Africa.' Reynolds (note 15 above).

[44] S Bekker & A Leildé 'Is Multiculturalism a Workable Policy in South Africa?' (2003) 5 (2) *Int J of Multicultural Societies* 119–134, 122.

[45] See *Doctors for Life* (note 25 above).

redressing the socio-economic inequalities inherited from apartheid and achieve some degree of social transformation.[46]

The system is not, however, without its limits. Firstly, since a PR electoral system is premised on representation through political parties, it does not enable those minorities who are not included in, or whose interest is not espoused by, any of the political parties in operation to be represented. The result is that peripheral minorities such as the San, Koi and Nama communities of South Africa might not be sufficiently represented, and have little, if any, voice in the national decision-making processes. Reference to this was made in the previous chapter, which suggested that to achieve the inclusion of such groups, it may be necessary to supplement the PR system with mechanisms that guarantee their representation. Given the political history of South Africa, it is, however, unlikely that any such mechanism of group-based representation could be a solution here.

Moreover, the effectiveness of these arrangements and the extent to which minorities are able to have meaningful participation and feel reasonably included is often constrained by the political and social structures within which they operate. In the current political power configuration of the country, South Africa is a one-party-dominant state.[47] Results from the three elections held so far show that the ANC's electoral support and, more accurately, parliamentary representation has shown a significant increase. In the last elections, in 2004, the ANC won 69 per cent of the votes cast, which is 7 per cent higher than the votes it won in the 1994 elections. This means that the ANC controls about two thirds of the seats in the legislature and dominates the institutions of government. This essentially renders minority parties and minority groups that are not sufficiently represented in the structures of the ANC peripheral to the political processes and the structure of government. As one observer puts it, 'although formal constitutional provisions and formalities appear to guarantee a multi-party system, the racial polarisation of the electorate decrees South Africa to be, *potentially*, a one-party "dominant" state for the foreseeable future'[48] if not until the end of the world as arrogantly declared by ANC's current President Jacob Zuma.

Given that PR electoral system gives a great deal of say to political parties rather than the electorate, the dominance of the national political scene by ANC also significantly undermines effective representation of the interests of

---

[46] See R Southall 'Introduction: The ANC State, More Dysfunctional Than Developmental' in S Buhlungu et al. (eds.) *State of the Nation South Africa 2007* (2007) 1, 6–8.

[47] See H Giliomee & C Simkins (eds.) *The Awkward Embrace: One-Party Domination and Democracy* (1999); *Challenges to Democracy by One-party Dominance: A Comparative Assessment* Konrad-Adenauer-Stiftung Seminar Report (October 2006). [Challenges to democracy]

[48] L Schlemmer 'Democracy or Democratic Hegemony: The Future of Political Pluralism in South Africa' in Giliomee & Simkins (ibid) 281, 282.

various sections of society in the NA unless it is espoused by the ANC. One of the manifestations of this has been the weakness of the NCOP in ventilating and effectively reflecting the interests of provinces and the communities constituting the provinces.

6.3.3. *The System of Provincial Government: Minority Accommodation through 'Federalism'*

Although FC s 1(1) proclaimed the Republic of South Africa to be 'one, sovereign state' and nowhere does it refer to South Africa as 'federal', the nature of the system of provincial government enunciated in the FC has clothed South Africa with the most salient attributes of a federal state.[49] As in any full-fledged federal system, the provinces enjoy legislative and executive authorities.[50] Their powers are original and constitutionally entrenched. They are represented in the national parliament through the NCOP. They can also adopt their own constitutions.[51] Besides, the Constitution and, most importantly, the division of powers are not subject to alteration by either the national or provincial government alone. Such amendment is subject to the involvement of both orders of government.[52] And the Constitutional Court serves as umpire to oversee the constitutional division of power as well as conflicts involving provinces, and those between provinces and the centre.

6.3.4. *Provincial Boundaries*

As noted in the previous chapter, the extent to which regional autonomy or federalism can address ethnic claims and accommodate diversity depends upon both the relative coincidence between the boundaries of regional governments and the territorial concentration of groups, and the nature and degree of autonomy constitutionally vested in sub-national governments. Some argue that the demarcation of provincial boundaries under the FC represents a rejection of ethnic-based political organisation.[53] This is not, however, entirely accurate. Although the boundaries of the nine provinces were not drawn merely on the

[49] In this regard, Haysom insightfully observed that '[i]f the South African constitutional schema were to be analysed against a formal federal checklist it could, with justification, be classified as federal'. N Haysom 'Federal Features of the Final Constitution' in Andrews & Ellmann (note 8 above) 504–524, 504. Also See *Ex Parte President of the Republic of South Africa: In Re Constitutionality of the Liquor Bill* 2000 (1) SA 732 (CC) [*Liquor Bill*]

[50] See T Madlingozi & S Woolman 'Provincial Legislative Authority' and C Murray & O Ampofo-Anti 'Provincial Executive Authority' in Woolman et al. (note 13 above) Chapters 19 & 20 respectively.

[51] See S Woolman 'Provincial Constitutions' in Woolman et al. (note 13 above) Chapter 21.

[52] See FC s 74.

[53] See for example A Egan & R Taylor 'South Africa: The Failure of Ethno-Territorial Politics' in J Coakley (ed.) *The Territorial Management of Ethnic Conflict* (2003) 99–117.

basis of territorial concentration of ethno-cultural groups, cultural and language realities were among the ten criteria used in the demarcation of provincial boundaries.[54] The spatial distribution of language groups further shows that many provinces have a relatively large concentration of particular ethno-cultural groups.[55]

In practical terms, this created the necessary territorial space to accommodate the interests of the Inkatha Freedom Party (IFP) and the NP, who mobilised particular groups in demanding the adoption of federalism to guarantee self-government for these groups.[56] In addition to its immediate role during the negotiations, the current boundary configuration of provinces also has the potential to accommodate the demand that territorially concentrated ethno-cultural groups may raise for self-government. According to Gloppen, '[i]f further political divisions should arise between ethnic groups within the African population, for instance along linguistic lines, the current provinces could provide several groups with provincial strongholds (for instance Xhosa speakers in the Eastern Cape, Sotho speakers in the Free State, Pedi speakers in Northern Provinces)'.[57] Indeed, notwithstanding that most of the ethno-linguistic groups that dominate various provinces have not made any such claim so far, the system nevertheless provided their members with the framework for political participation and representation, firstly within the structure of the provinces, promoting self-rule, and secondly through the NCOP in the NA, promoting shared rule. To this extent, it is possible to conclude that the system of provincial government, although mainly territorial in its design, serves the accommodation of minority claims to self-government and therefore also has important multicultural features. This can additionally be gathered from the nature of the division of power set by the Final Constitution.

6.3.4.1. *The Division of Power*

The matters over which provincial governments have legislative authority are defined in the FC.[58] Provinces have both exclusive and concurrent jurisdictions.[59]

---

[54] Ebrahim (note 5 above); B de Villiers *The Future of Provinces in South Africa – The Debate Continues* KAS Policy Paper Issue No 2 (October 2007) 8.

[55] In the Eastern Cape isiXhosa is first home language to 83.4 percent, in Kwazulu-Natal isiZulu to 80.9 per cent, in the Northern Cape Afrikaans to 68.0 per cent, in the North West seTswana to 65.4 per cent, in the Free State Afrikaans to 64.4 per cent, in the Western Cape Afrikaans to 55.3 per cent, and in Limpopo siPedi to 52.1 per cent. In Gauteng and Mpumalanga no single language group constitutes a majority and these are the only truly multicultural provinces. See Statistics South Africa *Census 2001* (2001) <http://www.statssa.gov.za/census01/html/>.

[56] See Henrard (note 8 above) Chapters 3 & 4. In the other provinces, there has not been similar group mobilisation for autonomy or self-government.

[57] Gloppen (note 8 above) 252.

[58] See V Bronstein 'Legislative Competence' in Woolman et al. (note 13 above) Chapter 15.

[59] See *Liquor Bill* case (note 49 above) paras. 40–52.

The functional areas over which provinces have exclusive jurisdiction are set out in Schedule 5. They also have the power to pass their own constitutions.[60] FC Schedule 4 lists the functional areas in respect of which provincial governments enjoy concurrent legislative competence with parliament pursuant to FC s 44(1)(a)(ii) and s 104 (1)(b)(i).

Although the functional areas of provincial exclusive jurisdiction are very limited and further subject to the limitations under FC s 44(2),[61] some are of particular importance to accommodate the claims of territorial minorities.[62] They provide a framework for promoting and preserving the history and culture of minorities within their localities. Similarly, subject to the limitations under FC s 146,[63] the functional areas under Schedule 4 provide even wider avenues to accommodate the interests and identities of minorities through the system of provincial government. These include, in particular: 'cultural matters', 'education at all levels, excluding tertiary education', 'indigenous law and customary law (subject to Chapter 12 of the Constitution)', 'language policy and the regulation of official languages (to the extent that the provisions of section 6 of the Constitution expressly confer upon the provincial legislatures legislative competence)', 'media services directly controlled or provided by the provincial government (subject to section 192)', 'traditional leadership' (subject to Chapter 12 of the Constitution)', and 'welfare services'. Provinces also have the power to designate as official languages at least two languages spoken within their respective jurisdictions. Although the powers assigned to provinces are not wide, which reflects the unitary bias of the South African 'federal' system, it is nevertheless clear from this that provinces are vested with important powers that allow self-government of territorially concentrated communities and promote their identities, including by designating regional languages as their official languages.

6.3.4.2. *Achievements and Challenges*

It can be concluded that from the perspective of this study the system of provincial government is one of the devices that the 1996 South African Constitution

[60] S 143 (1). The scope of the constitution-making powers of provinces was a subject of several cases decided by the CC. See Woolman (note 51 above).

[61] This provides that Parliament may intervene, by passing legislation in accordance with s 76 (1), with regard to a matter under Schedule 5, when it is necessary to maintain (a) national security, (b) economic unity, and (c) essential national standards, as well as (d) to establish minimum standards required for the rendering of services and (e) to prevent unreasonable action by a province which is prejudicial to the interests of another province or to the country as a whole.

[62] These include 'archives other than national archives', 'libraries other than national libraries', 'museums other than national museums' and the more general area of 'provincial cultural matters'. See Schedule 5 of the Constitution.

[63] This section stipulates that national legislation that applies uniformly across the country prevails over provincial legislation under certain defined circumstances.

deliberately employs to accommodate diversity. This it has done and continues to do in three ways. First, one of the factors leading to the adoption of provincial government was the need to avoid conflict and include all significant parties in the constitutional negotiation process. Seen from this perspective, the inclusion of the system of provincial government can be credited for preventing the possible collapse of the negotiations for the constitution.[64] It was only after several concessions were made and incorporated into the 1993 constitution that the IFP and other parties agreed to participate in the first national elections in 1994.[65] Secondly, the system is also intended to promote stability and national cohesion by creating multiple spheres of government so as to divide and share political power and economic resources among various sections of society. In this regard, another of the achievements of the system of provincial government in South Africa is the degree to which it minimised the centrifugal tendencies prevalent in some parts of the country, particularly KwaZulu-Natal and Western Cape.[66]

Thirdly, the system of provincial government is intended to serve as a mechanism to accommodate territorially concentrated minorities.[67] Despite the weakness of the provinces' powers and the strong centralist tendency of the constitutional framework, one would nevertheless agree with Murray and Simeon that it 'has provided some, albeit limited, space for minority empowerment'.[68] The system of provincial government also not only allowed mobilised ethno-regional minorities in KwaZulu-Natal and the Western Cape to form regional majorities and exercise a measure of control over key areas of their lives, but also created structure for power-sharing by regional elites and communities in other provinces as well. Moreover, in the prevailing political reality of ANC's dominance, it cannot be denied that it is a critical avenue for minority parties with strong support in these provinces to exercise political power. In effect, it serves as a power-sharing arrangement such that, while the party or coalition of the parties that constitute the majority in Parliament form the national government, other minority parties may form provincial or local governments, individually or by coalition, in those provinces where they enjoy strong support.[69] This also enhances the depth of South Africa's democracy by creating the opportunity for some provinces to serve as a bulwark against

---

[64] See N Steytler & J Mettler 'Federal Arrangements as a Peacemaking Device during South Africa's Transition to Democracy' (Fall 2001) 31 (4) *Publius: The J of Federalism* 93, particularly 96–99; Gloppen (note 8 above) 201–202.

[65] Ebrahim (note 5 above) 155.

[66] C Murray & R Simeon 'Multilevel Governance in South Africa' in B Berman, D Eyoh & W Kymlicka (eds.) *Ethnicity and Democracy in Africa* (2004) 277, 299.

[67] Henrard (note 8 above) 221.

[68] Murray & Simeon (note 3 above) 725.

[69] Gloppen notes that KwaZulu-Natal, the Western Cape and the Northern Cape 'have a demographic profile where national (ethnic/linguistic/racial) minorities (Zulus, Afrikaans speakers, coloureds) have a fair chance of winning power at provincial levels.' Gloppen (note 8 above) 252.

the one-party-dominated centre. These possibilities would not exist if South Africa were a full-fledged unitary state, where whoever controls the centre takes everything. It is clear from this that the system of provincial government has promoted both self-government of some groups through provinces, and shared government by all through representation and participation in the national legislative process via the NCOP. It also offers opportunities to deepen South Africa's democratic process by providing multiple avenues of participation, as well as checks on the power of the dominant centre.

The operation of the system of provincial government is not without limits. Currently, the ANC controls a staggering 297 seats in Parliament and is the ruling party in all the nine provinces. Politically speaking, this has the effect of weakening the constitutional scheme of multilevel government and particularly the ability of provinces to develop their own policies and experiment with their powers. This may weaken the accommodation of diversity through provincial autonomy, particularly in those provinces where there have been strong demands for autonomy. This danger is further accentuated by centralisation processes that have been witnessed over the course of the past decade. These trends are reflected not only in the dominant control that the centre has over fiscal sources, but also in the various laws and structures that have come to regulate important areas of the organisation and operation of provinces.

As in other African states, and probably even more so, there is also high degree of disparity among the country's nine provinces. As recent events surrounding the redefinition of provincial boundaries in Khutsong and Matatiele have shown, this problem has strong potential to fuel instability. One of the challenges that the system of provincial government faces in South Africa is therefore one of minimising and ultimately overcoming this disparity. In this regard, the effective, albeit admittedly complex, implementation of FC s 214 should receive serious attention.[70] Related to this are problems of administrative inefficiency and poor service delivery, particularly in the historically disadvantaged provinces.

Probably the most serious challenge facing the system of provincial government is the uncertainty of its continued existence. In 2007, the national government initiated a process for reviewing the system of provincial government.[71] Although no firm decision has as yet been taken, this has aroused fears of further centralisation and even the abolition of provinces.[72] Assessment of the operation of the system nevertheless reveals that the issue is not whether provinces should be

[70] Haysom (note 49 above) 518.

[71] See *Policy Process on the System of Provincial and Local Government: Background: Policy Questions, Process and Participation*, <http://www.dplg.co.za>, For a discussion on the merits or otherwise of this review process see De Villiers (note 54 above).

[72] See 'Provinces to be Scrapped' *Sunday Times* 26 October 2006; Resolution of the 32nd Annual Conference of the Inkatha Freedom Party held in Ulundi on 12–14 October 2007.

maintained. It is rather how to strengthen their administrative and managerial capacity, and allow them to exercise their powers independently to address the specific socio-economic and cultural needs of their population.[73] From the perspective of this study, the danger of a review of the system of provinces that involves diminishing or abolishing their role is that it may reverse the achievements made in terms of accommodation of diversity and the 'rainbowism' that has been in the making. This may also unleash ethnic mobilisation, not only in those provinces that are historically strongholds of opposition parties associated with particular groups, such as KwaZulu-Natal, but also in others, as elites in those provinces who benefit from the existing system seek to defend the status quo.[74] It may also lead to over-centralisation of power in the hands of the ANC, and in times of crisis within the party, as witnessed during and after the Polokwane Conference, this would threaten the proper functioning of democratic institutions. As Bertus de Villiers maintains, '[w]hile a review of the functioning of provinces is justified, the baby should not be thrown out with the bathwater; and worse, should not be drowned'.[75]

6.3.5. *Self-Determination*

From the discussion in the previous two chapters, it is clear that the institutional arrangements of representation and participation examined above, as well as the system of provincial government, constitute mechanisms of institutionalising internal self-determination. The only difference, in the context of the 1996 Constitution, is that these institutional arrangements are not *directly* intended to acknowledge, and do not seek to give express institutional recognition to, the various ethno-cultural groups as collectivities. Nevertheless, the Constitution does not either totally close the door on this possibility. Accordingly, FC s 235 recognises what it calls 'the notion of the right of self-determination of any community sharing a common cultural and language heritage within a territorial entity within the Republic or in any other way, determined by national legislation'.

The fact that this provision does not form part of the Bill of Rights and that it only recognises the notion of the right of self-determination indicates that self-determination is not recognised as a constitutional right, but enjoys only the status of a non-justiciable constitutional principle.[76] This marginal and ambivalent recognition is further reinforced by the incorporation of this

---

[73] See De Villiers (note 54 above); Simeon & Murray (note 66 above).

[74] The IFP has already expressed its grave concern over the process of revision. See Resolution No. 11 of the 32nd Annual Conference of the Inkatha Freedom Party held in Ulundi on 12–14 October 2007.

[75] De Villiers (note 54 above) 30.

[76] See Steytler & Mettler who argued that self-determination in the legal sense was reduced to, at most, a political claim (note 64 above) 100. But the clear enunciation of self-determination in

provision, like a footnote at the end of the Constitution, in a chapter entitled 'General Provisions'. Moreover, despite some views to the contrary,[77] this provision does not impose obligations but simply creates for parliament a constitutional discretion to operationalise it. As Nico Steytler and Johan Mettler point out, '[a]ny federating process along the route of self-determination would not be in the hands of any self-selected community, but will be governed by parliament'.[78] In legal terms, one can however, say, following the Supreme Court of Canada, that in the unlikely but not impossible event that the majority of members of a 'community sharing common culture and language' demand self-determination under FC s 235, it can be considered that this would impose on Parliament an obligation at least to negotiate. Obviously, the CC has a role to play in ensuring that constitutional procedures are duly followed and rights are respected in any such process. Nevertheless, there is no evidence currently that any group would in the foreseeable future successfully initiate this process.

6.4. Language Policy and the Accommodation of Linguistic Diversity

6.4.1. *Official Languages*

'Only in the imaginative provisions for the recognition of official languages,' Iain Currie insightfully observes, 'did the interim Constitution go beyond the minimum by specifically requiring positive action by the state to ensure the maintenance and development of minority languages.'[79] Indeed, the way the FC resolved the issue of the status of official languages is one of its few, if not necessarily the only, highly ingenious features of the FC with respect to the accommodation of diversity in South Africa. Arguably, as much as, if not more than, other aspects of the constitutional design, this plays a crucial role in resolving the challenges of ethnic diversity by comprehensively institutionalising in the public domain the recognition of the language diversity of the country. The FC s 6 (1) recognises 11 official languages of the Republic.[80] Of these, nine are indigenous languages that were subject to discrimination and neglect during apartheid. The official

---

the Constitution should surely be seen as making it more than a mere political ideal, hence the characterisation here as a non-justiciable constitutional *principle*.

[77] H Strydom H. *International Standards for the Protection of Minorities and the South African Constitution* (2002) <http://www.fwdklerk.org.za/download_docs/02_05_Int_Standard_Minorities_Publ_ PDF.pdf>.

[78] Steytler & Mettler (note 63 above) 100.

[79] I Currie 'Minority Rights: Education, Culture and Language' in Chaskalson et al. (eds.) *Constitutional Law of South Africa* (1996) Chapter 35, 35-4.

[80] The official languages are 'Sepedi, Sesotho, Setswana, siSwati, Tshivenda, Xitsonga, Afrikaans, English, isiNdebele, isiXhosa and isiZulu'.

recognition of these languages reflects the arguments advanced in this study regarding recognition of the culture of groups within the post-colonial African state, in that it is not only a commitment to remedy their past disadvantages, but also a guarantee for their survival and development in the political/public domain in addition to the social/private sphere.

FC s 6(1)'s main value is the recognition and institutional expression of the multi-linguistic and multicultural composition of South Africa. It symbolises the constitutional commitment to uphold and promote the diversity that is characteristic of the country.[81] This commitment is, however, not just symbolic. It is also substantive. Accordingly, FC s 6(2) encumbers the state with a constitutional duty 'to take practical and positive measures to elevate the status and advance the use of these (indigenous) languages' having regard to their 'historically diminished use and status'. When read with FC s 6(4), which requires that all languages be treated equitably, this demands that the state provide special support to the indigenous official languages.[82] Not only does this serve to achieve substantive equality among speakers of these historically marginalised languages, it also facilitates the process of national integration and transformation.

Other than the 11 languages designated as official, the FC additionally recognises other languages, such as the indigenous Khoi, Nama and San languages. As the CC has observed, these indigenous languages 'have suffered great historical neglect and are threatened with extinction'.[83] Accordingly, FC s 6(5)(*a*) requires the Pan South African Language Board (PSALB) to take special steps to 'promote and create conditions for the development and use of' these languages in addition to the 11 official languages.[84] A lower level of recognition and protection is extended to other languages, including the principal Indian languages.[85]

FC s 6(3) has two functions. The first is to tell us that the effect of the designation of the 11 languages as official is to make them languages that are to be used 'for the purpose of government'. According to Iain Currie, the phrase 'purposes of government' encompasses the various activities of government

---

[81] The preamble of the 1996 Constitution describes South Africa as belonging to 'all who live in it, united in *diversity*' (my emphasis).

[82] See Henrard (note 8 above) 119.

[83] First Certification Judgement (note 20 above) institutionalised languages but it also facilitates the process of national integration and transformation at para. 211.

[84] The CC seems to interpret this as mandating the Board to take special measures to protect those especially vulnerable indigenous languages. Ibid.

[85] FC s 6 (5) (*b*) uses the weaker formulation of 'promote and ensure respect for', compared to s (5) (a)'s 'promote and *create conditions for the development and use*' (my emphasis). Under the Pan South African Language Act of 1995, this distinction applied only between the 11 official languages and all other languages. This is nevertheless revised by the FC. See Henrard (note 8 above) 119–120.

including, in particular, legislation and administration.[86] This means that these 11 are the languages to be used in the making of laws, in communication with state agencies and for accessing public services. Since '[i]t will too often be practically and financially impossible to provide every type of service',[87] the second function of FC s 6(3) is to institutionalise the principle of the sliding-scale approach adopted in this study, by defining the considerations to be taken into account in determining the use of particular languages by the national and provincial governments. These are 'usage, practicality, expense, regional circumstances, and the needs and preferences of the population as a whole or in respective provinces'.[88] Like the sliding-scale approach, the effect of these considerations is that it is not constitutionally required for both national and provincial governments to use each of the official languages for all purposes of government. Accordingly, provinces can designate as official languages, on the basis of usage, from among the official languages that are principally spoken in the province. The national government can similarly decide the particular official languages for purposes of government. At the same time, to counter the possible dominance of one language in the public sphere at the national or provincial levels, this sub-section also provides that 'no national or provincial government may use only one official language'. It is clear from this that the FC seeks to accommodate language diversity through a policy of multilingualism at both national and provincial levels, but subject to the sliding-scale considerations for its application.

Admittedly, the considerations under FC s 6(3) offer both national and provincial governments relatively wide discretion to determine the use of languages for government purposes. As far as legislation is concerned, I share the view that the importance of language for public participation and the principle that laws ought to be intelligible to the people to whom they apply entail that '[l]egislation at the national level should, in principle, be published in all the principal languages of the state. Similarly, legislation at the provincial level should be published in the principal languages spoken in the province.'[89] This same logic dictates that legislative proceedings should take place in the principal languages of the state or of the province, as the case may be. Consistent with this account, the National Language Policy Framework (NLPF) envisages the use of all the official languages in 'all legislative activities' (publication of legislation and the conduct of legislative proceedings), including in *Hansard* publications,

---

[86] See I Currie 'Official Languages and Language Rights' in Woolman et al. (note 13 above) Chapter 65.

[87] Ibid, 65-14.

[88] It also provides that '[m]unicipalities must take into consideration the language usage and preferences of their residents'.

[89] Currie (note 86 above) 65-10.

as a matter of right, provided that in the case of provincial legislatures, regional circumstances will determine the language(s) to be used.'[90] [91]

For purposes of administration (in the provision of public services and communication involving government agencies), the various considerations under s 6(3) have more roles to play, but in the NLPF the general approach is in favour of using most of the official languages. Firstly, the NLPF envisages that official correspondence must be in the official language of the recipient's choice.[92] Secondly, '[w]here the effective and stable operation of government at any level requires comprehensive communication of information', government documents must be published in all the 11 languages or in all of the official languages of the province.[93] Thirdly, where this is not required, such documents should be published based on the principle of functional multilingualism.[94] Accordingly, based on the purpose of the communication, its public importance and its target audience, national government departments should publish communications in at least six languages simultaneously.[95] Consistent with this framework, the draft South African Languages Bill provides for publication of official documents in all 11 languages and where this is not possible in at least six languages, as laid down in the NLPF.

The aim of the official language policy is not only to protect the diversity of languages in South Africa, as required by CP XI, but also, by promoting the use of these languages for 'government purposes', to promote the participation of the public in the management of public affairs and to increase their access to public services. It also expresses the constitutional commitment to take the most important dimension of the identity of South Africans seriously and use it to ensure that speakers of the various languages have equal opportunities in various aspects of public life.[96] In this sense, multilingualism constitutes part of the overall constitutional scheme whose objective it is to 'heal the divisions of the past and establish a society based on democratic values, social justice and fundamental human rights'.[97]

---

90 NLPF para. 2.4.4.

91 On the details of the implementation of this see National Language Policy Framework (2002). For a comprehensive analysis of official languages and language rights see Currie (note 85 above).

92 NLPF para. 2.4.6.2.

93 NLPF para. 2.4.6.4.

94 NLPF para. 2.4.6.3.

95 NLPF para. 2.4.6.5.

96 According to the NLPF, the development of African languages is crucial to correct the imbalance that affects the speakers of these languages in terms of their communication with the government, and their access to government services, justice, education and jobs. See <http://www.saps.gov.za/saps_profile/components/language_management/downloads/implem_plan__english.pdf> [NLPF]

97 Preamble to the FC.

Notwithstanding the symbolic importance of the multilingual approach of official language policy and the rather wide language-policy framework, no adequate practical steps are being taken by the national government to give effect to the constitutional guarantees and this ambitious policy framework. The law that is supposed to give effect to important aspects of FC s 6 has not yet been passed by Parliament, although the draft bill has been around for some years now. At the political level, there seems to be little interest in and commitment to the constitutional promise of multilingualism. This problem is further compounded by the de facto dominance of English as lingua franca in the public domain, which is reinforced by the decision of the government in 2002 that state departments had to choose a single language for inter- and intra-departmental communication, which is inevitably English. This has given rise to a perception on the part of speakers of some languages, particularly Afrikaans, that the role of their languages is being diminished. Coupled with a general sense of powerlessness, this tends to engender a sense of alienation, particularly on the part of the Afrikaans-speaking population.[98] Naturally, this would undermine the constitutional objective of a South Africa that belongs to all who live in it, united in diversity. This is accordingly an area where there is clear divergence between the theory and practice of South Africa's constitutional design for accommodation of diversity.

6.4.2. *Other Language Guarantees*

One of the contentious issues that arose during the negotiations for the FC and continued to be an issue post-adoption of the FC is the status of single-medium public schools. This is addressed under FC s 29(2). The most important aspect of this sub-section from the perspective of this study is that it guarantees the right of everyone to 'receive education in the official language or languages of their choice in public educational institutions where that education is reasonably practicable.'[99] Although this is not a membership right, it nevertheless creates for members of the groups represented by the 11 official languages the right to education in *their* language if they so wish.

The controversy surrounding the use of language in education that continues to dominate the case law on the right to education relates to whether the right to education in a language of one's choice includes the right to single-medium institutions. Clearly, the FC envisages that this right may be given application through, among other means, single-medium institutions. According to Murray

[98] See M Schönteich & H Boshoff *'Volk', Faith and Fatherland: The Security Threat Posed by the White Right* ISS Monograph No. 81 (March 2003) 97–99.

[99] Practicability depends on, among other things, the number of students requesting teaching in the particular language and the availability of institutions providing education in the language.

and Simon, '[t]his clause attempts to straddle the interests of Afrikaners, by expressly permitting "single-medium institutions" … and the interests of the ANC, by emphasising equity and "the need to redress the results of past racially discriminatory laws and practices".'[100] In situations where a previously privileged group is now non-dominant in political and cultural terms, and seeks protection for its language by maintaining single-medium public schools, the challenge is to find the right balance between the rights of that group and the need, at the same time, to ensure equality of access to public schools for members of previously disadvantaged groups in the official language of their choices.[101] It is nevertheless clear from the provisions of the Constitution, as confirmed by the jurisprudence on the right to education,[102] that there is no right to a single-medium institution. Single-medium institutions are mentioned in the Constitution only as one means, among many others, of giving effect to the right to receive education in a language of choice subject to considerations of practicability, equity and the need to redress discriminatory practices.

From the perspective of this study, this is a model formulation that has given a robust constitutional expression to the vague, generally weak and highly qualified formulation of the rights of members of minorities to education under international law. It has also gone a step further than these international standards in that it envisages a positive obligation, under certain circumstances, to provide schools in minority languages. Unlike those international standards, however, under FC s 29(2) the right is couched as a purely individual right without any group dimension. This can be contrasted with FC s 31 which guarantees membership-based rights.

Consistent with the framework of minority rights adopted in this study, FC s 29 further provides communities with the right to establish and maintain, at their own expense, independent educational institutions. Accordingly, religious and cultural communities can establish and maintain educational institutions on the basis of *their religion, culture* and *language*, subject to non-discrimination on the basis of *race*.[103] Other requirements are registration and possession of standards not inferior to those at comparable public educational institutions.

---

[100] Murray & Simeon (note 3 above) 699.

[101] For a discussion on the court cases relating to education in minority languages, see S Woolman and M Bishop 'Education' in Woolman et al. (note 13 above) Chapter 57.

[102] See for example, *Laerckool Middlburg & 'n ander v Departementshoof, Mpumalanga Van Ondrways, & andre* 2003 (4) SA 160 (T).

[103] Kriegler J in this regard noted that this is the first qualification to the right of religious, cultural and linguistic minorities to establish and maintain educational institutions for the preservation of their religion, culture or language: 'A common culture, language or religion having racism as an essential element has no constitutional claim to the establishment of separate educational institutions. The Constitution protects diversity, not racial discrimination.' *Ex Parte Gauteng Provincial Legislature: In re Dispute Concerning the Constitutionality of the Gauteng School*

The FC provides additional language guarantees in the form of the prohibition of unfair discrimination against anyone on grounds of language under FC s 9. Discrimination on the basis of language in relation to the medium of schooling has been a subject of several cases.[104] These cases reveal that language cannot be used to exclude learners from access to public schools and that FC s 29 does not guarantee a right to a single-medium school. Moreover, the fact that the Bill of Rights is binding on both public authorities and private persons (both natural and juristic persons), by virtue of FC s 8(2), means that no entity that exercises public authority nor any private person can prohibit any person from using her language, or even any other language of her choice (FC s 30), in communication with others in public fora, in the media, in educational institutions, or in business.

Finally, FC s 6 establishes the PSALB. This institution is charged with two tasks. With respect to the official languages and the marginalised Khoi, Nama and San languages, as well as sign language, it has the responsibility to promote and create conditions for their development and use. As far as other languages used by various other linguistic communities and religious groups are concerned, the PSALB's role is to promote and ensure respect for them.

6.5. Rights of Religious and Cultural Communities

6.5.1. *The Relationship between s 30 and s 31*

FC s 30 provides for the right of *everyone* 'to use the language and to participate in the cultural life of their choice', subject to the Bill of Rights. It corresponds more with Article 15 of the ICESCR or Article 27 of the UDHR than with the minority rights guarantee under Article 27 of the ICCPR. This means that the right guaranteed under this section is essentially the freedom of individuals to be associated with a language or culture of *their choice* in general. Thus, unlike Article 27 of the ICCPR, it is not a right specific to members of specific ethno-cultural groups to their culture or language, although the choice involves that. In effect, it is a right that allows individuals to use even a language other than the language of their group or participate in the culture of a group other than their own.[105] As such, it is a right that guarantees individuals the freedom to

Education Bill of 1995 1996 (3) SA 165 (CC), 1996 (4) BCLR 537 (CC) para. 40. (*Constitutionality of the Gauteng School Education Bill*).

[104] See *Constitutionality of the Gauteng School Education Bill* (ibid) paras. 71 & 74; *Western Cape Minister of Education & Others v The Governing Body of Mikro Primary School* 2006 (1) SA 1 (SCA), 2005 (10) BCLR 973 (SCA); *Laerckool Middlburg & 'n ander v Departementshoof, Mpumalanga Van Ondrways, & andre* 2003 (4) SA 160 (T).

[105] See *Christian Education South Africa v Minister of Education* 2000 (4) SA 757 (CC), 2000 (10) BCLR 1051 (CC) para 26. For a contrary view see S Woolman 'Community Rights: Language, Culture & Religion' in Woolman et al. (note 13 above) Chapter 58, 58-49. He argues that FC s

determine which language to speak and which culture to be associated with, whether or not that language or culture is their own. In this sense, this is also a right that recognises the capacity of individuals to change their cultural or linguistic associations. One can conclude from this that as FC s 15 is to freedom of religion and belief, so FC s 30 is to language and culture. Accordingly, the relationship between FC s 30 and FC s 31 is similar to that between FC s 15 and FC s 31.

6.5.2. *S 31 Rights*

The formulation of FC s 31 to a large extent mirrors Article 27 of the ICCPR. Unlike FC s 30 rights, the rights under this section, like the rights under Article 27 of the ICCPR, are specifically applicable only to those who *belong to* a cultural, religious or linguistic community.[106] One can conclude from this that whereas FC s 30 rights are choice rights, FC s 31 rights are, by contrast, membership rights. Although the nature of the formulation of the rights under FC s 31 can further be examined, since that has in many ways been sufficiently addressed[107] it is important now to consider the ways in which FC s 31 rights serve to accommodate the linguistic, cultural and religious diversity of South Africa.

As we have seen in Chapter IV, the recognition of cultural groups can be approached from two perspectives. The first is the argument about culture. This is the argument that culture is central to defining an individual's identity and serves as an important source of meaning and framework for making meaningful choices in life. The right of people to be who they are is affirmed by various constitutional provisions. In particular, FC s 31 entails that people are not 'forced to subordinate themselves to the cultural and religious norms of others' and are 'able to enjoy what has been called "the right to be different"'.[108] Moreover, as the CC has held, 'if society is to be open and democratic in its fullest sense it needs to be tolerant and accepting of cultural pluralism'.[109] In other words, if individuals are to be free to pursue their life goals and make meaningful choices, their cultural attachments need both toleration and accommodation. Without this, members of minorities, in particular, cannot pursue, not only their cultural or religious commitments, which would be against their identity and dignity,

30's 'primary purpose is to regulate the horizontal relationships between individuals and other members of linguistic and cultural communities'.

[106] See Human Rights Committee, General Comment 23, Article 27 (fifth Session, 1994) UN Doc. HRI/GEN/1/Rev. 1 at 38 (1994) para. 14. [General Comment 23]

[107] See Woolman (note 105 above); P Lenta 'Religious Liberty and Cultural Accommodation' (2005) 122 *SALJ* 352.

[108] *Christian Education* (note 105 above) para. 24.

[109] Ibid, para. 23.

but also their conception of the good life in general, which would be contrary to their freedom.

The second perspective is the 'equality in difference' argument – that in multi-ethnic societies minorities can feel and be treated with equality only where their culture and religion are treated with equal concern and respect.[110] The implication of this is that the laws, practices and decisions of the state should be sensitive to and accommodative of the dictates of such religions and cultures on their members. Without this tolerance and accommodation, members of such religions or cultures cannot properly enjoy their FC s 9 right to 'equal protection and benefit of the law'. In this context, as Sachs J pointed out, 'equality lies not in treating everyone the same way, but in treating everyone with equal concern and respect'.[111] Accordingly, 'the state should, wherever reasonably possible, seek to avoid putting believers to extremely painful and intensely burdensome choices of either being true to their faith or else respectful of the law'.[112]

FC s 31 directly expresses a commitment on the part of the FC that it not only permits and affirms cultural, linguistic and religious diversity, but also 'promotes and celebrates it'.[113] This is given effect under the 1996 Constitution in at least two ways. As argued elsewhere in this study, one of the ways to give effect to the right to one's culture is through the legal recognition of customary laws. Accordingly, the recognition of customary law under the 1996 Constitution is an aspect of the ways by which the right to participate in one's culture under FC s 31 is given effect. The other one is through exemption from general rules that prohibit the pursuit of a certain religious or cultural commitment.

6.5.2.1. *The Right to Participate in One's Culture and the Recognition of Customary Law*

As in other African countries, one of the issues that arose in South Africa with respect to the right to culture is the constitutional status of customary laws and traditional institutions. Although colonialism deformed the customary law and traditional authorities of most African communities,[114] these institutions have

[110] See A Addis 'On Human Diversity and the Limits of Toleration' in I Shapiro & W Kymlicka (eds.) *Ethnicity and Group Rights* (1997) 112, 121. Also see D Miller 'Liberalism, Equal Opportunities and Cultural Commitments' in P Kelly (ed.) *Multiculturalism Reconsidered: Culture and Equality and its Critiques* (2002) 45, 48.

[111] *Christian Education* (note 105 above) para. 42. Sachs J made reference in the body of the judgement to *Prinsloo v Van der Linde and Another* 1997 (3) SA 1012 (CC), 1997 (6) BCLR 759 paras. 32–33.

[112] *Christian Education,* ibid, para. 35.

[113] See *Minister of Home Affairs and Another v Fourie and Another*; Lesbian and Gay Equality Project and Others 2006 (1) SA 524 (CC), 2006 (3) BCLR 355 (CC) para. 65. (Fourie).

[114] For details see GBN Ayittey *Indigenous African Institutions* (1991) Chapter 9; M Mamdani *Citizen and Subject: Contemporary Africa and the Legacy of Late Colonialism* (1996) 35–180; T Bennett & C Murray 'Traditional Leadership' in S Woolman et al. (note 13 above) Chapter 26, 26-8 – 26-15.

continued to play important roles in the lives of the majority of peoples in South Africa, as in most African countries.[115] As noted previously, the recognition of customary law and traditional institutions facilitates the integration of people who continue to rely on them into the processes of the state to the extent that they embody the culture, social values and traditions of such groups.[116]

Under the FC, customary laws and traditional institutions are given express recognition under Chapter 12. FC s 211(3) stipulates that 'the courts must apply customary law when the law is applicable, subject to the constitution and any other legislation that deals with customary law'. Moreover, in FC s 39(2) and (3) courts are called upon to develop customary law, along with common law, in accordance with 'the spirit, purport and objects of the Bill of Rights'. This constitutional recognition elevates the status of customary law to be an integral part of the legal system of South Africa with its own independent standing.[117] Accordingly, the courts (and legislature) are under a constitutional obligation to respect and accommodate customary law in the South African legal system. Similarly, the recognition of traditional authorities is a manifestation of the recognition of the structures of constituent ethno-cultural communities as forming part of the larger political system. But, as Gloppen notes, 'these structures are supplements to the democratically elected bodies, not alternative channels of government or of political representation'.[118]

Seen in the light of FC s 31, the importance of this is that it enhances the rights of members of indigenous cultural communities to participate in their culture by protecting the institutions that support such culture. For those people who run important aspects of their lives on the basis of customary law, its constitutional recognition and promotion marks a promise to a possible end of their historical alienation and marginalisation by and from the state, and opens an opportunity for their inclusion. It constitutes an important manifestation of the constitutional promise that 'South Africa belongs to all who live in it, united in our diversity'.

The recognition of customary law and the affirmation of its validity in the jurisprudence of the CC, even in cases in which a particular rule of customary law was found to be unconstitutional, as in *Bhe*, strengthens the right to participate in one's culture in more than one way. By affording a certain degree of

---

[115] See *Bhe v Magistrate, Khayelitsha & others* 2005 (1) SA 580 (CC), 2005 (1) BCLR (CC) para. 45 [Bhe] ; also see A Donkers & R Murray 'prospects and problems facing traditional leaders in South Africa' in B de Villiers (ed.) *The Rights of Indigenous People: A Quest for Coexistence* (1997) 39, 43–44.

[116] *Bhe* (ibid) paras. 41 & 45.

[117] See *Alexkor Ltd & another v Richtersveld Community & Others* 2004 (5) SA 460 (CC) para. 51, (stating that '[w]hile in the past indigenous law was seen through the common law lens, it must now be seen as an integral part of our law' and that 'the Constitution acknowledges the originality and distinctiveness of indigenous law as an independent source of norms within the legal system'). [Richtersveld]

[118] Gloppen (note 8 above) 237.

constitutional solicitude to customary law, it gives legal support to the institutions in which the culture and heritage of the community are embedded. This has the additional value of guaranteeing the preservation of this culture and heritage, and its transmission to future generations. Moreover, it expresses the commitment of the FC to take seriously and treat with equal concern and respect those cultures and ways of life that have historically been denigrated and undermined. It is, in a way, one of the ways by which the FC seeks to promote equality in difference, a concept of equality accepted under South African constitutional law.[119]

The extent to which the constitutional promise to take the culture and institutions of hitherto marginalised communities seriously can make a meaningful contribution to enhancing the quality of life of those communities that rely on it depends on how courts define the relationship of customary law to the Constitution, and in particular the Bill of Rights. As the CC warned in the First Certification Judgement, the 'confrontation between the Bill of Rights and legislation on the one side and indigenous law on the other need not take place in the manner that' frustrates the development of the latter.[120] One possible way of approaching the tension without undermining or threatening the survival of customary law is to treat it as a conflict between one right, often equality and/or dignity, and another right, the right to culture.[121] Accordingly, the process of defining this relationship is also a matter of reconciling and balancing the competing interests, wherever possible, in a way that permits the survival and development of indigenous law as recognition of the rights of those communities, hitherto marginalised, who depend on and wish to live under it, to be governed by their indigenous law.[122] This rests within the South African constitutional framework more on the rights to culture, as enunciated under s 31, and equality, under s 9, than on self-determination.

6.5.2.2. *Exemptions from General Rules*

Another important issue that arises with respect to FC s 31 is the question of how to accommodate and afford protection to those aspects of the identity of individuals and groups that do not conform to the standards of the mainstream society. One of the ways by which FC s 31 can give practical effect to this commitment is by requiring the state to *accommodate* even those aspects of the culture or religion of a community that mainstream society regards as unusual,

[119] See *Christian Education* (note 105 above); Fourie (note 112 above).

[120] *First Certification Judgment* (note 21 above) paras. 200, 202.

[121] See V Bronstein 'Reconceptualizing the Customary Law Debate in South Africa' (1998) 14 (3) *SAJHR* 388–410.

[122] Consider the argument presented by Ngcobo J in *Bhe* (note 115 above).

bizarre or even threatening.[123] This is generally established through judicial pronouncements.

As the internal limitation of FC s 31 and the general limitation under FC s 36 reveal, the rights guaranteed are not without limits. Accordingly, although the protection of the rights under this section entitles members of religious or cultural minorities to be exempted from general laws that interfere with the pursuit of their religion or culture, it does not do so all the time. The various cases decided by the CC reveal that exemption on the ground of culture or religion is justified where certain conditions are fulfilled. First, the practice with respect of which exemption is requested has to be a cultural or religious practice. However, as the CC held in *Pillay*,[124] it is not required that such a practice be obligatory. It suffices that it forms part of the culture or religion of the community to which the claimant belongs. Secondly, the practice must be one that is genuinely held by the claimant to be an important part of her religion or culture. Accordingly, as the CC held in *Pillay*, a claimant who merely appears to adhere to a religious or cultural practice, but is willing to forgo it if necessary, cannot demand the same adjustment from others as those whose identity will be seriously undermined if they do not follow their belief.[125] Thirdly, it must be impossible for the claimant to practice her strongly held culture or religion while respecting the law in question. In *Christian Education*, part of the reasoning of the CC for declining exemption seems to be that parents can follow the religious practice in question while respecting the particular law challenged. Similarly, as the CC in *Pillay* pointed out, the infringement that the law or the decision in question causes to the right of the claimant should be severe enough to require the exemption.[126]

The fourth condition, as envisaged under FC s 31(2), is that exemption should not lead to a violation of the rights of others. In *Christian Education*, the applicants challenged the law that prohibits corporal punishment of children in schools on account of their religious beliefs, and requested exemption from its application. In declining the request for exemption, one of the important considerations for the CC was the rights of children to personal security and dignity.[127] In the *Prince* case,[128] Sachs J puts this more broadly when he says in a strong minority judgement that 'where there are practices that might fall within a general prohibition, but *that do not involve any violation of the Bill of*

[123] See *Prince v President, Cape Law Society, & Others* 2002 (2) SA 794 (CC), 2002 (3) BCLR 231 (CC) para. 172; *Christian Education* (note 105 above) para 25; *Fourie* (note 112) para. 60.
[124] *MEC for Education, KwaZulu-Natal & Others v Pillay* 2008 (1) SA 474 (CC) (Pillay case).
[125] Ibid, para. 86.
[126] Ibid, para. 85.
[127] See *Christian Education* (note 105 above) paras 39–49.
[128] *Prince* (note 122 above).

Rights, the Constitution obliges the state to walk the extra mile'[129] in order to accommodate the religious or cultural commitments of minorities.

The fifth is that the law or practice can achieve its legitimate purpose while accommodating the religious or cultural commitments of minorities. In other words, where the law can achieve its purpose with less restrictive means, the claimant should be given exemption. In granting the exemption, the *Pillay* Court held that:

> the admirable purposes that school uniforms serve do not seem to be undermined by granting religious and cultural exemptions. There is no reason to believe, nor has the school presented any evidence to show, that a learner who is granted an exemption from the provisions of the school (uniform) Code will be any less disciplined or that she will negatively affect the discipline of others.[130]

The sixth condition is that the costs of the exemption should not be so great as to frustrate the legitimate aims of the law in question. Such a cost can be weighed in terms of both resources and the possibility of effective regulation. In the *Prince* case, for example, the majority held that the cost of exemption of Rastafarians from the Drugs and Drug Trafficking Act to allow the use of cannabis for their religious purposes was that it could not be effectively regulated, a cost found by the majority to be so high that it could frustrate the legitimate aim of the law, and hence declined the requested exemption. Sometimes the determination of the cost can be affected by the religious or moral convictions of sitting judges and/or, as in the *Prince* case, the court may not always get the assessment right.[131] It is important to note here that there could be cases where any form of exemption from the measures set by the law could seriously negate the legitimate purposes of the law. This is the case, according to the CC, where such measures 'have principled foundations and are deliberately designed to transform national civic consciousness in a major way'.[132] That is the case where the purpose of the law is to ban all instances of the act in question. In *Christian Education*, the court accordingly held that 'the whole symbolic, moral and pedagogical purpose of the measure (of prohibition of corporal punishment) would be disturbed, and the State's compliance with its duty to protect people from violence would be undermined'[133] if religious exemption from the prohibition of corporal punishment in schools were allowed.

An important aspect of the jurisprudence relating to exemptions from general rules is that it finds its defence on the basis of substantive equality. As Sachs J

---

129 Ibid, para. 149. (my emphasis).

130 *Pillay* case (note 123 above) para. 101.

131 For a critique of the failure of the CC to allow the exemption see Lenta (note 106 above) 356–358, 371–375.

132 *Christian Education* (note 105 above) para. 50.

133 Ibid.

aptly put it, '[e]quality means equal concern for and respect across difference … Equality therefore does not imply a leveling or homogenization of behaviors but an acknowledgement and acceptance of difference.'[134] If people of different religious and cultural membership are to be treated with equal concern and respect, and thus enjoy equality, it is necessary that their religious and cultural commitments are reasonably accommodated including, where possible, by exempting them from conforming to a general law. Langa CJ thus stated in *MEC for Education: Kwazulu-Natal and Others v Pillay*, such accommodation is necessary 'in order to allow all people to participate and enjoy all their rights equally. It ensures that we do not relegate people to the margins of society because they do not or cannot conform to certain social norms.'[135]

6.6. The CRCRLC

In addition to the generally common constitutional arrangements and protection mechanisms considered above, the FC has additionally provided for the establishment of a Commission for the Promotion and Protection of the Rights of Cultural, Religious and Linguistic Communities (CRCRLC or the Commission) as one of the Chapter 9 institutions supporting constitutional democracy. According to FC s 185(1), the primary objectives of the CRCRLC are

- to promote respect for the rights of cultural, religious, and linguistic communities;
- to promote and develop peace, friendship, humanity, tolerance, and national unity among cultural, religious, and linguistic communities, on the basis of equality, non-discrimination, and free association; and
- to recommend the establishment or recognition, in accordance with national legislation, of a cultural or other council or councils for a community or communities in South Africa.

In 2002, Parliament established the CRCRLC under the Commission for the Promotion and Protection of the Rights of Cultural, Religious and Linguistic Communities Act No 19 of 2002. In addition to those listed under FC s 84 (1), s 4 of the Act includes as the objectives of the CRCRLC:

- to foster mutual respect among cultural, religious and linguistic communities;
- to promote the right of communities to develop their historically diminished heritage.

---

[134] *Ministry of Home Affairs and Another v Fourie and Another* 2006 (1) SA 524 (CC), 2006 BCLR 355 (CC) para. 60.

[135] 2008 (1) SA 474 (CC); 2008 (2) BCLR 99 (CC) para. 73.

To this end, the Commission is vested with promotional, investigative, educational, conciliatory and advisory powers and functions necessary for achieving its objectives as set out in the Constitution and the enabling act. According to s 5 of the Act, the Commission is the body responsible for conducting various programmes for the promotion of both awareness of the various cultural, religious and linguistic communities and respect for and protection of their rights. As part of its promotional mandate, the Commission can recommend the establishment of community councils and recognise such councils, who can apply for financial assistance to the Commission or any other organ.[136] In addition to monitoring, investigating and researching on any issues concerning the rights of these communities, it also can recommend on any legislation that impacts on the rights of those communities, and inform the appropriate organs or authorities of the state on any relevant matter, and make recommendations for dealing with such matters. Most importantly, the Commission is mandated to facilitate the resolution of what the act calls 'frictions' between and within such communities or between any such community and an organ of a state, as well as to receive and deal with the requests related to their rights.

The availability of such an institution with such powers and functions is of particular importance to the achievement of the multicultural commitments of the FC. It provides a framework for promoting the rich cultural, religious and linguistic diversity of South Africa as an important source of meaning in the lives of many South Africans, and as a resource for overcoming the divisions of the past and building a common South African identity. One of the ways in which it can achieve this is by providing direct and easy access to people who wish to air their concerns and fears with respect to the enjoyment and preservation of their culture, religion or language. It is also more suited than the ordinary judicial process to address promptly situations of conflicts within and between communities, or between such communities and the state, as it is empowered to conduct investigation on its own motion. It is clear from this that the establishment of this Commission is part of the general commitment of the Constitution to accommodate South Africa's ethno-cultural diversity. As such, it serves a particular constitutional purpose whose pursuit could have been overlooked and could not have been effectively realised if it were under the Human Rights Commission, whose main object is to address mainstream human rights issues.

The extent to which it can serve its purposes and discharge its mandates, however, depends not only on how effectively the CRCRLC executes its mandate, but also on the degree of financial, resource and political support it gets from

[136] S 36 & 37 of the act.

government.[137] If the experience so far is anything to go by, the political will for the effective operation of the CRCRLC leaves much to be desired.

6.7. Equality beyond Recognition of Difference: Socio-Economic Guarantees, including Positive Measures

In South Africa, as in other African countries and multi-ethnic societies elsewhere in the world, racial, linguistic and religious diversity raises the question not only of recognition of diversity but also of redressing historical disadvantages and existing inequalities. Due to long history of discrimination that resulted from the practice of apartheid,[138] the question of redressing historical disadvantages and existing inequalities is perhaps more urgent in South African than in any other country. This is indeed expressly recognised in the 1996 Constitution and specific provisions are stipulated to achieve the objective of socio-economic equality in South Africa. Understandably, the constitutional commitment for equality is thus the most conspicuous and demanding of all. Equality is one of the fundamental values of on which the new South Africa is founded under S 1 of the Constitution. According to S 7(1), equality is also one of the three democratic values that underpin the bill of rights of guaranteed in Chapter II of the Constitution.

Reflecting the place of honour that is accorded to equality, the first right listed in the Bill of Rights is the rights to equality. The right as provided for under S 9 of the constitution consists not only of formal equality but also guarantees substantive equality. Thus, FC s 9 (1) provides that '[e]very one is equal before the law and has the right to equal protection and benefit of the law'. Most significantly, 'equality', affirms FC s 9 (2), 'includes the full and equal enjoyment of all rights and freedoms'. Accordingly, it further stipulates that '[t]o promote the achievement of equality, legislative and other measures designed to protect or advance persons, or categories of persons, disadvantaged by unfair discrimination may be taken.' As it is clear from this formulation, positive measures required for rectifying disadvantages resulting from historical discrimination are not exception to and derogation from the right to equality. Rather, they are, in the words of the CC, 'a substantive and composite part of, the equality protection envisaged by the provisions of section 9 and of the Constitution as a whole'.[139]

137 For a rather harshly critical review of the role of CRCRLC see S Woolman & J Soweto Aullo 'Commission for the Promotion and Protection of the Rights of Cultural, Religious and Linguistic Communities' in Woolman et al. (note 13 above) Chapter 24.

138 For a detailed account of South Africa's experience of inequality and discrimination see Sampie Terreblanche *A History of Inequality in South Africa 1652–2002* (2002).

139 *Minister of Finance v Van Heerden* 2004 (6) SA 121 (CC), 2004 (11) BCLR 1125 (CC) para. 32.

Various measures have been taken in the socio-economic spheres of South Africa in order to redress the pervasive inequalities among various race groups and sexes. These include measures in the areas of access to land rights, education, health, housing and employment, among others. One of the most notable measures adopted to achieve socio-economic equality include legislative measures regulating employment and economic empowerment. In line with the requirements of the Constitution under s 195 (1) (*i*) to make the public administration broadly representative of the South African people, the government adopted a policy of affirmative action.[140] The major normative framework underpinning the policy is the goal of redressing the imbalances in the composition of the public service and achieving substantive equality. This the policy has sought to pursue without seriously compromising the requirements of minimum competency and fairness as stipulated under s 195 (1) (*i*).

As part of the initiative to rectify the disadvantages of the past and ensure equality of opportunity for all, the government also adopted the Employment Equity Act.[141] The preamble to the act describes the purposes thereof 'to promote the constitutional right of equality and the exercise of true democracy, to eliminate unfair discrimination in employment, to ensure the implementation of employment equity to redress the effects of discrimination, to achieve a diverse workforce broadly representative of our people, to promote economic development and efficiency in the workforce and to give effect to the obligations of the Republic as a member of the International Labour Organization.' Section 2 of the Act further states the objective of the Act as being the promotion of equal opportunity and fair treatment in employment through the elimination of unfair discrimination; and the implementation of affirmative action measures to redress the disadvantages in employment experienced by designated groups, in order to ensure their equitable representation in all occupational categories and levels in the workforce. Chapter 3 of the Act prescribes affirmative action measures that designated employers are expected to take. Under s 15 of the Act, affirmative action measures are defined as 'measures design to ensure that suitably qualified people from designated groups have equal employment opportunities and are equitably represented in all occupational categories and levels in the workforce of a designated employer.' The designated groups to which affirmative action measures are applicable are 'black people, women and people with disabilities.'

Notwithstanding the fact that the various legislative and other measures taken aim at rectifying the injustices of the past and achieving substantive equality, the means and method used such as affirmative action measures unleashed heated

[140] For further discussion on these see Kristin Henrard *Minority Protection in Post-Apartheid South Africa: Human Rights, Minority Rights and Self-Determination* (2002) 179–180.

[141] Employment Equity Act 55 of 1998.

debate in the country. The major concern raised was how such measures can be pursued without seriously undermining the entitlement of all South Africans to equality. Most importantly, serious questions are being asked if equality can be achieved without changes in the current structure of the South African economy. The flexibility of the Constitution to allow the government to introduce such structural changes to the economy has been a subject of fierce debate in the country during 2011 and 2012.

6.8. Conclusion

This chapter is an attempt to explore the form that the proposed constitutional minority rights regime, in the robust sense defended in this study (constitutional design for accommodation of ethno-cultural diversity), takes in the context of the specific historical and political situation of particular countries and how it operates in practice. As the foregoing discussions revealed, at the political level, while rejecting group membership as a basis of political representation and participation, the FC has nevertheless established an inclusive democratic system that reflects the most important components of the constitutional design for accommodation of diversity outlined in the previous chapter and defended in this study in general. As reflected in the design of South Africa's democracy as set out under the FC, it has been identified above that this accommodative constitutional design has three important dimensions. The first is expressed by the principle of proportional representation which shaped not only the design of the electoral system but also the organisation and operation of the national and provincial legislative processes and the character of the public service. The second dimension relates to the principle of public participation which is interpreted by the CC as endowing South Africa with a deliberative form of democracy which guarantees all members of society a say in national policy-making processes. Last but not least, the aspect of the FC that also manifests the model defended in this study is the system of provincial government and the reference to the right to self-determination for a community sharing a common cultural and language heritage.

Consistent with the model defended in this study, the FC additionally provides certain rights and protection mechanisms for the identity of what it calls 'cultural, religious and linguistic communities'. Firstly, it adopts a multilingual policy regime. Accordingly, it designates 11 languages as official languages, which serve for government purposes at the national and provincial levels. It also recognises other languages and mandates their promotion and development. Moreover, the FC guarantees to everyone the right to receive education in the official language of one's choice. Finally, it prohibits discrimination on the basis of language both in the public and private spheres. Secondly, it also provides for the promotion of the cultural and religious identity of members of various cultural and religious groups. This is expressed within the framework of FC s 31 not only in the recognition of customary law and the institution of traditional leadership but also in exemptions from general rules elaborated in the jurisprudence of the CC. Thirdly, the FC establishes institutions for the promotion and enforcement of these various guarantees. Accordingly, apart from the CC, it established the PSALB and the CRCRLC with mandates to promote the rights of cultural, religious and linguistic communities.

Although this chapter did not investigate the actual operation of this system in depth, it has nevertheless been concluded that these various institutional arrangements and guarantees have been instrumental in the process towards achieving a South Africa that 'belongs to all who live in it, united in our diversity'.[142] Nevertheless, some of the issues identified also clearly illustrate that the constitutional design defended in this study is only a necessary, and not a sufficient, condition for a successful accommodation of ethno-cultural diversity. Political, social and economic conditions determine the extent to which the constitutional framework can operate optimally to achieve this objective. In the South African context, for example, notwithstanding their representation, minority groups and minority parties seem to have become peripheral to the processes of the state. This is not, however, due to the failure of the PR system. It is rather attributable to the South African political context that led to the evolution of a *de facto* one-party democracy. Given ANC's historical ambivalence towards some of the important aspects of the constitutional design, including the system of provincial government, this is making not only the implementation of some of these accommodative devices, but also their future, uncertain.

This greatly increases the importance of the CC's role in actively scrutinising the actions or inactions of the political organs of government that may threaten the application of the constitutional principles aimed at an inclusive and participatory democratic system. In this regard, the articulation of the nature of South Africa's democracy under the FC as being based on deliberation, with respect for and accommodative of the voices of minorities, such as in *Masondo* and *Doctors for Life*, among others, is a highly commendable development, which, if fully embraced by the CC, will help to rectify the functional deficits of South Africa's one-party-dominant democracy.

---

[142] See Preamble to the FC.

CHAPTER VII

THE CASE OF ETHIOPIA'S ETHNIC FEDERALISM

7.1. Introduction

Although the origin and process of the making of Ethiopia starkly differ from those of most African states, it is similar to those states in facing the challenge of managing its ethno-culturally diverse population.[1] One of the dominant features of its political history, particularly since World War II, has been the struggle between the forces of centralisation and unity, on the one hand, and ethno-regional minorities that sought equal recognition of their cultures, political representation and participation, and, most of all, territorial autonomy on the other. This struggle precipitated a civil war involving numerous armed liberation movements organised along ethnic lines.[2] When these movements, led by the Ethiopian Peoples Revolutionary Democratic Front (EPRDF), ousted the military regime of Mengistu Haile-Mariam in 1991, the most dominant agenda was the resolution of the so-called nationality question (the problem of minorities) through the structural and democratic transformation of the Ethiopian state. Although there was no agreement more on mechanisms for addressing the problem than on the nature of the problem itself,[3] the major political forces of the time considered it critical to deploy ethnicity, expressed in terms of national self-determination, as a principle of political organisation.[4] This led to the adoption of one of the most radical constitutions in Africa, if not in the world, in terms of the extent of its institutionalisation of ethnic diversity.[5]

---

[1] On the nature of ethno-cultural diversity in Ethiopia, see D Levine *Greater Ethiopia: The Evolution of a Multiethnic Society* (2000); A Habtu 'Ethnic Pluralism as an Organizing Principle of the Ethiopian Federation' (2004) 28 *Dialectical Anthropology* 91, 93–97; K Tronvoll *Ethiopia: A New Start?* (2000) 6–11.

[2] On the eve of the fall of the military regime, there were about 17 armed movements mobilised for the recognition and protection of the rights and distinct identity of particular communities. See *Be Ethiopia Ye Dimocraci Sirat Ginbata Gudayoch* (Ginbot 1994 E.C.) 26.

[3] Assefa Fesseha offers a comprehensive analysis of the various perspectives, their convergence and divergence. A Fiseha *Federalism and the Accommodation of Diversity in Ethiopia: A Comparative Study* (2005/2006) 52–79.

[4] See L Aalen *Ethnic Federalism in a Dominant Party State: The Ethiopian Experience 1991–2000* (2002) 39–41.

[5] See Habtu (note 1 above) 91–123. Will Kymlicka notes in this regard that what makes Ethiopian federalism strikingly distinct from other multi-nation federal systems is the 'explicitness, at constitutional level, of its affirmation of the national self-determination and the logical consistency with which it attempts to institutionalize that principle'. W Kymlicka *Emerging Western Models of*

If there is one overriding concept discernible throughout Ethiopia's 1994 Constitution,[6] it is the concern with the rights of what it calls the 'nations, nationalities, and peoples' of Ethiopia.[7] In a word, ethnicity is the one issue to which the Constitution primarily addresses itself and it constitutes the epicentre of the constitutional framework. According to the Preamble to the Federal Democratic Republic of Ethiopia (FDRE) Constitution, the objects of the federalisation of Ethiopia, with the rights of ethnic minorities as its main organising principle, are, among others, to build 'a political community … capable of ensuring lasting peace, guaranteeing democratic order, and advancing our economic and social development'[8] and to rectify historically unjust relationships.[9] Against the background of these objectives and the general framework established in Chapter V, this chapter examines Ethiopia's constitutional design for the accommodation of diversity. This serves not only as a further illustration of the practical institutionalisation and operation of the constitutional design defended in this study, but also to point to the form that this design should not take and the pitfalls that must be avoided.

7.2. Federalism as the Only Viable Option

Unlike South Africa, for Ethiopia a unitary form of state structure was not an option at all. There were at least two reasons for this, one conceptual and another practical. Firstly, a unitary system cannot coexist with sub-national communities that possess sovereignty and retain the right to withdraw unilaterally from the union. Thus, Dr Samuel Assefa of Rutgers University, now Ethiopia's Ambassador to the United States, aptly captures the incompatibility between unitarism and sub-national sovereignty:

> The attempt to combine these discrepant constitutional commitments – to vest all authority permanently in the centre, on the one hand, and, on the other, to recognize the right of some or all local units to secession and independence – would yield a most unwieldy hybrid, a genuinely neurotic constitution, one might say.[10]

Multination Federations: Are They Relevant for Africa? Paper delivered at the Seminar on Ethnic Federalism: The Challenges for Ethiopia held on 14–16 April 2004 in Addis Ababa.

[6] Proclamation No. 1/1995 Proclamation of the Constitution of Federal Democratic Republic of Ethiopia *Federal Negarit Gazeta* 1st Year No. 1 Addis Ababa 21 August 1995 adopted on 8 December 1994, came into effect on 21 August 1995. [FDRE Constitution]

[7] At least 23 articles of the Constitution, including the Preamble, make direct or indirect reference to 'nations, nationalities and peoples'.

[8] See Preamble to FDRE Constitution.

[9] Ibid.

[10] S Assefa 'Of Federalism and Secession' in *Constitutionalism: Reflections and Recommendations, Symposium on the Making of the New Ethiopian Constitution* (1993) 113–125, 115.

Secondly, central to the war that various groups fought against the military regime was the high degree of concentration of power at the centre and the corresponding political and economic marginalisation and cultural domination of the various population groups constituting Ethiopia.[11] After the fall of the Dergue, the mood of the new forces was decidedly for making a sweeping break from this politically unitarist and culturally exclusive past and creating a new political system.[12] One is inclined to agree with Samuel Assefa's categorical statement that a unitary system 'is not a *live option* for Ethiopia – it does not lie within the horizon of what is actually possible, given where we [in Ethiopia] stand today'.[13] There has been general agreement across the political divide that there is no alternative to federalism.[14]

As a result, the FDRE Constitution 'establishes a Federal and Democratic State structure'.[15] As Fasil Nahum observes, the formula 'We the nations, nationalities and peoples of Ethiopia' is applied 'to its fullest extent in the Constitution' to create a multinational federation with the constituent ethnic groups as its foundation.[16] Whereas under the South African Constitution provinces are not created merely on the basis of ethnic boundaries and enjoy only very limited, albeit not insignificant, competences, under the FDRE Constitution the member states of the federation are constituted mainly on the basis of ethnic boundaries, and ethnic groups form the foundation of the federation and are entitled to substantial political rights. This is further outlined below.

---

[11] See Habtu (note 1 above) 96–101; Fiseha (note 3 above) 11–79; K Abraham *Ethiopia from Bullets to the Ballot Box* (1994); K Mengisteab 'New Approaches to State Building in Africa: The Case of Ethiopia's Ethnic Based Federalism' (1997) 40 *African Studies Review* 111–132; J Abbink 'Breaking and Making the State: The Dynamic of Ethnic Democracy in Ethiopia' (1995) 13 *Journal of Contemporary African Studies* 149–163.

[12] At the Constituent Assembly the dominant view was that, given the history of the country, the constitutional empowerment of the constituent ethnic groups through the right to self-determination was the only way to redeem and rectify the wrongs of the past. See Minutes of the Constitutional Assembly (Nov. 1994), Minutes No. 20 of Hidar 12 and 13, 1987 E.C. For more see also *Be Ethiopia Ye Dimocraci Sirat Ginbata Gudayoch* (note 2 above) 23–30. According to EPRDF, the policy on the rights of ethnic communities is essentially an expression and guarantee of the freedom and equality of the diverse groups that together constitute Ethiopia. Ibid, 23–41.

[13] Assefa (note 10 above) 115.

[14] There is, however, disagreement among various sections of society and political parties as to the form that federalism should take. Many reject ethnicity as the basis for federalising Ethiopia. The only political parties that opposed the federalisation of Ethiopia were the All Amhara Peoples Organisation and Ethiopian Democratic Union Party. Aalen (note 4 above) 42–43.

[15] Article 1. Proclamation No. 1/1995 Proclamation of the Constitution of Federal Democratic Republic of Ethiopia *Federal Negarit Gazeta* 1st Year No. 1 Addis Ababa 21 August 1995.

[16] F Nahum *A Constitution for a Nation of Nations: The Ethiopian Prospect* (1997) 52.

7.2.1. *The Founding Principles and Peculiar Features of Ethiopia's Federation*

It has been noted above that ethnicity is probably the most important issue to which the FDRE Constitution addresses itself. This is also reflected in the normative premises of the federation that this Constitution establishes. One of these is the constitutional importance of ethnic groups. The Preamble to the FDRE Constitution distinctly depicts the place of honour that the numerous ethno-linguistic groups of the country occupy in the new constitutional order. It is not with the familiar words 'We the people ...' that the Preamble commences, but rather with 'We the Nations, Nationalities and Peoples of Ethiopia ...'.

The difference between the two formulations is not one of terminology alone; there is a qualitative and even paradigmatic difference. Whereas 'We the people' signifies the existence only of one demos, 'We the nations, nationalities and peoples' suggests the existence of more than one demos constituting Ethiopia. This is essentially a rejection of the monolithic conception of the state as a nation-state – a state with a singular and homogenous identity.[17] As Fasil Nahum puts it, these words signify that the Constitution 'is not a constitution of the Ethiopian citizens simply lumped together as a people'. Elaborating on this, he writes that 'the Ethiopian citizens are first categorized in their different ethno-linguistic groupings and then these groupings come together as authors of, and beneficiaries from, the Constitution of 1994'.[18]

Moreover, whereas in the nation-state model individual citizens are the foundation of the society and hence the constitutional order, in this case the various ethno-linguistic groups are the point of departure. This changes the definition of the state-society relationship from that between the individual and the state (as in the dominant liberal constitutional tradition) into a relationship mainly between ethnic minorities and the state. Consequently, in contrast to the liberal constitutional tradition in which the individual takes a central place,[19] in the Ethiopian constitutional model ethnic communities are the ultimate agents and bearers of rights. It is clear from this that the Ethiopian Constitution is more communitarian in its theoretical premises and content than libertarian and egalitarian.

---

[17] Nahum writes: 'We the nations, nationalities and peoples' recognizes Ethiopia as a Nation of Nations.' Ibid, 51. Also see Habtu (note 1 above) 102.

[18] Nahum, ibid.

[19] The concern of liberal constitutionalism is securing the rights and liberties of individuals. See G Walker 'The Idea of Nonliberal Constitutionalism' in I Shapiro & W Kymlicka (eds.) *Ethnicity and Group Rights* (1997) 154. As a result, its preoccupation is that of defining the nature of the relationship between the individual and the state. In the words of Buchanan, therefore, 'the problem of constitutional design was thought to be that of insuring that such (state) power would be effectively limited' to secure the maximum possible freedom for the individual. See JM Buchanan 'Notes on the Liberal Constitution' (1993) 14 *The Cato Journal* <http://www.cato.org/pubs/journal/cj14n1-1.htm>.

In consonance with this, Article 8 provides: 'All sovereign power resides in the Nations, Nationalities and Peoples of Ethiopia'. Reaffirming that the Constitution is a covenant among the various ethnic communities rather than among citizens as individuals, the second paragraph of this article states that 'the Constitution is an expression of their sovereignty'. Once again, it departs from the dominant constitutional paradigm of the liberal nation-state. Conventionally, popular sovereignty is formulated in a way that ascribes sovereignty to the entire people of a state, made up of individual citizens and their shared will.[20] In the formulation of Article 8, sovereignty does not reside in the Ethiopian people in their entirety. Instead, it is shared, to use the terminology of the Constitution, among the 'nations, nationalities and peoples' of Ethiopia.

Another distinguishing feature, which underlies all the above, is the principle of national self-determination. It was first introduced as a constitutional principle into the Ethiopian legal order under the 1991 Transitional Period Charter of Ethiopia. According to the Preamble of this Charter, 'self-determination of all peoples shall be one of the governing principles of political, economic and social life'. As set out under Article 39 of the FDRE Constitution, 'every Nation, Nationality and People in Ethiopia has an unconditional right to self-determination including the right to secession'. This gives the various ethno-linguistic communities in the country the highest possible level of constitutional recognition and right. Viewed from this perspective, ethnicity is established as a constitutionally valued main basis for political organisation. Thus, the legitimacy of the structures and processes of the state largely depends on the extent to which they reflect the demands of ethno-linguistic diversity in the country. Accordingly, the federal system is designed as a means for recognising and accommodating the interests and distinct identity of the various groups, the foundation of the constitution. To say that this is one of the most controversial clauses of the Ethiopian constitution may be an understatement.[21]

---

[20] See, for example, the popular sovereignty clause of the US Constitution and that of the Republic of South Africa.

[21] For some, Article 39 is laid down to legitimise constitutionally the eventual dismemberment of Ethiopia as a state. See M Haile 'The New Ethiopian Constitution: Its Impact upon Unity, Human Rights and Development' (1996) 20 *Suffolk Transnational LR* 1–84; Assefa (note 10 above); YC Metiku, 'Ethiopia's Right to 'Life' in International Law', (1994) 2 *New Trends in Ethiopian Studies* 205, 208–210; B Haile-Selassie *Ethiopia: A Precarious Ethno-Federal Constitutional Order* (Unpublished SJD dissertation, University of Wisconsin Law School, 2002); JW Harbeson 'A Bureaucratic Authoritarian Regime' (October 1999) 9 *Journal of Democracy* 62. For the protagonists of this article it is a guarantee against abuse by the state. Nahum (note 14 above) 53; PH Henz 'A Political Success Story' (October 1999) 9 *J of Democracy* 40. But one cannot understand why secession was included in the first place without examining the political reality of Ethiopia immediately after the fall of the Dergue regime and its historical origins in the political history of the country. That was a time when the different parts of the country were under the control of various ethnic-based armed liberation fronts, and one cannot be certain that without the right to secession these forces would have been willing to participate in the 'Democratic and

It is within this framework that the Constitution sets up the structure of Ethiopia's federation.[22] One of the consequences of these normative premises is the assignment of the power of constitutional adjudication to a political body, the House of the Federation (HoF).[23]

7.2.2. *Member States of the Federation*

As noted previously, the capacity of a federation to accommodate territorially based ethno-cultural diversity depends upon the delimitation of the boundaries of constituent units along ethno-cultural lines. Article 47 of the Constitution of Ethiopia designates as member states of the federation nine *states* or *regional states*,[24] varying enormously in population size, level of development, geographic area and level of diversity.[25] We have noted above that the main purpose of Ethiopia's federal system, according to the Constitution, is to prevent the recurrence of the civil war which was caused by what it calls 'unjust historical relationships', through accommodation of diversity. Ethnicity has therefore been the main, if not the only, consideration in the demarcation of the boundaries of the regional states. Article 46(2) provides that the states are to be constituted 'on the basis of the settlement patterns, language, identity and consent of the people concerned'. These factors to a large extent reflect ethnicity. Thus, they are substantially similar to the elements of the definition of 'nations, nationalities and peoples' under Article 39(5) of the Constitution.[26] In accordance with these provisions, Article 47 established the nine regional states. Many of the federal states are designated as 'mother states' for the majority ethnic group inhabiting them. The names of the six major groups to which six of the nine states are designated are reflected

---

Peaceful Transitional Conference' of July 1991 which established the transitional government. In a way, it was a necessary condition to bring all the armed struggle movements to the negotiating table and a means for building their lost confidence and trust in the central government. See A Eshseté 'Ethnic Federalism: New Frontiers in Ethiopian Politics' in *First National Conference on Federalism, Conflict and Peace Building* (2003) 142, 150–159 [First National Conference]; A Habtu 'Multi-Ethnic Federalism in Ethiopia: A Study of the Secession Clause in the Constitution' (2005) 35(2) *Publius: The J of Federalism* 313–337.

[22] On self-determination and federalism under the FDRE Constitution see PH Brietzka 'Ethiopia's "Leap in the Dark": Federalism and Self-determination in the New Constitution' (1995) 39 (1) *J of African L* 19.

[23] This is one of the two houses of parliament in which 'nations, nationalities and peoples' are represented.

[24] This is a reduced number from 14 at the time of the Transitional Period. See Proclamation No. 7/1992 A Proclamation to Provide for the Establishment of National/Regional Self-Governments *Negarit Gazeta* 51st Year No. 2 Addis Ababa 14 January 1992.

[25] Aalen (note 4 above) 65–74.

[26] The elements of the definition of 'nations, nationalities and peoples' under Article 39 are a) a group of people; b) possession of common culture or similar custom; c) language; d) identity; e) psychological makeup; and f) territory.

in their nomenclature.[27] The remaining three are multicultural states inhabited by a variety of ethnic groups.

As several states are composed of diverse groups, to actualise the right of all groups to self-government and the constitutional requirement that autonomous units of government be established at lower levels of government, some of the administrative structures within these states are recognised to serve as self-government structures for the groups that individually constitute them. These self-government structures take two forms: for relatively large groups at Zonal level, and for smaller groups, of not less than 100,000, at Woreda (district) level. As they have political power vested in executive and legislative bodies for the self-government of the particular community, these specific Zones and Woredas are qualitatively different from others, which simply serve as lower administrative entities of the regional states.[28] They are therefore called special Zones and Woredas.

Although the basis for defining the boundaries of the regional states was mainly ethnicity, there is no congruence between the nine states and the constituent ethnic groups. All nine states are multicultural, although the degree of diversity of each varies. Notwithstanding this, it is clear that Ethiopia's federalism is a full-fledged multinational federalism and stands in the rank of the federations of Canada, Switzerland, Belgium and India, although the degree and nature of its explicit institutionalisation of ethnicity differs tremendously from theirs. The way the federal units have been designated has served to fulfil the aspirations of those groups seeking self-government and thus addressed their historical need for their recognition through the provision of such structures. As these structures are instituted on an egalitarian basis, many believe that the arrangement rectifies what the Constitution calls 'unjust historical relationships'.[29] But, as we will see below, Ethiopia's federalism has structural flaws and other limits.

7.2.3. *Division of Powers*

Unlike the federal constitutions of many states, the Ethiopian Constitution has engendered little agreement among scholars regarding the nature of the balance of power between the federal and state governments. Broadly speaking, one can discern two dominant but opposing perspectives in the literature. On the one hand, some scholars argue that the power vested in the member states of the federation is so wide that Ethiopia's is not a proper federation.[30] These

---

[27] These are Tigray, Afar, Amhara, Oromia, Harari and Somali.

[28] The nine regional states consist of 70 Zones. The Zones are further divided into about 600 Woredas. Only some of them serve as self-government structures. Mostly, they are administrative entities without any autonomous political power.

[29] Preamble to the FDRE Constitution para. 5.

[30] See Haile (note 21 above); Assefa (note 10 above).

scholars approach the issue of federal division of powers through the prism of the Constitution's commitment to very wide ethnic rights, such as, in particular, the right to self-determination, including secession.

In the first place, the authors of the Constitution are the 'nations, nationalities and peoples' of Ethiopia. Secondly, Article 8 provides that '[a]ll sovereign power resides in the Nations, Nationalities and Peoples of Ethiopia'. The second paragraph of this article further states that 'the Constitution is an expression of *their* sovereignty'. In this formulation, sovereignty does not reside in the Ethiopian people in their entirety.[31] Instead, it is shared among the 'nations, nationalities and peoples'. This entails that the primary and ultimate bearers of sovereignty are the various constituent ethnic groups. The sovereign power with which the Ethiopian state is clothed is a delegated one. And yet, even the delegation is only partial as the constituent units reserve part of their sovereign power when joined together to constitute the Ethiopian state anew.[32] Thirdly, and most importantly, the Constitution guarantees to the various groups the right to self-determination, including secession.[33] Fourth, contrary to the conventional understanding of federalism and the practice of almost all federal countries, including South Africa, the power of constitutional adjudication is assigned, not to an independent judicial body, but to the House of Federation (HoF), a political body of the federal government in which 'nations, nationalities and peoples' are represented.[34] Moreover, as a further expression of the sovereignty of the states, in the federal division of powers, residual powers are allocated to the states.[35]

These aspects of the Ethiopian federal system are expressions that the states hold ultimate powers and make the union the Constitution envisages subject to the will of each state singularly for its survival. In such a system the political and

---

[31] Haile (ibid) 21.

[32] This seems to imply that Ethiopia's is a 'coming together' federation, a federation formed from previously independent entities, although this has not actually been the case. In reality Ethiopia's is very much like a 'holding together' federation, a federation formed from a previously unitary state. On the distinction between 'holding together' and 'coming together' federations see A Stepan 'Federalism and Democracy: Beyond the U.S. Model' in D Karmis & W Norman (eds.) *Theories of Federalism: A Reader* (2005) 255, 257–258.

[33] The procedure for exercising this right is laid down under Article 39 (4). This is the most controversial aspect of the Constitution among both academics and citizens of the country. See Habtu (note 1 above) 92. Also see note 21 above.

[34] Some argue that the nature of the composition and political attributes of the HoF is such that where a dispute arises over distribution of power between the centre and the states, 'its propensity is likely to favour the augmentation of the power of the state at the expense of federal power'. Haile (note 21 above) 28. Indeed, Haile considers the assignment of the power of constitutional interpretation to the HoF as a further confirmation that 'there is no genuine federalism under the constitution and that the subunits are the real sovereigns'. Ibid. On the political implications of the nature of the composition of this body see Haile-Selassie (note 21 above) 154–160.

[35] Article 52(1).

legal bond of the units to the centre is too weak as states can unilaterally walk out of the union. This clearly makes it akin to a confederation, for it is only in a confederation that the constituent units can unilaterally withdraw from the union.[36] Hence the conclusion that the balance of power is strongly in favour of centrifugal forces, and the characterisation that Ethiopia's is too weak a union to qualify properly as federal.[37] Some have gone further and stated that 'the constitution can be said to have juridically extinguished Ethiopia as a sovereign entity and created nine sovereign tribal entities in its place in the same territory'.[38]

Scholars in the second category maintain that the power constitutionally assigned to states is so minimal that Ethiopia's is a system in which the centre is tremendously predominant.[39] For these scholars, the main focus of the analysis is the content of the division of federal power and the political and socio-economic framework within which that federal division of power operates. Firstly, although the Constitution under Article 52 (1) assigns to the states all powers that are not assigned to the federal government, either exclusively or concurrently with the states, the analysis of the exclusive powers of the federal government reveals that what is left for the states is essentially a very limited, one can say secondary, legislative space. Accordingly, Article 51 (2) & (3) empower the federal government to 'formulate and implement the country's policies, strategies and plans in respect of overall economic, social and development matters' and to 'establish and implement national standards and basic policy criteria for public health, education, science and technology as well as for the protection and preservation of cultural and historical legacies'. It is clear from this that the federal government is the one with powers to determine economic, social, health and development policies and laws.[40]

Secondly, the power to legislate on commercial, labour, intellectual-property and criminal matters is entirely assigned to the federal government,[41] which can also enact civil laws that the HoF deems necessary to establish and sustain one economic community.[42] As far as land and natural resources are concerned,

---

[36] As Duchacek argued, when the constituent units can unilaterally withdraw from the union, the political arrangement between the centre and the constituent units is more similar to a confederation without strong sub-national control than a federation. ID Duchacek, *Comparative Federalism: The Territorial Dimension of Politics* (1987) 207.

[37] Assefa (note 10 above) 121–125.

[38] Haile (note 21 above) 21–22.

[39] Esheté (note 21 above); EJ Keller 'Ethnic Federalism, Fiscal Reform, Development and Democracy in Ethiopia' (2002) 7 (1) *African J of Political Science* 21–50; Brietzka (note 22 above) 26–30.

[40] In practice the economic, agricultural, health, education and population policies of the country have indeed been formulated by the centre, and many of them are so detailed that they leave almost no room for the states.

[41] See Articles 55 (2) (g), (3), (4) & (5).

[42] This qualification is wide and leaves for states, from the sphere of civil laws, only family-law matters and probably succession. In its opinion on a petition from the Ethiopian Justice and Legal System Research Institute, the CCI held that since such civil laws as the law of contract and the

states only have the power to 'administer', while the federal government is empowered to enact laws on their utilisation and conservation.[43] Thirdly, the federal government also has the power to intervene in a regional state when such state is unable to maintain peace and order or where any state, in violation of the Constitution, endangers the constitutional order.[44] Although states enjoy some fiscal authority, the distribution of fiscal authority set out under the Constitution and Proclamation 33/1992 shows, according to Andreas, that 'the richest sources of revenue belong to the central government: all international trade and 88 percent of indirect taxes'. He further observes that '[t]he federal state controls more than 80 percent of domestic revenue, and with control of most external assistance, and 90 percent of total revenue'.[45] The Constitution also expresses deep commitment to building a common political community and maintaining one economic community.[46] A further manifestation of the centralist bias of the Ethiopian federation is that – contrary to the principle of federalism and the practice of almost all federal systems, in which federal units share policy-making power with the centre through representation in an upper house of parliament, and unlike the provinces in South Africa that participate in national policy making through the NCOP – the states of the Ethiopian federation are not involved in federal law making as the HoF does not participate in the law-making process.[47]

It is clear from the above analysis that it is only with respect to matters that deeply implicate the culture and religion of groups that many of the powers assigned to states apply.[48] Accordingly, with respect to civil law matters, except

---

law of deeds and acts are necessary for one economic community and hence should be regulated on a nationwide basis, the making of such laws is not within the jurisdiction of states. *Opinion of the CCI on the Making of the Law on Deeds and Notorial Acts* (Unpublished) 3–5.

[43] Despite this clear stipulation of the Constitution, when the CCI in one case was requested to determine whether the regional state had the power to legislate on land rights, it ruled that since this power forms part of the residual power of states, the land-law proclamation made by the Amhara state is not unconstitutional. *Biyadglegn Meles & Others v The Amhara Regional State* 30 Miazia 1989 E.C.

[44] Article 55 (16) and Article 62(9). See H Tewfiq 'Conflict Management Structures and Intervention under the Ethiopian Constitution' in First National Conference (note 21 above) 226–242.

[45] Eshetė (note 21 above) 166.

[46] See *Issues in the Ethiopian Democratization Process*, a publication that sets out the policy of the government which articulates the powers and rights of ethnic groups guaranteed under the Constitution as instruments for democracy, individual and group equality, and, most of all, for building a common political community and one economic community.

[47] See, for more on this, Fiseha (note 3 above) Chapter III; Aalen (note 4 above) 61.

[48] See J Abbink 'Ethnicity and Constitutionalism in Contemporary Ethiopia' (1997) 41 *J African L* 159–174, 168. Even in this instance, on important matters such as education, one of the most crucial tools for preserving and promoting the culture of groups, the federal government enjoys the main policy-making authority. As far as the formulation and implementation of economic and development policies are concerned, Abbink maintains that 'the present-day regional states may not be the most effective'. Ibid.

in those cases regarded by the HoF to be necessary to establish and maintain one economic community, states have the main legislative authority.[49] Other important matters for state regulation in this area include customary and religious laws, subject to the limitations of the federal constitution.[50] Most importantly, states are empowered to determine their own official language/s.[51]

Against the foregoing, Andreas concludes: '[E]thnic federalism, aside from the protection of ethnic equality and diversity, consists chiefly in administrative decentralisation. What is dispersed to regional states is executive power.'[52] Similarly, Keller concluded:

> In spite of the fact that the Constitution gives a great deal of power and administrative authority to regional states, the overwhelming amount of political power in this system rests with the central government. Because of this, in practice, Ethiopia operates more like a unitary state, with regional states closely following the policy lead of the center, mainly as represented in the TPLF's [Tigray Peoples Liberation Front's] Five Year Program, rather than asserting their policy independence.[53]

This same view is also expressed by, among others, Brietzka.[54]

These opposing perspectives partly reflect the attempt on the part of the architects of the Constitution to balance out two seemingly opposing political ideals and forces: sovereignty of ethno-national groups and a political union through a federal compact. On the one hand, they sought to institutionalise the self-determination and sovereignty of the 'nations, nationalities and peoples' and to make this the foundation for the new political order. On the other hand, they also tried to create a political union, tying these constituent groups together through a federal compact. The result is that, based on analysis of the text of the Constitution, the position of scholars on both sides of the debate is not inaccurate. The conclusion that naturally flows from this is that the determination of the balance of power between the centre and the states depends upon the power configuration that exists at any point in time. Developments during the past 14 years show that by almost all standards the balance tilts too much away

---

[49] See *Ruling of the Council of Constitutional Inquiry on the Petition from the Prime Minister's Office* Miazia 26 1994 E.C. (unreported). In this ruling on a petition from the Office of the Prime Minister on whether the federal government has the power to legislate a family law with nationwide application, the CCI, the body responsible for advising the HoF on matters of constitutional interpretation, held that the power to enact family law is a state power. One of the reasons for this finding was that family law is very much intertwined with the culture, tradition and religion of communities, which express the diversity whose regulation is, in the overall scheme of constitutional division of powers, left to the states.

[50] Article 91 of FDRE Constitution envisages the cultures and traditions of the various communities to be 'compatible with fundamental rights, human dignity, democratic norms and ideals, and the provisions of the Constitution'.

[51] See Article 5 (3) FDRE Constitution.

[52] Eshetè (note 21 above) 167.

[53] Keller (note 39 above) 34.

[54] See Brietzka (note 22 above) 29.

from states, in favour of the centre. To begin with, like South Africa, Ethiopia is a one-party-dominant state.[55] Like the ANC, the ruling Ethiopian Peoples Revolutionary Democratic Front (EPRDF) not only controls both levels of government, but also operates on the basis of the principle of democratic centralism.[56] This has left the states totally subservient to the centre, with no substantively real autonomy for independent policy making. Secondly, as important sources of revenue are assigned to the centre and the states lack the capacity to raise sufficient revenue, they are dependent on the centre for their fiscal needs.[57] As a result states have been conducting themselves as if they were administrative structures of the centre, mimicking the policies and plans of the centre and executing them. Nevertheless, given that none of the states had any historical experience of self-government, this dependence is also not entirely structural.

It seems that it is how the federal system evolves that will eventually determine whether the overall constitutional division of power will result in a cohesive democratic order. Although for now, because of the historical and political situation of the country, it is operating in favour of the centre, as many have rightly pointed out, and the experience of India attests, with the emergence of parties with strong regional support this may entirely change. This is especially so given that, unlike in India, states under FDRE possess the ultimate right of secession.[58]

7.3. Representation and Participation

We have seen earlier that the South African Constitution provides for an indirect system of representation and very wide avenues for public participation. In Ethiopia, consistent with the constitutional principle on the rights and equality of 'nations, nationalities, and peoples' as the basis of the new political order, the system of representation is based on the right of 'nations, nationalities and peoples' to equitable representation in federal and state governments.[59] As the highest organ of the federal government, arguably the most important body in which the various communities need representation is the legislature. The federal Constitution establishes two Houses of Parliament: the House of Peoples' Representatives (HPR) and the HoF. Article 50(3) proclaims that the HPR is the

[55] Aalen (note 4 above); Esheté (note 21 above) 167–168.

[56] See Aalen, ibid, 81–85; Fiseha (note 3 above) 378–379. According to Ivo D Duchacek, under a federal constitution, if lawmaking 'is fully controlled by a monolithic authoritarian party that does not permit dilution of its powers, obviously, any decentralization in favour of another group, territorial, or political is severely limited or outrightly excluded'. I Duchacek, *Power Maps: Comparative Politics of Constitutions* (1973) 131.

[57] Keller (note 39 above) 35–38; Aalen (note 4 above) 74–81; Fiseha (note 3 above) 156–157; Esheté (note 21 above) 166–167.

[58] Assefa (note 10 above); Esheté (note 21 above) 168; Haile-Selassie (note 21 above) 7.

[59] Article 39(3) FDRE Constitution.

highest authority of the federal government. It is the only house with legislative power on matters assigned to the federal government.[60] We turn now how the issue of representation in these bodies of national policy making, particularly the HPR, is addressed under the FDRE Constitution. This is essentially a function of the electoral system.

The most important provision of the Constitution on the design of the electoral system is Article 54(2). According to this provision, '[m]embers of the House (Peoples' Representatives) shall be elected *from candidates in each electoral district by a plurality of the votes cast*' (my emphasis). It is clear from the words emphasised that the electoral system chosen by the framers of the Constitution is what is known as the 'first-past-the-post system' (FPPS). In this system, elections are held in single-member districts, and the winner is the candidate who receives the support of the largest number of voters in a constituency. This is provided for under Article 13(2) of the electoral law:[61] 'A candidate with more votes received than that by other competitors within the constituency shall be declared the winner.'

As far as the representation of ethno-cultural groups is concerned, this system works best if electoral districts are constituted on the basis of the settlement patterns of the various groups. Given the requirement of Article 39(3) for equitable representation of all groups, it is imperative that electoral districts are constituted to ensure equitable representation of all the various ethnic groups.[62] According to Article 15(1) of the electoral law, the country is divided into permanent electoral constituencies by taking the Woreda (district) as its basis. What this means is that outside of Addis Ababa and other ethnically mixed

---

[60] Article 50(3) FDRE Constitution.

[61] Proclamation no. 111/1995 Proclamation to Ensure the Conformity of the Electoral Law of Ethiopia Proclamation with the Constitution of the Federal Democratic Republic of Ethiopia *Federal Negarit Gazeta* 54th Year No. 9 (hereinafter the Electoral Law).

[62] Fiseha argues that the requirement of Article 39 (3) for equitable representation at the federal level does not apply to the legislature. He says: 'Although the Constitution guarantees the various nationalities equitable representation in the federal government, close observation of Article 39 (3) and 62 reveals that the right to equitable representation in federal government only ensures the various nationalities in the federal executive, in the mostly non-legislative House of the second chamber and perhaps the other agents, but not in the federal legislature.' It is not, however, clear why the requirement of equitable representation does not apply in particular to the body which is, according to the Constitution, 'the highest authority of the federal government'. If at all there is a body in which the various ethnic groups, particularly the smaller ones, need representation it can only be such a body, with the highest authority of the federal government. This is indeed the message that one gathers from Article 54 (3) of the Constitution which reserves 20 seats for 'minority nationalities and peoples'. It is to ensure the representation of those population groups whose size is not large enough to constitute an electoral constituency that the Constitution provides for their special representation. See Aalen (note 4 above) 56. Given that Article 39 (3) speaks of equitable representation in federal government (clearly in its entirety) and that the HPR is the highest authority of the federal government, it is only logical that Article 39 (3) applies to the HPR as well.

major cities, electoral districts either coincide with the self-government unit of minority ethnic groups within the multi-ethnic regions, or are drawn within ethnically defined constituencies. Since representatives to the HPR are elected from districts which are mostly inhabited by members of a particular ethnic group, the composition of the HPR accordingly mirrors the ethno-cultural diversity of the country.[63] To provide for the representation of those ethnic groups whose population size is smaller than the size of an electoral district,[64] the Constitution and electoral law envisage special representation.[65] So, although the Constitution declares that members of the legislature are representatives of the Ethiopian people as a whole, it is clear from the above that the electoral system effectively makes members of the HPR accountable to the constituency from which they are elected, which are formed by members of particular ethnic groups. This is sanctioned by the Constitution itself. Article 12(3) guarantees the people the right to recall an elected representative in case of loss of confidence. Similarly, it is provided that a member of the HPR may lose her mandate of representation upon loss of confidence by the electorate.[66] In legal, if not in political, terms this means that members of the HPR ultimately represent and are accountable to the particular communities that voted for them. Politically, they are mainly responsible for the party that they represent.

7.4. Language and Culture

7.4.1. *Official Language*

Given the centrality of culture and language in the historical development of the Ethiopian state and the resultant ethnic claims for recognition and equality underlying the conflicts that led to the current constitutional order, language and culture receive particular attention in the Constitution. In general terms, as

[63] If one looks at the representation of ethnic groups at the federal level by reference to regional states, it takes the following proportions: the 547 seats of the HPR are filled by 40 representatives from Tigray (including from Addis Ababa), 8 from Afar, 149 from Amhara (including from Addis Ababa), 185 from Oromia (including from Addis Ababa), 123 from the SNNPRS (including from Addis Ababa), 19 from Somali, 6 from Benshangul Gumuz, 3 from Gambela, 1 from Harari and 13 independent representatives.

[64] Although the National/Regional Self-Government Establishment Proclamation No. 7/1992 is no longer in force, it is the foundation for the division of the country into various self-government units. According to this Proclamation a Woreda, which constitutes an electoral district, is comprised of 100,000 people.

[65] See Article 54(3) of the Constitution & Art. 2(5) & 15(3) of the Electoral Law. One notes here that the Constitution makes a distinction between the term 'nation' and the words 'nationalities and peoples'. Nations are apparently groups with a large enough population size not to need special representation, whereas nationalities and peoples are generally numerically inferior to nations, hence their minority status.

[66] Article 54(7).

indicated earlier, language is one of but the major defining elements of a 'nation, nationality or people' as defined under Article 39(5) of the Constitution. Specific recognition and protection of languages is envisaged in several constitutional provisions. Article 5(1) states: 'All Ethiopian languages shall enjoy equal state recognition.' Unlike s 6 of the South African Constitution, which outlines in detail the obligations that arise from the different forms of recognition of languages (official and non-official languages), no where does the Ethiopian Constitution define the obligation that 'equal state recognition' entails. According to Nahum, however, 'state recognition of every Ethiopian language means that efforts for its development – i.e., the preservation of its literature; the provision for a script, where such does not exist; the documentation of its oral literature; and the further study of each language via grammatical, vocabulary and overall publication and enhanced use of the language – will be done with both state blessing and state support to the extent possible'.[67] Nevertheless, given the practical differences among the various languages spoken in the country, the declaration that all languages enjoy equal state recognition is a rhetorical one that, in a poor country of more than 80 different languages, is near impossible to achieve.

Where the determination of the use of languages for official purposes is concerned, Article 5(2) designates Amharic as 'the working language of the Federal Government'. The effect of this is that Amharic becomes the language in which federal organs conduct their activities. Similarly, all interactions between the federal and state governments are to be conducted in Amharic. One would logically expect that regional states should use Amharic in the discharge of federal functions delegated to them, although this is not clearly provided for in the Constitution. As is happening in practice, it may as well be the case that Amharic serves as a medium of communication in inter-state relations. This is attributable to various factors, in addition to the constitutional status of Amharic as the working language of the federal government. It manifests the demographic utility of the language as a medium of communication for a large number of peoples belonging to different ethnic groups, and seems to be largely dictated by the need for a common language.[68] Since Amharic is the most widely spoken language in the country and thus serves as the principal medium of

---

[67] Nahum (note 16 above) 55.

[68] Of course, for those whose language is Amharic, its choice as the working language gives it the further advantage of getting additional support not available for those that are not working languages. It also offers original speakers of Amharic more chance for federal employment and of reaching the higher echelons of the state structures. From the perspective of national unity and integration, however, the provision of one common, preferably neutral language is important. In the case of Amharic, although it is not neutral as between the various groups, since it has, as a result of the accident of history, established itself to be a lingua franca for members of different language groups in the country, it has the distinct advantage of being accepted by members of most of, if not all, of the language groups. This can, for example, be gathered from the decision of many of the regional states to adopt Amharic as their working language.

communication for members of different ethnic groups, it has already achieved the status of the lingua franca of Ethiopia. This can be gathered from, among other things, the fact that it serves as the official language not only at the federal level, but also in five of the nine regional states. From the perspective of this study, the existence of one common medium of communication in the form of Amharic is necessary for national integration and to prevent the emergence of the Tower of Babel that some fear might happen in the future.[69]

Not everyone is happy with this choice. There are thus those who argue that Oromiffa, as the language of the largest group in the country, should be accorded the status of a working language of the federation. However, it is not clear how this can be normatively defended. Oromiffa is no more disadvantaged than other languages of the country. Indeed, it has been one of the few to receive public support as it is among the few for which, among others, public broadcast frequencies have been allocated. Furthermore, in terms of continued survival, Oromiffa is no more endangered than many of the other languages. It is rather one of the few languages whose continued survival is guaranteed, by virtue of the fact that it serves as official language in Oromia and Harari states. From a normative and international minority rights perspective, there is little to support the view that a minority's size alone can justify the recognition of its language as an official or national language.[70] If Oromiffa claims such status, there seems little to prevent other languages from doing the same. Accordingly, although within the framework of this study the claim for the use of a minority language for public purposes may be legitimately defended, this does not necessarily entail granting such a language official or national status.

Space is provided for the recognition of languages at the regional state level. Article 5(3) gives member states of the federation the power to determine by law their respective working languages. Accordingly, those other languages designated by regions as working languages would, like Amharic, enjoy state support, albeit only at regional levels. The choice of working language by the nine regional states reveals three patterns. The first includes states that have chosen the working language of the federal government, Amharic, as their working language. Five have adopted this approach. For Gambella, Benshangul-Gumuz and the South Nations, Nationalities and Peoples Regional State (SNNPRS), the choice of Amharic as a working language is motivated by their multi-ethnic

---

[69] Haile (note 21 above) 36.

[70] The literature and the practice in this area show that although size is one of the considerations, by itself alone it is not decisive to support a claim for official recognition of a language. See Francesco Capotorti *Study on the Rights of Persons Belonging to Ethnic, Religious and Linguistic Minorities* (1979) Sales No. E. 78XIV. 1; F De Varennes *Language, Minorities and Human Rights* (1996); K Henrard *Devising an Adequate System of Minority Protection: Individual Rights, Minority Rights and the Right to Self-Determination* (2000); A Addis 'Individualism, Communitarianism, and the Rights of Ethnic Minorities' (1992) 67 *Notre Dame LR* 615.

composition; they are composed of people who speak no less than three indigenous languages. The State of Afar has chosen Amharic as a temporary measure, until its own Afar language is developed in its script form to render it suitable for running the bureaucracy. For the state of Amhara, the rationale for choosing Amharic, the major language of the region, as a working language is no different from those states that follow the second pattern, which is to choose the major language of their respective territories. This is what Tigray, Oromia and Somali have done. Of the nine regional states, Harari has the distinction of choosing two languages, Harari and Oromiffa, as its working languages, and represents the third pattern. In all of these states, consistent with Article 39(3), the various ethnic groups are entitled to use their languages at least for primary education, and in Zonal or Woreda councils and administration. However, the use of nationality languages at these lower levels as a medium of instruction or in administrative communications is often limited by availability of resources in terms of finance, manpower and materials, as well as the level of literary development of many of the languages.

The adoption of Amharic as working language in the three multi-ethnic states has the danger of marginalising indigenous language speakers particularly in terms of access to public services including employment opportunities in the public service. According to Dereje, for example, despite the fact that non-indigenous groups in Gambella State constitute only 24 percent of the population in the region, they nevertheless make up 'more than 40 percent of the skilled labour in the new regional bureaucracy.'[71] As he further rightly noted, as things stand the choice of Amharic as the working language of the regional state will ultimately disadvantage the local people who are not conversant with Amharic. Clearly in these three multi-ethnic regions, there is a need for providing facilities 'to improve the local people's competence in Amharic'.[72]

As previously mentioned, some fear that the policy of multilingualism reflected in the choice of working language or official language of regional states may hinder national integration and lead to a Tower of Babel situation. For this reason, Minassie advocates for the general use of Amharic, with the eventual aim of making it the national language.[73] The problem with this view is not only that the fear is not born out by events, but also that it ignores the interest of speakers of other languages in using their language for government purposes. It must, however, be admitted that the language arrangement envisaged by the Constitution has its drawbacks. It wrongly assumes that there is an exact fit between regional boundaries and language boundaries, and as a result

[71] Dereje Feyissa 'The Exeprience of Gambella Regional State' in David Turton (ed.) *Ethnic Federalism: The Ethiopian Experience in Comparative Perspective* (2006) 216.
[72] Ibid.
[73] Haile (note 21 above) 36.

overlooks the need to address the situation of those members of society who might not speak, or who choose not to speak, the designated official languages of their federal units. For purposes of both addressing the lack of 'fit' between regional and linguistic boundaries and promoting the constitutional objective of building one political and economic community, following the example of countries such as Russia and India it may be necessary to encourage and even require the use of Amharic along with regional languages in those states where Amharic is not a working or official language. This situation reflects some of the important principles that should regulate the operation of multicultural federal systems, including equality and non-discrimination.

7.4.2. *Language and Education*

As far as language use for educational purposes is concerned, unlike in the South African Constitution, the matter is not specifically addressed in the Ethiopian Constitution. The only clause that may be said to have an effect on it is Article 39(2), which provides that '[e]very nation, nationality and people in Ethiopia has the right to speak, to write and to develop its own language'. It cannot be doubted from this that minorities have a right to establish educational institutions that offer education in the minority language. One can also conclude from this and the granting of the right to self-government to all minorities that government bears some obligation to provide education in minority languages, at least at primary school level. This is particularly so where the language is represented by a large enough number of speakers, and they demand the provision of education in their language. Indeed, under the current education policy, each regional state can choose its own language of instruction in primary schools. Further, within each regional state, municipalities, zones and districts can choose their own language(s) of instruction.

Available information indicates that due to low levels of development of local vernaculars, including a lack of writing systems, adequate teaching material, and teaching staff in the local language, as well as to pragmatic considerations such as prospects of employment and social mobility, many communities have chosen Amharic as their language of instruction. Despite this dominance of Amharic, of some 80 local languages spoken in the country, 22 are now in primary school use.[74] These include the eight local languages chosen as medium of instruction in the multi-ethnic SNNPRS.[75] The various limitations mentioned above and financial constraints have in other cases led to the imposition by authorities

[74] Habtu (note 1 above) 104.

[75] See GPE Cohen 'Language and Ethnic Boundaries: Perceptions of Identity Expressed through Attitudes Towards the Use of Language Education in Southern Ethiopia' (2000) 7 (3) *Northeast African Studies* 189–206, 190.

of artificially constructed languages. In the SNNPRS, the attempt by regional authorities to homogenise the languages of four ethnic groups into one language to be used in education was rejected, particularly, by one of those groups as a threat to their distinct identity as recognised in the Constitution. This development clearly illustrates the imperative to give members of the various language communities sufficient opportunity to express their views and their interests, and for authorities to inform and consult them sufficiently before implementing language policies.

7.4.3. *Rights to Language and Culture*

Like FC s 31, the 1994 Ethiopian Constitution guarantees the rights to language and culture. Article 39(2) guarantees every nation, nationality and people the right to speak, write and develop their own languages. This article is nevertheless different from FC s 31, under which the right is essentially an individual right. Under the 1994 Ethiopian Constitution, the right is vested in the various ethnic groups qua groups. Despite this, there is no substantive difference in the nature of the protection these two provide. This is partly because FC s 31 gives recognition to the group context in which speakers of a particular language can use their language. Thus, since both FC s 31 and Article 39(2) seek to recognise and protect language as an attribute of the identity of members of particular language groups, they provide more protection to languages than what freedom of expression or the press alone could provide.

The right to culture is also recognised and guaranteed in various ways. According to Article 39(2), every nation, nationality and people has the right 'to express, to develop and to promote its culture and to preserve its history'. This provision identifies different dimensions of the right to culture. The right to express one's culture involves, among other things, the performance of the rituals and cultural practices and the use of the cultural symbols, jewellery, cosmetics and dress of one's group. Development may consist in the adoption and production by members of a group of the various aspects of its culture in new and modified forms, adapted to changing circumstances and needs. Promotion involves the recording, reproduction and communication of the way of life and the cultural norms and values of the community concerned. The right to culture is given further support under Article 91(1). According to this article, '[g]overnment shall have the duty to support, on the basis of equality, the growth and enrichment of cultures and traditions'. However, an issue left unaddressed under the FDRE Constitution is whether and what kind of language rights regional minorities who do not speak the official language of the region may have. This is particularly important given that the use of the working language of the federation by states is not constitutionally sanctioned.

Unlike under FC s 31, no internal limitation is attached to the various components of the right to culture as stipulated under Article 39(2). One area of serious concern that this commonly gives rise to is whether the right to culture, articulated as the right of a group qua group, can be made consistent with individual rights of members of the group, particularly women. A holistic reading of the Constitution seems to warrant a strong conclusion that the right to culture under Article 39(2) cannot be exercised in a manner inconsistent with the rights of individuals. One can deduce this from paragraph two of the Preamble,[76] Article 10(1),[77] the interpretation clause under Article 13(2),[78] and the guarantees on the rights of women under Article 35.[79] Article 91(1), in particular, limits the obligation of government to support cultures and traditions only to those 'that are compatible with fundamental rights, human dignity, democratic norms and ideals, and the provisions of the Constitution'. It is clear from this that although the right to culture is vested in ethnic groups, it does not entitle any part of these groups to use this right for limiting the rights and freedoms of their members or the rights of others.

7.5. Equality Beyond Recognition of Difference: Socio-economic Guarantees, Including Positive Measures

Due to the nature of the process of state formation in the country, Ethiopia, like many other African countries, exhibits socio-economic as well as political/administrative inequalities along ethnic and regional lines. One of the ways by which the Ethiopian Constitution sought to rectify this imbalance in the socio-economic conditions and opportunities of members of different ethnic groups and achieve the restructuring of the Ethiopian state was through federalism. Federalism is used to redistribute resources and empower hitherto marginalised ethnic groups and regions of the country. Referring to one of the most marginalised regions of the country and the local communities in the region, Dereje in this regard stated '[w]hichever criteria were used to determine the

---

[76] This paragraph emphasises full respect for human rights as the basis of the new constitutional order.

[77] This article stipulates that 'human rights and freedoms, emanating from the nature of mankind, *are inviolable and inalienable*'. This is as distinct from Article 10 (2), which merely calls for respect for the democratic rights of citizens and of peoples.

[78] This provides that the rights under Chapter III shall be interpreted in a manner conforming to the principles of the UDHR, International Covenants on Human Rights and international instruments adopted by Ethiopia.

[79] This article guarantees the equality of women in marriage; in the acquisition, administration, control, use and transfer of property, including land; and in the inheritance of property. It further enjoins the state to enforce the right of women to eliminate the influences of harmful customs, and prohibits laws, customs and practices that oppress or cause bodily or mental harm to women.

establishment of regional states, the creation of the Gambella Peoples' National Regional State (GPNRS), appears to have been one of the most visible political steps ever taken by the Ethiopian state to integrate its historical minorities.' He goes on to say that '[b]y a sheer political fiat, Gambella was transformed from an obscure district to a regional state, resulting in tremendous flow of financial resources from the federal government to the GPNRS, to meet the demands of the new political reality.'[80]

The Constitution in the chapter on national policy principles and objectives additionally commits the government to 'provide special assistance to nations, nationalities and peoples least advantaged in economic and social development'.[81] In the distribution of revenues to regional governments, one of the considerations for determining the amount of the transfer from federal to regional governments has been the fact that a region is least advantaged in economic and social development. Although it is not assigned the same percentage from year to year, level of development has been given upto 25 percent in calculating the allocation of federal grants to regional states.[82]

Affirmative action measures have also been introduced at the level of regional states as well. These have included the preferential treatment of individuals belonging to communities indigenous to the region for employment. As Dereje explains in Gambella, for example, '[t]he preferential treatment includes employment opportunities for the locals as "birth-right" and a two-year experience bonus to give them competitive advantage' over others.[83]

7.6. Assessment of the Constitutional Design

7.6.1. *The Limits of the Constitutional Design*

7.6.1.1. *The Flaws in its Paradigmatic Basis*

It is clear from the foregoing that Ethiopia's federation suffers from multiple structural limitations. The country's constitutional design has many flaws, the most fundamental of which is its communitarian foundation and characteristics, from which flow all other limitations discussed below. This is expressed by the Constitution's conception of the nature of ethnic groups in general, and those in Ethiopia in particular. It defines ethnic groups in absolute communitarian terms as natural communities that are internally homogenous, possess defined boundaries and exist independently of each other (not just in cultural terms, but

80 Feyissa (note 71 above) 213.
81 Art. 89 (4).
82 See Solomon Negussie *Fiscal Federalism in Ethiopian Ethnic-based Federal System* (2008).
83 Feyissa (note 71 above) 214.

territorially as well). The conception of groups in such essentialist terms tends to see difference as given and static, rather than as relationally constructed.[84] Most disturbingly, unlike the framework adopted in this study, which merely recognises the important role of communities in the lives of people, the necessary implication of the Constitution's communitarian conception is that it assumes the primacy of the community over the individual, and does not consider that individuals can abandon their cultural or communal attachments. It rather assumes that each Ethiopian fits neatly within a particular ethnic group and necessarily identifies herself with that group. The institutional implication of such a conception of community is 'the emergence and proliferation of insulated and exclusionary communities'.[85]

7.6.1.2. *Discrepancy Between Theory and Fact: The Neglect of Regional Minorities*

Contrary to the Constitution's essentialist view that Ethiopia's ethnic groups inhabit ethnically homogenous territories, a long history of population movement and inter-ethnic interactions of various kinds means that all regions of the country are multi-ethnic, albeit to varying degrees. In such circumstances, where elements of diversity within a federation do not fall neatly and precisely into geographical units,[86] for the Constitution to define federal units expressly as belonging to particular ethnic groups endangers residents of those units who are not members of the group to which the unit is constitutionally recognised to belong. Depriving these regional minorities of legal recognition and political membership, this renders them second-class citizens at best and unwelcome aliens at worst. As Assefa notes, '[T]he danger is that the respective regional states and the dominant ethnic groups consider themselves "owners" of the "mother state". Other citizens of different ethnic background or those who do not like to associate themselves with any ethnic group have politically no place.'[87] Consequently, regional minorities constantly face the danger of domination,

[84] Addis (note 70 above) 648.

[85] Ibid, 646.

[86] RL Watts 'Federalism and Diversity in Canada' in Yash Ghai (ed.) *Ethnicity and autonomy* (2001) 29, 41. This can also be seen from the composition of the members of the Ethiopian federation. The Oromo region is inhabited by a large number of Amhara and people from the South, in addition to intra-group cultural and regional variations among the Oromo. Amhara, apart from the majority Amhara (who have different province-based historical identities as Wollo, Gonder, Gojam and Showa), is inhabited by Agaw, Oromo and Argoba peoples. Tigray is composed of the Kunama, Erob and the majority Tigrayan people. The predominantly homogenous Afar and Somali regional states (whose principal populations also have clan-based identities) also have significant numbers of people belonging to other ethnic groups.

[87] Fiseha (note 3 above) 266.

exclusion and even persecution by regional authorities, a situation characterised by some as the threat of local tyranny.[88]

What is troubling is not just that the Constitution assigns particular regions for particular ethnic groups, but rather its failure to recognise and address the situation of intra-regional diversity that results from the discrepancy between regional and cultural boundaries. As Paul Henze notes, one manifestation of this is that 'the resolution of conflicts between individual rights and ethnic pressures, including the protection of individuals within "nations, nationalities and peoples" is not specifically considered'.[89] Similarly, unlike many federal systems, the Constitution does not envisage rights for regional minorities and how they can be reconciled with the power of regional majorities. Clearly, one of the structural limitations of Ethiopia's ethnic federalism is its utter failure to provide mechanisms for the protection of the regional minorities that its institutionalisation has created. Seen from the perspective of this study, this obviously does not cohere with the limits of minority rights and the principles that regulate their operation.

7.6.1.3. *Threat to Individual Rights*

As can be gathered from the above, the sovereignty of states and the right to secession, coupled with the assignment of ownership of federal units to particular ethnic groups, pose even greater dangers to fundamental rights and the bonds of common citizenship in ways contrary to the framework adopted in this study.[90] Rights that are particularly at risk include equality and non-discrimination, freedom of movement and political participation. Since state power is assigned on the basis of ethnicity, there is a fear that the exercise and enforcement of many individual rights become dependent upon group membership. The regional majority ethnic group may be disposed 'to frame and enforce rules and practices calculated to enhance its status as a political community and

---

[88] Fiseha (note 3 above) 260–276; D Turton 'Four Questions about Ethiopia's Ethnic Federalism' (2005) 1 (2) *STAIR* 88–101. This danger has already materialised in the Oromia Regional State. According to some reports, several lives and properties were lost when the regional authorities employed force to extricate from Wollega members of the non-indigenous highland communities, who are largely people of Amhara origin. See A Kefale 'Federalism: Some Trends of Ethnic Conflicts and their Management in Ethiopia' in AG Nhema (ed.) *The Quest for Peace in Africa* (2004) 51, 61–62; T Girshaw 'Conflict Mapping in the FDRE for the Year 1994 (E.C.)' in First National Conference (note 21 above) 66.

[89] P Henze 'Comments on the Ethiopian Draft Constitution of 1994', Washington, D.C. Unpublished paper quoted in Abbink (note 48 above) 171.

[90] See A G Selassie 'Ethnic Federalism: Its Promise and Pitfalls for Africa' (Winter 2003) 28 *Yale J of Int L* 51; John Boye Ejobowah 'Liberal Multiculturalism and the problems of institutional instability' in Bruce Berman, Dickson Eyoh & Will Kymlicka (eds.) *Ethnicity and Democracy in Africa* (2004) 301, 313–314; Assefa (note 10 above); G Assefa 'The Protection of Fundamental Rights and Freedoms in Ethiopian Federalism' in First National Conference (note 21 above) 252.

privilege its members as individuals'.[91] Employment opportunities, access to public resources, and other opportunities might also be limited to the 'sons of the soil' or members only, although in the case of disadvantaged regions this can operate as an important aspect of justified special measures.

Since non-members have no guarantee of equal access to jobs and other opportunities, their right to move freely across regional boundaries and freely determine their residence is far from secure. Individuals living in a state controlled by an ethnic group to which they do not belong 'face the prospect of being expelled from their lands, fired from their jobs, and forced to return to their "homelands"'.[92] Non-indigenous groups in Oromia, Gambella and Benshangul-Gumuz states have at different times been victims of violent attacks, forcible expulsion from their lands and exclusion from opportunities, including access to jobs.[93] There are, however, no available data to show the extent of this problem and its effect in restricting peoples' movement across regional boundaries.

In many of the regional states, non-indigenous peoples have no political right to representation at the regional level. While in some regions they are disqualified on account of language requirements, in others they do not have any political recognition or representation as they are not taken to belong to the region by membership. In Benshangul-Gumuz, the indigenous ethnic groups who account for 53 per cent of the total population constituted 100 per cent of those with political recognition and regional government representation. The other 47 per cent are individuals belonging to non-indigenous ethnic groups, who apparently had no political recognition and representation in the regional government at all. In Oromia, Amhara, Tigray, Somali and Harari, members of non-indigenous groups who are not conversant with the language of the regional governments do not have political representation and cannot stand for election. As a result, contrary to international norms and the principle of mutual recognition or reciprocity as discussed in Chapter V, a large percentage of people are effectively disenfranchised.

The recognition and institutionalisation of ethnicity as the main marker of peoples' identity also has the effect of forcing people into identifying themselves with a particular ethnic group and hence restricting freedom of self-identification and association. Samuel Assefa rightly observes that 'it is fair to say that the institutions presently in place accommodate only' one type of diversity and Ethiopian nationalism, the nationalism predicated upon particularist attachments to a given ethnic group.[94] The essentialist assumption of this framework that all

[91] G Selassie (ibid) 94.
[92] Ibid, 95.
[93] See Kafale (note 88 above); Fiseha (note 3 above).
[94] S Assefa 'Two Concepts of Sovereignty' a paper prepared for a Symposium held in Mekelle on the occasion of the 25th anniversary of the TPLF, February 2000 7.

individuals belong to a particular group, and necessarily identify with it, denies recognition to the identity of a substantial portion of the population that 'is of mixed ethnic background or unsure of which ethnic group they belong to or wish to identify with'.[95] Even for those who identify with particular groups, it closes for them the possibility of choosing not to be identified by their group membership, and, by tying them to their particular groups, it restricts their freedom of association.

There are, however, no data to substantiate these fears and provide conclusive evidence. Indeed, not all of them have been borne out by events. This is partly attributable to the existence of a dominant party, as well as the high degree of dependence of states on the federal government, which commits them simply to pursuing federally formulated policies.[96] Notwithstanding the constitutional framework, in practice, therefore, the political system operates in a way that minimises the threat that the communitarian bias of the constitution poses to individual rights.

7.6.1.4. *Threat of the Fragmentation of the Political System and the Common National Economy*

The constitutional promise of self-government structures coupled with the right of secession to all ethnic groups is also an invitation for the fragmentation of the country along ethnic lines.[97] This is a classic case of the problem of opening Pandora's Box. It encourages further divisions as 'citizens who might not have been aware of their ethnicity regroup under its banners purporting to be a distinct people'[98] and demand their own self-government structures. This is exactly what has happened in the three multi-ethnic states.[99] Thus, for example, although the SNNPRS originally had only nine Zones (a self-government structure below states) this has since increased to 13 Zones and five special Woredas. The danger of this is that as more and more groups claim their own self-government structure, the political process becomes more and more fragmented.

This entails the danger of fragmenting society into different ethnic islands and permanently freezing such divisions, and creates further administrative complications. Contrary to the minority rights framework articulated in this study, the Ethiopian framework restricts the capacity of individuals to associate

---

[95] C Clapham 'The Political Framework: Controlling Space in Ethiopia' in W James, D Donham, E Kurimoto & A Triulzi (eds.) *Remapping Ethiopia: Socialism and After* (2002) 9–30, as quoted in Fiseha (note 3 above) 246.

[96] Assefa (note 88 above) 5.

[97] Haile (note 21 above) 32–35; Ejobowah (note 90 above), 305–308.

[98] G Selassie (note 90 above) 86; Ejobowah (note 90 above) 305.

[99] These are Gambella, Benshangul-Gumuz, and the SNNPRS. In the SNNPRS, the most diverse of all the states, it is believed that there are more than 50 ethnicities.

freely with others and think outside of their ethnic group. Instead, it forces them into associating themselves with their kin and seeing things only through the prism of their ethnicity. This makes it impossible not only to maintain a uniform system of human rights for all, but also to maintain a common citizenship. Under such circumstances, it is clear that the project of building a common political community envisaged by the Constitution becomes an ideal that might never see the light of the day.[100] And it would indeed be admirable if it were possible to maintain the integrity of the country. So far, what seems to have helped to hold the centre are the existence of a dominant party and the high degree of state dependence on the federal government. It is not impossible to imagine the materialisation of the threat of fragmentation should the ruling party lose control of any of the federal units, particularly the major ones.

One consequence of using ethnicity as the principal basis for designing the federation is the creation of hugely unequal units. The federation includes regional units ranging from the large Oromiya state, with more than 20 million people and an area of 360,000 square kilometres, to the tiny Harari state, which includes less than 150,000 people dispersed over 300 square kilometres. The two largest regional states, Amhara and Oromiya, account for 30 per cent each of the total population. In the long run, therefore, one axis of division or fragmentation might be that which involves the rivalry between these two states as they seek to gain the support of smaller ethnic groups.

The current arrangement has the additional danger of fragmenting the national economy or preventing the emergence of a common economic community, as envisaged by the Constitution, by creating regional barriers on the basis of ethnicity. As Selassie points out, ethnic federalism 'has the potential to restrict the mobility of labour, goods, and capital across subnational jurisdictions, and thus to undermine the notion of a common market'.[101] Despite the constitutional guarantees of freedom of movement, and freedom to choose residence[102] and pursue an economic activity of one's choice in any part of the

---

[100] It is on this account that many doubt if the kind of ethnic federalism adopted in Ethiopia coupled with the right of secession could succeed in addressing the country's ethnic problems. Markakis concludes that 'it remains to be seen if it will succeed'. J Markakis *Resource Conflict in the Horn of Africa* (1998) 139. Similarly, Assefa holds that 'one can see problems arising for the smooth functioning of the federal arrangement if one or two non-EPRDF parties, or parties that do not accept the core values of EPRDF, come to power in regional states'. Note 88 above, 6. Brietzke considers the constitutional design to be 'a recipe for disaster'. Note 22 above, 35. Cohen fears that it may even encourage demands for secession. J Cohen 'Ethnic Federalism in Ethiopia' (New Series 1995) 2 (2) *Northeast African Studies* 168. For Ehrlich, as for Brietzke, Ethiopia's experiment is as bold as it is suicidal. C Ehrlich 'Ethnicity and Constitutional Reform: The Case of Ethiopia' (1999) 6 *IALSA J Int & Comparative L* 51, 62.

[101] G Selassie (note 90 above) 89. This is mainly attributable to the fact that in such a system the ethnic factor takes precedence over the demands of the market. Also see Abbink (note 48 above) at 169.

[102] Article 32 (1).

national territory,[103] the requirement of free movement of capital and labour, on the one hand, and the ethnic-based federal arrangement, on the other, have shown competing tendencies. The main reason for this has been that regional authorities, with their newly achieved powers, seeking to create economic enclaves of their own, have sought to view everything through the prism of ethnicity, consequently discriminating in favour of their members in terms of access to economic resources and facilities such as land, credit and licences to operate businesses.[104] Federal officials have admitted that this has indeed been one of the challenges that the Ethiopian federation experienced. GebreAb Bernabas, who was State Minister of the Ministry of Federal Affairs, stated:

> There were incidents of conflict where some sectarian elements of some states slowed down or even arrested the free flow of capital within Ethiopia. In the name of giving priority to indigenous peoples, Ethiopian investors were either prevented from transferring their capital to the states or sabotaged once they did so.[105]

It is clear that under these circumstances the constitutional project of building one economic community would be a dream that could never be realised.[106] As Bernabas observes, 'the phenomenon is inimical to our ideal of creating a common economic space'.[107]

7.6.1.5. *Horizontal Relationship Between Various Groups: The Unregulated Domain*

With the exception of the inadequately defined principle of equitable representation enshrined under Article 39(3), the Constitution provides no sufficient mechanisms to regulate relations between minorities. The creation of new centres of power without sufficiently defining how they are to be shared among the various minorities constituting, particularly, the four multi-ethnic states, has induced rivalry for control of these new political structures, leading in many instances to violence. It has also led to the transformation of existing resource-based and territorial conflicts between neighbouring ethnic groups into a conflict for the control or a share of political power at the local level.[108]

---

[103] Article 31 (1).

[104] 'In the process,' argues G Selassie, 'market rules of competition are either superseded or otherwise manipulated, with the result that members of other ethnic communities are excluded from participation in the local economy.' Note 90 above, 89.

[105] G Bernabas 'Ethnic and Religious Policies of the Federal Democratic Republic of Ethiopia' in First National Conference (note 21 above) 213. As far as free movement of labour is concerned, Bernabas writes that 'again there is a reluctance on the part of those, in the receiving end, to welcome fellow citizens to come, work and live with them'. Ibid, 214.

[106] Also see Assefa (note 88 above).

[107] Bernabas (note 99 above) 213.

[108] See D Feyissa *Ethnic Federalism in Ethiopia: The Experience of Gambella Regional State*, paper presented at the Seminar on Ethnic Federalism: The Challenges for Ethiopia, Addis Ababa

Post-1991 Ethiopia has therefore witnessed escalation in regional conflicts within these states. The SNNPRS, and more particularly Gambella, are the worst hit.[109] In Benshangul-Gumuz Regional State (BGRS), the disproportionately small number of Woredas and percentage of representation provided for the Berta, the largest ethnic group in the region, gave rise to a tension between the Berta and the regional government. This ultimately led to violence, and the Berta withdrew from the regional government and threatened to secede from it.[110] With mediation from the HoF, the immediate tension was resolved with the agreement of the parties provisionally to allocate additional representatives to the Berta in the regional council, in return for their return to the legislature.[111]

7.6.1.6. *Lack of Effective and Independent Constitutional Adjudication Mechanism*

As the experience of multicultural societies, particularly Canada, Spain, South Africa and Bosnia-Herzegovina, shows, the existence of an independent constitutional adjudication body is the key to the success of a constitution that seeks to accommodate diversity. Such a body is clothed with all the necessary qualities for 'facilitating adaptation of the federal system without resort to constitutional amendment'.[112] Moreover, constitutional adjudication through a judicial body allows a principled, transparent and coherent interpretation and elaboration of the constitution, which is a necessary condition for building and enhancing public confidence in the system and, most importantly, for keeping the diverse groups participating in the political process committed to the rules of the constitution. Experience in South Africa,[113] Canada[114] and Bosnia and Herzegovina[115] also shows that independent constitutional adjudication is important to provide authoritative frameworks that help resolve sensitive politico-legal disagreements that arise under a constitution, and to rectify the limits or omissions of the constitution in a coherent and constitutionally and morally defensible way. From the perspective of this study, without such a body, the constitutional design for accommodation of diversity becomes susceptible to the dictates of political

---

April 14–16, 2004; M Tadesse Gambella: The Impact of Local Conflict on Regional Conflict ISS/CPRD Paper (May 2007) 11–13.

[109] See Kefale (note 88 above) 56–61; Fiseha (note 3 above) 267–276; Feyissa (ibid) 8–9.

[110] See Kefale (note 88 above) 59–60; EA Baylis 'Beyond Rights: Legal Processes and Ethnic Conflicts' (2004) 25 *Michigan J Int L* 529, 538–539.

[111] For details on the process see Baylis (ibid) 562–564.

[112] Watts (note 86 above) 45.

[113] H Klug *Constituting Democracy: Law, Globalism and South Africa's Political Reconstruction* (2000) Chapter 8.

[114] S Tierney *Constitutional Law and National Pluralism* (2004) 247–270.

[115] J Woelk 'Federalism and Consociationalism as Tools for State Reconstruction? The Case of Bosnia & Herzegovinia' in GA Tarr, RF. Williams & J Marko (eds.) *Federalism, Subnational Constitutions, and Minority Rights* (2004) 177, 188–190.

expediency and even manipulation. In other words, it becomes a constitution without sufficient mechanisms for its proper enforcement or constitutionalism.

This is another area that makes the Ethiopian approach to the accommodation of diversity once again distinct from that of South Africa. Under the FC, the CC is an important component of the constitutional design for accommodation of diversity. Indeed, the various guarantees provided in the text of the FC aside, the CC is the key institution that has made South Africa's transition to democracy a success and the process of transformation legitimate. In the case of Ethiopia, no comparable body is available. Another outcome of the constitutional entrenchment of ethnicity as the main organising principle was the assigning of the role of constitutional adjudication to a political body. According to the framers of the Constitution, since it is the expression of the sovereignty of 'nations, nationalities and peoples' of Ethiopia, it is only they, as authors, who should be vested with the power of interpreting the Constitution.[116] Accordingly, the body that is charged with the power of constitutional interpretation is the HoF, the second house of parliament, which is constituted by representatives of the 'nations, nationalities and peoples'.[117] Under Article 62(2) of the Constitution, the HoF has the power to interpret the Constitution. Article 83, the clause on interpretation of the Constitution, further provides that all constitutional disputes shall be decided by the HoF.

The consequence of this is that not only disputes involving ethnic rights provided for in the Constitution and disputes involving the various spheres of government, but also those cases involving fundamental rights, are to be decided by the HoF. Article 84(3) envisages that where an ordinary court is seized of a matter the disposition of which requires the interpretation of the Constitution, it should refer such matter to the Council of Constitutional Inquiry (CCI), the body with the power to investigate constitutional disputes and submit its recommendations thereon to the HoF for final decision.[118] Similarly, Article 21(2) of Proclamation 250/2001 stipulates that 'the Court handling the case shall submit it to the CCI only if it believes that there is a need for constitutional interpretation in deciding the case'.

The problem is not just that the power of judicial review is assigned to a non-judicial body. It is rather, first, that the HoF lacks the qualities of a judicial body that are necessary for properly enforcing the rules of the Constitution. According to Article 61(1), the HoF is composed of 'representatives of nations, nationalities and peoples'. By its composition, it is clear that the main purpose of the HoF is not the enforcement of the rules of the Constitution, but the

---

[116] See Ye Ethiopia Hige Mengist Gubae Vol. 4 Hidar 14–20, 1987 E.C. (Minutes of the Constitutional Assembly, November 1994) discussions on Articles 59, 61 and 62.

[117] Article 61(1) FDRE Constitution.

[118] Article 84(1) FDRE Constitution.

protection of the interests of the groups it represents.[119] Moreover, its members are to be elected by the State Councils, the highest organ of member states of the federation.[120] Given that the State Councils are controlled by political parties, and more particularly the ruling political party, the representatives that they elect to the HoF are accordingly members of the ruling party. Even if members of the HoF are in constitutional terms representatives of 'nations, nationalities, and peoples', as members of the ruling party, politically speaking they are also essentially its representatives. This means that, at least in political terms, the power of constitutional interpretation is in the hands of the ruling party. It is clear from this that the HoF does not have the requisite independence and impartiality for enforcing the constitutional design for accommodation of minorities in an independent, normatively coherent and principled way. Unfortunately, the existence of the CCI does not at all rectify this deficiency since it has only an advisory role and at any rate itself lacks the qualities of a judicial body.

The second problem with the existing arrangement for constitutional interpretation is the need for constitutionalism, rule of law and, most importantly, the protection of fundamental rights. As part of its power to interpret the Constitution, the HoF is the main body that has the responsibility to enforce the Chapter on the Bill of Rights through constitutional interpretation. Indeed, this is explicitly provided for under Article 23(1) of Proclamation 250/2001: 'Any person who alleges that his fundamental rights and freedoms have been violated by the final decision of any government institution or official may present his case to the CCI for constitutional interpretation.'[121] The result is that the interpretation of fundamental rights is taken away from the judiciary and placed in the hands of a purely political body. Whatever role that courts have is very minimal and of negligible importance.[122] This renders the enforcement of human rights to be a matter mainly in the hands of the political organs of the state. At least politically speaking, to the extent that the body interpreting the constitution is under the control of the ruling party one can legitimately conclude that Ethiopia's is a constitution without sufficient constitutionalism. From the perspective of this study, the problem with this is that it leaves fundamental rights without sufficient mechanism for judicial enforcement and undermines constitutionalism and rule of law, which are all the necessary conditions for an effective operation of the constitutional design for accommodation of minorities.

---

[119] M Habib *Role and Function of the House of the Federation* <http://www.hofethiopia.org/pdf/The%20role%20of%20the%20House%20in%20EFDRE%20constition.pdf>.

[120] Article 61 (3) provides that '[t]he State Councils may themselves elect representatives to the House of the Federation, or they may hold elections to have the representatives elected by the people'.

[121] Council of Constitutional Inquiry Proclamation, *Federal Negarit Gazeta* 7th Year, No. 40 Addis Ababa, 6 July 2001.

[122] See M Tadese (Vice President of the Federal Supreme Court and Vice Chairman of the CCI) *Yeethiopia higna fitihi getsitawochi* (Addis Ababa, 1999 E.C.) 162.

7.6.2. *Achievements*

Notwithstanding the above limitations, Ethiopia's constitutional design has achieved important successes in terms of accommodation of diversity that would not otherwise have been possible. The Ethiopian federal system has at least five achievements to its credit. First, not only has it ended the decades of civil war that afflicted the country but it also prevented the danger of disintegration facing Ethiopia after the fall of the military regime of Mengistu Haile-Mariam.[123] Kidane Mengisteab thus argues that EPRDF's policy measures, such as ethnic-based federalism, were 'essential to stop the perpetual bloodshed, to avert the country's total disintegration and to mend ethnic relations'.[124] It was a crucial condition for many of the dominant ethnic-based forces of the time to abandon armed struggle and accept participation in the unfolding new political system. By dispersing the centres of power, it also contributed to the diffusion of conflicts to regions, thus preventing the recurrence of the nation-wide civil war characteristic of the military era. According to David Turton, 'it has provided peace and security for the majority of the population following a violent civil war and laid down, for the first time in the history of Ethiopia, "the legal foundation for a fully fledged democracy"',[125] although the adequacy of the legal framework for democracy is contested.

Secondly, the egalitarian orientation of Ethiopia's ethnic pluralism is also expected to enhance social cohesion and national integration, notwithstanding the suggestion of some aspects of the constitutional design to the contrary. Alem Habtu is among those who hope that 'the drive toward egalitarian ethnic pluralism has the potential to enhance ethnic harmony based on mutual respect and reciprocity'.[126] Indeed, some studies have concluded that 'the EPRDF government is making some headway in engendering a sense of Ethiopian identity that either transcends or coexists with a clear sense of ethnic identity among the country's nationality groups'.[127]

Thirdly, Ethiopian federalism also served to end the political and cultural hegemony of the dominant culture. This entailed the demise of the many years of patterns of domination, ethno-cultural assimilation and centralisation. It also marked a rejection of the denigration of the cultures, languages and histories of minorities and the resultant damage to the dignity and self-respect of their

---

[123] See J Abbink 'Breaking and Making the State: The Dynamic of Ethnic Democracy in Ethiopia' (1995) 13 *J of Contemporary African Studies* 149–163, 151; J Young 'Ethnicity and Power in Ethiopia' (1996) 70 *Review of African Political Economy* 531–542, 532.

[124] Mengisteab (note 11 above) 126.

[125] Turton (note 88 above) 93.

[126] Habtu (note 1 above) 114.

[127] See EJ Keller 'Making and Remaking State and Nation in Ethiopia' in RR Larémont (ed.) *Borders, Nationalism and the African State* (2005) 87, 130.

members. Most importantly, it also rejected the uneven patterns of development and the socio-economic neglect or marginalisation of many of the minorities in the country.

Corresponding to this is the political recognition and institutional affirmation of the cultures, languages and histories of hitherto marginalised minorities, and their equality. An important feature of the new constitutional order is its complete break from the centrally imposed singular Ethiopian identity, and the redefinition of Ethiopia as a multicultural state committed to the accommodation its diversity. Leenco Leta, prominent figure of the separatist Oromo Liberation Figure, captures this paradigmatic change as follows:

> The recognition of the right of self-determination of nationalities was conceptualised and the reconfiguration of the Ethiopian state was to bring about wide-ranging changes. The policy of Ethiopian identity, which was traditionally projected to coincide with Amhara identity, was to undergo fundamental changes. The previous policy of gradual homogenisation through amharaization was to be abandoned. Instead of imposing a single Ethiopian identity, a mosaic was to be projected. Contrary to the previous practice of defining Ethiopian identity in a manner that excluded or failed to embrace the identities of the various nationalities, a more inclusive image was to be projected.[128]

The fourth achievement is the high level of representation of minorities in the political structures of the state. Mainly on account of the group-based politics of recognition, unlike the imperial and the military regimes, under the current federal system almost all minorities constituting the country are represented in the national political processes. This can be seen in the composition of the Parliament and the federal executive. For the first time in the history of the country, it has now become possible to find members of all linguistic, religious and cultural groups in the federal Legislature and, more directly, in the HoF. Similarly, despite the perceived or real dominance of some groups, the executive in its entirety is more vividly diverse in its linguistic, cultural and religious composition than at any other time in the history of the country. Institutions of the federal government and the civil service are more and more mirroring the diversity of the country.

Despite many problems and its downsides for inter-ethnic relations, particularly due to the perceived dominance of some groups in national politics, constitutional change has at some level contributed to inter-group relations and mutual recognition. It has also brought about on the part of most, if not all, minorities a sense of being included and accommodated in the national project. As a result, many are now able to see themselves as full Ethiopian citizens with equal rights and entitlements. As Assefa rightly points out, this has contributed

---

[128] L Lata 'The Making and Unmaking of Ethiopia's Transitional Charter' in Asafa Jalata (ed.) *Oromo Nationalism and the Ethiopian Discourse: The Search for Freedom and Democracy* (1998) 51.

to members of the various ethnic groups regaining group pride and a sense of self-respect and dignity.[129] Obviously, for those whose Ethiopian identity is intimately associated with their group membership, this has increased their sense of belonging to and identification with the state. This is expressed not only during peace, but also at times of national emergency. For example, some reasonably maintain that 'the sentiment of Ethiopian nationalism exhibited by many volunteers (during the Ethiopia–Eritrea war in 1998–2000) owes a great deal to the institutional recognition and protection that is extended to particularist identities under the new federal arrangement'.[130]

Finally, at the local level, it has created a framework for the political empowerment of minorities on the basis of self-government, which also serves as a basis for equitable access to resources and the socio-economic empowerment of historically disadvantaged minorities. According to Dereje, who studied the effect of Ethiopia's constitutional change in one of the historically disadvantaged states, the Gambella Peoples National Regional State (GPNRS), 'the implementation of ethnic federalism has created a new political space and institutional design to further promote local empowerment … the creation of [the GPNRS] appears to be one of the most visible political steps ever taken by the Ethiopian state to integrate its historic minorities'.[131] There is also hope that this could enhance the democratic space and enable people actively to participate in the political processes. Thanks to the federal scheme and the constitutional requirement of equitable distribution of resources,[132] for the first time in the history of the country, not only people at the centre but also those at the periphery are more equitably taking part in and benefiting from the development processes of the country.

More and more communities are now beneficiaries of social services, including health, sanitation and education. Indeed, education is one area that has shown huge expansion in the various regional states. Many minority languages that have achieved the required degree of literary development have been given support to become medium of instruction, particularly at elementary levels. In the Afar, Somali, Benshangul-Gumuz, Southern, and Oromia regional states, pilot nomadic schools and boarding schools have been established and/or are planned in order to provide educational access to children in pastoral communities, in most cases for the very first time.[133] Plans are also under way for Regional Education Media Units to design and transmit educational programs

---

[129] Fiseha (note 3 above) 244.
[130] Assefa (note 94 above) 7.
[131] Feyissa (note 108 above) 7.
[132] See Article 43 (3), Article 62, Article 89 (1) (2) & (4) & Article 94 (2).
[133] Habtu (note 1 above) 104.

in local languages.[134] In addition to this, the coverage of secondary and higher education has been expanded, and Ethiopia's higher education institutions are now becoming increasingly diverse in terms of their ethno-cultural representation.

7.7. Conclusion

This case study, like the previous one, shows that the issue of minorities may be addressed through the provision of constitutional guarantees and mechanisms for the accommodation of ethno-cultural diversity. Unlike the constitutional design of South Africa, which is mainly inspired by the liberal constitutional framework, Ethiopia's reflects a huge communitarian influence. This chapter illuminates the effect of this difference, in terms of the nature of the constitutional guarantees and institutional mechanisms, on the constitutional accommodation of ethno-cultural diversity. In this regard, it has been noted that some of the institutional limitations identified with the Ethiopian constitutional design are attributable to the ethno-nationalist or communitarian paradigmatic foundation of the Constitution. Generally, this case study illustrates the limits of constitutional accommodation of minorities and the pitfalls that must be avoided in institutionalising mechanisms for accommodation of ethno-cultural diversity.

Unlike the case of South Africa, ethno-cultural conflict in Ethiopia has mainly involved the struggle of members of various ethno-linguistic groups for the recognition of their equality not just as individual citizens but as members of their respective groups. As it can be concluded from the foregoing discussion, in such cases the group-rights approach of constitutional design for accommodation of ethno-cultural diversity may not only provide a framework for achieving ethno-cultural justice but also lead, as a result, to a fair amount of political instability.

It can also be gathered that generally, the use of the group-rights approach of constitutional design for accommodation of minorities creates tension between group rights and individual rights or the rights of regional minorities. In the case of the Ethiopian constitutional design, it is true that this approach both arrested the violent conflict that raged in the country for over three decades and contributed to the prevention of its disintegration. Nevertheless, it clearly came out that the lack of sufficient attention to this fundamental tension and the flaws in the Constitution's conception of the nature of group rights resulted in a seemingly unresolvable structural tension between group-rights and individual rights and/or the rights of regional minorities. Accordingly, even if it brought ethno-cultual justice for the country's historically marginalised groups and

[134] Ibid.

achieved fair amount of stability, it has created new threats to individual rights and the rights of regional minorities.

At least three conclusions can be drawn from this. First, if ethno-cultural justice and peaceful co-existence are to be achieved between members of various groups in a multi-ethnic society with a conflict history of the type in Ethiopia, it might be imperative to use the group-rights approach to constitutional accommodation of minorities. Second, where the group-rights approach is used, it is almost inevitable that there will be tension between group rights and individual rights, albeit such tension is not necessarily irresolvable. Finally, the requirement of justice for and peaceful co-existence between members of different ethno-cultural groups may not in some cases be achieved without limiting the rights of individuals and/or regional minorities. It is clear from this that any constitutional design committed to both these objectives and those implementing such a constitution should pay equal attention to these two requirements to achieve a balance in such a way that the limits that the requirements of justice and stability put on individual rights is not of such a nature that frustrates the fundamentals of the protection of individual rights or regional minorities. Equally importantly, the democratic and principled implemetation of the constitutional framework for accommodation of diversity is best pursued through an independent constitutional adjudication mechanism.

CHAPTER VIII

CONCLUSION, FINDINGS AND FINAL OBSERVATIONS

8.1. Introduction

In this age of multiculturalism, the issue of minorities is a topical subject in the political and legal discourse of many states and international organisations and one that has received wide scholarly attention in various fields, including philosophy, social sciences and law. Despite its currency and its centrality to the institutional crisis that currently afflicts the post-colonial African state, manifested by ethnic conflicts and civil wars that have caused the loss of countless human lives and resources, the issue of minorities has received scant attention in the legal literature and the constitutional framework of African states. There are also no studies that have comprehensively examined and elaborated the role that minority rights (particularly in the broad sense, as defended in this study) can play, and the kind of constitutional guarantees and institutional arrangements that are necessary to translate them into an adequate constitutional framework for the accommodation of diversity in Africa.

The central aim of this study has been to examine and defend the nature and content of a robust minority rights framework that can serve in Africa as a basis for the constitutional accommodation of ethno-cultural diversity and for achieving a (more) legitimate political and socio-economic structure of social co-operation. To address this, the study employed three lines of investigation. The first focused on the background and problematisation of the subject of the study. This was addressed in the first three chapters. The second line of investigation consisted of the resolution aspect of the study. This involved examination of normative political theory and the relevant norms of international human rights law, within which aspects of constitutional design necessary for addressing the issue of minorities in Africa were identified, analysed and elaborated. The third line of investigation examined the actual institutionalisation and operation of such constitutional designs in Africa. To this end, the study employed the case studies of South Africa and Ethiopia. This chapter presents the findings of the study and outlines the conclusions.

8.2. The Core Arguments and Findings of the Study

Chapter I of this study outlined the structure of the minority rights framework defended in this study and examined the concept of minorities in Africa. It was submitted that in the African context the term minorities as commonly used in international legal discourse would be too limited to capture the particular characteristics of ethno-cultural diversity and state-society relationship that define the issue of minorities in Africa. The chapter accordingly examined the concept of minorities based on Francesco Capotorti's definition of the term, and proposed a more nuanced conceptualisation and understanding, capable of reflecting the nature of the issue of minorities in Africa. Accordingly, it defines 'minorities', as the term applies in the African context, as referring to the situation of those ethno-culturally identifiable population groups constituting the post-colonial African state who suffer political, socio-economic and cultural marginalisation or are vulnerable to such marginalisation. Conceptualising the term in this way leads to a distinction between minorities with ascriptive identity markers transmitted across time and generations, and marginalised social groups identified by shared personal characteristics. For the purposes of this study, the latter groups are not considered as minorities.

Consistent with this understanding of minorities in Africa, the chapter formulated the minority rights framework more broadly to refer not only to cultural, linguistic and religious rights of minorities,[1] but also to other policies and institutional arrangements that together establish an effective constitutional design for the accommodation of ethno-cultural diversity, and more broadly for defining a just political and socio-economic framework of social co-operation in the post-colonial African state. This also reflects the premise of this study that the issue of minorities in Africa is not about ethno-cultural diversity or about identity per se. It is rather a product of the process by which the post-colonial African state was made, and the failure of its basic structure as a common framework of social co-operation acceptable to all members of the various ethno-cultural communities that were forcibly brought together to constitute the state.

In Chapter II, the study examined two issues. The first was the historical, socio-economic and political processes that led to the genesis of the issue of minorities in Africa. In this regard, it was argued that this issue cannot be understood independently of the process of the making of the African state and the way this has historically defined the relationships of members of various groups with the state. This revealed that the forcible amalgamation of socio-politically and culturally distinct and unequal communities under one central

[1] These limited sets of rights constitute minority rights as commonly used in international legal discourse.

authority, the colonial state, is what in the first place set the stage for the genesis of the issue of minorities. The most important historical and political factors are, however, the divisive and discriminatory patterns of colonial governance and the resulting post-colonial ethnic and ethno-regional imbalances in the control of political power and distribution of socio-economic goods and opportunities. These, together with the centralised organisation of political power and control of societal resources, define one of the characteristics of the issue of minorities in Africa. This is the unequal and discriminatory patterns of power relations and the failure of state structures to reflect, embody and protect fairly the interests of members of all the communities that were forcibly lumped together to constitute the African state. Here the issue of minorities finds its expression, not only through the inequalities among various groups and ethno-regions in terms of share of political power and access to resources and opportunities, but also in explosive ways through the resultant rivalry for domination and control of the state machinery.

Given the nature of the making of the African state and its evolution, the issue of minorities has other dimensions as well. The first of these is the lack of affinity between the institutions and norms of the state, on the one hand, and the norms and social structures of the diverse population constituting the state on the other. The result is that the institutions of the post-colonial state in most cases continue to operate as alien entities to which minorities in particular have no access and in which they have no say. The other and related dimension of the issue is the colonial and post-colonial non-recognition and even denigration, devaluation and suppression of the cultures and languages of the constituent minorities. This has undermined the cultural and linguistic integrity of various groups and brought on their members a sense of insecurity about their identity.

The other matter examined in the chapter was the question of the nature and types of claims to which the issue of minorities has given rise. It was found that one can identify four types of minority claims in Africa. The first is the claim of what I call ethno-political minorities. These are groups who seek to take part and have their say in the political structures and processes of the state. This is often expressed by the contention of members of various groups, through either political parties or armed struggle, for control or a share of political power. The second is the claim of cultural minorities for legal and political recognition of their cultural traditions and languages, and the institutionalisation of those cultures and languages as part of the character that defines the state in which they live. This is not simply a claim for the freedom to use and develop one's culture and language. It is mainly about achieving cultural and language equality in public life. Thirdly, there is also the related but qualitatively different claim of peripheral minorities, such as those identified as indigenous peoples of Africa who, having historically been left out of state processes, experience a high degree of political, socio-economic and cultural marginalisation. Their situation raises seemingly irreconcilable claims of integration into, or more accurately inclusion in, the processes of the state and, at the same time, the recognition and protection of their distinct way of life and the interests associated with it – most importantly, protection of their attachment to and dependence on their territories and the resources therein. Finally, there are those ethno-national/regional minorities, who, due to various historical and political processes particular to the countries to which they belong, have developed a separate socio-political and cultural identity attached to the territory they historically inhabited. As a result, they seek and demand self-government, and sometimes even secession.

The argument drawn from the above is that addressing these claims is a matter of justice, and will accordingly require the redefinition of the character of the post-colonial African state, with the adoption of constitutional mechanisms and guarantees capable of accommodating these claims. Accordingly, in Chapter III, the major question that was examined was the approach of the post-colonial African state to the issue of minorities. It was established that the issue of minorities has been approached on the basis of the nation-state model of the policy of nation-building and the dominant liberal nation-state constitutional model.

Post-colonial nation-building assumed that existing ethnic cleavages characteristic of the population of the African state were antithetical to national unity and political stability. The achievement of national unity was accordingly considered to require that a common national identity be established by welding together or transcending existing ethnic memberships. As a result, the process of nation-building has been ethno-culturally homogenous in its objects and authoritarian and coercive in its application. In this regard, Chapter III demonstrated that post-colonial nation-building has been conceptually flawed, morally indefensible and unsuccessful in its outcome. The assumption of the mutual exclusivity of national integration and ethno-cultural diversity is factually wrong or at least highly exaggerated. Ethnic diversity alone neither detracts from the goal of national integration nor causes instability. The process of assimilation into a common national identity at the expense of ethnic membership can also violate rights to dignity and identity. Not only did this process eventually fail to bring about national integration, but it even entrenched divisions, and in many cases led to the eruption of violent conflicts and the disintegration of some states.

The liberal nation-state constitutional model followed by African states fared no better. Indeed, it provided the necessary legal framework for the post-colonial state in its pursuit of the homogenising nation-building process. This has been so for various reasons. Its first attribute of national sovereignty discussed in this chapter emphasises national unity and the common identity of the state, and as such tends to support assimilation into the national identity or the dominant culture. Similarly, the provision of universal citizenship that emphasises equal rights and state neutrality and relegates cultural membership to the private domain, outside of the public realm, is also not only assimilative, but has discriminatory effects in the context of multi-ethnic African societies. This is because it gives a semblance of legitimacy to the domination of the state by members of particular groups to the exclusion of others, and it allows and even perpetuates the continuation of existing socio-economic, political and cultural inequality among groups and ethno-regions. Similarly, the exclusive focus of the liberal nation-state constitutional model on individual rights makes it inhospitable to the articulation and defence of membership rights. It led in Africa to an emphasis on individual (often formal) equality and non-discrimination, which it was believed would suffice to prevent membership discrimination and overcome ethnic divisions. As part of the discourse of nation-building, this was accordingly taken to mean that people relate to the state only as individuals not as members of particular ethnic groups.

It was accordingly maintained in this analysis that although national integration, electoral democracy and common citizenship are necessary, maintaining difference-blind structures and guaranteeing individual rights, including formal equality and non-discrimination, do not address the socio-economic and political marginalisation of many minorities and/or their vulnerability to such marginalisation, nor do such mechanisms guarantee the equal recognition of the cultures and languages of all minorities forming the post-colonial African state. The recognition of this fact means that the constitutional recognition of ethno-cultural diversity and the provision of mechanisms for its accommodation are necessary, not only to address adequately the issue of minorities within a democratic framework, but also to achieve legitimate structure of government necessary for a fair distribution of the burdens and benefits of social co-operation within the post-colonial African state.

In Chapter IV, the study launched an examination and elaboration of a robust minority rights framework that justifies and offers the basis for appropriate constitutional recognition and mechanisms for the accommodation of ethno-cultural diversity in Africa. Based on an analysis of normative political theory and international law relevant to the subject, we determined and identified that such a robust minority rights framework, particularly relevant to the African context, has three elements. The first is the recognition of cultural identity. Based on a defence of the importance of cultural membership to the identity of individuals and to their capacity to make meaningful choices, and of the need to rectify the colonial and post-colonial non-recognition and denigration of minority cultures and languages, the study contended that an effective constitutional design for the accommodation of diversity should provide guarantees and policy frameworks that recognise the use of indigenous languages, not only in the private domain, but also in the public sphere, including in communication with state agencies.

It should also give institutional expression and support to the cultures and religions of the various minorities. This was shown to be a necessary condition if members of such minorities are to have their identity duly recognised and respected, and to be treated with equal concern and respect.

The second component of the required minority rights framework defended in this study is equality. Considering the nature of the issue of minorities in Africa, a distinction was made between universal equality and substantive equality. While universal equality, involving the provision of the same rights and status universally to individuals, provides the basis for a common bond of citizenship, substantive equality is concerned with the membership rights of minorities necessary both to offset their political and socio-economic vulnerabilities and to prevent their future exclusion, as well as to recognise and affirm their particularity or cultural distinctness. Here, equality operates not only as a justification for recognising the particular cultural attributes of minorities that give meaning to the lives of their members, but also for developing constitutional guarantees and mechanisms for rectifying structures and patterns of socio-economic and political inequalities among various groups and ethno-regions. In the political field, this dictates that states adopt institutional arrangements that provide fair and adequate representation and participation for members of all groups. It is also important that there exists a socio-economic regime that rectifies past patterns of socio-economic marginalisation or deprivations, and institutionalises a fair system of distribution of the burdens and benefits of living under a common government.

The third component of the minority rights framework (broadly understood in this study as various policies and mechanisms for accommodation of diversity) is self-determination. Self-determination mainly captures the historical and political context of the issue of minorities. Accordingly, a certain formulation of self-determination was examined and defended to address the illegitimate historical process of the making of the state and the failure of its basic structure to reflect, embody and serve the interests of members of all groups equitably, as well as the continuing alienation of members of various groups from state processes. This is based on James Anaya's distinction between substantive self-determination and remedial self-determination.

Substantive self-determination, which applies to the institutions of government under which human beings live, entails that the governing institutional order of a society be one that is (a) a product of the equal and free participation and consent of individuals and groups constituting the society (constitutive aspect) and (b) managed on an ongoing basis through the equal participation and freely and equally expressed will of the people/peoples concerned (ongoing aspect). Within this framework, we considered the institutions of colonial rule that deprived the state's constituent minorities of their freedom to exist independently, and the continuing alienation of members of minorities from the processes of the post-colonial state under which they live, as a violation of self-determination.

Remedial self-determination, which refers to the particular form by which self-determination is given application, is accordingly employed to identify and develop mechanisms that rectify such violation. This can include various mechanisms and guarantees identified on the basis of culture and equality. But in addition, it includes providing ethno-national/regional minorities with self-government structures and recognising and protecting the interests of peripheral minorities, such as indigenous peoples, over the land and resources to which they have cultural and socio-economic attachment. Beyond rectifying such violations, the application of self-determination in these various forms in redesigning the governing institutional order of the post-colonial African state also constitutes a way of giving proper application to the right of self-determination in its internal dimension, which is in the process of recognition under international law.[2]

Chapter V considered the question of how this framework should be translated into specific constitutional arrangements and guarantees 'to consolidate the framework of the modern African state while giving recognition and maximum utility to the component elements of ethnicities, cultures, and aspirations for self-determination'.[3] Accordingly, the chapter outlines the necessary institutional mechanisms and constitutional guarantees that define the structure and content of the framework defended in Chapter IV (the constitutional design for accommodation of diversity in Africa). These include: institutional mechanisms that guarantee minorities adequate representation and participation in national policy-making structures; self-government, particularly in the form of federalism; a socio-economic regime that redresses historical inequities and institutionalises a fair system of distribution; a policy framework that recognises and determines the use of indigenous languages in the public sphere, particularly in communication with state institutions, in education and in the media; and cultural and religious rights, including the recognition and enforcement of customary law and religious family law.

The nature, limitations and principles that regulate the operation of these mechanisms and constitutional guarantees were also identified and examined. It was maintained that minority guarantees as identified and defended in this

[2] Okafor calls this the 'righting of the post-colonial African state'. This, according to Okafor, 'refers primarily to the international legal imperative of utilizing and adhering to international human rights law norms (especially those relating to self-determination and minority rights) in the process of state-formation or even state-disintegration in Africa (as elsewhere).' Brackets in the original. OC Okafor '"Righting," Restructuring, and Rejuvenating the Post-Colonial African State: The Case for the Establishment of an AU Special Commission on National Minorities' (2007) 13 *African Yearbook of Int L* 2005 43.

[3] FM Deng 'Ethnicity: An African predicament' (1997) 15 (3) *The Brookings Review* 28–31, 28.

study are generally regarded as group rights not because they are exercised or held by the group as a collectivity, but mainly because they are membership rights and protect the interests of individuals as members of particular ethno-cultural groups. The institutional mechanisms and constitutional guarantees are not, and should not be, of such a nature that they trample upon individual rights and democratic principles. Although tensions can arise in particular situations between the two and may even be inevitable, generally they go together and can, in many ways, be interdependent and complementary. But in designing a group-rights based constitutional design for accommodation of minorities, attention must be paid to articulate in sufficient detail and clarity the principles and the limits that define the boundary and regulate the application of group rights.

In Chapters VI and VII, the translation of these proposed constitutional arrangements and guarantees into an actual constitutional design and how it operates in practice are illustrated by examining the design of the 1996 Constitution of South Africa and the 1995 Constitution of Ethiopia, although the constitutional design of these countries is also a product of the politics of a particular time of the two countries. This examination is conducted within the framework of the outline set in Chapter V. Chapter VI showed that even if the particular history and political context of South Africa is not generally hospitable to the articulation of constitutional forms and guarantees that give expression to group membership, the FC nevertheless provides a sufficiently sophisticated design both to overcome the divisions and inequalities inherited from the apartheid past and to accommodate the interests and identities of members of various groups. This design involves institutional mechanisms that facilitate the *participation and representation* of members of all communities, a deliberative policy-making process, and a federal-like state structure involving the system of provincial government. This is accompanied by a multilingual policy framework involving the recognition of all the major languages spoken by 99 per cent of the population and other guarantees, including the right to education in an official language of one's choice, the rights of cultural and religious groups, and the establishment of institutions charged with the promotion and protection of the rights of cultural, religious and linguistic communities.

The actual operation of South Africa's constitutional design shows that these mechanisms and constitutional guarantees form an important part of what makes the terms of social co-operation in South Africa just and legitimate for all South Africans. They have accordingly helped South Africa's successful transition to democracy and allow members of all sections of society to identify with the Constitution and the institutions it established, although questions have been raised in 2011 and 2012 as to the flexibility of the Constitution to achieve the structural transformation of the South African economy for overcoming the inequalities and divisions inherited from the apartheid past. They also constitute important aspects of the Constitution, whose object it is to realise on a continuous basis the constitutional promise that 'South Africa belongs to all who live in it, united in diversity'.[4] Generally, this case study dispelled the often exaggerated fears and views prevalent in post-colonial Africa that the recognition of ethno-cultural diversity frustrates national integration. It proved that not only can the two indeed be pursued together, but also the recognition of diversity in numerous ways supports the goals of national integration, although such integration has yet to happen in South Africa.

At the same time, it was also noted that the efficacy and success of the constitutional design for the accommodation of diversity defended in this study depends both on the nature of its institutionalisation, and on the particular historical, socio-economic and political contexts within which it operates and is given effect. In the context of South Africa, although, objectively speaking, the Final Constitution provided a reasonably sophisticated design for the accommodation of diversity as an essential feature of South Africa's constitutional democracy, while some of its aspects are rendered ineffective due to the evolution of the country into a dominant-party democracy, others are not fully implemented due to political inattention (e.g. language rights) or else face possible abandonment (e.g. the system of provincial government).

Chapter VII examined the design of Ethiopia's FDRE Constitution as a further illustration of the constitutional application and actual operation of the mechanisms and constitutional guarantees outlined in Chapter V and generally defended in this study. The Ethiopian case study is particularly interesting, both on account of its radical features and because it offers important insights into the limits of constitutional accommodation of minorities and the pitfalls that must be avoided in institutionalising minority rights and/or mechanisms for accommodation of diversity. In other words, it tells us what the framework of minority rights defended in this study should not be about. That is minority rights as defended in this study should not be instituted in a way that undermines democratic ideals of universal reach including human rights and national integration. It also illustrates in concrete terms the discussion in Chapter V on the limitations and principles that regulate the operation of minority rights (the proposed institutional mechanisms and constitutional guarantees).

We noted that Ethiopia's constitutional design for the accommodation of diversity has some structural limitations. Many attribute these to its full institutionalisation of ethnicity. This may well be the case. It was, however, further argued that the limitation is attributable to a more fundamental problem. This involves (a) the Constitution's conception of the characteristics of ethnic groups in general and the nature of Ethiopia's ethnic diversity in particular, and (b) the

[4] Preamble to the South African Constitution 1996 Act No 108.

particular characteristics of the institutional mechanisms and constitutional guarantees. First, the Constitution defines ethnic groups in absolute communitarian terms as natural communities that are internally homogenous and possess defined boundaries and exist independently of each other (not just in cultural terms but territorially as well). It also assumes that each Ethiopian fits neatly within a particular ethnic group and necessarily identifies herself with that group. These are all assumptions that fly in the face of the interdependencies and overlaps between the different cultures and the possession by individuals of multiple layers of identification whose importance differs from individual to individual. Secondly, the Constitution prescribes radical constitutional forms, including the legal affirmation that each ethnic group is sovereign and entitled to the right to self-determination, including secession, and an ethnic federation in which major ethnic groups are assigned their own homelands.

Notwithstanding the above, in addition to illustrating the application of the discussion in Chapter V about the nature and limits of minority rights and the principles governing their operation, the Ethiopian case study additionally offered a further illustration that the provision of mechanisms and constitutional guarantees for the accommodation of diversity is a necessary condition for equality and justice in the multi-ethnic societies such as the ones we have in Africa. It revealed that for multi-ethnic societies with ethno-cultural conflict is of the kind Ethiopia has experienced, a group-rights regarding constitutional design is a *sine qua non* to justice for and peaceful co-existence between members of various groups.

8.3. Overall Conclusions and Final Observations

This study defended a robust minority rights framework involving certain constitutional guarantees for the cultures, religions and languages of minorities and institutional arrangements that ensure the representation and participation of members of minorities in the processes of the state and give them control over some aspects of their membership interests. Such a robust minority rights framework provides the necessary mechanisms not only to rectify the cultural, socio-economic and political marginalisation of minorities, but also to secure the substantive inclusion of their members in the management of public life. Minority rights as elaborated in this study are accordingly treated as essential components of the requirement of justice in the context of the ethno-cultural diversity and inequality that characterise the post-colonial African state.

The framework defended in this study addresses the various dimensions of the issue of minorities in Africa. The institutional arrangements that it dictates, outlined in Chapters IV and V, demand the redefinition of the existing structure and distribution of power of the post-colonial African state so as to remedy existing ethnic and ethno-regional political and socio-economic inequalities. In other words, they establish the necessary conditions for members of all groups to have their fair share in the processes of the state.

Together with the constitutional guarantees accorded to the cultures, languages or religions of the various ethno-cultural groups, these institutional arrangements dismantle the highly centralised organisation of political power and control of societal resources of the post-colonial African state that has entrenched the winner-take-all politics of the 'zero-sum game' which precipitated the violent conflicts witnessed in many African countries. They lead to the empowerment of members of all groups, particularly those who feel alienated from the state or are vulnerable to marginalisation. This helps to diminish and ultimately eliminate the alienation of minorities from the state. As the state protects the cultural and linguistic identity of minorities and reflects in its structures and processes the symbols and relevant social values of members of all groups, it becomes possible for all citizens to feel included and identify with the state and its processes. This facilitates the integration of the institutions and norms of the state on the one hand and the norms and cultures of the diverse constituent groups on the other. Needless to say, this also reflects and advances the objective of national integration that all African states seek to achieve.

The last three chapters of this book elaborated these constitutional mechanisms and guarantees and examined their nature and limits, as well as the principles that regulate their operation once they are institutionalised. Some conclusions and general observations are made below, particularly with respect to self-government (federalism), representation and participation, and constitutional policy and guarantees on language, culture and religion.

8.3.1. *Federalism*

Federalism is one of the mechanisms through which the minority rights framework defended in this study may be translated into an adequate constitutional design for the accommodation of diversity in Africa. In its multicultural form in particular, it creates structures both for self-government and for members of minorities to be represented and to participate in national policy making. It therefore has, so the study argued, the necessary institutions and norms for addressing some of the important claims of minorities. Probably its most important value is in dismantling the centralised organisation of political power, and control of resources that is characteristic of the post-colonial African state and which often leads to fierce rivalry and even violence among various groups and/or ethno-regions. It disperses power and resources territorially, allowing members of various groups or regions to have their fair share. The multiple centres of power it creates give members of different ethno-cultural groups multiple avenues for effective participation. The case study of South Africa, although still in its early stage of development, supports most of these conclusions.

The argument for multicultural federalism may also be supported by the fact that other alternatives, such as the unitary state which signifies the continuation of the status quo, have previously failed and are not better options. This is for example illustrated by the Ethiopian case study. The other alternative to federalism, that is the redrawing of the borders of the post-colonial African state, is not practical either. This is particularly true where there is no demand for independence, as in most of the ethnic struggles and conflicts in African states. Besides, except for very limited, exceptional cases, addressing minority issues through secession is not considered to be a viable option, whether in normative political theory or in international law and the practice of states. This study accordingly maintains that, from all angles, federalism, particularly in its multicultural form, is probably the most optimal institutional device to provide an effective constitutional design for the accommodation of diversity in Africa.

As far as its actual effect is concerned, we have observed that although federalism is necessary, it is not sufficient. Its efficacy depends, among other things, on the particular form in which it is institutionalised and the political and socio-economic context of the country within which it operates. With respect to South Africa, we observed that although the constitutional text establishes a system of provincial government suitable for the South African reality, its role as a device for distributing power and accommodating diversity has not been optimal due in part to the ANC's political dominance both nationally and provincially. This is also observed with respect to the Ethiopian case. Politically speaking, this has the effect of weakening the constitutional scheme of multilevel government and particularly the ability of provinces to develop their own policies and experiment with their powers.

One observation that can be made in this regard is that in these circumstances, if the system of provincial government is to achieve its constitutional purposes, a separation must be maintained between party and government. The judiciary can play a great part in this. In addition, the provincialisation of the ANC or the emergence of strong provincial support for either new or existing opposition parties would also create the political space for the effective operation of the system of provincial government.

The most serious challenge facing the system of provincial government in South Africa is its possible diminishment or abolition. This is not, however, because provinces have become of no use or undermine national unity. There is no evidence to suggest this. Although problems of service delivery might have contributed to it, this rather seems to be a move for more centralisation. From the perspective of this study and the particular reality of South Africa as well, we pointed out that there are very strong reasons to maintain the system of provincial government. It has been noted that there is a strong view that the policy question should be how to strengthen the capacity of provinces and make them more effective, rather than scrapping them. One can suggest in this regard that improving the administrative and fiscal capacity of provinces may allow them to emerge as critical instruments, not only for continuous accommodation of South Africa's diversity, but also for deepening the process of democratisation and socio-economic transformation. Moreover, it is also indispensable to rectify existing socio-economic and administrative imbalances or reduce them to an acceptable level. In conclusion, it is fair to say that whether and how the system of provincial government would continue to facilitate the accommodation of diversity and actualise its potential for enhancing South Africa's democracy depend on not only addressing these existing difficulties, but also how the political and socio-economic, as well as judicial, developments affect its evolution.

As far as Ethiopia's federalism is concerned, one can say that its role in accommodating the country's diverse population could be enhanced, and even its survival guaranteed, only if its multiple structural limitations are rectified through constitutional amendment. It is also important in this regard that such a process involves the participation of all sections of society for it to gain legitimacy. In terms of the limitations, one point that has emerged is that the Constitution has not effectively institutionalised the principles that regulate the operation of minority rights (discussed in Chapter V) to ensure that the institutions that these rights justify do not undermine both individual rights and the constitutional objective of maintaining national unity and achieving an integrated economic system. This is probably where the reform should start. First, it is imperative to develop effective mechanisms for the promotion and enforcement throughout the country of the individual human rights and freedoms guaranteed in the Constitution. This may in particular include establishing a commission charged with, among other responsibilities, ensuring that federal and state practices and decisions adhere to the principles of equality and non-discrimination.

Secondly, the nature of the relationship between group and individual rights, including the obligation of regional authorities vis-à-vis, in particular, regional minorities, must be clearly defined. Most importantly, there is also a need for reform of the Constitution's conception of Ethiopian society as a collection of distinct communities. This requires reducing its communitarian characteristics and emphasising its commitment to building a bond of common citizenship as members of one political and economic community. The basis of representation and participation in regional authorities should also be changed from ethnic membership to residence, while securing institutional guarantees to protect the interests of local communities and historically marginalised groups.

Although some of these reforms require constitutional amendment, many can be implemented through judicial pronouncement. But the Ethiopian federal system also lacks a proper judicial mechanism for effecting constitutional change – making this one of the crucial areas where the Constitution needs amendment. This can be achieved, for example, by transforming the existing CCI into a constitutional court, and the HoF into the organ of the legislature in which the interests of members of the federation or the various minorities constituting them are to be represented. This would also correct the existing lack of regional participation in national policy, which is contrary to the principle of federalism.

8.3.2. *Representation and Participation*

The most important dimension of the issue of minorities in Africa is the struggle for a meaningful role in state processes. This is essentially a question of representation and participation. Given the context of ethno-cultural diversity and existing patterns of unequal power relations, it is suggested that a legitimate and sustainable democratic system can be achieved only through institutional arrangements and policy-making processes that give proportional representation and effective participation to minorities. Existing institutional arrangements and processes in which the winner takes all should be abandoned.

This study concluded that the principle of proportional representation and deliberative policy-making are best suited to effect the institutional arrangements and processes that give members of all groups a stake in the multi-ethnic African state. At the same time, the aim is not to entrench ethnic cleavages in the political processes. Accordingly, group representation through a quota system or reservation of seats is not regarded as the primary option. Rather, emphasis is put on proportional electoral design. It is, however, argued that where this happens to be ineffective in ensuring the participation of peripheral minorities such as indigenous peoples, the proportional electoral design should be supplemented by group representation on the basis of the quota system or reservation of seats, or any similar mechanisms, albeit temporarily. Emphasis is also put on deliberative processes that ensure that minorities have their say and are listened to. In addition, the principle of proportional representation is also given application within the public service.

In the South African case study, one of the issues noted was that although there seems to be wide agreement on the need for a PR electoral system, the current closed-list system is not working optimally. This is partly due to its emphasis on political parties rather than representatives or the electorate, and partly to ANC dominance and the recently scrapped floor-crossing that increasingly pushed other parties to the margins. Other forms of PR system that give more control to the electorate and the removal of the floor-crossing law may deliver a better result. Another issue raised was that the PR system may not guarantee that peripheral minorities such as the Koi, San and Nama communities get representation. Although group representation does not seem to be a live option in the context of South Africa, it is nevertheless clear that there may be a need to rectify the defects in the existing system of representation to give a voice to these communities. One possible option could be the provision of technical and financial assistance for the establishment and running of organisations by members of these communities that articulate and promote their interests.

Equally important for ensuring the voice of minorities is the existence of deliberative processes. In this regard, the constitutional requirement for a participatory legislative process offers the legal basis for elaborating standards on the nature and mechanisms of deliberation. The emerging jurisprudence of the CC elaborating these standards is a highly commendable development in the right direction. The importance of this lies in creating sufficient avenues for minorities not only to have their say, but to be listened to as well.

In the Ethiopian case, instead of the proportional electoral system proposed in this study, the first-past-the-post system is adopted. Although this system delivers representation of the population diversity due to the delimitation of electoral districts following ethnic boundaries or within ethnic territories, it was found to be flawed for various reasons. First, it tends to emphasise the geography of ethnicity and hence to entrench divisions in the electoral system. Secondly, minority parties that genuinely espouse the interests of particular groups have not achieved representation, and even if represented they did not get parliamentary seats in proportion to their electoral support. In practice this has entrenched the dominance of the ruling coalition while the position of minority parties has been weakened or has failed to show significant improvement. Thirdly, it has limited the thriving of political pluralism and genuine representation of population diversity that would have been possible under the PR system. This book accordingly suggests that the electoral system be reformed along the lines of PR system. This naturally calls for the amendment of the Constitution, which is best effected as part of the federal structure reform suggested above.

Within the states of the federation, regional minorities face exclusion and discrimination which is expressed in terms of, among other things, a lack of representation and participation in regional governments. The conflicts that have emerged within the multi-ethnic states for control of new centres of power are also partly attributable to the lack of constitutional principles that require a well articulated and fair system of representation. It has accordingly emerged that mechanisms that give adequate voice to regional minorities as well as all other communities should be developed. This can be given effect through the establishment of either (a) bicameral regional legislatures where the second chamber is composed of representatives of all the constituent communities, or (b) consultative bodies in which all members of the different communities are to be represented, or (c) one legislative body in which members of all the different communities get representation but the group/s indigenous to the region would have veto powers over clearly defined cultural matters and socio-economic interests.

8.3.3. *Language, Culture and Religion*

In terms of language policy, the study advocated a multilingual approach. This should be given effect through a language regime that recognises and determines the use of indigenous languages in the public domain, including in communication with public authorities, in education and in the media. The application of this nevertheless depends upon the combination of various factors, including the size of the group speaking the particular language, its territorial concentration, the nature of the public service in question and the capacity of the state. Accordingly, the larger and the more territorially concentrated the group is and the more vital the public good is, the higher the obligation of the state to recognise the language as a medium of communication either for all public purposes, or for the more vital ones, in the region in which the speakers of the language live. This, however, does not mean that even in such regions the local vernacular becomes an exclusive medium of public communication. To give people living in those regions choices, the local vernacular should be made to operate alongside the official language/s.

With respect to South Africa, it has been noted that the FC provides for a robust policy framework for multilingualism expressed most significantly in the recognition of 11 official languages. As envisaged in the FC, this is expected to lead to the enactment of relevant legislation to articulate in detail mechanisms for the implementation of the framework under FC s 6. A bill drafted in 2000 has not yet been adopted. This reluctance to implement the constitutional obligations concerning multilingualism and the dominance of English as the lingua franca in various areas of public life has led to fears of linguistic marginalisation, particularly on the part of Afrikaans-speakers. If the constitutional recognition of the 11 official languages is to be more than a hollow gesture, it is imperative that the implementing legislation is adopted. The PSALB and the CPPCRLC should also be given adequate financial and political support if they are to implement their mandates contributing to the constitutional objective that South Africa belongs to all who live in it, united in diversity.

Under the Ethiopian Constitution, the equality of all Ethiopian languages is recognised in Article 5(1). The equality that is envisaged here is merely formal equality. In reality, these various languages are unequal, and no obligation is envisaged under the constitution to achieve the substantive equality of the different languages. The problem with such a policy of formal equality of the languages of the country is that it does not address the historical disadvantages and inequalities suffered by many of the languages. At the same time, given the resource implications of substantive linguistic equality in a country with more than 80 languages and with very limited resources, the provision of substantive equality would not have been realistic.

Notwithstanding the formal equality of all Ethiopian languages, for practical reasons Amharic is chosen as the working language of the federal government. Regional states are authorised to designate as official or working language/s the language/s of their choice. To the extent that regional states are not required to use their working languages alongside with the working language of the federation, there is a danger that regional minorities would suffer various forms of discrimination as the language requirement of the federal unit to which they belong would put severe limit on their ability to fully exercise many of their basic rights. This is one area where the country may have problems in the not-so-distant future if the problem is not addressed.

BIBLIOGRAPHY

Books and Journal Articles

Aalen, L *Ethnic Federalism in a Dominant Party State: The Ethiopian Experience 1991–2000* (Bergen: Chr. Michelsen Institute Development Studies and Human Rights, 2002)

Abbink, J. 'Breaking and Making the State: The Dynamic of Ethnic Democracy in Ethiopia' 13 *Journal of Contemporary African Studies* (1995) 149

Abdulahi Ahmed An-Na'im (ed.) *Human Rights Under African Constitutions* (2003)

Abdulahi, A.M. 'The Refugee Crisis in Africa as a Crisis of the Institution of the State' 6(4) *Int'l J. Refugee L.* (1994) 562

Abkin, J. 'Breaking and Making the State: The Dynamic of Ethnic Democracy in Ethiopia' (1995) 13 *Journal of Contemporary African Studies* 149

Acheampong, K.A. 'The African Charter and the Equalization of Human Rights' 12 *Scandinavian Human Rights Journal* (1994)

Ackermann, L.W.H. 'Equality and non-discrimination: Some analytical thoughts' 22(4) *South African Journal on Human Rights* (2006) 597

Adamolekun, L. & Kincaid, J. 'The Federal Solution: Assessment and Prognosis for Nigeria and Africa' 21 *Publius: The Journal of Federalism* (1991)

Addis, A. 'Individualism, Communitarianism, and the Rights of Ethnic Minorities' 67 *Notre Dame Law Review* (1992) 615

Addis, A. 'On Human Diversity and the Limits of Toleration' in Ian Shapiro and Will Kymlicka (eds.) *NOMOS XXXIX: Ethnicity and Group Rights* ((New York: New York University Press, 1997) 112

Aka, P.C. 'Nigeria: The Need For An Effective Policy Of Ethnic Reconciliation In The New Century' 14 *Temp. Int'l & Comp. L.J* (2000) 351

Akermark, A.S. *Justification of Minority Protection in International Law* (The Hague: Kluwer Law International, 1996)

Albertyn, C. & Goldblatt, B. 'Equality' in S Woolman, et al. (eds.) *Constitutional law of South Africa* (2nd Edition, OS, 2007) Chapter 35

Albertyn, C. 'Equality'in Elisje Bonthuys & Cathi Albertyn (eds.) *Gender, Law & Justice* (2007) 87

Alexander Jr., A.S. 'The Ivory Coast Constitution: An accelerator, not a brake' 3(1) *The Journal of Modern African Studies*' (1963) 293

Alfredsson, G. 'Minority Rights: International Standards and Monitoring Procedures' in Norman Taku (ed.) *From human wrongs to human rights – Part VII* (Centre for Human Rights, University of Pretoria: 2000) 37

Anaya, S.J. 'On Justifying Special Ethnic Group Rights: Comments on Pogee' in Ian Shapiro and Will Kymlicka (eds.) *Ethnicity and Group Rights* (1997) 222

Anaya, S.J. 'Self-determination as a collective Human Right under International Law' in Pekka Aiko & Martin Scheinin (eds.) *Operationalizing the Right of Indigenous Peoples to Self-determination* (2000) 3

Anaya, S.J. *Indigenous Peoples in International Law* (Oxford: Oxford University Press, 1996)

Anaya, S.J. *Indigenous Peoples in International Law* (Oxford: Oxford University Press, 2004)

Anderson, B. *Imagined Communities: Reflections on the origin and spread of nationalism* (London and New York: Verso revised ed., 1991)

An-Na'im, A.A. 'Introduction: Expanding legal protection of human rights in African Countries' in Abdulahi Ahmed An-Na'im (ed.) *Human Rights Under African Constitutions* (2003)

Arendt, H. *The Origins of Totalitarianism* (New York: World Publishing, 1972)

Asante, S.K.B. 'Nation Building and Human Rights in Emergent African Nations' 2 *Cornell International Law Journal* (1969) 83

Assefa, S. 'Of Federalism and Secession' in *Constitutionalism: Reflections and Recommendations, Symposium on the Making of the New Ethiopian Constitution* (Addis Ababa: Inter Africa Group, 1993) 113–125

Ayittey, G.B.N. *Indigenous African Institutions* (Transnational Publications, 1991)

Barker, E. *Principles of social and political theory* (Oxford: Clarendon Press, 1951)

Barry, B. *Culture and Equality: An Egalitarian Critique of Multiculturalism* (Cambridge, Massachusetts: Harvard University Press, 2001)

Baylis, E.A. 'Beyond rights: Legal processes and ethnic conflicts' 25 *Michigan J. Int'l L.* (2004) 529

Bekker, S. and Leildé, A. 'Is multiculturalism a Workable Policy in South Africa?' 5(2) *International Journal of Multicultural Societies* (2003) 119

Berkeley, B. *Liberia: A Promise Betrayed* (New York: Lawyers Committee for Human Rights, 1986)

Boon, C. *Political Topographies of the African State: Territorial Authority and Institutional Choice* (Cambridge: Cambridge University Press, 2003)

Bronstein, V. 'Reconceptualizing the Customary Law Debate in South Africa' 14 (3) *SAJHR* (1998) 388

Brownlie, I. *African Boundaries: Legal and diplomatic encyclopedia* (London, Berkeley and Los Angeles: C. Hurst and Co. (Publishers) Ltd., and University of California Press, 1979)

Brownlie 'The Rights of Peoples in Modern International Law' in James Crawford (ed.) *The Rights of Peoples* (Oxford: Clarendon Press, 1988) 1

Buergenthal, T. *International human rights in a nutshell* (1988)

Busia Jr., N.K.A. 'The right to self-determination, the state and the quest for democracy in Africa: An explanatory analysis' *Proceedings of the 4th Annual Conference of African Society of International and Comparative Law* (1992)

Busia, Jr., N.K.A. 'The status of human rights in pre-colonial Africa: Implications for contemporary practices' in Eileen Mccarthy-Arnolds et al. (eds.) *Africa, human rights and the global system: The political economy of human rights in a changing world* (Westport, Connecticut and London: Greenwood Press, 1994) 225

Busia, K . A. *Africa in Search of Democracy* (London: Routledge and Kegan Paul, 1976)

Canefe, N. 'Sovereignty without nationalism? A critical assessment of Minority Rights Beyond the Sovereign Nation-state Model' in Mortimer Sellers (eds.) *The New World Order Sovereingty, Human Rights, and the Self-determination of Peoples* (Oxford/Washington, D.C.: Berg Publishers, 1996) 91

Capotorti, F. *Study on the Rights of Persons Belonging to Ethnic, Religious and Linguistic Minorities* (New York: United Nations, 1979) Sales No. E.78XIV.1

Casalas, N.T. *Group Rights as Human Rights: A Liberal Approach to Multiculturalism* (Dordrecht: Springer, 2006)

Castellino, J. 'Order and Justice: National Minorities and the Right to Secession' 6 *International Journal on Minority and Group Rights* (1999) 389

Clapham, C. 'Ethnicity and the national question in Ethiopia' in P Woodward and M Forsyth (eds.) *Conflict and peace in the Horn of Africa: Federalism and its alternatives* (Aldershot: Dartmouth Publishing Co. Ltd, 1994) 27

Clay, J.W. 'Nation, Tribe and Ethnic Group in Africa' 9 *Cultural Survival Quarterly* (1985) 2

Cobbah, J.A.M. 'African Values And The Human Rights Debate: An African Perspective' 9 *Human Rights Quarterly* (1987) 309

Cohen, G.P.E. 'Language and Ethnic Boundaries: Perceptions of Identity Expressed through Attitudes towards the use of Language Education in Southern Ethiopia' 7(3) *Northeast African Studies* (2000) 189

Compagnon, D. 'Somali Armed Movements: The Interplay of Political Entrepreneurship and Clan-Based Factions' in Chiristopher Clapaham (eds.) *African Guerrillas* (Bloomington: Indiana University Press, 1998) 73

Cornwell, R. 'Somalia: Fourteenth Time Lucky?' *Occasional Paper 87* (Pretoria: Institute for Security Studies, April 2004)

Crawford, J. 'The rights of peoples: "Peoples" or "Governments"? in James Crawford (ed.) *The rights of peoples* (Oxford: Clarendon Press, 1988) 55

Currie, I. 'Minority Rights: Education culture and language' in Matthew Chaskalson, Janet Kentridge, Jonathan Klaaren, Gilbert Marcus, Derek Spitz, Stuart Woolman (eds.) *Constitutional law of South Africa* Chapter (Cape Town: Juta and Co. Ltd, 1st ed., 1996) Chapter 35

Currie, I. 'Minority Rights: Education, Culture and Language' in Chaskalson et al. (eds.) *Constitutional law of South Africa* Chapter 35
Davidson, B. *The Black Man's Burden: Africa and the Curse of the Nation-State* (London: James Currey, 1992)
De Lupis, I.D. *International Law and the Independent State* (Aldershott: Gower 2nd ed., 1987)
De Varennes, F. *Language, Minorities and Human Rights* (The Hague: Kluwer Law International, 1996)
De Varennes, F. 'A Guide to the Rights of Minorities and Language' COLPI Paper No. 4 (2001)
De Varennes, F. *Towards Effective Political Participation and Representation of Minorities* E/CN.4/Sub.2/AC.5/1998/WP.5
De Villiers, B. 'The Constitutional Principles: Content and Significance' in Bertus de Villiers *Birth of a constitution* (Cape Town: Juta & Co. Ltd, 1994) 41
De Villiers, B. 'The Constitutional Principles: Content and Significance' in Bertus De Villiers (ed.) *Birth of a Constitution* (Cape Town: Juta and Co Ltd., 1994) 41
De Villiers, B. *The Future of Provinces in South Africa – The Debate Continues* Konrad-Adenauer-Stiftung Policy Paper Issue No 2 (Johannesburg: KAS, October 2007)
Decalo, S. 'Chad: The roots of centre periphery strife' 79 *African Affairs* (1980) 491
DeLancey, M.W. 'The Construction of the Cameroon Political System: The Ahidjo Years 1958–1982' 6 *Journal of Contemporary African Studies* (April 1987) 3
Deng, F.M. 'Ethnicity: An African Predicament' 15 (3) *The Bookings Review* (Summer 1997) 28
Deng, F.M. 'Sudan's Turbulent Road to Nationhood' in Ricardo René Larémont (ed.) *Borders, Nationalism and the African State* (Boulder, Colorado: Lynne Rienner Publishers, Inc., 2005) 33
Dersso, S.A. 'The Jurisprudence of the African Commission on Human and Peoples' Rights With respect to Peoples' Rights' 6 (2) *African Human Rights Journal* (2006) 358
Dersso, S.A. *Promotion of Human Security in Africa: The Role of African Human Rights Institutions* ISS Monograph Series No. 145 (June 2008)
Deveaux, M. *Cultural Pluralism and Dilemmas of Justice* (Ithaca & London: Cornell University Press, 2000)
Dinstein, Y. 'Collective Human Rights of Peoples and Minorities' 25 *International and Comparative L. Quarterly* (1976) 102
Diop, C.A. *Pre-colonial black Africa* (Westport, Connecticut: Lawrence Hill, 1987)
Donders, Y.M. *Towards a Right to Cultural Identity?* (Antwerp: Intersentia, 2002)
Donkers, A. and Murray, R. 'Prospects and Problems Facing Traditional Leaders in South Africa' in Bertus de Villiers (ed.) *The Rights of Indigenous People: a Quest for Coexistence* (Pretoria: HSRC, 1997) 39
Du Plessis, L. M 'A background to drafting the chapter on fundamental rights' Bertus de Villiers *Birth of a constitution* (Cape Town: Juta & Co. Ltd, 1994) 89
Duchacek, I.D. *Comparative Federalism: The Territorial Dimension Of Politics* (Lanham, Md.: University Press of America, 1987)
Duchacek, I. *Power Maps: Comparative Politics of Constitutions* (Santa Barbara: American Bibliographical Center-Clio Press, Inc., 1973)
Dugard, J. 'A Legal Basis For Secession – Relevant Principles And Rules' in Julie Dahlitz (ed.) *Secession and international law* (The Hague: T.M.C. Asser Press, 2003) 92
Dworkin, R. 'Constitutionalism and Democracy' 3 *European Journal of Philosophy* (1995) 1
Dworkin, R. 'Liberal Community' 77 *California Law Review* (1989) 479–504
Ebrahim, H. *The Soul of a Nation: Constitution-Making in South Africa* (Cape Town: Oxford University Press, 1998)
Egan, A. and Taylor, R. 'South Africa: The Failure of Ethno-Territorial Politics' in J. Coakley (ed.) *The Territorial Management of Ethnic Conflict* (London: Frank Cass, 2003) 99
Eide, A. 'Cultural Rights and Minorities: Essay in Honour of Erica-Irene Daes' in Alfredson, G. & Stavropoulou, M. (eds.) *Justice Pending: Indigenous Peoples and Other Good Causes: Essays in Honour of Erica-Irene A. Daes* (The Hague: Kluwer Law International, 2002) 83
Eide, A. 'Minority Protection and World Order: Towards A Framework for Law and Policy' in Alan Philips and Allan Rosas (eds.) *Universal Minority Rights* (Turku/Abo: Institute for Human Rights, 1995) 87
Eide, A. 'Minority Situations: In Search of Peaceful and Constructive solutions' 66 *Notre Dame L. Rev.* (1991) 1311

Eide, A. *Commentary to the Declaration on the Rights of Persons Belonging to National or Ethnic, Religious or Linguistic Minorities* Working Paper, Working Group on Minorities (6th Sess.) E/CN.4/Sub.2/AC.5/2000/WP.1

Eide, Asbjørn, Catarina Krause, and Allan Rosas (eds.) *Economic, social and cultural rights: A Textbook* (The Hague: Kluwer Law International, 2nd rev. ed. 2001)

Ejobowah, J.B. 'The Limits and Possibilities of Conflict-Reduction Strategies in Africa's Polyethnic States' in E Ike Udogu (eds.) *The Issue of Political Ethnicity in Africa* (2001) 149

Elazar. D. *Federalism and the Way to Peace* (Kingston, Ontario: Queen's University, Institute of Intergovernmental Relations, 1994)

Erlich, H. 'The Eritrean autonomy 1952–1962: Its failure and its contribution to further escalation' in Yoram Dinstein (ed.) *Models of autonomy* (New Brunswick (USA) and London: Transaction Books, 1981)

Esheté, A. 'Ethnic Federalism: New Frontiers in Ethiopian Politics' in *First National Conference on Federalism, Conflict and Peace Building* (Addis Ababa: United Printers, Plc., 2003) 142

Ezetah, C.R. 'International law of self-determination and the Ogoni question: Mirroring Africa's post-colonial dilemma' 19 *Loyola of Los Angeles International and Comparative Law* (19997) 814

Ezetah, C.R. 'Legitimate Governance and Statehood in Africa: Beyond the Failed State and Colonial-Self-determination' in Edward Kofi Quashigah & Obiora Chinedu Okafor (eds.) Legitimate Governance in Africa: International and Domestic Legal Perspectives (The Hague: Kluwer Law International, 1999) 15

Fawcett, J. *The Law of Nations* (Harmondsworth: Penguin Books, 1971)

Forrest, J.B. *Subnationalism in Africa : Ethnicity, Alliance, and Politics* (Boulder, Colorado: Lynne Rienner Publishers, Inc., 2004)

Freeman, M. *Human Rights: An Interdisciplinary Approach* (Cambridge: Polity Press, 2002)

Friedman, S & Humphries, R (eds.) *Federalism and its Foes* (1993)

Fru, A.N. 'The Reunification Question in Cameroon History: Was the Bride an Enthusiastic or a Reluctant One' 47(2) *Africa Today* (Spring 2000) 91

G. Selassie, A. 'Ethnic Identity and Constitutional Design for Africa' 29 (1) *Stanford Journal of International Law* (Fall 1992–1993) 1

G. Selassie, A. 'Ethnic Federalism: Its promises and Pitfalls for Africa' 28 *Yale Journal of International Law* (Winter 2003) 51

Gagnon, A. & Tully, J. (eds.) *Multicultural Democracies* (2001) 1;

Garet, R.R. 'Community and Existence: The Rights of Groups' 56 *South Carolina Law Review* (1983) 1001

Gellner, E *Nations and Nationalisms: New Perspectives on the Past* (London Blackwell, 1983)

Gellner, E. *Nations and nationalism* (Ithaca, New York: Cornell University Press, 1983)

Ghai, Y. 'Autonomy as a Participatory Right in Modern Democratic State: Public Participation, Autonomy and Minorities' in Zelim A. Skurbaty (eds.) *Beyond a One Dimensional State: An Emerging Right to Autonomy?* (Leiden & Boston: KoninKlijke Brill NV, 2005) 3,

Gilbert, G. 'The Legal Protection Accorded to Minority Groups in Europe' *Netherlands Yearbook of International Law* (1992) 67

Giliomee, H & Simkins, C (eds.) *The Awkward Embrace: One-Party Domination and Democracy* (Capetown: Tafelberg Publishers Ltd, 1999)

Gloppen, S. *South Africa: The Battle over the Constitution* (Aldershot: Ashgate,1997)

Gudina, M. *Ethiopia: Competing Ethnic Nationalisms and the Quest for Democracy 1960–2000* (Addis Ababa: Shaker Publishing, 2003)

Gurr, T.R. and Scarritt, J.R. 'Minority Rights at Risk: A Global Survey' 11 *Human Rights Quarterly* (1989) 375

Gurr, T.R. *Minorities at Risk: A Global View of Ethnopolitical Conflicts* (Washington D.C.: USIP,1993)

Gurr, T.R. *Peoples Versus States: Minorities at Risk in the New Century* (Washington, D.c.: USIP, 2000)

Habtu, A. 'Ethnic Pluralism as an Organizing Principle of the Ethiopian Federation' 28 *Dialectical Anthropology* (2004) 91

Habtu, A. 'Multi-Ethnic Federalism in Ethiopia: A Study of the Secession Clause in the Constitution' 35(2) *Publius: The Journal of Federalism* (2005) 313

Haile, M. 'The New Ethiopian Constitution: Its Impact upon Unity, Human Rights and Development' 20 *Suffolk Transnational L. Rev.* (1996) 1

Haile-Selassie, B. *Ethiopia: A Precarious Ethno-Federal Constitutional Order* (Unpublished SJD dissertation, University of Wisconsin Law School, 2002)
Hannikainen, L. 'Self-determination and autonomy in international law' in Marku Suksi (ed.) *Autonomy: Applications and Implications* (The Hague: Kluwer Law International, 1998) 97
Hannum, H 'Contemporary Developments in the International Protection of the Rights of Minorities' 66 *Notre Dame L. Rev.* (1991) 1431
Hannum, Hurst *Autonomy, Sovereignty and Self-Determination – The accommodation of conflicting rights* (Philadelphia: University of Pennsylvania Press, 1990)
Harbeson, J.W. 'A Bureaucratic Authoritarian Regime' 9 *Journal of Democracy* (Oct.1999) 62
Henrard, K. *Devising an Adequate System of Minority Protection: Individual Rights, Minority Rights and the Right to Self-determination* (2000)
Henrard, K. *Minority protection in post-apartheid South Africa* (Westport, CT: Praeger Publishers, 2002)
Henz, P.H. 'A Political Success Story' 9 *Journal of Democracy* (Oct. 1999) 40
Heraclides, A. *Self-determination of minorities in international politics* (Portland, Oregon: Frank Cass, 1991)
Heyns, C. (ed.) *Human Rights Law in Africa* Vol. I (Leiden/Boston: Martinus Nijhoff, 2004)
Higgins, R. 'Post-Modern Tribalism and the Right to Secession, Comments' in Catherine Brölmann et al. (eds.) *Peoples and Minorities in International Law* (1993) 29
Hitchcock, R.K. 'Human rights and Indigenous peoples in Africa and Asia' in David P. Forsythe and Patrice C. McMahon (eds.) *Human rights and diversity* (Lincoln and London: University of Nebrasaka Press, 2003) 209
Hobbes, T. *Leviathan* C.B. Macpherson's (ed.) (London: Penguin Group, 1968)
Horowitz, D.L. *A Democratic South Africa? Constitutional Engineering in a Divided Society* (1991)
Horowitz, D.L. *Ethnic Groups in Conflict* (1985)
Howard, R.E. *Human Rights in Common Wealth Africa* (New Jersey, Rowman and Littlefield, 1986)
Humphrey, J.P. *No distant Millennium: The international law of human rights*, (New York: UNESCO, 1989)
Ihonbvere, J. 'The "irrelevant" State, ethnicity and the quest for nationhood in Africa' 17 *Ethnic and Racial Studies* (1994) 42
Ihonvbere, J.O. 'Politics of Constitutional Reforms and Democratization in Africa' 41 *IJCS* (2000) 1
Ihonvbere, J.O. 'The State and Ethnicity in Africa' in E Ike Udogu (ed.) *The Issue Of Political Ethnicity In Africa* (Aldershot: Ashgate Publishing Ltd, 2001) 59
James, W. & Hadland, A. 'Shared Aspirations: The Imperative of Accountability in South Africa's Electoral System' in *Electoral Models for South Africa: Reflections and Options* Electoral Task Team Review Roundtable Konrad-Adenaur-Stiftung Seminar Report No 18 (2nd ed.) (KAS: Johannesburg, January 2007) 15
Jinadu, L.A. *Explaining and Managing Ethnic Conflict in Africa: Towards a Cultural Theory of Democracy* Claude Ake Memorial Papers No. 1 (Uppsala: Nordic Africa Institute, 2007)
Johannesen, C. *Kingship in Uganda: The role of the Buganda Kingdom in Ugandan politics* CMI Working Papers 8 (Bergen: CHR. Michelsen Institute, 2006)
John S Mbiti *African Religions and philosophy* (New York: Boubleday, 1970) 141
Jovanović, M.A. 'Recognizing Minority Identities through Collective Rights' 27 *Human Rights Quarterly* (2005) 625
Justino, P. & Litchfield, J. *Economic Exclusion and Discrimination: The Experience of Minorities and Indigenous Peoples* (London: Minority Rights Group International, 2003)
Kaballo, S. 'Human Rights and Democratization in Africa' in David Beetham (ed.) *Politics and Human Rights* (Oxford: Blackwell Publishers, 1995) 189
Kadima, D. & Kasenally, R. 'The Formation, Collapse and Revival of Political Party Coalitions in Mauritius: Ethnic Logic and Calculation at Play' in Denis Kadima (ed.) *The Politics of Party Coalitions in Africa* (Johannesburg: EISA & KAS, 2006) 73
Karmis, D. & Norman, W. (eds.) *Theories of Federalism: A Reader* (2005)
Kasfir, N. 'Cultural Sub-nationalism in Uganda' in Victor A. Olorunsola (ed.) The Politics of Cultural Sub-nationalism in Africa (Garden City, New York: Anchor Books, 1972) 51

Kaspin, D. 'Tribes, regions and Nationalism in democratic Malawi' in Ian Shapiro and Will Kymlicka (eds.) *Ethnicity and group rights* (New York and London: New York University Press, 1997) 464

Kefale, A. 'Federalism: Some trends of ethnic conflicts and their management in Ethiopia' in Alfred G Nhema (ed.) *The quest for peace in Africa* (Addis Ababa: OSSREA, 2004) 51

Keller, E.J. 'Making and Remaking State and Nation in Ethiopia' in Ricardo René Larémont (ed.) *Borders, Nationalism and the African State* (Boulder, Colorado: Lynne Rienner Publishers, 2005) 87

King, P. 'Federation and Representation' in M Burgess & A. Gagnon (eds.) *Comparative Federalism and Federation* (London: Harvester, 1993) 95

Kishindo, P. 'The impact of a national language on minority languages: The case of Malawi' 12(2) *Journal of Contemporary African Studies* (1994) 138

Kiwanuka, R. 'The meaning of 'people' in the African Charter on Human and Peoples' Rights' 82 *American J Int'l L* (1988) 80

Klabbers, J and Lefeber, R. 'Africa: Lost Between self-determination and *uti possidetis*' in C Brölmann, R Leteber & M Zieck (eds.) *Peoples and minorities in International law* (Dordrecht: Martinus Nijhoff Publishers, 1993) 37

Klug, H. 'How the Centre Holds: Managing Claims for Regional and Ethnic Autonomy in a Democratic South Africa' in Yash Ghai *Autonomy and Ethnicity: Negotiating Competing Claims in Multi-ethnic Societies* (Cambridge: Cambridge University Press, 2000)

Klug, H. *Constituting Democracy: Law, Globalism and South Africa's Political Reconstruction* (Cambridge: Cambridge University Press, 2000)

Koenig, Matthias & Guchteneir, Paul de 'Political Governance of Cultural Diversity' in Matthias Koenig & Paul de Guchteneir (eds.) *Democracy and Human Rights in Multicultural Societies* (Aldershot: UNESCO Publishing/Ashgate, 2007) 3

Kuper, L . 'Genocide and mass killings: Illusion and reality' in B.J Ramacharan (ed.) *The right to life in International Law* (Martinus Nijhoff Publishers, Dordrecht, 1985) 117

Kymlicka, W. (ed.) *The rights of Minority cultures* (Oxford: Oxford University Press,1995)

Kymlicka, W. 'Federalism, Nationalism and Multiculturalism' in Dimitrios Karmis & Wayne Norman (eds.) *Theories of Federalism: A reader* (New York: Palgrave Macmillan, 2005)

Kymlicka, W. 'Nation-building and Minority Rights: Comparing Africa and the West' in Bruce Berman, Dickson Eyoh & Will Kymlicka (eds.) *Ethnicity and Democracy in Africa* (Oxford/ Athens: James Currey & Ohio, 2004) 54

Kymlicka, W. *Finding Our Way: Rethinking Ethno Cultural Relations in Canada* (Toronto: Oxford University Press, 1998)

Kymlicka, W. *Multicultural Citizenship: A Liberal Theory of Minority Rights* (Oxford: Oxford University Press, 1995)

Kymlicka, W. *Liberalism, Community and Culture* (Oxford: Clarendon Press, 1989)

Laakso, L. & Olukoshi, A. 'The Crisis of the Post-colonial Nation-State Project in Africa' in A Olukoshi & L Laakso (eds.) *Challenges to the Nation-State in Africa* (Uppsal: Nordic Africa Institute, 1996) 15

Larémont, R.R. (ed.) *Borders, nationalism and the African state* (Boulder Colorado: Lynne Rienner Publishers, Inc., 2005)

Le Vine, V.T. 'The Fall And Rise Of Constitutionalism In West Africa' 35(2) *The Journal of Modern African Studies* (1997) 181

Legum, C. 'Africa's Quest for Nationhood and Stability' in *Black Africa Twenty-Five Years After Independence: Lessons for the Future* (Africa Institute of South Africa, Conference, 1985)

Lehmann, K 'Aboriginal title, indigenous rights and the right to culture' 20 (1) SALJ (2004) 86

Lemarchand, R. 'The Limits of Self-Determination: The Case of the Katanga Secession' 56(2) *American Political Science Review* (1962) 404–416

Lemarchand, R. *Burundi : Ethnic conflict and Genocide* (Woodrow Wilson Centre Press and Cambridge University Press, 1996)

Lenta, P. 'Religious Liberty and Cultural Accommodation' 122 *SALJ* (2005) 352

Lerner, N. 'The Evolution Of Minority Rights In International Law' in Catherine Brölman, René Lefeber and Marjolein Zieck (eds.) *Peoples and minorities in international law* (1993) (Dordrecht/Boston/London: Martinus Nijhoff Publishers, 1993)75

Levine, D *Greater Ethiopia: The Evolution of a Multiethnic Society* (Chicago: The University of Chicago Press, 2000)
Lewis, A. *Politics in West Africa* (London: George Allen & Unwin Ltd,1965)
Lewis, I.M. 'The Tribal Factor in Contemporary Africa' in Colin Legum and John Drysdale (eds.) *Africa: Contemporary record 1969–1970* (1971) A 13
Lijphart, A. *Democracies: Patterns of majoritarian and consensus government in the twenty-one century* (New Haven: Yale University Press, 1984)
Lijphart, A. *Democracy in plural societies* (New Haven & London: Yale University Press,1977)
Liphart, A. 'The Alternative Vote: A Realistic Alternative for South Africa?' 18 *Politikon* (June 1991) 9
Locke, J. *Two Treatises of government* Peter Laslett (ed.)
Lodhi, A 'The Language Situation in Africa Today' 2(1) *Nordic Journal of African Studies* (1993) 79
Macklem, P. *Indigenous Difference and the Constitution in Canada* (Toronto: University of Toronto Press, 2001)
Makkonen, T. 'Is Multiculturalism Bad for the Fight against Discrimination?' in Martin Scheinin & Reetta Toivanen (eds.) *Rethinking Non-Discrimination and Minority Rights* (Turku/Åbo, Berlin: Institute for Human Rights Åbo Akademi University & German Institute for Human Rights, 2004) 155
Malaquias, A.V. 'The Political Economy of Angola's Ethnic Conflict' in S MacLean F. Quadir and T.M. Shaw (eds.) *The Crises of Governance in Asia And Africa* (Burlington: Ashgate, 2001) 207
Mamdani, M. *Citizen and Subject: Contemporary Africa and the Legacy of Late Colonialism* (Princeton, New Jersey: Princeton University Press, 1996)
Margalit, A. & Raz, J. 'National Self-determination' in Will Kymlicka (ed.) *The Rights of Minority Cultures* (Oxford: Oxford University Press, 1995) 79
McDougal, J. *History And The Culture Of Nationalism In Algeria* (Cambridge: Cambridge University Press, 2006)
McGarry, J. and O'Leary, B. (eds.) *The Politics of Ethnic Conflict* Regulation: *Case Studies of Protracted Ethnic Conflicts* (London and New York: Routledge, 1993)
Mckean, W. *Equality and Discrimination under International Law* (Oxford: Clarendon Press, 1983)
Mengisteab, K. 'New Approaches to State Building in Africa: The Case of Ethiopia's Ethnic-Based Federalism' 40(3) *African Studies Review* (1997) 111
Meredith, M. *The State of Africa: A History of Fifty Years of Independence* (Johannesburg: Jonathan Ball Publishers, 2005, 2006)
Metiku, Y.C. 'Ethiopia's Right to 'Life' In International Law' 2 *New Trends in Ethiopian Studies* (1994) 205
Michelman, F.I. 'Constitutional Authorship' in Larry Alexander (ed.) *Constitutionalism: Philosophical Foundations* (Cambridge: Cambridge University Press, 1998) 64
Mill, J.S. *Considerations on representative government* in H Acton (ed.) *Utilitarianism, liberty, representative government* (London: J.M. Dent, 1972)
Miller, D. 'Liberalism, Equal Opportunities and Cultural Commitments' in Paul Kelly (ed.) *Multiculturalism Reconsidered*: Culture and Equality *and its Critiques* (Cambridge: Polity Press, 2002) 45
Miller, D. *On Nationality* (Oxford: Clarendon Press, 1995)
Mojekwu, C.C. 'Self-determination: The African perspective' in Y Alexander & R A Friedlander (eds.) *Self-determination: National, Regional & Global Dimensions* (Boulder: Westview Press, 1980)
Mulikita, N. M 'A False Dawn? Africa's Post-1990 Democratization Waves' 12(4) *African Security Review* (2003) 105
Murray, C. and Simeon, R. 'Recognition without empowerment: Minorities in a democratic South Africa' 5(4) *I.CON* (2007) 699
Mutua, M.W. 'Putting Humpty Dumpty Back Together: The Dilemmas of the Post-colonial African State' 21 *Brooklyn Journal of International Law* (1995) 505
Mutua, M.W. 'The Banjul Charter and the African Cultural Fingerprint: An evaluation of the Language of Duties' 35 *Virginia J. Int'l L.* (1995) 339
Mutua, M.W. 'Why redraw the map of Africa: A moral and legal inquiry' 16 *Mich. J. Int'l L.* (1995) 1113
Nahum, F *A Constitution for a Nation of Nations: The Ethiopian Prospect* (Lawrenceville, NJ & Asmara: The Red Sea Press, Inc, 1997)

Neuberger, B. 'State and Nation in African Thought' in Johan Huchinson & Anthony D. Smith (eds.) *Nationalism* (Oxford: Oxford University Press, 1994) 231

Neuberger, B. *National Self-Determination in Postcolonial Africa* (Boulder, CO: Lynne Rienner Publishers, 1986)

Ngugi, J. 'The Decolonization-Modernization Interface and the Plight of Indigenous Peoples in Post-Colonial Development Discourses in Africa' 20 *Wisconsin International Law Journal* (2002) 279

Nkrumah, K. *I Speak of freedom* (New York: Prager, 1961)

Nnoli, O. *Ethnicity and development in Nigeria* (Aldershot: Avebury, 1995)

Nowak, *UN Covenant on Civil and Political Rights: CCPR Commentary* (Kehl am Rhein, Strasbourg, Arlington, Va: N.P. Engel Publishers, 1993)

Nwabueze, B. *Constitutional Democracy in Africa* (Ibadan: Spectrum Books Ltd., 2004 Vol. 1 & 5)

Nwabueze, B.O. *Constitutionalism in the Emergent States* (London and Enugu, Nigeira: C. Hurst & Co. (Publishers) Ltd., & Nwamife Publishers Ltd., 1973)

Okafor, O.C. '"Righting," Restructuring, and Rejuvenating the Post-colonial African State: The Case for the Establishment of an AU Special Commission on National Minorities' 13 *African Yearbook of International Law* 2005 (2007) 43

Okafor, O.C. *Re-Defining Legitimate Statehood: International Law and State Fragmentation in Africa* (2000)

Okere, B.O. 'The Protection of Human Rights in Africa and the African Charter on Human Rights and Peoples' Rights: A comparative Analysis with the European and American Systems' 6 *Hum Rts. Q.* (1984) 141

Okwa-Okafor, O.C. 'Self-determination and the struggle for ethno-cultural autonomy in Nigeria: The Zangon-Kafaf and Ogoni problems' 6 ASIL Proc. (1994) 52

Oloka-Onyango, J. 'Reinforcing Marginalized Rights in an Age of Globalization: International Mechanisms, Non-State Actors, and the Struggle for Peoples' Rights in Africa' 18 *American University Int'l L. Rev.* (2003) 851

Oloka-Onyango, J. 'The Question Of Buganda In Ugandan Contemporary Politics' 15(2) *Journal of Contemporary African Studies* (1997) 173

Osaghae, E. E 'The Ogoni Uprising: Oil politics, minority Agitation and the Future of the Nigerian State' 94 *African Affairs* (1995) 325

Osaghae, E.E. 'Ethnicity, the State and Constitutionalism in Africa: Preliminary Observations' in Okon Akiba (ed.) *Constitutionalism and society in Africa* (2004) 95

Ouguergouz, F. *The African Charter on Human and Peoples' Rights: A Comprehensive Agenda for Human Dignity and Sustainable Democracy in Africa* (The Hague: Kluwer Law International, 2003)

Owusu, M. 'Domesticating democracy: Culture, civil society and constitutionalism in Africa' 39(1) *Comparative Studies in Society and History* (January 1997) 120

Packer, J. 'On the Content of Minority Rights' in J Räikkaä (ed.) *Do We Need Minority Rights?* (The Hague: Kluwer Law International, 1996) 121

Parekh, B. *Rethinking multiculturalism: Cultural diversity and political theory* (2000) 239

Patten, A. & Kymlicka, W. 'Introduction: Language Rights and Political Theory: Context, Issues, and Approaches' in Alan Patten and Will Kymlicka (eds.) *Language Rights and Political Theory* (Oxford: Oxford University Press, 2003) 1

Patten, A. 'The Rights of Internal Linguistic Minorities' in Avigail Eisenberg & Jeff Spinner-Halv (eds.) *Minorities within Minorities: Equality, Rights and Diversity* (Cambridge: Cambridge University Press, 2005) 135

Peaslee, A (eds.) *Constitutions of Nations* (The Hague: Martinus Nijhoff, 1965) Vol. 1 Africa

Pejic, J 'Minority Rights In International Law' 19 *Human Rights Quarterly* (1997) 666,

Penelope Andrews & Stephen Ellmann (eds.) *The Post-Apartheid Constitutions: Perspectives on South Africa's Basic Law* (Johannesburg: University of the Witwatersrand, 2001)

Pentassuglia, G. 'State Sovereignty, Minorities and Self-determination: A Comprehensive Legal View' 9 *Int'l Journal on Minority and Group Rights* (2002) 303

Pham, J.P. 'African Constitutionalism: Forging New Models for Multiethnic Governance and Self-determination' in Jeremy I Levitt (ed.) *Africa: New Boundaries in International Law* (Oxford, Portland: Hart Publishing, 2008)

Plattner, M. and Diamond, L. 'The Challenge of Ethnic Conflict' 4(4) *Journal of Democracy* (1993)
Porto, J.G. 'Cabinda, Notes On A Soon-To-Be-Forgotten War' *Occasional Paper 77* (Pretoria: Institute for Security Studies, August 2003
Posner, D.N. *Institutions and ethnic politics in Africa* (New York: Cambridge University Press, 2005)
Prunier, G. *The Rwanda Crisis: History of a Genocide* (London: Hurst, 1995)
Räikkä, J. (ed.) Do We Need Minority Rights? (The Hague: Kluwer Law International, 1996)
Räikkä, J. 'Is a Membership-Blind Model of Justice False by Definition?' in J Räikkä (ed.) Do We Need Minority Rights? (The Hague: Kluwer Law International, 1996) 3
Ramaga, P V 'Relativity of the Minority Concept' 14 *Human Rights Quarterly* (1992) 104,
Ramaga, P.V. 'The Group Concept in Minority Protection' 15(3) *Human Rights Quarterly* (1993) 575
Ramchanran, B.G. 'The Protection of Minorities in Africa' in Gudmundur Alfredsson & Stavropoulous, M. (eds.) *Justice Pending: Indigenous Peoples and Other Good Causes: Essays in Honour of Erica-Irene A Daes* (The Hague: Kluwer Law International, 2002) 99
Ramchanran, B.G. 'The Protection of Minorities in Africa' in Gudmundur Alfredsson & Maria Stavropoulous (eds.) *Justice Pending: Indigenous Peoples and Other Good Causes: Essays in Honour of Erica-Irene A Daes* (The Hague: Kluwer Law International, 2002) 99
Rawls, J. *Political Liberalism* (2005)
Rawls, J. *Political Liberalism* (New York: Columbia University Press, expanded edition 2005)
Reader, J. *Africa: A Biography of the Continent* (London: Penguin Books, 1998)
Rein, S. 'Sierra Leone: Between the prison houses of nationalism and transnationalism' in Malinda S. Smith (ed.) *Globalizing Africa* (Asmara: Africa World Press, Inc., 2003) 127
Reynolds, A. 'Constitutional Engineering in Southern Africa' 6(2) *Journal of Democracy* (April, 1995) 86
Reynolds, A. 'The Case for Proportionality' 6(4) *Journal of Democracy* (Oct. 1995) 117
Reynolds, A. *Report: Electoral system and the protection and participation of minorities* (London: Minority Rights Group International, 2006)
Reyntjens, F. 'Authoritarianism for Francophone Africa from the Colonial to the Post-Colonial State' *Third World Legal Studies* (1988) 59
Reyntjens, F. 'Recent Developments in Public Law of Francophone African States' 30 (2) *The Journal of Modern African Studies* (1986) 75
Rivkin, A. *Nation-building in Africa: Problems and prospects* (New Jersey: Rutgers University Press, 1969)
Roach, S.C. 'Minority Rights and an Emergent International Right to Autonomy: A Historical and Normative Assessment' 11 *Int'l J on Minority and Group Rights* (2004) 411
Robinson, J. 'Federalism and the Transformation of the South African State' in Graham Smith *Federalism: The Multiethnic Challenge* (London, New York: Longman, 1995) 255
Rosas, A. 'Internal Self-determination' in Christian Tomuschat (ed.) *Modern Law of Self-determination* (Dordrecht: Martinus Nijhoff Publishers, 1993) 225
Rothchild, D. 'Reconfiguring State-Ethnic Relations in Africa: Liberalization and the Search for New Routines of Interaction' in Peter Lewis (ed.) *Africa: Dilemmas of Development and Change* (Boulder: Westview Press, 1998) 215
Rothchild, D. and Olorunsola, V.A. (eds.) *State versus ethnic claims: African policy dilemmas* (Boulder, Colorado: Westview Press, 1983)
Said, A. 'Afar ethnicity in Ethiopian politics' in Mohamed Salih and John Markakis (eds.) *Ethnicity and the state in eastern Africa* (1998) 108
Samuel Huntington *The third Wave of Democratization in the late twentieth century* (Norman; The University of Oklahoma Press,1991)
Schlemmer, L. 'Democracy or Democratic Hegemony: The Future of Political Pluralism in South Africa' in Herman Giliomee & Charles Simkins (eds.) *The Awkward Embrace: One-Party Domination and Democracy* (Capetown: Tafelberg Publishers Ltd, 1999) 281
Schönteich, M. & Boshoff, H. *'Volk', Faith and Fatherland: The Security Threat posed by the White Right* ISS Monograph No. 81 (Pretoria: Institute for Security Studies, March 2003)
Schraeder, PJ 'Ethnic Politics in Djibouti: From "Eye of the Hurricane" to "Boiling cauldron"' 92 *African Affairs* (1993) 203
Schumpeter, J.A. *Capitalism, Socialism and Democracy* (London & New York: George Allen & Unwin Publishers, 1943 reprinted by Routledge 1996)

Seleoane, M 'Recognition of indigenous peoples in international law: Recent developments' in D de Villiers (ed.) *The rights of indigenous people: A quest for coexistence* (Pretoria: HSRC, 1997)1
Shaw, M.N. 'The Definition of Minorities in International Law' in Yoram Dinstien (ed.) *The Protection of Minorities and Human Rights* (Dordecht: Kluwer Academic Publishers, 1992) 1
Shivji, I.G. 'State and Constitutionalism: A New Democratic Perspective' In his *State and Constitutionalism: An African Debate on Democracy* (Harare: SAPES Trust, 1991) 27
Sigler, J.A. *Minority rights – A comparative analysis* (Westport, Connecticut: Greenwood Press, 1983)
Sithole, M. 'Ethnicity and democratization in Zimbabwe' in Harvery Glickman (Ed.) *Ethnic conflict and democratization in Africa* (Atlanta, Georgia: African Studies Association Press, 1995) 121
Skurbaty, Z. *As if peoples mattered: Critical appraisal of 'peoples' and 'minorities' from the international human rights perspective and beyond* (The Hague: Martinus Nijhoff Publishers, 2000)
Smith, G. 'Mapping the Federal Condition: Ideology, Political Practice and Social Justice' in Graham Smith (ed.) *Federalism: The Multiethnic Challenge* (1995)
Smock, D & Bentsi-Enchill, K. (eds.) *The Search for National Integration in Africa* (1976)
Solway, J.S. 'Reaching the limits of universal citizenship: "Minority" struggles in Botswana' in Bruce Berman et al. (eds.) *Ethnicity and democracy in Africa* (Oxford: James Currey; Athens: Ohio University Press, 2004) 129
Sonko, B. 'The Casamance Conflict: A forgotten Civil War? 3 & 4 *CODESERA Bulletin* (2004) 30
Southall, R. 'Introduction: The ANC state, more dysfunctional than developmental' in Sakhela Buhlungu et al. (eds.) *State of the Nation South Africa 2007* (Cape Town: HSRC Press, 2007) 1
Stamatopoulou, E. *Cultural Rights in International Law: Article 27 of the Universal Declaration of Human Rights and Beyond* (Leiden: Koninklijke Brill NV, 2007)
Stavenhagen, R. 'Cultural Rights: A Social Science Perspective' in Asbjørn Eide, Catarina Krause, and Allan Rosas (eds.) *Economic, social and cultural rights: A Textbook* (The Hague: Kluwer Law International, 2001) 85
Steiner, H.J. 'Political Participation as a Human Right' *Harvard Human Rights Yearbook* (1998) 77
Stepan, A. 'Federalism and Democracy: Beyond the U.S. Model' in Dimitrios Karmis & Wayne Norman (eds.) *Theories of Federalism: A Reader* (New York: Palgrave Macmillan, 2005) 255
Tamir, Y. *Liberal Nationalism* (Princeton, New Jersey: Princeton University Press, 1993)
Taylor, C. 'Nationalism and modernity' in John A. Hall (ed.) *The State of the Nation: Ernest Gellner and the Theory of Nationalism* (Cambridge: Cambridge University Press, 1998) 191
Taylor, C. 'Nationalism and Modernity' in John A. Hall (ed.) *The State of the Nation: Ernest Gellner and the Theory of Nationalism* (1998)
Taylor, C. 'The Politics of Recognition' in Amy Guitmann (ed.) *Multiculturalism: Examining the Politics of Recognition* (1994) 25
Thio, L. 'Battling Balkanization: Regional Approaches Towards Minority Protection Beyond Europe' 43 *Harvard Int'l L. J* (Summer 2002) 409
Thornberry, P. 'Is there a phoenix in the ashes? International Law and Minority Rights' 15 *Texas Int'l L.J.* (1980) 421
Thornberry, P. 'The UN Declaration on the Rights of Persons Belonging to National or Ethnic, Religious and Linguistic Minorities: Background, Analysis, Observation, and an Update' in Alan Philips and Allan Rosas (eds.) *Universal Minority Rights* (1995) 13
Thornberry, P. *International Law and the Rights of Minorities* (Oxford University Press, 1991)
Tierney, S. *Constitutional Law and National Pluralism* (Oxford: Oxford University Press, 2004)
Topperwien, N. 'Participation in the Decision-Making Process as a Means of Group Accommodation' in G Alan Tar, Robert F Williams & Joseph Marko (eds.) *Federalism, Subnational Constitutions and Minority Rights* (Westport, CT: Praeger Publishers, 2004) 41
Touré, S. *Toward Full Reafricanisation* (Paris: Presence Africaine, 1959)
Tronvoll, K. *Ethiopia: A new Start?* MRG Report (London: Minority Rights Group International, 2000)
Tully, J. *Strange Multiplicity: Constitutionalism in an Age of Diversity* (Cambridge: Cambridge University Press,1995)
Turton, D. 'Four questions about Ethiopia's Ethnic Federalism' (2005) 1 (2) *STAIR* 88
Udogu, E.I. (eds.) *The Issue Of Political Ethnicity In Africa* (Aldershot: Ashgate, 2001)
Udombana, N.J. 'The Unfinished Business: Conflicts, the African Union and the New Partnership for Africa's Development' 35 *Geo. Wash. Int'l L. Rev.* (2003) 55

Umozurike, U O *Self-Determination in International Law* (Hamdon, CT: Archon Books,
Van Dyke *The cultural rights of peoples* 2(2) *Universal Human Rights* (April-June 1980) 2
VandenHole, W *Non –Discrimination and Equality in the View of the UN Human Rights Treaty Bodies* (Antwerp: Intersentia, 2005)
Walker, G. 'The Idea of Nonliberal Constitutionalism' in Ian Shapiro and Will Kymlick (eds.) *NOMOS XXXIX: Ethnicity and Group Rights* ((New York: New York University Press, 1997) 154
Wani, I.J. 'Cultural Preservation and the Challenges of Diversity and Nationhood: The Dilemmas of Indigenous Cultures in Africa' 59 *UMKC L Rev.* (1991) 611
Watts, R.L. 'Federalism and Diversity in Canada' in Yash Ghai (ed.) *Autonomy and Ethnicity: Negotiating Competing Claims in Multi-ethnic Societies* (Cambridge: Cambridge University Press, 2000) 29,
Watts, R.L. 'Federalism, Federal Political Systems, and Federations' 1 *Annual Review of Political Science* (1998) 117
Watts, R.L. *Comparing Federal Systems* (Montreal & Kingston: McGill-Queen's University Press, 1999)
Weiss, H.F. & Carayannis, T. 'The Enduring Idea of the Congo' in Ricardo René Larémont (ed.) *Borders, Nationalism and the African State* (Boulder, Colorado: Lynne Rienner Publishers, Inc., 2005) 135–178
Welsh, D. 'Ethnicity in Sub-Saharan Africa' 72 *International Affairs* (1996) 477
Wheatley, S. 'Deliberative Democracy and Minorities' 14 (3) *European Journal of International Law* (2003) 507
Williams, M.S. 'Memory, history and membership: The moral claims of marginalized groups in political representation' in J Raikka (ed.) *Do we need minority rights?* 85–119, 105, 110
Williams, M.S. 'The Uneasy Alliance of Group Representation and Deliberative Democracy' in Will Kymlicka & Wayne Norman (eds.) *Citizenship in Diverse Societies* (Oxford: Oxford University Press, 2000) 124
Wilson, H.S. *The imperial experience in Sub-Saharan Africa since 1870* (Minnesota: University of Minnesota Press; Oxford: Oxford University Press, 1977)
Wilson, J. 'Ethnic Groups and the Right to Self-Determination' 11 *Connecticut Journal of International Law* (Spring 1996) 433
Woolman, S., Roux, T. and Bishop, M. et al. *Constitutional Law of South Africa* (Cape Town: Juta & Co. Ltd, 2006 2nd revised ed.)
World Directory of Minorities (London: Minority Rights Group International ed., 1997)
Wunsch, J S 'Foundations of Centralization: The Colonial Experience and the African Context' in J S Wunsch & D Olowu (eds.) *The Failure of the Centralized State: Institutions and Self-Governance in Africa* (1990) 34
Xnathaki, A. 'The Right to Self-determination: Meaning and Scope' in Nazila Ghanea & Alexandra Xanthaki (eds.) *Minorities, peoples & Self-determination: Essays in Honour of Patrick Thornberry* (2005) 15
Xydis, D.P. (ed.) *Constitutions of the World* (The Hague: Martinus Nijihoff, 1974)
Young, C. 'Competing Images of Africa: Democratization and its Challenges' in Okon Akiba (ed.) *Constitutionalism and society in Africa* (2004) 141
Young, C. 'Democratization in Africa: The Contradictions of a political imperative' in Widner, J.A. (ed.) *Economic change and political liberalization in Sub-Saharan Africa* (Baltimore: The Johns Hopkins University Press, 1994) 230
Young, C. 'Ethnic Diversity and Public Policy: An Overview' in his *Ethnic Diversity and Public Policy: A Comparative Inquiry* (Hampshire, New York: Mackmillan Press, 1998) 1
Young, I M. 'Differing Group Representation' in Ian Shapiro and Will Kymlicka (eds.) *NOMOS XXXIX: Ethnicity and Group Rights* (New York & London: New York University Press, 1997) 349
Young, I.M. 'Polity and Group Difference: A Critique of the Ideal of Universal Citizenship' in Robert E. Goodin & Philip Pettit *Contemporary Political Philosophy: An Anthology* (Malden, MA: Blackwell Publishing, 1997) 256
Young, I.M. *Justice and the Politics of Difference* (Princeton, New Jersey, 1990)
Young, J. 'Ethnicity and Power in Ethiopia' 70 *Review of African Political Economy* (1996) 531
Zewde, B. *Modern Ethiopian History 1855–1974* (London: James Currey; Athens: Ohio University Press; Addis Ababa: Addis Ababa University Press, 1991)

Table of Cases

Alexkor Ltd & another v Richtersveld Community & Others 2004 (5) SA 460 (CC)

Bhe and Others v Magistrate, Khayelitsha, and Others (Commission for Gender Equality as Amicus Curiae*); Shibi v Sithole and Others; South African Human Rights Commission and Another v President of the Republic of South Africa and Another* 2005 (1) SA 580 (CC); 2005 (1) BCLR 1 (CC)

Case U 5/98, Request for Evaluation of Constitutionality of Certain Provisions of the Constitution of Republika Srpska and the Constitution of the Federation of BiH, Partial Decision (Constitutional Ct. Bosn. & Herze. July 1, 2000), available at <http://ccbh.ba/decisions>

D.A.V. College, Jullunder v Punjab, A.I.R. (1971) S. Ct. 1731

Democratic Alliance & Another v Masondo NO & Another 2003 (2) SA 413 (CC),

Doctors for Life International v Speaker of the National Assembly 2006 (6) SA 416 (CC), 2006 (12) BCLR 1399 (CC)

Ex Parte Chairperson of the Constitutional Assembly: In Re Certification of the Constitution of the Republic of South Africa 1996 (4) SA 744 (CC), 1996 (10) BCLR 1253 (CC)

Ex Parte Gauteng Provincial Legislature: In re Dispute Concerning the Constitutionality of the Gauteng School Education Bill of 1995 1996 (3) SA 165 (CC), 1996 (4) BCLR 537 (CC)

Ex Parte President of the Republic of South Africa: In Re Constitutionality of the Liquor Bill 2000 (1) SA 732 (CC)

Ex Parte Speaker of the Western Cape Provincial Legislature: IN Re First Certification of the Constitution of the Province of the Western Cape (1997) (4) SA 795 (CC), 1997 (9) BCLR 1167 (CC)

John Ballantyne and Elizabeth Davidson, and Gordon Mcintyre v Canada (Communications Nos. 359/1989 and 385/1989) UN Doc. U.N. Doc. CCPR/C/47/D/359/1989 and 385/1989/Rev.1 (1993)

Ivan Kitok v Sweden (Communication No. 197/1985) UN Doc. Supp. No. 40 (A/43/40) 221 (1988) (HRC)

Ilmari Länsman et al. v Finland (Communication No. 511/1992) UN Doc. Supp. No. 40 (A/50/40) 66 (1992) (HRC)

Jouni E. Länsman et al. v Finland (Communication 671/1995) UN Doc. Supp. No. 40 (A/52/40) 191 (1996) (HRC)

Kamanakao and others v Attorney-General and Another (2002) *African Human Rights Law Reports* (AHRLR) 35 (BwHC 2001)

Katangese People Congress v Zaire (2000) AHRLR 72 (ACHPR 1995) [Communication 75/92 8th Annual Activity Report, 1994–1995]

Laerckool Middlburg & 'n ander v Departementshoof, Mpumalanga Van Ondrways, & andre 2003 (4) SA 160 (T)

Minority Schools in Albania PCIJ (Ser. A/B) No. 64 (1935)

Malawi African Association, Amnesty International, Ms. Sarr Diop, Union Interafricaine des droit de l'Homme and RADDHO, Collectif des Veuves et Ayants-droit & Association Mauritanienne des Droits de l'Homme v Mauritania (2000) AHRLR 149 (ACHPR 2000) Communications 54/91, 61/91, 98/93, 164/97, 196/97 & 210/98 (13th Annual Activity Report ACHPR,1999–2000)

MEC for Education, KwaZuu-Natal & Others v Pillay 2008 (1) SA 474 (CC)

Minister of Home Affairs and Another v Fourie and Another; Lesbian and Gay Equality Project and Others v Minister of Home Affairs and Others 2006 (1) SA 524 (CC), 2006 (3) BCLR 355 (CC)

Opinion of the CCI on the making of the law on deeds and Notorial acts (Unreported)

Prince v President, Cape Law Society, & Others 2002 (2) SA 794 (CC), 2002 (3) BCLR 231 (CC)

Reference re the Secession of Quebec (1998) 2 SCR 217

Ruling of the CCI *Biyadglegn Meles & Others v The Amhara Regional State* 30 Miazia 1989 E.C. (Unreported)

Ruling of the CCI on the Petition from the Prime Minister's Office 26 Miazia 1994 E.C. (unreported)

Sandra Lovelace v Canada (Communication No. 24/1977) U.N. Doc . Supp. No. 40 (A/36/40) 166 (1981) (HRC)

SERAC & CESR v Nigeria Communication No. 155/96 decided at ACHPR's 30th Ordinary Session held in Banjul, The Gambia from 13–27 October 2001

Western Cape Minister of Education & Others v The Governing Body of Mikro Primary School 2006 (1) SA 1 (SCA), 2005 (10) BCLR 973 (SCA)

Internet sources

Assefa, S. 'Two Concepts of Sovereignty' paper prepared for a symposium held in Mekelle on the occasion of the twenty-fifth anniversary of the TPLF, February 2000 published in the weekly Addis Tribune 24 February 2000 accessed from <http://www.addistribune.com/Archives/2000/03/24-03-00/Two.htm> last accessed on 7 September 2005

Buchanan, J.M. 'Notes on the Liberal Constitution' 14 *The Cato Journal* (1993) available at <http://www.cato.org/pubs/journal/cj14n1-1.htm> accessed on 24 October 2006

Donald R Snodgrass *Successful economic development in a multiethnic society: The Malaysian experience* available at <http://www.earthinstitute.columbia.edu>

Habib, M. *Role and Function of the House of the Federation* available at <http://www.hofethiopia.org/pdf/The%20role%20of%20the%20House%20in%20EFDRE%20constition.pdf> accessed on 9 April 2008

<http://www.earth.columbia.edu/sitefiles/File/about/director/pubs/503.pdf> accessed on 13 March 2008

Minorities At Risk data of the University of Maryland on Lunda and Yeke of the DRC available at <http://www.cidcm.umd.edu/mar/assessment.asp?groupId=49005>

National Language Policy Framework available at <http://www.saps.gov.za/saps_profile/components/language_management/downloads/implem_plan__english.pdf> accessed on 17 Oct. 2007

Pitsch (1995) Ovimbundu of Angola a case from University of Maryland's Minorities at risk project <http://www.bsos.umd.edu./cidcm/mar/angovim.htm>

Prunier, G. 'Kenya: Roots of Crisis'; Roger Southall 'South African Lessons for Kenya' both available at <http://www.opendemocracy.com>

Reynolds, A. 'South Africa: Electoral System, Conflict Management And Inclusion' available at <http://aceproject.org/ace-en/topics/es/esy/esy_za>

Rozès, A. 'Angolan deadlock, Chronicle of a war with no solution' 10 *African Security Review* (2001) available at <http://www.issafrica.org/Pubs/ASR/10No3/Rozes.html>

Statistics South Africa, Mid-year estimates for South Africa by population group and sex, 2007 available at <http://www.statssa.gov.za/PublicationsHTML/P03022007/html/P03022007.html> accessed on 22 November 2007

Violations of linguistic and cultural rights of minority groups in Botswana statement of Ramahobo, L. to the UN Working Group on Minorities (March 1, 2004) available at <http://www.unhchr.ch/minorities/statements10/MCB3a.doc> last accessed on 2006/09/27

Others

Minority Rights Human Rights Fact Sheet No. 18 (Rev. 1) (Geneva: United Nations, 1998)

Lund Recommendations on the Effective Participation of National Minorities in Public life

Electoral models for South Africa: Reflections and Options Electoral Task Team Review Roundtable Konrad-Adenaur-Stiftung Seminar Report No 18 (2nd ed.) (KAS: Johannesburg, January 2007)

The International Panel of Eminent Personalities to Investigate the 1994 Genocide in Rwanda And the Surrounding Events *Rwanda: The Preventable Genocide* (1994) available at <http://www.africa-union.org/Official_documents/Reports/OUA-Rapport%20sur%20le%20genocide%20au%20Rwanda.pdf>

Human Rights Committee, *The Right to Self-determination of Peoples (Art. 1) : 13/04/84. CCPR General comment 12*, 1984

Vienna Declaration and Programme of Action of 1993 UN Doc A/CONF.157/23

Human Rights Committee, General Comment 23, Article 27 (fifth Session, 1994) UN Doc. HRI/GEN/1/Rev.1 at 38 (1994)

The Document of the Copenhagen Meeting of the Conference on the Human Dimension of the Conference on Security and Cooperation in Europe (CSCE)

Be Ethiopia Ye Dimocraci Sirat Ginbata Gudayoch (Addis Ababa: Ministry of Information, Ginbot 1994 E.C.)

Minutes of the Constitutional Assembly (Nov. 1994)

Human Rights Watch/Africa *Mauritania's Campaign of Terror: State-Sponsored Repression of Black Africans* (New York: Human Rights Watch, 1994)

INDEX

www.ingramcontent.com/pod-product-compliance
Lightning Source LLC
LaVergne TN
LVHW020652300926
849161LV00004B/908